WHY *HUMANAE VITAE* IS STILL RIGHT

Why *Humanae vitae* Is Still Right

Edited by Janet E. Smith

IGNATIUS PRESS   SAN FRANCISCO

Cover design by Enrique J. Aguilar

© 2018 by Ignatius Press, San Francisco
All rights reserved
ISBN 978-1-62164-266-4
Library of Congress Control Number 2018941777
Printed in the United States of America ∞

To Sacred Heart Major Seminary

CONTENTS

FOREWORD

Since the Second Vatican Council, our Holy Fathers, the popes, have insistently called the People of God to live out the Council's vision by making evangelization our first priority. As Blessed Paul VI put it: "Evangelizing is in fact the grace and vocation proper to the Church, her deepest identity. She exists in order to evangelize."[1] Most recently, Pope Francis reaffirmed this conviction with his own straight-to-the-point style: "We no longer say that we are 'disciples' and 'missionaries,' but rather that we are always 'missionary disciples'."[2] Accepting the Good News of Jesus Christ includes accepting the commission to share that Good News with our world.

The Good News we proclaim is that Jesus Christ has definitively rescued the human race from our fallen condition, and in that deliverance he has raised us up to a state even more marvelous than what our first parents enjoyed when they were molded by God at the dawn of creation.

Because being sexual is integral to being human, it comes as no surprise that the Lord Jesus' saving work includes saving human sexuality. By rising in the flesh, the Lord has lifted up every dimension of our fleshly existence. He has fulfilled his mission of restoring our sexuality, and the marriage covenant that is its proper context, to what the Father had in mind "from the beginning" (Mt 19:4).

As part of rescuing us from "the father of lies" (Jn 8:44), our Savior has rescued marriage and sexuality from the falsehoods that have in every age obscured their nature. Jesus brought back into the light the truth, the Creator's own truth, about marriage and sexuality. And not

---

[1] Paul VI, apostolic exhortation *Evangelii nuntiandi* (December 8, 1975), no. 14, http://w2.vatican.va/content/paul-vi/en/apost_exhortations/documents/hf_p-vi_exh_19751208_evangelii-nuntiandi.html.

[2] Francis, apostolic exhortation *Evangelii gaudium* (November 24, 2013), no. 120, http://w2.vatican.va/content/francesco/en/apost_exhortations/documents/papa-francesco_esortazione-ap_20131124_evangelii-gaudium.html.

only has he done for us this incomparable service of disclosing for all time the nature of this essential dimension of being human; he has won for us the grace of being able to live out this truth. In Christ we know the abiding truth of marriage and sexuality, and we are empowered to live this truth.

Fifty years ago, in the face of the world's objections to this saving truth, Blessed Paul VI stood as a courageous witness to it. He testified to the nature of marriage and sexuality as established by the Creator, by reaffirming what they exist for: both intimacy and procreation, neither one without the other. In giving this witness, Blessed Paul VI, at no little personal cost, was living out for himself his call to the Church to evangelize. He offered a powerful witness to the Good News that Christ has saved humanity, saved it in all of its dimensions.

As a pastor who is fully committed to leading my fellow disciples in moving forward to answering the call to take up the New Evangelization, I am deeply grateful to the authors of this collection of essays. By their careful scholarship and considered reflection they offer a rich range of insights into the truth about marriage and sexuality to which Blessed Paul VI offered his witness in *Humanae vitae*. These essays are a much-needed resource for all who work so devotedly to share with our age the Good News about human sexuality restored in Christ Jesus. This great effort is a work of love: love for our friends and neighbors, since living this truth is the path to flourishing in time and to blessedness in eternity; love for God, so that his glory will shine out ever more brightly in our world. It is the work of Jesus Christ, and so it cannot fail.

—Archbishop Allen Vigneron
Archdiocese of Detroit

INTRODUCTION

Fifty years after *Humanae vitae* was promulgated, it is neither a forgotten nor an embraced document. There is still much rejection of the teaching of *Humanae vitae* among many theologians and lay Catholics, but there is also a strong current in the Church of theologians and laity who have developed solid defenses of this magisterial teaching and who are, with some considerable success, winning the hearts and minds of others. There are too many reasons for the upswing in support for *Humanae vitae* to list here, but among them were the 1992 publication of the *Catechism of the Catholic Church* and Pope John Paul II's 1993 encyclical *Veritatis splendor*. Those magisterial documents did not succeed in quenching dissent, but they did bring orthodoxy more into the mainstream; today those who support Church teaching on both moral and doctrinal matters are an influential part of the Church's structure in terms of teaching at Catholic colleges, universities, and seminaries, as well as at national, diocesan, and parish levels.

More and more people are seeing the horrific consequences of the nearly universal use of contraception. Mary Eberstadt catalogues those consequences as well as commenting on the underlying stunted anthropology that has produced them. Dr. Angela Lanfranchi notes that the modern science on pheromones provides support for the teaching of *Humanae vitae*, unknown to Pope Paul VI at the time. Prof. Deborah Savage testifies to how the availability of the Pill during her college years in the seventies radically changed how men and women interrelated and illuminates the damage it has done to a woman's fundamental identity and how it distorts the true meaning of masculinity. Obianuju Ekeocha reports on the devastating impact of imperialistic Western promotion of contraception in Africa, a very pro-life and pro-child continent.

As far as defenses of *Humanae vitae* go, none can match the influence of Pope Saint John Paul II's Theology of the Body, which has lead millions to understand the wisdom and beauty of the Church's teaching on contraception. No single individual has done more to bring that teaching to the modern world than Christopher West, whose essay here makes fascinating connections between Fatima, Marx, and the Theology of the Body and also addresses the differences between contraception and natural family planning. Prof. Michael Waldstein performed an enormous service in providing a consistent translation on the Theology of the Body (along with a tremendously useful introduction). Here, in a surprisingly effective juxtaposition of the modern and the ancient, he combines a critique of the modern worldview based on Descartes' rejection of the person as union of body and soul with a moving analysis of the ancient story of Odysseus, Penelope, and their marital bed.

This volume contains a special and original essay in which Prof. Joseph Atkinson situates the teaching of *Humanae vitae* within the context of Scripture, within the context of creation itself as a call to holiness. Certainly, the Theology of the Body is fundamentally rooted in Scripture as no defense of *Humanae vitae* has been before; but the Theology of the Body is a series of meditations on key texts, whereas Atkinson digs deeply into the concepts that are the most foundational to Scripture and shows how contraception is completely incompatible with the life-giving thrust of creation.

While there are now (much more than twenty-five years ago) many theological and scriptural defenses of *Humanae vitae*, philosophical defenses remain important. Prof. Maria Fedoryka's essay is a beautiful and profound meditation on how fruitfulness is inextricably bound to the very meaning of love and that it is that meaning, rather than a strict focus on the biological purpose of sexuality, that justifies the Church's condemnation of contraception. Prof. Janet Smith's essay on natural sex takes another tack and uses the thought of Thomas Aquinas and Martin Luther to show how the procreative power of the sexual act is central to the analysis of the morality of sexual acts. Prof. Michele Schumacher studies how contraception has reduced the act of sexual intercourse to largely a physical act and even a counterfeit act that no longer partakes in the transcendent nature of sexuality. Prof. William Newton writes on how contraception leads to abortion, both because it leads people to have sex without concern for pregnancy and also because contraception diminishes the value of human life and the receptivity to new life.

Saint John Paul II was a fervent advocate and defender of the Church's teachings on sexual morality throughout his priesthood and pontificate.

Unknown to many is the document here called the Krakow report (only recently translated in English), a document written by him—when he was a cardinal—and a group of Krakovian moral theologians in reply to the work of the special commission established to advise Pope Paul VI on the question of contraception. It clearly influenced Paul VI in his writing on *Humanae vitae*. Indeed, in the view of George Weigel, *Humanae vitae* would have been a better document had it followed the Krakow report more closely. Weigel provides some important background on the Krakow document.

Those who dissent from *Humanae vitae* often claim that the "rights" of conscience permit couples to use contraception. Prof. Janet Smith tailors her discussion of conscience to the work of physicians who, when true to their profession and faith, would not be party to prescribing contraception. Prof. Derek Doroski's essay demonstrates a marvelous truth: that when medicine honors the truths of creation, solutions to problems such as infertility will be more readily found—solutions that are moral and effective.

Many of those who reject the teaching of *Humanae vitae* claim that the "nonreception" of the teaching by the laity indicates that the teaching is not required by the faith. Prof. Janet Smith's essay on the *sensus fidelium* or "sense of the faithful" explains precisely what the *sensus fidelium* is and how it is properly used to determine which teachings are compatible with the faith.

One of the most important initiatives of the U.S. bishops in decades was its opposition to the U.S. Department of Health and Human Services (HHS) mandate that required that all employers pay for insurance policies that provide contraception. Prof. Peter Colosi reports on what a challenge it was for the bishops to defend religious liberty when most Americans seem to value free contraception more than religious freedom. He notes that the widespread rejection by Catholics of the Church's teaching on contraception, due in large part to a lack of catechesis on the matter, impeded the bishops' efforts. He lauds the bishops for recent initiatives to promote the teachings of *Humanae vitae* and encourages further engagement.

The final chapter in this book is an essay that is a comprehensive defense of the Church's teaching. It was written by a team of scholars with expertise in several areas in response to a challenge to *Humanae vitae* being launched by dissenters from *Humanae vitae* at the United Nations.

It sketches out the wide range of justifications that can be made for *Humanae vitae* and should be a handy resource that should lead many to desire to read the more fulsome presentations of various defenses as presented in this book.

Readers of this volume may even be moved to read the precursor volume: *Why Humanae Vitae Was Right: A Reader,*[1] published upon the occasion of the twenty-fifth anniversary of *Humanae vitae*. There, more of the initial challenges to *Humanae vitae* spawned by proportionalism were considered, such as the principle of totality and the claim that *Humanae vitae* was not infallible. It includes some of the classic defenses of *Humanae vitae*, such as those by the distinguished analytic philosopher G. E. M. (Elizabeth) Anscombe and the notable personalist, phenomenologist Dietrich von Hildebrand. The first volume is not at all outdated—the essays there remain timely and complement the essays in this book. This new volume demonstrates that there are still many riches of *Humanae vitae* to be discovered, both in terms of helping us understand why the modern world is in such a state of revolt in respect to sexuality and also in terms of the tremendous honor and responsibility that God has bestowed on spouses by inviting and enabling them to be co-creators with him.

* * * * *

I would like to express my heartfelt appreciation to all the authors represented in this volume, for their dedication to explaining unpopular truths and their patience with the process of bringing such a collection to completion. A particular thanks to Maria Fedoryka, who provided assistance at a crucial moment. Those with whom I worked at Ignatius Press could not have been more professional and accommodating, particularly Mark Brumley and Diane Eriksen.

---

[1] Janet E. Smith, ed., *Why Humanae Vitae Was Right: A Reader* (San Francisco: Ignatius Press, 1993).

The Prophetic Power of
*Humanae vitae**

Mary Eberstadt

One recurring theme in Pope Francis' teaching is that human realities trump scholarly abstractions: "La realidad es superior a la idea" ["Realities are greater than ideas]."[1] His signature phrase about pastors who have the "smell of the sheep"[2] is the folk version of this maxim. Cautions about "rigidity", "empty rhetoric", and getting "stuck in pure ideas" appear often in his work,[3] and in that of his inner circle, too. What matters most are "the realities people face in their daily lives", as Blase Cardinal Cupich put it in a speech at Cambridge recently.[4]

Attention to "reality" is especially fitting as we mark this fiftieth anniversary year of one of the most famous, and infamous, encyclicals in Church history. Ten years ago, on its fortieth anniversary, *First Things*

---

*This essay was originally published in "The Prophetic Power of *Humanae vitae*: Documenting the Realities of the Sexual Revolution", *First Things*, April 2018, https://www.firstthings.com/article/2018/04/the-prophetic-power-of-humanae-vitae.

[1] Francis, apostolic exhortation *Evangelii gaudium* (November 24, 2013), no. 233, (hereafter cited as *EG*), Spanish translation, http://www.vatican.va/evangelii-gaudium/sp/files/assets/basic-html/page177.html; English translation, http://w2.vatican.va/content/francesco/en/apost_exhortations/documents/papa-francesco_esortazione-ap_20131124_evangelii-gaudium.html.

[2] Chrism Mass, Homily of Pope Francis (March 28, 2013), in Dennis Coday, "Pope's Quotes: The Smell of Sheep", *National Catholic Reporter* (blog), October 29, 2013, https://www.ncronline.org/blogs/francis-chronicles/pope-s-quotes-smell-sheep.

[3] *EG*, nos. 45, 231.

[4] Blase Cardinal Cupich, "Amoris Laetitia as a New Paradigm of Catholicity" (the Annual Von Hugel Lecture, Cambridge University, February 9, 2018), https://www.youtube.com/watch?v=AxbgtpUYkoQ.

published my "Vindication of *Humanae vitae*".[5] Citing contemporary evidence from many sources, including sociology, psychology, history, and contemporary women's literature, I argued:

> Four decades later, not only have the document's signature predictions been ratified in empirical force, but they have been ratified as few predictions ever are: in ways its authors could not possibly have foreseen, including by information that did not exist when the document was written, by scholars and others with no interest whatever in its teaching, and indeed even inadvertently, and in more ways than one, by many proud public adversaries of the Church.[6]

Of course, to say that proof abounds is not to say that a valid argument falls always and everywhere on happy ears—not fifty years ago, not ten years ago, and not today. The promise of sex on demand, unencumbered by constraint, may be the strongest collective temptation humanity has ever encountered. That's why, since the invention of the Pill, resistance to the traditional Christian code has been unremittingly ferocious, and why so many among the laity and clergy wish that this rule—among others—were less taxing. As the disciples of Jesus Christ complained upon hearing his teaching about marriage, these lessons are "hard".[7]

But to confuse "hard" with "wrong" is a fundamental error. If we are truly to lean into *realidades* (realities), there is only one conclusion to be drawn from the mass of empirical evidence now out there. It's the same conclusion that was visible ten years ago, and that will remain visible ten, or one hundred, or two hundred years from now. It is simply this: The most globally reviled and widely misunderstood document of the last half century is also the most prophetic and explanatory of our time.

Let us set aside theology, philosophy, ideology, and other abstractions and count up the new realities vindicating *Humanae vitae*, one by one.

The first empirical reality is this: if we leave out individual intentions and assess nothing but uncontroversial facts, it is transparently clear

---

[5] Mary Eberstadt, "The Vindication of *Humanae vitae*", *First Things*, August 2008, https://www.firstthings.com/article/2008/08/002-the-vindication-of-ihumanae-vitaei.

[6] Ibid.

[7] See Mt 19:3–12 and Mk 10:2–12.

that the increased use of contraception has also increased abortion. Fifty years ago when contraception became commonplace, many people of goodwill defended it precisely for the reason that they thought it would render abortion obsolete. Reliable birth control, they reasoned, would prevent abortion. But the concomitant rise in contraceptive use and abortion since the 1960s shows this commonly held logic to be wrong.[8] Many studies have emanated from the social sciences during the past decades that try to explain what secular wisdom regards as a puzzling fact. Far from preventing abortion and unplanned pregnancies, contraception's effects after the invention of the Pill run quite the other way: rates of contraception usage, abortion, and out-of-wedlock births have all exploded *simultaneously*.

Writing in the *Quarterly Journal of Economics* twenty-two years ago, economists George A. Akerlof, Janet L. Yellen, and Michael L. Katz summarized these unexpected connections:

> Before the sexual revolution, women had less freedom, but men were expected to assume responsibility for their welfare. Today women are more free to choose, but men have afforded themselves the comparable option. "If she is not willing to have an abortion or use contraception," the man can reason, "why should I sacrifice myself to get married?" By making the birth of the child the physical choice of the mother, the sexual revolution has made marriage and child support a social choice of the father.[9]

In other words, contraception has led to more pregnancy and more abortion because it eroded the idea that men had equal responsibility in case of an unplanned pregnancy. Contraception, as these economists explain, sharply reduced the incentive for men to marry—including to marry their pregnant girlfriends. In the new, post-Pill order, pregnancy became the woman's responsibility—and if birth control "failed", that was not the man's problem.

[8] See William Robert Johnston, "Historical Abortion Statistics, United States", Johnston's Archive, February 23, 2017, www.johnstonsarchive.net/policy/abortion/ab-unitedstates.html.

[9] George A. Akerlof, Janet L. Yellen, and Michael L. Katz, "An Analysis of Out-of-Wedlock Childbearing in the United States", *Quarterly Journal of Economics* 111, no. 2 (May 1996), at Brookings Policy Brief Series, August 1, 1996, https://www.brookings.edu/research/an-analysis-of-out-of-wedlock-births-in-the-united-states/.

Then there is the fact that contraception and abortion are bound together juridically. As Michael Pakaluk, among other scholars, has recently pointed out:

> As regards jurisprudence, the fruit of contraception is abortion. Until the 1960s, Comstock Act laws were on the books in many states, making the sale of contraceptives illegal even to married couples. These laws were overturned in 1965 by the Supreme Court's muddled *Griswold* decision. But by 1973—only eight years later—the Supreme Court in *Roe v. Wade* had inferred from the right to contraception a right to abortion.[10]

Putting that point differently: legal reasoning justifying freedom to contracept has been used to justify freedom to abort—a linkage that undermines the claim that a hard-and-fast line can be drawn between the two. Or, we might say, freedom to contracept was not enough. People needed the added freedom to terminate a "product of failed contraception".

History connects the same causal dots. The push to liberalize abortion laws in countries around the world did not begin until the first third of the twentieth century, as birth-control devices came into wider circulation, and American states did not start liberalizing abortion laws until after the federal approval of the Pill in 1960.[11] *Roe v. Wade* comes after the Pill, not before. As a matter of historical fact, the mass use of contraception called forth the demand for more abortion.

---

[10] Michael Pakaluk, "The Link between Contraception and Abortion", *First Things*, January 23, 2018, https://www.firstthings.com/web-exclusives/2018/01/the-link-between -contraception-and-abortion.

[11] See, for example, the timeline in Marge Berer, "Abortion Law and Policy around the World", *Health and Human Rights Journal*, June 19, 2017. As noted, "the first country to reform its abortion law was the Soviet Union" in 1920. See also the timeline of Supreme Court cases concerning "reproductive freedom" compiled by the American Civil Liberties Union (ACLU). In 1965, *Griswold v. Connecticut* strikes down state proscriptions against the sale and use of contraceptives for married couples. Seven years later, in *Eisenstadt v. Baird*, the Court establishes the right of unmarried couples to contraceptive use. One year later, *Roe v. Wade* establishes the right to abortion on demand. Plainly, abortion was not liberalized and then legalized *independent* of the increasing circulation and de-stigmatization of contraceptives. The timeline of U.S. jurisprudence alone suggests a causal chain. See ACLU, "Timeline of Important Reproductive Freedom Cases Decided by the Supreme Court", accessed April 17, 2018, https://www.aclu.org/other /timeline-important-reproductive-freedom-cases-decided-supreme-court.

Writing in the *National Catholic Bioethics Quarterly* in 2015, researcher Scott Lloyd likewise concluded that contraception leads to abortion—not inevitably in individual cases, of course, but repeatedly and reliably as twinned social phenomena: "Because the lower risk perceived with contraceptives enables sexual encounters and relationships that would not occur otherwise, it invites pregnancies that occur in situations where women do not feel ready to become pregnant."[12]

As we review the record, mercy and forgiveness are patently in order—toward the postwar generation that championed contraception, that is. Who, back then, could have anticipated that contraception would lead to abortion on a scale never before seen? Would the uproar over *Humanae vitae* have been much diminished had all critics known then what the ledger shows now? Might not some of those dissenting Catholics—and others—who publicly rebuked the Church have acted differently if they had realized that embracing contraception would open the way to vastly more abortion? It is plain in hindsight that the "lowering of moral standards" foreseen by *Humanae vitae*[13] would come to include disrespect not only for women, but for the human fetus, too.

Reality since 1968 has made it impossible to pretend that contraception has not played a decisive role in the scourge of abortion. Pope Francis has called abortion "a very grave sin" and a "horrendous crime".[14] The old defense of birth control as the alternative to abortion has been overruled by facts. The reality that it is an accelerant to abortion has been confirmed by time.

In part because fifty years of experience have established reality number one, a second reality has become evident. People outside the Catholic Church—most notably, though not only, some leading Protestants—have come to see *Humanae vitae* in a new and more favorable light. One of the least reported religious stories of our time, this potent trend may

---

[12] Scott Lloyd, "Can We Be Pro-Life and Pro-Contraception?", *National Catholic Bioethics Quarterly* 15, no. 2 (Summer 2015): 234.

[13] Paul VI, encyclical letter *Humanae vitae* (July 25, 1968), no. 17 (hereafter cited as *HV*), http://w2.vatican.va/content/paul-vi/en/encyclicals/documents/hf_p-vi_enc_25071968 _humanae-vitae.html.

[14] Pope Francis used these words in a 2016 interview with the Italian Catholic media outlets TV2000 and Blu Radio. See Inés San Martin, "Pope Francis Calls Abortion 'Horrendous Crime' and 'Very Grave Sin'", *Crux*, November 20, 2016, https://cruxnow.com /vatican/2016/11/20/pope-francis-calls-abortion-horrendous-crime-grave-sin/.

reconfigure Christianity, replacing disunity over birth control with a new unity. Observing what the sexual revolution has wrought, more and more Protestant voices now question yesterday's nonchalance about contraception. This reconsideration is far from a majority view—yet. But it manifests what any minority view must have in order to win over others: evidence and moral energy. Consider the following examples from the last ten years.

> Protestants have done themselves a disservice by ignoring *Humanae Vitae's* substantial statement on human anthropology and sexuality.... Protestants would be well-served to study Paul VI's encyclical and take heed of its warnings. (Evan Lenow, professor at Southwestern Baptist Theological Seminary)[15]

> Many evangelicals are joining the discussion about birth control and its meaning. Evangelicals arrived late to the issue of abortion, and we have arrived late to the issue of birth control, but we are here now. (R. Albert Mohler, Jr., president, Southern Baptist Theological Seminary)[16]

> For evangelicals, an anticontraception position is not seen as exclusively Roman Catholic, as it would have been in the past. (Jenell Paris, anthropologist, Messiah College, Pennsylvania)[17]

> Whenever current events touch on life issues, evangelicals like me become increasingly uncomfortable with the contraception culture. We realize we have much more in common with Catholics, who revere life, than the radical feminists who revere the rights of women above all else. (Julie Roys, evangelical author and blogger)[18]

> "There has been a shift in evangelical thinking about contraception". (*New York Times*, 2012)[19]

---

[15] Evan Lenow, "Protestants and Contraception", *First Things*, January 2018, https://www.firstthings.com/article/2018/01/protestants-and-contraception.

[16] R. Albert Mohler, Jr., "The Pill Turns 50—TIME Considers the Contraceptive Revolution", AlbertMohler.com, April 26, 2010, https://albertmohler.com/2010/04/26/the-pill-turns-50-time-considers-the-contraceptive-revolution/.

[17] Quoted in Mark Oppenheimer, "Many Evangelicals See Something to Admire in Candidates' Broods", *New York Times*, January 20, 2012, http://www.nytimes.com/2012/01/21/us/more-protestants-oppose-birth-control.html.

[18] Julie Roys, "Rethinking Contraception", blog, March 1, 2012, http://julieroys.com/rethinking-contraception/.

[19] Oppenheimer, "Evangelicals See Something to Admire".

These second thoughts among Protestants and other non-Catholics are less a radical break from Christian tradition than a return to it. Church teaching on contraception, including Protestant teaching, has followed an unbroken line through the centuries. Not until the Anglican Communion made the first exception to the prohibition at the Lambeth Conference of 1930 did Catholics and Protestants divide on this moral teaching. The famous Resolution 15 was intended for married couples only, and in carefully delineated circumstances, but it ushered in contraception for convenience. Its language matches the terminology deployed by would-be Catholic "reformers" today:

> In those cases where there is such a clearly felt moral obligation to limit or avoid parenthood, and where there is a morally sound reason for avoiding complete abstinence, the Conference agrees that other methods may be used, provided that this is done in the light of the same Christian principles.[20]

Then, as now, Protestants who were not at ease with abandoning traditional teaching turned to Rome for authority. Charles Gore, the bishop of Oxford, objected to Resolution 15. He had "manifold reason to believe that in the case of Birth Prevention the 'very strong tradition in the Catholic Church' has been in the right, and has divine sanction".[21] The move by some Protestants toward *Humanae vitae* today is in part a tacit declaration that, in retrospect, the bishop of Oxford's side might have been the right one.

In Africa, both Protestants and Catholics lean toward traditionalism in Christian moral teaching. Here as elsewhere in history, the maxim delivered by sociologist Laurence R. Iannaccone holds: "Strict churches are strong"—and concomitantly, lax churches are weak.[22] It is in tradition-minded Africa that Christianity has grown explosively in the years since

---

[20] "Resolution 15—The Life and Witness of the Christian Community; Marriage and Sex", Anglican Communion Office, accessed April 17, 2018, http://www.anglicancommunion.org /resources/document-library/lambeth-conference/1930/resolution-15-the-life-and-witness -of-the-christian-community-marriage.aspx?author=Lambeth+Conference&year=1930.

[21] Charles Gore, *Lambeth on Contraceptives* (London: Mowbray, 1930), under "Is It Then Wrong in Itself?", http://anglicanhistory.org/gore/contra1930.html.

[22] Laurence R. Iannaccone, "Why Strict Churches Are Strong", *American Journal of Sociology* 99, no. 5 (March 1994): 1180–211, https://www.journals.uchicago.edu/doi/abs /10.1086/230409.

Humanae vitae—as opposed to those nations whose Christian leaders have struggled, and struggle still, to change the rulebook.

As the Pew Research Center put it in a report a few years ago, "Africans [are] among the most morally opposed to contraception."[23] Substantial numbers of people in Kenya, Uganda, and other sub-Saharan countries—Catholic and otherwise—agree with the proposition that contraception use is "morally unacceptable"; in Ghana and Nigeria, it is more than half the population. Despite decades of secular proselytizing, many in Africa have resisted the attempts of reformers to bring them into line with the Western sexual program—which includes, of course, diminishing the number of Africans.

Nigerian-born Obianuju Ekeocha, author of the new book *Target Africa: Ideological Neo-Colonialism of the Twenty-First Century*, wrote an open letter to Melinda Gates, whose foundation dedicates impressive resources to spreading birth control among Africans: "I see this $4.6 billion buying us misery. I see it buying us unfaithful husbands. I see it buying us streets devoid of the innocent chatter of children.... I see it buying us a retirement without the tender loving care of our children."[24]

Africans are not the only intended beneficiaries of campaigns to expand the contraceptive *Weltanschauung*. Nor are they alone in abjuring the idea that the world would be better off with fewer of them in it. As one notable Indian targeted with the same message some years back put it, "It is futile to hope that the use of contraceptives will be restricted to the mere regulation of progeny. There is hope for a decent life only so long as the sexual act is definitely related to the conception of precious life."[25] The author of these sentences is not moral philosopher Elizabeth Anscombe, whose famous 1972 essay "Contraception and Chastity" defended *Humanae vitae* with this same logic.[26] It is instead Mahatma

---

[23] Michael Lipka, "Africans among the Most Morally Opposed to Contraception", Pew Research Center, Factank News in the Numbers, April 16, 2014, http://www.pewresearch .org/fact-tank/2014/04/16/africans-among-the-most-morally-opposed-to-contraception/.

[24] Obianuju Ekeocha, *Target Africa: Ideological Neo-Colonialism of the Twenty-First Century* (San Francisco: Ignatius Press, 2018), p. TK.

[25] M. K. Gandhi, *Self-Restraint vs. Self-Indulgence: Gandhi's Views on Self-Discipline* (Greenleaf Books, 1999).

[26] Elizabeth Anscombe, "Contraception and Chastity", in *Why Humanae Vitae Was Right*, 1st ed., ed. Janet Smith (1972; repr., San Francisco: Ignatius Press, 1993).

Gandhi—one more non-Catholic to affirm the reasoning behind Christian moral teaching. "I urge the advocates of artificial methods to consider the consequences," he explained elsewhere. "Any large use of the methods is likely to result in the dissolution of the marriage bond and in free love."[27]

There is also sound reason for the enduring fear that "public authorities" might "impose" these technologies on the citizenry—as *Humanae vitae* also warned.[28] This has happened, of course, in China, via its long-standing, barbaric "one child" policy, replete with forced abortions and involuntary sterilizations. A softer kind of coercion has appeared in the United States and other Western nations where efforts have been made to link desired outcomes with mandatory birth control. In the 1990s and beyond, for example, some U.S. judges backed state-imposed implantation of long-term contraceptives on women convicted of crimes. Such implied force has provoked criticism by (among others) the American Civil Liberties Union (ACLU). "The recent attempts to coerce women to use Norplant represent a reversion to an era of overt racism and eugenics," the ACLU explained.[29]

Another reality concerns the state of modern women. Contraception, it was and is perennially asserted, will make women happier and freer than ever before. Has it? Evidence points to the contrary—from social science suggesting that female happiness across the United States and Europe has been declining over time, to the dolorous notes so often struck in academic and popular feminism, to the growing worry among secular women that marriage has become impossible and it is time to go it alone.[30] A decade after I documented those trends, there is much more that could be added to the ledger suggesting that *Humanae vitae* was right to spy an impending increase in divisiveness between the sexes. Consider in passing just two evocative snapshots.

In 2012, Amazon U.K. announced that E. L. James' *Fifty Shades of Grey* had replaced J. K. Rowling's *Harry Potter* books as the bestselling

---

[27] Mohandas Karamchand Gandhi, *Collected Works of Mahatma Gandhi*, vol. 31 (New Delhi: Publication Division, Ministry of Information, 1995), p. 99.

[28] *HV* 17.

[29] "Norplant: A New Contraceptive with the Potential for Abuse", under "Have the Coerced Uses of Norplant Been Discriminatory?", ACLU, press release, accessed April 18, 2018, https://www.aclu.org/other/norplant-new-contraceptive-potential-abuse.

[30] Eberstadt, "Vindication of *Humanae vitae*".

volume in its history.[31] This signals an extraordinary commercial demand *by women* for the tale of a rich and powerful man who humiliates, bullies, and commits violence against a woman, over and over. Sadomasochism is a prominent theme elsewhere in popular culture—including, again, popular women's culture. Concerning the fashion industry, John Leo observed, "I first noticed the porn-fashion connection in 1975, when *Vogue* magazine ran a seven-photo fashion spread featuring a man in a bathrobe battering a screaming model in a lovely pink jumpsuit ($140 from Saks, picture by Avedon)."[32] *Harper's Bazaar* has seconded the point: "Long before [the] *50 Shades* fever hit, designers had been mining BDSM for sartorial inspiration. From literal crops to all forms of waist, wrist and ankle ties—not to mention the sheer volume of leather—it's clear Christian Grey would be proud."[33]

Implied and even overt violence against women saturates video games and, of course, pornography. The sadomasochistic look has become widespread in popular music, too; the number of globally recognized female singers who have *not* paid homage to pornography and degradation is vanishingly small.[34] Why are so many women subsidizing a self-image of subjugation and dejection at a time when their freedom is greater than ever before? Does the success of *Fifty Shades* tell us that men have become so hard to get that any means of finding one will do, no matter how degrading?

Joy does not abound in another post-Pill reality: the continuing secular sex scandals of 2017 and 2018, and the #MeToo movement. It appears that the sexual revolution licensed predation. That is not a theological judgment, but an empirical one—foreseen in part by social scientist Francis Fukuyama. His 1999 book *The Great Disruption* made a

---

[31] "*Fifty Shades* Trilogy Outsells *Harry Potter* on Amazon UK's Website", *Guardian*, August 1, 2012, https://www.theguardian.com/books/2012/aug/01/fifty-shades-outsells-harry-potter-amazon.

[32] John Leo, *Two Steps Ahead of the Thought Police*, 1st ed. (New York: Simon and Schuster, 1994), p. 223.

[33] Keri Pieri, "The Best Bondage on the Runway: Fashion Has Loved Bondage since Long before *50 Shades of Grey*", *Harper's Bazaar*, February 13, 2015, https://www.harpersbazaar.com/fashion/fashion-week/g5263/best-runway-bondage-fashion/.

[34] For an overview, see Mary Eberstadt, "Jailhouse Feminism: What the Raging Gets Right", *National Review*, February 19, 2015, https://www.nationalreview.com/2015/02/roots-female-rage/.

point that echoes in *Humanae vitae*, though based on a thoroughly secular analysis:

> One of the greatest frauds perpetrated during the Great Disruption was the notion that the sexual revolution was gender-neutral, benefiting women and men equally.... In fact the sexual revolution served the interests of men, and in the end put sharp limits on the gains that women might otherwise have expected from their liberation from traditional roles.[35]

Almost twenty years later, that point is irrefutable. The abuse scandals show that the revolution democratized sexual harassment. No longer does a man have to be a king or a master of the universe to abuse or prey upon women in unrelenting, serial fashion, and for a long time, with no punishment. One needs only a world in which women are assumed to use contraception—the world we've had since the 1960s, the world that *Humanae vitae* foresaw.

This brings us to still another reality: fifty years into the sexual revolution, one of the most pressing, and growing, issues for researchers is not overpopulation, but its opposite: *underpopulation*. Ten years ago, I reviewed evidence for the claim that the overpopulation scares of the late 1960s were just that: scares. They happened not so coincidentally to be ideologically useful to partisans who wanted the Church to change her moral teaching. As I noted in 2008:

> So discredited has the overpopulation science become that this year Columbia University historian Matthew Connelly could publish *Fatal Misconception: The Struggle to Control World Population* and garner a starred review in *Publishers Weekly*—all in service of what is probably the single best demolition of the population arguments that some hoped would undermine church teaching. This is all the more satisfying a ratification because Connelly is so conscientious in establishing his own personal antagonism toward the Catholic Church.... *Fatal Misconception* is decisive [secular] proof that the spectacle of overpopulation, which was used to browbeat the Vatican in the name of science, was a grotesque error all along.[36]

---

[35] Francis Fukuyama, *The Great Disruption: Human Nature and the Reconstitution of Social Order* (New York: Free Press, 1999), pp. 121–22.

[36] Eberstadt, "Vindication of *Humanae vitae*".

The past decade has made reality plain. Not only is "overpopulation" a shifting ideological chimera, but the *reverse* obtains. A great many people, especially in the increasingly barren and graying West, are suffering instead from what experts in those stricken societies call an "epidemic" of loneliness. This finding would not surprise Pope Francis, who in an interview with *La Repubblica* in 2013 called the "loneliness of the old" one of the worst "evils" in today's world.[37] Fifty years after the embrace of the Pill—undeniably, *because* of the embrace of the Pill—loneliness is spreading across the materially better-off countries of the planet. Toward the end of last year, the *New York Times* published a harrowing story about what the birth dearth looks like from the other end of time's telescope.

> "4,000 lonely deaths a week," estimated the cover of a popular weekly magazine.... Each year, some of [Japan's elderly] died without anyone knowing, only to be discovered after their neighbors caught the smell.
>
> The first time it happened, or at least the first time it drew national attention, the corpse of a 69-year-old man living near Mrs. Ito had been lying on the floor for three years, without anyone noticing his absence. His monthly rent and utilities had been withdrawn automatically from his bank account. Finally, after his savings were depleted in 2000, the authorities came to the apartment and found his skeleton near the kitchen, its flesh picked clean by maggots and beetles, just a few feet away from his next-door neighbors.[38]

The story goes on to note, "The extreme isolation of elderly Japanese is so common that an entire industry has emerged around it, specializing in cleaning out apartments where decomposing remains are found." According to another recent report in the *Independent*, cleanup firms are burgeoning and insurance companies offer policies to protect landlords in case a "lonely" happens on their property.[39]

---

[37] "The Pope: How the Church Will Change", interview with Eugenio Scalfari, *La Repubblica*, October 1, 2013, http://www.repubblica.it/cultura/2013/10/01/news/pope_s _conversation_with_scalfari_english-67643118/.

[38] Norimitsu Onishi, "A Generation in Japan Faces a Lonely Death", *New York Times*, November 30, 2017, https://www.nytimes.com/2017/11/30/world/asia/japan-lonely-deaths -the-end.html.

[39] Anna Fifield, "Japan's Lonely Deaths: A Growing Industry Is Now Devoted to Cleaning Up after Japanese People Dying Alone", *Independent*, January 30, 2018, https://www .independent.co.uk/news/long_reads/lonely-deaths-japan-die-alone-clean-apartments -japanese-industry-next-homes-clear-a8182861.html.

Japan is just one country facing post-Pill demographic change. "Loneliness is becoming a common phenomena [*sic*] in France," *Le Figaro* reported several years ago.[40] Citing a study on the "New Solitudes" by the Fondation de France (French Foundation), the article names the prime driver of this loneliness: "family rupture", especially divorce. In a similar vein, a 2014 study on "Socio-Demographic Predictors of Loneliness across the Adult Life Span in Portugal" agreed that divorce increases the likelihood of loneliness—though it did not ask whether having children in the picture might ameliorate the problem.[41] Oddly, one can read through many "loneliness studies" without seeing reference to children, a striking omission that says a good deal about our era.

The secular culture is taking note. In Sweden, a 2015 documentary *The Swedish Theory of Love* questioned the dominance of "independence" in that country as an ideal. It seems more a curse than a blessing when one half of Swedes now live in households of one. As a report put it,

> A man is alone in his flat. He has been lying there dead for three weeks—people only noticing his demise when an awful smell appeared in the communal hallways. As the Swedish authorities scrutinise the case, they discover that the man has no close relatives or friends. It is highly likely that he lived lonely and alone for years, sitting solitary in front of his TV or computer. After a while, they discover that he has a daughter, but she proves impossible to locate.... It becomes apparent that he actually had quite a lot of money tucked away in the bank. But what does that help when he had no one to share with.[42]

And then there's Germany. In an article in *Der Spiegel* titled "Alone by the Millions: Isolation Crisis Threatens German Seniors", the German Centre of Gerontology reports:

> Over 20 percent of Germans over the age of 70 are in regular contact with only one person—or nobody. One in four receives a visit less than

[40] Michael Cosgrove, "Loneliness Is Becoming a Common Phenomena in France", *Le Figaro*, February 7, 2010, http://plus.lefigaro.fr/note/loneliness-is-becoming-a-common-phenomena-in-france-20100702-236888.

[41] Félix Neto, "Socio-Demographic Predictors of Loneliness across the Adult Life Span in Portugal", *Interpersona* 8, no. 2 (2014), https://interpersona.psychopen.eu/article/view/171/html.

[42] *The Swedish Theory of Love*, documentary, directed by Erik Gandini (Sweden, 2015).

once a month from friends and acquaintances, and nearly one in 10 is
not visited by anyone anymore. Many old people have no one who still
addresses them by their first name or asks them how they are doing.[43]

Such human poverty abounds in societies awash in material wealth.
This ironic juxtaposition, too, was not foreseen by those who argued for
and against *Humanae vitae* in 1968. Yet without doubt, what unites these
tragic portraits is the sexual revolution, which by the 1970s was operat-
ing at full throttle in Western nations, driving up divorce rates, driving
down marriage rates, and emptying cradles.

In addition to its destructive force at the beginning and end of the
human lifespan, the sexual revolution also continues to generate per-
mutations of sexuality unheard-of in the history that preceded our own.
There are the scores of "gender identities" that have achieved sacrosanct
status in much the way that medieval seals and shields once signified a
different kind of elemental belonging—and the ongoing accommodations of law and custom to such radical ideas. So unexpected and pervasive are these new transformations that several books outlining the new
sexual cartography have appeared within the last year alone, including
Ashley McGuire's *Sex Scandal: The Drive to Abolish Male and Female*,[44]
about the social and political enforcement of androgyny; Mark Regnerus' *Cheap Sex: The Transformation of Men, Marriage, and Monogamy*,[45]
an economic analysis of how the revolution and especially pornography
have radically changed incentives for marriage; and Ryan T. Anderson's
groundbreaking examination in *When Harry Became Sally: Responding to
the Transgender Moment*.[46]

The shifting boundaries mapped by these and other new analyses of
the revolution's fallout are no mere abstractions, but poignant facts for
many millions of manifestly confused and suffering human beings. At the
outermost reaches of the revolution's changes, phenomena never before

---

[43] Guido Kleinhubbert and Antje Windmann, "Alone by the Millions: Isolation Crisis
Threatens German Seniors", *Der Spiegel*, January 10, 2013, http://www.spiegel.de/international
/germany/germany-faces-epidemic-of-lonely-and-isolated-seniors-a-876635.html.

[44] Ashley McGuire, *Sex Scandal: The Drive to Abolish Male and Female* (Washington, DC:
Regnery Publishing, 2017).

[45] Mark Regnerus, *Cheap Sex: The Transformation of Men, Marriage, and Monogamy* (New
York: Oxford University Press, 2017).

[46] Ryan T. Anderson, *When Harry Became Sally: Responding to the Transgender Moment*
(New York: Encounter Books, 2018).

seen continue to percolate up from the social atomization. Elderly people without grandchildren buy talking robotic toys whom they treat as babies.[47] Japan is also home to the phenomenon of "herbivores", meaning men who live gently, including by avoiding sex, which has lately been the subject of much worried commentary in a country already over a demographic precipice; how much this phenomenon is driven by chronic pornography use is another open question that did not exist in the prerevolutionary era.[48]

A further reality to ponder is historical, and worth reiterating at a time when hope burns eternal in some precincts that the Catholic Church will cease its intransigent insistence on supposedly retrograde points of doctrine. The churches that have accommodated themselves to the sexual revolution have imploded from within. As a headline in the *Guardian* put it simply in 2016, on the eve of a contentious conference at Lambeth where African representatives of the Anglican Communion dissented once more from changing moral teaching, "The Anglican Schism over Sexuality Marks the End of a Global Church".[49]

In 1930, people would have been shocked if told that the doctrinal war over sex would shatter the Anglican Communion; that parts of the Communion would go to legal war over churches and jurisdictions as well as doctrine; that the separation of North and South, Episcopal and Anglican, Africa and Europe, would yield divisions and subdivisions, sorrow and acrimony, on a global scale.

In 1998, Bishop John Shelby Spong of Newark, New Jersey, a leader of the Episcopalian church who urged an embrace of the sexual revolution, published a book called *Why Christianity Must Change or Die*, agitating for still more dismantling of the tradition.[50] The Christianity of which he spoke *did* change, exactly as he and others hoped. And now the retooled version they fought for is dying. According to David

---

[47] Duncan Bartlett, "Japan's Toys for the Elderly", *Business Daily, BBC World Service*, April 30, 2006, http://news.bbc.co.uk/2/hi/business/4919606.stm.

[48] Greg Wilford, "Young Japanese People Are Not Having Sex", *Independent*, July 8, 2017, https://www.independent.co.uk/news/world/asia/japan-sex-problem-demographic-time -bomb-birth-rates-sex-robots-fertility-crisis-virgins-romance-porn-a7831041.html.

[49] Andrew Brown, "The Anglican Schism over Sexuality Marks the End of a Global Church", *Guardian*, January 8, 2016, https://www.theguardian.com/commentisfree/2016/jan /08/anglican-schism-sexuality-end-global-church-conservative-african-leaders-canterbury.

[50] John Shelby Spong, *Why Christianity Must Change or Die: A Bishop Speaks to Believers in Exile* (San Francisco, CA: HarperSanFrancisco, 1998).

Goodhew, editor of the 2016 volume *Growth and Decline in the Anglican Communion: 1980 to the Present*, research by Jeremy Bonner on the Episcopal Church shows that

> around [the year] 2000 serious decline set in.... Average Sunday attendance dropped by nearly one third between 2000 and 2015.... The rate of baptism has been cut almost in half over a thirty-year-period.... The most dramatic data is for marriages.... In 2015 the Episcopal Church married less than a quarter of the number it married in 1980.[51]

The sad facts of religious history in favor of Paul VI's prophetic stance make their own case. Disaster descended on the Anglican Communion for doing exactly what dissenters from *Humanae vitae* want the Catholic Church to do: make exceptions to rules that people find difficult. Surely anyone urging Rome to follow Lambeth's lead today must first explain how Catholicism's fate will be different. As David Goodhew also noted in his online piece "Facing Episcopal Church Decline", "If we believe Christian faith is good news, we should be seeking its proliferation, and be worried when it shrinks."[52]

"Manuscripts don't burn."[53] In Mikhail Bulgakov's twentieth-century masterpiece *The Master and Margarita*, a despairing author trapped under oppressive Soviet rule tries to destroy his own unpublished book in a fire—only to learn, in the redemptive denouement, that it's impossible. Bulgakov could see with his soul what he would never witness with his eyes. Too dangerous to publish under Communism, *The Master and Margarita* itself would not appear until 1967, almost thirty years after the novelist's death in 1940—whereupon it became, and remains, a literary sensation around the world.

"Manuscripts don't burn", one of the most famous lines in *The Master and Margarita*, became an immortal rallying cry on behalf of the indomitable nature of truth. Truth, artistic or otherwise, may be unwanted,

[51] David Goodhew, *Growth and Decline in the Anglican Communion: 1980 to the Present*, 1st ed. (New York: Routledge, 2016), quoted in David Goodhew, "Facing Episcopal Church Decline", *Covenant*, weblog of the Living Church Foundation, July 24, 2017, https://living church.org/covenant/2017/07/24/facing-episcopal-church-decline/.

[52] Goodhew, "Facing Episcopal Church Decline".

[53] Mikhail Bulgakov, *The Master and Margarita*, trans. Richard Pevear and Larissa Volokhonsky (New York: Penguin Books, 2016), p. 287.

inconvenient, resented, mocked in all the best places—even harassed, suppressed, and forced underground. But that does not make it anything other than truth.

In this moment of watchfulness inside and outside the Church, a global fellowship knows the truths of *Humanae vitae* and related teachings *as* truths, however unwanted or hard. They are among the latest pilgrims in a line stretching two thousand years back. They have sacrificed to stand where they do, and they sacrifice still—including by relinquishing the good opinion of a mocking world.

These cradle Catholics and converts and reverts, fellow-traveling non-Catholics, clergy and laity alike, have the consolation of one final *realidad*, which may be the most important reality of all. Whatever the anxieties of the moment, however prominent or widespread the disgruntlement, the ever-growing empirical record continues to vindicate Paul VI's encyclical. *Humanae vitae* does not burn.

Hormones and *Humanae vitae*

The Impact of Oral Contraceptives on Pheromones and Sexual Behavior and Preferences, and on Women's Mortality[*]

Angela Lanfranchi, M.D.

Humanae vitae instructed that sexual activity should be observant of natural law. Natural law asserts that by virtue of our human nature (endowed by our Creator) there are universal human values and rights knowable through reason. The arguments against contraception in *Humanae vitae* are largely philosophical in nature: they are based on the nature or meaning of marital intercourse. But there are also scientific studies unknown prior to the publication of *Humanae vitae* that support the conclusions of Pope Paul VI. Two scientific developments that have made the words of Pope Paul VI so prescient are the growing understanding of the role of pheromones in human sexual behavior and of the effect on a woman's body of synthetic hormones found in hormonal contraception such as the Pill, Depo Provera, Norplant, and the "patch", among others. These new findings particularly support the prediction made in *Humanae vitae* that widespread use of contraception would be damaging to a woman's physical and psychological health. Moreover, as we shall see, what is harmful to her psychological and physical health is also harmful to her relationships.

---

[*] This article is a much-revised version of "A Scientific Basis for Humanae Vitae and Natural Law: The Role of Pheromones on Human Sexual Preferences by Oral Contraceptives and the Abortifacient Effects of Oral Contraceptives", *Linacre Quarterly* (April 12, 2018), http://journals.sagepub.com/doi/abs/10.1177/0024363918756191?journalCode=lqra.

Our fallible and willful human nature often rebels when a restriction meant for our well-being is placed upon what is considered our freedom for our cherished choices. Understandably, we want to have a reason for the restriction. We say, "Prove why it is better for me to change my behavior," or, "Prove to me why contraception is wrong and will hurt me."

The evidence that existed long before 1973 that an embryo is a living human being should have been sufficient to have kept abortion illegal. But had the justices who decided *Roe v. Wade* been able to see a moving and audible ultrasound image of a three-week-old embryo's beating heart, they may have been swayed to protect the life, once they could see and hear it with their own senses. Similarly, had clergy and laity known how tampering with a woman's natural hormones impacts her physiologically and psychologically, and consequently her relationships as well, they may have more easily come to accept the teaching of *Humanae vitae*. That information was not available in 1968. Indeed, the science illustrating the reason hormonal contraceptives affect sexual behavior and "mate" preference could only be obtained after a large number of women used the Pill and the sociological changes in the male-female relationship became painfully apparent.

Had Pope Paul VI known the physiological changes caused by the Pill that result in behavioral changes, he would have come to the same conclusions on the Pill's effect on human behavior that he arrived at, by moral doctrine on marriage taught by natural law and the Magisterium of the Church. In fact, he would likely have been surprised at the range of evidence that supports the Church's teaching.

How Hormonal Contraceptives Work

A woman using hormonal contraceptives is in a very unnatural state. It is natural for women from puberty to postmenopause to be cycling through fertile and infertile phases or to be pregnant. Hormonal contraceptives prevent a woman from getting pregnant by preventing ovulation, changing the viscosity of the mucus that carries a sperm to meet an ovum, and changing the quality of the endometrium. We know from in vitro fertilization studies that for good implantation rates for the embryo, the endometrium should be 8.5 millimeters thick.

Women on the Pill fail to develop a thickness over 6 millimeters.[1] Moreover, hormonal contraceptives change the very biochemistry of the women at the molecular level to impede pregnancy. For instance, the Pill interferes with a protein, interlueukin-1 beta. This protein causes the preimplanted embryo to orient itself properly so that it can implant itself into the endometrium, much like the space shuttle needs proper orientation to dock to the space station.[2] Simply stated, hormonal contraceptives attempt to put a woman's body into a condition that mimics pregnancy (nonovulation, no fertile mucus, a nonreceptive endometrium), because when a woman is pregnant, she cannot get pregnant.

So a woman using a hormonal contraceptive is in a state of pseudo pregnancy, a very unnatural state. That very unnatural state profoundly affects her relationships with males. Studies are showing that one of the reasons for the changes in male-female relationships is due to the impact of hormonal contraceptives on pheromones.

Pheromones

Pheromones are chemical compounds produced and secreted that influence the behavior and development of members of their own species. In animals, there is a vomeronasal organ (VNO) located in the nasal passages, which detects pheromones. It was thought that humans may not have pheromones. While the VNO exists in the human fetus, there is no such clear organ in adult humans. However, recent studies have shown that humans react to pheromones.

There are pits in nasal mucosa that react to pheromones in mammals, even when the VNO duct is obstructed. It is now believed that humans can react to pheromones directly through the olfactory nerve, which transmits smell to the brain. Over the last fifty years, this has been an area of significant scientific research. There is a rich and deep literature

[1] T. Rabe et al., "The Effects of Monophasic and Triphasic Oral Contraceptives on Ovarian Function and Endometrial Thickness", *European Journal of Contraception and Reproductive Health Care* 2 (1997): 39–51.

[2] John Wilks, "The Impact of the Pill on Implantation Factors—New Research Findings", *Ethics and Medicine* 16, no. 1 (2000): 15–22.

that supports the existence of human sexual pheromones. This research ranges from the chemical and molecular biology of putative human pheromones to those relating the effects on social behavior.

As in other areas of scientific research, there remains some controversy. Indeed, some scientists even question whether or not human pheromones exist. While it is simpler to demonstrate that one chemical, a pheromone, affects the behavior of an insect, human research is much more complex. Not only must ethical guidelines be met by the researcher, but the human is much more complex than an insect. Experiments and studies must have controls for many more variables that are difficult to quantify, such as the emotional states of subjects. Moreover, human behavior is controlled by many factors other than purely physical cues, such as moral and social conditioning and norms. On this controversy, Richard Doty's book *The Great Pheromone Myth* maintains that much of human behavior is learned and that "mammals are not insects".[3] Elsewhere, he also critiques some well-known research as having methodological flaws.[4]

It is no surprise that other researchers do not find Roty's rejection of the existence of human pheromones persuasive. In "Ecological Validity in Study of Human Pheromones", Tamsin K. Saxton, Anthony C. Little, and S. Craig Roberts give persuasive evidence that human pheromones do exist.[5] After reviewing the literature and history of human pheromonal research, they report on an experimental study that was constructed using the social context of "speed-dating" that studied twenty-five females and twenty-two males using a putative pheromone androstadienone in different concentrations with controls of water and of clove. They found a significant effect of androsteindienone on female judgments of male attractiveness.[6]

Regardless of whether or not human pheromones exist or not, it is clear that hormones affect human behavior. A study in Denmark

---

[3] Richard L. Doty, *The Great Pheromone Myth* (Baltimore, MD: Johns Hopkins University Press, 2010), p. 32.

[4] Richard L. Doty, *Human Pheromones in Neurobiology of Chemical Communication*, ed. C. Mucignat-Caretta (Boca Raton, FL: CRC Press/Taylor & Francis, 2014), chap. 19.

[5] Tamsin K. Saxton, Anthony C. Little, and S. Craig Roberts, "Ecological Validity in the Study of Human Pheromones", chap. 10 in *Chemical Signals in Vertebrates 11*, ed. Jane L. Hurst et al. (New York: Springer Science+Business Media, 2008).

[6] Ibid., p. 111.

showed that after just two months of women taking hormonal contraception, there was a statistically significant increase in the incidence of suicidal attempts and suicides among these women—an increase that the researchers themselves correlated to the use of hormonal contraception.[7] Perhaps we don't yet know whether pheromones affected by hormonal contraceptives are responsible for the changed behavior in women, or whether it is a more complex set of reactions mediated through hormonal exposure that causes the changed behavior, but it is clear that hormones do provoke changes in women's behavior. It does seem, however, that there is enough evidence that human pheromones exist and that hormonal contraceptives affect those hormones—that it is reasonable to use studies that connect hormonal contraceptives, pheromones, and changes in human behavior.

Pheromones in Humans

The first evidence of pheromone effects in humans was made by an observation of Martha McClintock. McClintock first noticed menstrual synchrony in the 1970s when soon after moving into a female college dormitory, all the women had menstrual cycles that were near synchronous. Data addressing how one woman could affect the hormonal cycle of another was nonexistent. It was plausible that pheromones were responsible. There was data that these pheromones were associated with underarm secretions.[8]

It took until 1998 for McClintock and Kathleen Stern to show that fluids collected from a donor woman's underarms, when applied to the upper lip of another female, could hasten or delay the recipient's menstrual period. The study fell short of identifying the exact chemicals responsible, but even many skeptics agree that it provides strong evidence for the existence of human pheromones.[9]

---

[7] Charlotte Wessel Skovlund et al., "Association of Hormonal Contraception with Suicide Attempts and Suicides", *American Journal of Psychiatry* 175, no. 4 (April 1, 2018): 336–42, https://doi.org/10.1176/appi.ajp.2017.17060616.

[8] Martha McClintock, "Menstrual Synchrony and Suppression", *Nature* 229 (January 22, 1971): 229, 244–45.

[9] Comment on Kathleen Stern and Martha K. McClintock, "Regulation of Ovulation by Human Pheromones", *Nature* 392 (March 12, 1998): 177–79, in A. Weller, "Human Pheromones: Communication through Body Odour", *Nature* 392 (March 12, 1998): 126–27.

In 1999, Noam Sobel used functional magnetic resonance imaging (MRI) to show that the human brain responded to androstadienone, even when subjects were unable to smell it.[10] In 2001, Ivanka Savic, using PET (positron emission tomography) scans and MRIs, reported that androstadienone and estratetraenol (male and female compounds, respectively) affected men's and women's brains differently. The male compound stimulated hypothalamic activity only in women, while the female compound increased hypothalamic activity only in men.[11] Since the hypothalamus influences the pituitary gland's release of hormones, it is in a key position to affect reproductive behavior. Almost twenty years later, there is significant research concerning human pheromones and unconscious social and psychological behavior. We have yet to sort out how all these chemical differences between men and women affect their relationships, but we do have significant evidence that they do, and in many ways. There have been many studies confirming that women are more attractive in their fertile phase. A 2003 study[12] revealed that women were found to be most attractive to men at midcycle when they were fertile. On the other hand, there was no fluctuation of attractiveness in women on the Pill. In 2007, psychologists from the University of New Mexico found that there was a connection between the menstrual cycles of female strippers and the tips they earned during a given night. Women in their fertile phase made higher tips than in their nonfertile phase.[13]

There is also evidence that shows differences in facial appearance preferences of partners in women who are taking the Pill.[14] With the initiation of the Pill, women decreased their preference for male facial masculinity, but they did not change their preference of same-sex faces.

---

[10] Noam Sobel et al., "Blind Smell: Brain Activation Induced by an Undetected Air-borne Chemical", *Brain* 122 (1999): 122, 209–17.

[11] Ivanka Savic, "Smelling of Odorous Sex Hormone-like Compounds Causes Sex-Differentiated Hypothalamic Activations in Humans", *Neuron* 31, no. 4 (2001): 661–68.

[12] Seppo Kuukasjärvi et al., "Attractiveness of Women's Body Odors over the Menstrual Cycle: The Role of Oral Contraceptives and Receiver Sex", *Behavioral Ecology* 15, no. 4 (July 2004): 579–84.

[13] Geoffrey Miller, Joshua M. Tybur, and Brent D. Jordan, "Ovulatory Cycle Effects on Tip Earnings by Lap Dancers: Economic Evidence for Human Estrus?", *Evolution and Human Behavior* 28, no. 6 (November 2007): 375–81.

[14] Anthony C. Little et al., "Oral Contraceptive Use in Women Changes Preferences for Male Facial Masculinity and Is Associated with Partner Facial Masculinity", *Psychoneuroendocrinology* 38, no. 9 (September 2013): 1777–85.

In fact, the faces of partners chosen while the women were taking the Pill were less masculine than the partners chosen when women were not taking the Pill. Studies show that women who are already pregnant are more attracted to "companionable males". It is thought that a woman who is already pregnant or in a pregnancy-like state induced by the Pill would prefer close relatives for support, while those women who are not pregnant would seek men as possible mates who are geneti-cally different and not closely related. David I. Perrett and others found that "enhancing masculine facial characteristics increased both perceived dominance and negative attributions (for example, coldness or dishon-esty) relevant to relationships and paternal investment."[15] According to S. Craig Roberts, "As might be expected, masculine faces are seen as more dominant but not as possessing traits that would be desirable in a long-term partner. Initiation of pill use impacts on preferences for these traits, suggesting that associated hormonal changes alter the balance in favour of cooperative feminine partners over dominant/healthy mascu-line partners."[16]

Information from Primate Studies

In 1999, anthropologist Dr. Lionel Tiger wrote a book entitled *The Decline of Males*, in which he examined how the Pill brought about profound sociological changes in the relationship of men and women.[17] In 1972, less than ten years after widespread use of the Pill began, when searching for the reasons for this sea change in male-female rela-tionships, he and colleagues from Rutgers University and its medical school created an experiment, described in his book. They established a colony of macaque monkeys on an isolated island off Bermuda that closely mimicked their natural African environment. The first three-month phase documented the behavior of the troop. The alpha male had three consorts with which he had regular sexual episodes. There

[15] David I. Perrett et al., "Effects of Sexual Dimorphism on Facial Attractiveness", *Nature* 394 (September 1998): 884.
[16] Little et al., "Oral Contraceptive Use in Women Changes Preferences for Male Facial Masculinity", p. 1783.
[17] Lionel Tiger, *The Decline of Males* (New York: St. Martin's Press, 1999).

were another five mature females and some immature females and adult males on the island.

After a three-month period of documenting their natural behavior, five adult females were injected with Depo-Provera, a hormonal contraceptive that has an effect for three months. Two of the females that were injected were the alpha male's consorts. Although he was still interactive with them, he stopped sexual activity with them and replaced them with two hormone-free females for sexual episodes.

After three months when the effect of the Depo-Provera was dissipated, the other adult females were injected with Depo-Provera. This again caused the alpha male to reject the injected females, and he interacted sexually only with the noninjected one.

The last three-month phase was observation, when all adult females were injected with Depo-Provera. According to the book, this caused the adult alpha male to "attempt rape, masturbate and behave in a turbulent and confused manner. He approached females, inserted his fingers into their genitalia, stroked and sniffed them, however anxiously."[18] He stopped having sexual intercourse. Once the Depo-Provera effects dissipated, behavior returned to baseline.

Of course, these studies on monkeys may not be completely applicable to human behavior. However, it may be responsible for a millennial generation adage: "I started on the Pill because I started having sex. Now I'm on the Pill and I'm not having sex." According to the Centers for Disease Control and Prevention, 82 percent of all women of reproductive age have taken the Pill.[19] In his book, *The Decline of Males*, Lionel Tiger makes a point that after the Pill became common, "there emerged a stunning array of candidly erotic and voluptuous novelties such as the abandonment of bras, the shortening of skirts, the popularity of tight jeans, and even the astonishing topless fashion at various resorts."[20] He did postulate that "perhaps chemically pregnant females have to employ more vigorous external signals."[21] It may also explain the more provocative style of today's fashions for women.

---

[18] Ibid., p. 9.

[19] Kimberly Daniels, William D. Mosher, and Jo Jones, "Contraceptive Methods Women Have Ever Used, 1982–2010", *National Health Statistics Reports*, no. 62 (February 14, 2013): 4, https://www.cdc.gov/nchs/data/nhsr/nhsr062.pdf#x2013;2010 [PDF - 251 KB]</a>.

[20] Tiger, *Decline of Males*, p. 45.

[21] Ibid., p. 44.

In his book, Dr. Tiger makes a very strong case that the Pill caused a major shift in male-female sexual relations. Separating sexual and reproductive behavior has led to the restructuring of the human family from a male-female pair raising children to the growth of large numbers of single-parent families. These families are usually headed by females, with the attendant financial stresses and greater difficulties in providing for the care of children. Dr. Tiger bemoaned the fact that men who had largely used condoms before the Pill were now unaware if contraception was being used or not. He also wrote of the counterintuitive problems brought on by the Pill, such as an increase in unplanned pregnancies and induced abortions.

The Pill and Violence against Women

In 2010, fifty years after the debut of the Pill, the *British Medical Journal* published a study regarding the mortality of Pill users. The only statistically significant difference found between users and nonusers of the Pill was the risk of dying a violent death. Violent death was almost double among Pill users. There was a 192 percent statistically significant increase in risk of dying a violent death.[22] For women who took the pill for eight years or longer, the risk increased and more than doubled. The authors reported that their finding was real but that they could not explain it. Almost immediately a "Rapid Response" was published online in a letter to the editor by S. Craig Roberts, then a senior lecturer in the field of behavioral ecology/evolutionary psychology at the University of Liverpool in the United Kingdom. He wrote:

> Hannahford et al. (2010)[23] report convincing evidence for reduction in mortality from several forms of cancer and other disease in women who have used oral contraception compared to never users. However, they also find a higher rate of violent death among ever users, and that the rate of violent death increases with longer duration of oral contraceptive use, but they are unable to explain these intriguing results. I suggest

---

[22] Philip C. Hannaford et al., "Mortality among Contraceptive Pill Users: Cohort Evidence from Royal College of General Practitioners' Oral Contraception Study", *British Medical Journal* 340 (March 12, 2010): c927.

[23] Ibid.

that recent evolutionary insights into human partner choice may provide a clue.

There is evidence that use of oral contraception alters women's baseline preferences for men,[24] such that pill users prefer men who are relatively similar to themselves at loci in the major histocompatibility complex (MHC), i.e., to particular spots on that gene in our DNA.[25] One consequence of being partnered with relatively MHC-similar men is that such women express lower sexual responsivity toward their long-term partner compared with women in relatively MHC-dissimilar couples, reject sexual advances from their partner more frequently, and report having had more extra-pair partners.[26] Other evidence points to the fact that MHC-similar couples are more likely to experience problems conceiving children and having less healthy children due to lower MHC heterozygosity.[27] Cumulatively, these effects could have real impact on the quality of spousal relationships.

It is not unreasonable to suspect that such effects could also influence rates of intimate partner violence. This is the most common cause of non-fatal injury among women[28] and accounts for more than a third of women murdered in the US.[29] Furthermore, ex-partners are a key risk factor, which could further emphasise the risk for pill users if the behavioural effects of pill use ultimately influence rates of marital breakdown.[30]

[24] S. Craig Roberts et al., "MHC-Correlated Odour Preferences in Humans and the Use of Oral Contraceptives", *Proceedings of the Royal Society B: Biological Sciences* 275 (July 12, 2008): 2715–22; Alexandra Alvergne and Virpi Lummaa, "Does the Contraceptive Pill Alter Mate Choice in Humans?", *Trends in Ecology and Evolution* 25, no. 3 (March 2010): 171–79.

[25] In each cell, there is a structure called a nucleus that contains a complete copy of our DNA. DNA is a code in the form of a double helix that contains the information so that a cell can produce whatever proteins are needed for the function of that cell. A gene is a unit of heredity that controls a hereditary trait, such as eye color, and is composed of a particular sequence of DNA at a specific location (locus) on a chromosome. Humans have forty-six chromosomes, and we are thought to have twenty thousand to twenty-five thousand genes.

[26] Christine E. Garver-Apgar et al., "Major Histocompatibility Complex Alleles, Sexual Responsivity, and Unfaithfulness in Romantic Couples", *Psychological Science* 17 (2006): 830–35.

[27] Jan Havlicek and S. Craig Roberts, "MHC-Correlated Mate Choice in Humans: A Review", *Psychoneuroendocrinology* 34 (May 2009): 497–512.

[28] Demetrios N. Kyriacou et al., "Risk Factors for Injury to Women from Domestic Violence", *New England Journal of Medicine* 341 (1999): 1892–98.

[29] Arthur L. Kellermann and James A. Mercy, "Men, Women, and Murder: Gender-Specific Differences in Rates of Fatal Violence and Victimization", *Journal of Trauma* 33 (1992): 1–5.

[30] S. Craig Roberts, "Contraceptive Pill Use and Violent Death", *BMJ* (March 20, 2010), http://www.bmj.com/cgi/eletter-submit/340/mar11_1/c927?title=Re%3A+Contraceptive+pill+use+and+violent+death.

Surely the Pill and its influence on mate selection and divorce does not account for all the male violence against women, but not to allow that it may play a significant role is to ignore some important facts.

Impact on Children Conceived by Those with Closely Related MHC Genes

The effect of poor selection of mates because of the MHC factor may also have an impact on the children conceived with those poorly chosen mates. Women choosing men who are similar to them in those genes can be choosing those men more closely related to them genetically. Choices of mates closely related in the MHC genes would likely tend to lead to the kind of illness prevalent in communities that closely inter-marry. The MHC (or HLA) genes are the group of genes that control our response to infections and have a role in autoimmune diseases. We match transplant donors and recipients by how closely their MHC genes are alike. Through intermarriage, the diversity of those genes lessen (because of fewer different alleles) and thus cause fewer responses to an infectious agent; altered autoimmune responses result in more autoim-mune diseases.[31] Thus the children of those marriages would be more susceptible to infections and have more autoimmune diseases.

How the Pill Kills Women

There are five ways that the Pill can actually lead to the death of the women taking them:

1. They cause your blood to clot. These clots can form in your heart and brain, and travel to your lungs from the leg causing heart attacks, strokes, and pulmonary emboli. Women on the Pill should be tested for hereditary conditions that cause their blood to more readily form clots. Those conditions should preclude women from

[31] Vasiliki Matzaraki et al., "The MHC Locus and Genetic Susceptibility to Autoimmune and Infectious Diseases", *Genome Biology* 18, no. 76 (April 27, 2017), https://genomebiology .biomedcentral.com/articles/10.1186/s13059-017-1207-1.

taking the Pill, as they are put at such high risk of complications and even death. The risk of heart attack doubles on the Pill. This risk is increased even higher if the woman has other risk factors such as hypertension (five times the risk), diabetes (sixteen times the risk), and high cholesterol (twenty-three times the risk). There is over twice the risk of stroke.[32] The risk of leg clots increases five times.[33]

2. The Pill enables promiscuous sex and thus leads to more potentially lethal infections of HPV (human papilloma virus) and HIV (human immunodeficiency virus).[34] Due to changes caused by the Pill, the cervical transformation zone (the location where viruses invade, causing infection and cancer) is more exposed. Women on the Pill are twice as likely to develop HPV and HIV infections if they are exposed to these viruses while taking the Pill.

3. Some forms of the Pill cause breast, cervical, and liver cancer, according to the World Health Organization's International Agency on Research of Cancer.[35] The longer a woman takes the Pill, the greater her risk of cervical cancer. Forms of the Pill are responsible for approximately 15 percent of all premenopausal breast cancer.[36] A meta-analysis showed a 44 percent increase in breast cancer if a woman took the Pill prior to pregnancy.[37]

4. As noted above, women on the Pill are more likely to die a violent death. As explained above, the Pill causes women to choose mates

[32] Leslie Allison Gillum, Sai Kumar Mamidipudi, and S. Claiborne Johnston, "Ischemic Stroke Risk with Oral Contraceptives: A Meta-Analysis", *JAMA* 284 (July 5, 2000): 72–78.

[33] A van Hylckama Vlieg et al., "The Venous Thrombotic Risk of Oral Contraceptives, Effects of Oestrogen Dose and Progestogen Type: Results of the MEGA Case-Control Study", *BMJ* (August 13, 2009): 339:b2921; Øjvind Lidegaard et al., "Risk of Venous Thromboembolism from Use of Oral Contraceptives Containing Different Progestogens and Oestrogen Doses: Danish Cohort Study, 2001–2009", *BMJ*, October 25, 2011; 343:d6423.

[34] Esther Roura et al., "The Influence of Hormonal Factors on the Risk of Developing Cervical Cancer and Pre-Cancer: Results from the EPIC Cohort", *PloS One* 11, no. 1 (January 25, 2016): e0147029; C. Wang et al., "Risk of HIV Infection in Oral Contraceptive Pill Users: A Meta-Analysis", *JAIDS* 21, no. 1 (May 1999): 51–58.

[35] "Combined Estrogen-Progestogen Contraceptives and Combined Estrogen-Progestogen Menopausal Therapy", *IARC Monographs on the Evaluation of Carcinogenic Risks to Humans* 91 (2007), http://monographs.iarc.fr/ENG/Monographs/vol91/mono91.pdf.

[36] D.M. Parkin, "Cancers Attributable to Exposure to Hormones in the UK in 2010", *British Journal of Cancer* (2011): 105, S42–S48, doi:10.1038/bjc.2011.483.

[37] Chris Kahlenborn et al., "Oral Contraceptive Use as a Risk Factor for Premenopausal Breast Cancer: A Meta-Analysis", *Mayo Clinic Proc* 81, no. 10 (2006): 1290–302.

that are similar to themselves in the MHC genes. These unions are more unstable, as the women refuse sexual relations more frequently and have more "extra-pair bondings"—that is, adultery or "affairs".

5. As mentioned above, there is a study done in Denmark that showed that women on the Pill have a 97 percent increase in suicide attempts and a 208 percent increase in suicide after just two months of use.[38] More precisely, in a nationwide prospective study, the researchers followed a group of young women who turned fifteen between 1996 and 2013 and who took hormonal contraceptives. Among "nearly half a million women followed on average 8.3 years", there were 6,999 first suicide attempts and 71 suicides. Compared to women who never used hormonal contraceptives, there was a 97 percent statistically significant increase in suicide attempts and an over 200 percent statistically significant risk of suicide.[39]

A Way Forward

Although many in the general public consider the Pill to be a very effective form of contraception, according to the Centers for Disease Control, every year 9 percent of women who use the Pill will get pregnant.[40] Too few women pay sufficient attention to failure rate—and other dangers—of contraception. Even when they know of some of the serious problems with the Pill, they often feel there isn't any method which is better. Yet there is.

Modern methods of natural methods of fertility control, generally referred to as methods of natural family planning (NFP), can be used instead of the carcinogenic Pill. Multiple studies have shown NFP to

---

[38] Charlotte Wessel Skovlund et al., "Association of Hormonal Contraception with Suicide Attempts and Suicides", *American Journal of Psychiatry* 175, no. 4 (April 1, 2018): 336–42, https://doi.org/10.1176/appi.ajp.2017.17060616.

[39] See ibid., p. 336.

[40] "Effectiveness of Family Planning Methods", Centers for Disease Control and Prevention, 2011, https://www.cdc.gov/reproductivehealth/contraception/unintendedpregnancy/pdf/Contraceptive_methods_508.pdf.

have the same efficacy of the Pill.[41] These methods rely upon a woman recognizing her own body's signs of fertility and communicating with her spouse to postpone or achieve pregnancy. There are no bad physical side effects of using natural family planning. Of great importance is that a woman's natural hormones continue to operate.

Some may argue that there is little moral difference between the use of the Pill and the use of NFP as the end goal may be the same when postponing pregnancy. However, there are very real differences—especially if one considers taking care of one's health a moral imperative. One involves taking a Group 1 carcinogen;[42] the other requires the woman to be aware of her fertile and infertile cycles and to share that information with her spouse. Abstinence requires significant self-control on the part of both spouses. Another difference is that periodic abstinence generally requires a close and intimate communication between partners, which can foster those qualities in other aspects of the marital relationship.

In short, In the case of contraception, a woman works against her body; in the case of NFP, a woman respects the natural workings of her body. An analogy would be a woman who wants to lose excess weight. She could practice bulimia and eat her food only to vomit after eating. Or she could use self-control and moderation by using portion control for healthy foods. Both using NFP and dieting are difficult, but both can yield tremendous results. Also, there is usually a very different way that contracepting couples respond to an unintended pregnancy from how couples using NFP respond. Contracepting couples often attempt to negate the baby-making power of the sexual act, and should a pregnancy occur, they sometimes speak of it as an "accidental pregnancy", which causes a crisis. Couples using NFP are very conscious of the baby-making power of the sexual act and are not quite as unsettled by an

[41] Crista Warniment, "Is Natural Family Planning a Highly Effective Method of Birth Control? Yes: Natural Family Planning Is Highly Effective and Fulfilling", *American Family Physician* 86, no. 10 (November 15, 2012); European Society for Human Reproduction and Embryology, "Natural Family Planning Method as Effective as Contraceptive Pill, New Research Finds", *ScienceDaily*, February 21, 2007, www.sciencedaily.com /releases/2007/02/070221065200.htm.

[42] Vincent Cogliano et al., "Carcinogenicity of Combined Oestrogen-Progestoagen Contraceptives and Menopausal Treatment", *Lancet Oncology* 6 (August 6, 2005): 552–53; "Combined Estrogen-Progestogen Contraceptives and Combined Estrogen-Progestogen Menopausal Therapy", *IARC Monographs on the Evaluation of Carcinogenic Risks*.

unintended pregnancy; more often they consider their sexuality, their fertility, and babies as gifts from God, and, while a pregnancy may be inconvenient, it is not really a surprise to them since they understand the meaning of the conjugal act.

In *Humanae vitae*, on the basis of the Church's understanding of human nature, Paul VI predicted some of the consequences that result from violating that nature. Others have amply demonstrated that those predictions by Pope Paul VI have sadly come true, at great expense to human happiness.[43] Fifty years later, we have learned that there are reasons for those consequences that he could not have known at the time. Truly, the body is fearfully and wonderfully made (pheromones!), and we seem just to be starting to learn how destructive it is, in many ways, to interfere with the delicate ecological balance of a woman's body. What we know about pheromones is revealing an enormous amount about a woman's psychological and physical health as well as her relationships. Catholics know that science and faith support each other. Here is just another example!

Armed with this information, both the laity and clergy can more persuasively educate not only the faithful but others as well about the beauty and intelligence of *Humanae vitae*, so that it will be embraced today as it should have been almost a half century ago.

---

[43] See the essay by Mary Eberstadt, "The Prophetic Power of *Humanae Vitae*", in this volume.

Rethinking *Humanae vitae*

Deborah Savage, Ph.D.

When Pope Blessed Paul VI promulgated his landmark encyclical *Humanae vitae* in July 1968, I was just getting ready to enter my junior year in high school. I knew nothing of the controversy that swirled around the document at the time. Though it seems unbelievable in light of our contemporary context, I was blissfully unaware that anything like contraception even existed, let alone that the birth control pill had only recently been invented, or that its use had even more recently been legalized. I was more or less a "normal" sixteen-year-old, at least what passed for it then—a diligent student and an athlete, looking forward to college. But I well understand now why, throughout the world, the Catholic Church and those who think with her and listen to her are taking the time to mark the fiftieth anniversary of *Humanae vitae*'s publication. Because by the time I got to college in 1970, everything had changed. It was there that I actually witnessed firsthand what the Holy Father's teaching was intended to avert. And although the cultural transformation that took place during that time is widely considered to have been "liberating", I now recognize those events as the beginning of a new kind of slavery.

There can be no question that *Humanae vitae* was a prophetic document; virtually every prediction it included has come to pass.[1] But the certainty I feel about the truth it proclaims is based only secondarily on moral concepts or indisputable sociological data. In the first place, it is grounded in my own lived experience—and that of the young women

---

[1] See Mary Eberstadt, "The Prophetic Power of *Humanae Vitae*", *First Things*, no. 282 (April 2018): 33–39; Mary Eberstadt, "The Vindication of *Humanae Vitae*", *First Things*, August 2008, https://www.firstthings.com/article/2008/08/002-the-vindication-of-ihumanae-vitaei; and Mary Eberstadt, *Adam and Eve after the Pill: Paradoxes of the Sexual Revolution* (San Francisco: Ignatius Press, 2012), pp. 134–49.

I knew—of the beginnings of the so-called sexual revolution. Since virtually everyone—from secular humanists, to academics, to feminists, to
Pope Francis—gives pride of place to human experience as the touchstone of truth, it seems timely now to give an account of mine.

When the birth control pill was introduced into the culture in the
mid-1960s, it entered into an already sexually loaded atmosphere that
had begun a decade before. People have forgotten now about the influence of Jean-Paul Sartre and his paramour, Simone de Beauvoir (one of
the matriarchs of second-wave feminism), and the pervasive presence
of the mores of the so-called beatnik generation. "Free love" was
already on the radar screen of most "twenty- and thirty-somethings"
as the decade began. But it was still accompanied by the unfortunate
"unintended" consequences that naturally occur from sexual intercourse: women have an "inconvenient" tendency to get pregnant.
When the first oral contraceptive became available in 1960, for the
first time in history, we were medically equipped to "cure" the fertility
problem. We were finally poised to remove the one remaining obstacle
to unfettered access to sex without a penalty—or so we thought. But at
the time, contraception was illegal, even for married couples.[2] All that
remained was to make it a matter of law.

The watershed event of the decade actually took place in 1965: the
Supreme Court's *Griswold v. Connecticut* decision to legalize contraception.[3] When *Humanae vitae* was promulgated barely three years later
in 1968, it simply reaffirmed the Church's perennial teaching: that the
"unitive and procreative dimensions" of the marital act are both essential
to its meaning.[4] But the *Griswold* decision had legalized what amounted

---

[2] In 1950, Margaret Sanger launched and funded the research that led to the invention
of the Pill in 1960. See Kirsten M.J. Thompson, "A Brief History of Birth Control in the
U.S.", Our Bodies Ourselves, December 14, 2013, https://www.ourbodiesourselves.org
/health-info/a-brief-history-of-birth-control/.

[3] For full information about *Griswold v. Connecticut*, see the website of Justia's U.S. Supreme
Court Center at https://supreme.justia.com/cases/federal/us/381/479/case.html. It is worth
noting that *Griswold* marks the Court's ultimately monumental discovery of the "right to
privacy" in sexual matters.

[4] The Lambeth Conference, a decennial event of the Anglican Communion, approved
of contraception in 1930. Until that time, most, if not all, Protestant denominations were
against the use of birth control. But the Anglican Communion wielded significant influence
over the Protestant community—though it would not be until the Lambeth Conference of
1958 that reasons were articulated, namely, that the "consciences of married couples should
be respected", most Protestants followed suit after the 1930 declaration and began approving
and using contraceptives.

to a human fiat to tear asunder these dimensions. There was no going back. The pope's encyclical sparked a firestorm of controversy in a culture that thought it had, finally, taken hold of the forbidden fruit. People abandoned the Church in its wake; priests and pastors were afraid even to discuss the issue with those who remained. But it was a firestorm that blazed almost entirely beyond the consciousness of people like me. Young people, especially young women, had no idea what was actually already underway.

I was born in San Francisco and went to a college barely an hour's drive from the famous Haight-Ashbury district, ground zero of the then-burgeoning free love movement. I guess you could say that I had a front-row seat at the beginning of what we now refer to as the sexual revolution. I watched firsthand, as the young women around me dropped like flies in the face of its onslaught. It was only later that I learned that the more experienced young men who lined up to watch the freshman girls arrive on campus actually competed with one another for who would make the most "scores". They literally put notches in their belts to keep a tally, placing bets on who would win the game. But it was not a game, not for me and not for the young women around me. We had entered into college life full of hope; for many, that hope lost its sheen in the meaningless sexual encounters that lay in wait for us.

The first indication that one of my dorm mates had "done it" was most often morning-after tears, followed soon by a kind of despair as it dawned on them that the young men to whom they had given themselves had no intention of calling back. The second was the heavy sense of desperation that filled the halls of the dorm as we all waited with baited breath for someone's menstrual cycle to begin. When it did, there was usually some kind of party; when it did not, the girl just disappeared. Abortion on demand, the one thing remaining that would ensure complete sexual freedom, was still out of reach. But it just no longer made sense to say no to young men so intent on their desires; at least it didn't make sense to *them*. The advent of the Pill had opened the door to sex without consequences, apparently even if you weren't taking it. Or such was the assumption. Most of us didn't really know yet that one simply needed to visit the campus clinic and procure a prescription for those magical birth control pills. It had all happened so fast. And anyway, to do so was an open admission that one had decided to "do it" on a regular basis. And, at least at first, that was a hard step to take. It gradually became clear that almost no one was likely to acquire a steady boyfriend. The average guy was looking for conquests. The women took their chances on every date—and every date brought with it the same tussle. No? Yes? No? Until, finally, one by one, the women, exhausted, surrendered.

Though I was Catholic, I knew nothing about *Humanae vitae* or its teaching. It simply was not on my radar screen. I was at a public university and it never really came up. I have no recollection of the priests at the Newman Center ever mentioning it—nor do I remember the priest at my home parish preaching about it. I knew what sex was but had little experience of it. What I did know for sure was that it was darn hard to get a date those days unless you had somehow hinted that you might be ready or willing to "go all the way". One young man said to me—when I protested that I did not do that sort of thing—"Well, I would like to hear your reason, but it had better be a good one." I remember feeling panicky as I realized I actually wasn't completely sure why; I did not know how to explain my reasons for saying no to his demand for sex. It was just an instinct really for which I had no coherent explanation. But I was fairly certain that to tell him that my mom told me not to was not going to fly. After all, he had taken me out for a nice dinner.

The sexual revolution defined my generation. Its aftermath has continued to define the experience of young people ever since, on college campuses, in bars and at parties, in the normal search for love. It has encroached on the workplace, insinuated itself into every form of media, shackled relationships, and destroyed marriages. It has led directly to the situation we now face. For when the sexual act is divorced from its procreative dimension, or from the sacramental love that ought to accompany it, there is no reason to rule out any kind of sexual encounter. Like the diseases that have spread as a result, it is itself a virus, a sort of permanent, culturally transmitted STD, one that now lurks in almost every interaction between men and women, young and old alike.

Though the irony is lost on most of today's thought leaders, it is patently obvious to any honest observer that the excesses of the "hook-up culture"—revealed so profoundly by the #MeToo phenomenon—are merely the logical consequences of the tacit decision, midway through the twentieth century, that it was time to agree to separate sex from a loving, committed relationship. At the end of the day, we were all complicit. And once we all agreed to it, there was nowhere to go except exactly where we find ourselves now—in a state of total confusion about human relationships. If only we had given it a moment's thought, we might have realized that this could have been predicted.

Oh—but wait—it actually *was* predicted. It was predicted by Pope Blessed Paul VI in 1968.[5]

And so, when, in recent months, I began hearing the persistent whispers that a movement was underway at the highest levels of the Church to "rethink" the teaching of *Humanae vitae*, I really couldn't believe it. I scoffed at the possibility at first. "Preposterous!" I declared with blustery confidence to friends and colleagues. The Catholic Church will *never* change that teaching, I said. Not now, not after decades of reflection on the theology of the body. Not now, when abortion has claimed the lives of millions of innocent children.[6] Not now, when it should be clear to anyone willing to consider the data that Pope Blessed Paul VI was a prophet of the first order. When the Harvey Weinstein scandal broke the dam on the #MeToo phenomenon, I felt the matter would soon be put to rest. Surely everyone will get it now, I thought. Surely it will finally be clear that the sexual "liberation" movement was anything but what it claimed to be.

I regret to say that the rumors appear to be true. The stage has indeed been set for a "rethinking" of *Humanae vitae*. In fact, what had been unthinkable just a few short years ago has apparently already begun. Recent news reports point to what may be the most explicit indication thus far that things are on the move. A yearlong lecture series on the document is in progress at the Pontifical Gregorian University in Rome. Hosted by the university's faculty of social sciences and moral theology, the purpose of the series is to take a new look at the 1968 encyclical "in a context of time and change".[7] The third talk in the series was given late last year by Father Maurizio Chiodi, a prominent Italian moral theologian; it was entitled "Re-Reading *Humanae Vitae* in Light of *Amoris Laetitia*". There are "circumstances", said Father Chiodi, "[and] I refer

[5] Eberstadt, "The Prophetic Power of *Humanae Vitae*".

[6] The link between contraception and abortion is quite clear. For one recent analysis, see Michael Pakaluk, "The Link between Contraception and Abortion", *First Things*, January 23, 2018, https://www.firstthings.com/web-exclusives/2018/01/the-link-between -contraception-and-abortion.

[7] Edward Pentin, "Pontifical Gregorian University Hosts Series of Talks to Take New Look at Humanae Vitae", *National Catholic Register*, October 21, 2017, http://www.ncregister.com /blog/edward-pentin/gregorian-university-hosts-series-of-talks-to-take-new-look-at-humanae.

to *Amoris Laetitia*, Chapter 8—that precisely for the sake of responsibility, require contraception."[8] Father Chiodi is the newest member of the Pontifical Academy for Life, a group recently reconstituted by Pope Francis; it now includes a number of dissenters from *Humanae vitae*. Father Chiodi is one of them.

It is no coincidence that the series at the Gregorian University marks the fiftieth anniversary of the promulgation of *Humanae vitae*. It seems that the moment is viewed by its detractors as an opportunity to rethink and reconsider the teaching contained in the controversial document. This is an inexplicable development in light of the insurmountable evidence that Pope Paul VI was a prophet of his own time.[9] Indeed, the excesses of the sexual revolution have reached proportions that even he did not anticipate. Our culture is committing a kind of slow suicide, and everyone knows it. Just a cursory glance at the data, most of it compiled by those with no commitment to the moral teaching of the Church, reveals some stunning facts. Let us consider just a few. The National Center for Health Statistics reports that U.S. birth rates fell to an all-time low in 2016: 62 births per 1,000 women ages fifteen through forty-four, down 1 percent from 2015 and just below the replacement rate after accounting for immigration.[10] The worldwide fertility rate has been cut in half since the latter half of the twentieth century; it stands now at 2.5 births per woman.[11] The CDC reports that the spread of STDs is at an all-time high and calls for urgent action to prevent further transmission.[12] The U.S. Census Bureau reports that one out of three children live without a father in the home,[13] even as the proof mounts that the

---

[8] Edward Pentin, "Academy for Life Member Uses *Amoris Laetitia* to Justify Contraceptive Use", *National Catholic Register*, January 9, 2018, http://www.ncregister.com/blog/edward-pentin/academy-for-life-member-uses-amoris-to-justify-contraceptive-use.

[9] See Eberstadt, "Vindication of *Humanae Vitae*". See also Bradford Wilcox, "The Facts of Life and Marriage: Social Science and the Vindication of Christian Moral Teaching", *Touchstone*, January/February 2005.

[10] Brady E. Hamilton et al., *Births: Provisional Data for 2016*, report no. 2 (Hyattsville, MD: National Center for Health Statistics, 2017), https://www.cdc.gov/nchs/data/vsrr/report002.pdf.

[11] Max Roser, "Fertility Rate", *OurWorldInData.org*, last modified December 2, 2017, https://ourworldindata.org/fertility-rate.

[12] "STDs at Record High, Indicating Urgent Need for Prevention", Centers for Disease Control and Prevention, press release, September 26, 2017, https://www.cdc.gov/media/releases/2017/p0926-std-prevention.html.

[13] "The Proof Is In: Father Absence Harms Children", National Fatherhood Initiative, accessed May 10, 2018, https://www.fatherhood.org/father-absence-statistic.

absence of a father in the home is the single most reliable *predictor* of family poverty.[14] We could go on.

And yet, here we are. A reversal is sought *in spite* of all the data, in the face of every indication that the contraceptive mentality that permeates our culture has led, not to the "liberation" it promised, but to a situation in which there is no moral norm discouraging sexual activity outside of marriage, leaving many of the women it was supposed to liberate feeling unequipped to say a simple no.[15] It is a matter of some irony that women are reporting what economists refer to as the "paradox of declining female happiness".[16] When I first heard that analysis, I laughed out loud. Let's just say for now that to call this a "paradox" is a kind of category error.

How could something so patently obvious be lost on some of those entrusted to shepherding God's people and protecting the deposit of faith—the truth? Do they not realize that the Catholic Church is literally the last line of defense in the battle to protect the dignity of both men and women? Can they not see that relinquishing our hold on the teaching of *Humanae vitae* is the final act of a drama written for us by the serpent in the Garden? Can a few highly placed theologians really decide for the rest of us that the Church should *declare as a matter of Catholic doctrine* that, at least in "some cases" (who are we kidding?), it is right to engage in practices that will, in the end, inevitably result in

[14] We know, with statistical certainty, that such households are four times *more* likely to be subsisting at or below the poverty line than families with husbands and fathers, whether biological or not, living in the home (*Children's Living Arrangements and Characteristics: March 2011*, table C8 [Washington, DC: U.S. Census Bureau, 2011]). Children living in families headed by females without a spouse present had a poverty rate of 47.6 percent, over four times the rate in families of married couples ("Information on Poverty and Income Statistics: A Summary of 2012 Current Population Survey Data", ASPE Issue Brief, U.S. Department of Health and Human Services, September 12, 2012, https://aspe.hhs.gov/basic-report /information-poverty-and-income-statistics-summary-2012-current-population-survey-data).

[15] See Heather MacDonald, "Policing Sexual Desire: The #MeToo Movement's Impossible Premise", *City Journal*, January 14, 2018, https://www.city-journal.org/html/policing -sexual-desire-15669.html.

[16] Betsey Stevenson and Justin Wolfers, "The Paradox of Declining Female Happiness", National Bureau of Economic Research, Working Paper No. 14969, May 2009, http:// www.nber.org/papers/w14969; for less scholarly and arguably superficial treatments, see Anna Petherick, "Gains in Women's Rights Haven't Made Women Happier: Why Is That?", *Guardian*, May 18, 2016, https://www.theguardian.com/lifeandstyle/2016/may/18 /womens-rights-happiness-wellbeing-gender-gap; Andrea Tantaros, "Five Ways Feminism Has Made Women Miserable", *Observer*, May 3, 2016, http://observer.com/2016/05 /five-ways-feminism-has-made-women-miserable/.

women being treated as sexual objects and in the debasement of men? After all that Christ has wrought—and that humanity has suffered? I can only hope that this "rethinking" is either simple ignorance or, at best, a well-intentioned, if dangerously misguided, effort to make the Church finally "relevant" to a world in the throes of a sex-induced hypnosis, a thoughtless lust that has now claimed the minds and hearts not only of men, but, for all practical purposes, of women as well.

The truths of *Humanae vitae* not only need to be upheld; they need to be more widely proclaimed and offered as an antidote to the sad situation the world is in today. For many of my peers, the ensuing years were spent pursuing happiness in all the wrong places. We share a common responsibility for the impact our experiment in disordered freedom has had on those who came after and the contraceptive ideology that found its way into virtually every arena of modern life.[17] It should be our mission to proclaim with all the *parresia* of faith that the way out will only be found by grasping once again the true meaning of human love and human sexuality.

Unfortunately for me, it wasn't until years later that I encountered in any real way the teaching of *Humanae vitae* and the work of Pope Saint John Paul II. Many in the world, some of them sitting in the pews at Mass each Sunday, still have had no real introduction to these teachings. In *Love and Responsibility* and the Theology of the Body I found too late the language I ultimately had had to work out for myself, the rationale that would have enabled me to respond to the young man who had demanded my reasons for saying no. In John Paul II's Apostolic Letter on the Dignity and Vocation of Women *Mulieris dignitatem* (August 15, 1988), I discovered an account that unequivocally affirmed the dignity that is rightfully mine. Most tragic, it was not until I went through my own marriage preparation that I encountered the profound intelligence at the core of natural family planning: I learned that my own body can alert me to the signs of my fertility. Who knew?

Are we really going to abandon that wisdom now? Is the Church, now, in the twenty-first century, actually going to deny, as a matter of doctrine, something that has disappeared from view—that, at least until relatively recently, it was women's simple no that had provided the

---

[17] Dr. Jennifer Roback Morse, *The Sexual Revolution and Its Victims* (San Marcos, CA: Ruth Institute Books, 2018).

antidote to the sometimes animalistic impulses of men? Only animals have sex without thinking about it. And it is women who *know*, if only inchoately, the significance of that often instinctive refusal. They know it for what it is: an act of self-preservation that simultaneously safeguards the personal integrity of man and the sacred potency of their union. For it is chastity that leads to an experience of a properly human eros, lifting the natural animal sexuality of both beyond an attachment to the merely gratifying, elevating it to a love of the beautiful and the truly good.

It is *because* women say no that men are called to confront their own, often chaotic, desire for sex. Without this no, men are held captive by their instincts; their development is stunted—they are prevented from becoming fully themselves. They become mired in an endless child-hood, driven by the wish for instant gratification, unable or unwilling to grow up.

But woman recognizes the greatness that lies in potency in the man; it is her very refusal that invites him into a deeper reflection on who *he is* or could be. It calls him to forge a will capable of ordering itself to a life of heroic virtue destined to be lived out in continual acts of self-sacrifice and devotion to family and the good of the wider human community. As Alan Bloom told us years ago, female modesty avoids the trap of "reducing sex to the thing-in-itself" and "extends sexual differentiation from the sexual act to the whole of life. It makes men and women *always men and women*."[18] In contrast, too many men *and* women in our culture now seek their happiness in thoughtless sexual encounters devoid of human purposes or meaning. They are mere couplings driven by lust or a misunderstood desire for love, in which Bloom's insight has proven to be manifestly true: the sexual act has indeed been reduced to "the thing-in-itself". And so we see that men have lost their way—because women lost theirs.

Though ridiculed today by many as mere sexual repression, woman's instinct to refuse the sexual advances of man is in fact a reflection of a profound wisdom, held in the deep recesses of her very being. It issues from the aquifer coursing through every woman's body. It is a knowl-edge that manifests in every sexual encounter, wanted and unwanted. Men, especially men seeking the heroic virtue characteristic of authentic

[18] Alan Bloom, *The Closing of the American Mind* (New York: Simon and Schuster, 1987), p. 102, emphasis added.

masculinity, can and do understand this intellectually. But they must be *summoned* to that effort; they must be *invited* to it. A man simply *cannot* know the full meaning of the sexual act as a woman does, for it actualizes a potency that only she possesses. It was and still is—whether they admit it or not—*women* who understand what is at stake in their simple yes or no, women who understand, often in a completely *preverbal* way, something about sex that is organically unknowable to men: that it is her very own *selfhood*, along with its live-giving potencies, that is on the table. For the truth is that all of humanity has no choice other than to pass through the womb to its human destination. Every woman contains within herself, at least potentially, all future humanity.[19] It is this inchoate, hidden understanding that is now laughed at by those who, unaccountably, have won the right to tell everyone what to think. Except Catholics, that is—at least, until now.

What has gone unacknowledged is the fact that the stories behind the #MeToo movement predate the Weinstein affair literally by *millennia*. Indeed, it is a familiar tale to almost every woman who has ever lived. Its provenance is the story of our first parents and their loss of innocence in the Garden of Eden. Man and woman *both* sinned in that moment and both share equally in the burden it imposed. In the aftermath, the gifts that had been theirs by natural right, instead of giving life, became a source of tension, confusion, and fear.[20] But though man and woman share the same guilt, they do not share the same consequences. And the consequences are playing out before our eyes.

A careful look at Genesis 3:1–24 reveals the truth at the heart of this state of affairs. Both Scripture and human experience attest to the fact that the effects of original sin manifest in different ways in men and women. Man's gift, which had been a particular insight into the nature of the created order, suddenly becomes his burden. He will struggle with

---

[19] Louis Bouyer, *Woman in the Church* (San Francisco: Ignatius Press, 1976), p. 34.

[20] I can only point to the proof of this claim here. For a more complete account of woman and man and the impact of original sin on both of them, please see Deborah Savage, "The Nature of Woman in Relation to Man: Genesis 1 and 2 through the Lens of the Metaphysical Anthropology of Aquinas", *Logos* 8, no. 4 (2013): 71–93. For an analysis more focused on the masculine genius, see "The Genius of Man", in *Promise and Challenge: Catholic Women Reflect on Feminism, Complementarity, and the Church*, ed. Mary Hasson (Washington, DC: Our Sunday Visitor, 2015), pp. 129–54. These were preliminary studies. A newer, more complete, and refined account is awaiting publication.

creation now. Those things he named as his own in Genesis 2 will now yield their fruits only with suffering and back-breaking toil. Instead of occupying the place of secure and confident steward of God's creation, he will now have to fight with it. And in forfeiting his natural relationship with the things of creation, he also loses sight of the gift that woman was and is. He forgets what he had understood in his first glimpse of her: that she was "bone of [his] bones and flesh of [his] flesh" (Gen 2:23), a *person*, his match in every way. Man will now tend to treat everything, including woman, as an *object*. Thus is woman made into a some*thing* rather than a some*one*. She becomes for him a "thing" to be mastered.

While Eve, whose special status as the mother of all mankind earns her the right to a name, and whose very creation marks the entrance of human relationship and community into human history, finds her own individuality and dignity compromised: her desire will now be for her "husband", even though he often wishes to "dominate" her—even when she knows he is using her. It is a narrative that has repeated itself throughout history. It repeats itself every day in our contemporary period—in one-night stands, in drunken encounters on college campuses, in the tragedy of domestic abuse, in the horrific spread of pornography. What had been bestowed on each as a kind of genius, reflected in man's capacity for productive use of the goods of creation, and woman's infinite capacity for the person, are now turned upside down, diminished, distorted.

The account of the Fall actually serves as a potent theory of history, its diagnostic power mostly overlooked. For the #MeToo phenomenon is really the story of original sin playing out as it has throughout the ages. What distinguishes this moment is that, this time, it is on full display on the world stage: Man tends to treat everything, including women, like objects. Woman, uncertain of her worth, aims to please.

How I wish that *someone* would have pulled me aside in 1970 and helped me to understand the danger my generation and I were in. Where were the priests, the ministers—the *adults*—then? They were either silent, afraid to preach or speak out about it, or applauding from the sidelines, regretful that such a revolution had come too late for them. Had I known then what I know now, about my body, about my dignity as a woman, about the meaning of truly fruitful love, how different my life—and the lives of countless young women who came of age in that era—would have been. And what of the hundreds of thousands of young women who have struggled since—who continue to struggle now—to overcome their natural instinct toward modesty and their predisposition to decline male advances outside of a committed, loving relationship. Though many women are still secretly hoping for a "steady boyfriend", many more are well on their way to finally replacing that instinct with their own, now hyperactive libido.[21] Having finally accepted that what they are looking for is merely a romantic myth they absorbed by watching *Cinderella* when they were little, they have now moved on to the theme from *Frozen*: "Let it go. No right, no wrong, no rules for me." Following the prompts of a disordered understanding of freedom, women seem to be dangerously close to the "liberation" they were promised so many years ago. It has taken a while. Should we not warn them that they have finally fallen into the same trap foisted on humanity by the so-called Enlightenment that the only thing that really matters is absolute, individual autonomy? Do you think we should help them understand the flaw in the modern conviction that to be "free" means to have the "right" to be free of even the desire for a relationship? Are we really hoping that women will finally accept that isolation is the goal, that commitment is for fools, and that children are merely a burden or a commodity? Even though, in her heart of hearts, it is relationship she seeks, woman is now—finally—poised at the possibility that real freedom means the right to liberate oneself from one's nature.[22] Freedom now means the freedom to refuse something already given—the gift of who one actually is.

Do you really think this is what the Reverend Martin Luther King Jr. had in mind when he envisioned the moment of liberation? Will it

---

[21] For a scholarly article, see Paul J. Wright, "United States Women and Pornography through Four Decades", *Archives of Sexual Behavior* 42, no. 7 (October 2013): 1131–41. For a more accessible analysis, see Trillia Newbell, "The Secret Women's Porn Problem", *Christianity Today*, October 2013, https://www.christianitytoday.com/women/2013/october/secret-womens-porn-problem.html. The article reports that Nielsen estimated that one in three visitors to porn sites in 2007 were women; the number is increasing every year.

[22] That this is the goal of the sexual libertinism of our time is clear, if left mostly unstated. There is probably no clearer articulation of this than that found in Camille Paglia's 1994 essay "No Law in the Arena: A Pagan Theory of Sexuality". There she states: "Nature exists whether academics like it or not and in nature, procreation is the single, relentless rule. That is the norm.... However, my libertarian view, here as regard to abortion, is that we have not only the right but the obligation to defy nature's tyranny. The highest human identity consists precisely in such assertions of freedom against material limitation." *Vamps and Tramps: New Essays* (New York: Vintage Books, 1994), p. 70.

finally be time to declare ourselves "Free at last! Thank God Almighty—free at last!"?

But here's the problem. What happens if women, the bearers of life, finally accept that the ideal way to live is to model their lives on the patterns suggested by the impulses of the average teenage boy? The contemporary, sexually active woman may not grasp the source of her discomfort, or her bitterness. But it is not hard to comprehend. For though it is never acknowledged, promiscuity, the hook-up culture, thoughtless sexual encounters, meaningless sex—all these factors, though certainly primary contributors to the decline of manhood in our culture, are actually destructive of women in a way that simply cannot be said of men.

Man's fundamental orientation is an external gaze; he faces outward. From his bodily design, to the objects of his attention, to the types of activities that engage him, he is turned toward the world. For him, the sexual act is itself ordered outwardly. His seed literally *leaves* his body; his involvement is momentary. Not so for woman. Woman's gaze is toward the internal. She bears everything on the inside. Who women are, from the design of our bodies, to the things that concern us, to the life of the child we have the capacity to carry—all this is *immanent*, hidden. It is the inner life that catches the woman's attention.

What simply must be understood is that, for a woman, the sexual act is an invitation to the man—or at least an agreement—to enter *inside* her, to enter *into* her very being. Sexual intercourse is an actual penetration of woman's inner self. When not accompanied by love and commitment, it is an act of pure, unadulterated theft, a theft that is permanent, of something that cannot be retrieved. She will not recover when she is used for the pure pleasure of it, no matter how hard she tries to feel whole again, for she holds within herself the memory of having been entered—and of what was lost.

To those who are ready to "rethink" *Humanae vitae* I offer this undeniable truth: it is woman who holds the union of the procreative and unitive dimensions together *in her very body*. In some silent, organic way, she grasps the truth of John Paul II's claim in *Love and Responsibility*, that the sexual act is man's participation in the very *transmission of existence*.[23]

---

[23] Karol Wojtyła, *Love and Responsibility* (San Francisco: Ignatius Press, 1981), p. 54. Wojtyła describes sexual intercourse as the moment when the couple enters into the "cosmic stream by which existence is transmitted" (p. 17).

And because this transmission travels along the axis that links heaven and earth, it has the force of an electrical current. Deny its nature and it is like trying to grab a power line. Come too close without the right formation, or without the right intention, and there will be a short. Human sexuality is *at the core* of man's essence, which is why the serpent never tires of meddling in it.

But the woman who is *grounded* in this profound self-knowledge, even if unspoken, is the equivalent of a heat sink.[24] Somehow she understands, even if only tacitly, that in the sexual act, she will discover her capacity for self-gift. She knows in the depths of her being that it is a gift that must be radical and total for it to have the full meaning it has, not only in the eyes of God, but for *her*. And she knows that in making that gift to a man who truly loves her, she reveals *to him* the gift that *he is*. In offering herself as a gift, and in accepting the gift of her beloved, she illuminates the nature of the gift that is at the heart of married love. Woman is called to be the guardian, the keeper of the gift of self, because it is only in *her* body that the fruits of that gift—new life—take root, grow, and are born.

If, as Pope Francis has declared, we need a "theology of women",[25] what is it going to include if not this reality?

The contraceptive mind-set that governs our culture is an affront to the dignity of women because it is a declaration that who she is, in her very being, is *not wanted*. Woman's fertility is *not* a disease; it is not an inconvenience. It is at the heart of the gift she is to the world. Whether or not a woman becomes a mother in the physical sense, or in the spiritual, her infinite capacity for the other is a feature of who she *is*. It is her task to remind all of us that *all human activity must be ordered toward human flourishing*.[26] Perhaps this is why the Church Fathers declare in the *Compendium of the Social Doctrine of the Church* that "the feminine genius is needed in every aspect of the life of society. Therefore the presence of women in the workplace must be guaranteed."[27] Women have rights

---

[24] In scientific terms, a heat sink is a device or substance for absorbing excessive or unwanted heat.

[25] See Pia de Solenni, "'Theology of Women in the Church' Only Beginning to Be Revealed", commentary, *National Catholic Register*, August 16, 2013, http://www.ncregister.com/daily-news/theology-of-women-in-the-church-only-beginning-to-be-revealed.

[26] See Savage, "Nature of Woman in Relation to Man", p. 92.

[27] *Compendium of the Social Doctrine of the Church* (Vatican City: Libreria Editrice Vaticana, 2004), p. 295.

because they are *human*, not because they are (finally) able to act like men. They are not men. Stop trying to make their bodies behave as though they are.

To those who couldn't care less about a Catholic teaching written five decades ago, I plead with you to *wake up*. For unless we acknowledge what is truly at stake here, the tragedy we have witnessed will play out for yet another generation—and another, and another. Unless and until woman's full destiny—and that of the human person—is seen for what it is, our world will always be populated with one generation after another of permanently adolescent males and wounded women.[28] The dignity of woman cannot be understood in any real sense *apart* from her natural capacity to bear and nurture life, but only *inclusive* of it. To deny this capacity is to refuse to see the integral whole that woman is; it is to reject her—and to ask her to deny herself. And it makes it impossible for her to fulfill her role in living out the mission given to both man and woman in the divine creation.

There can be no question that women and men are equally human; both are instantiations of the same substantial form—a rational soul. Both possess intellect, will, and freedom in equal measure. But their equality is not the equivalent of a mathematical equation; they are not interchangeable. Men and women are also different. Each brings *distinct* gifts to the world and to each other. Both are essential to the task of realizing the Church's social vision in the work of returning all things to Christ. Indeed, it is this very complementarity that gives them their *mission*. As Pope Saint John Paul II states in his *Letter to Women*: "To this 'unity of the two' God has entrusted not only the work of procreation and family life, but the creation of history itself."[29]

We are witnessing the final act of a drama that began in the Garden, that fatal moment when the relationship between man and woman first lost its footing. There will be no going back this time. For without a

[28] See Nicholas Eberstadt, "Who Is He? A Statistical Portrait of the Un-Working American Man", chap. 5 in *Men without Work: America's Invisible Crisis* (West Conshohocken, PA: Templeton Press, 2016), pp. 61–96. Dr. Eberstadt reports that the percentage of men in prime working years (ages twenty-five through fifty-four) dropped almost 10 percent during the period from 1965 through 2015 (p. 61). This is *not* due primarily to a lack of employment opportunity; men, especially unmarried men or men without children, have simply stopped looking for work in any formal sense (p. 64).

[29] John Paul II, *Letter to Women* (June 29, 1995), no. 8, https://w2.vatican.va/content/john-paul-ii/en/letters/1995/documents/hf_jp-ii_let_29061995_women.html.

doubt, in the end, the real question will go unanswered, since it will now become unanswerable: How will *we* explain it to *our* sons and daughters, those precious gifts to mankind who, in their beautiful innocence, have trusted us—their parents, their priests, their ministers, their teachers—to guide them through the turbulent waters of puberty and onto a flourishing adulthood? Without the wisdom of centuries to inform and support her, how will my own beloved daughter respond when her instinct for self-preservation is awakened, when the silent recognition arises that she possesses a fundamental dignity that seeks expression and affirmation? How will *she* respond when a young man says to *her*: "Well, I would like to know your reason, but it had better be a good one"?

To those who would "rethink" *Humanae vitae* in the name of Holy Mother Church, I offer this fervent plea: Please, Your Excellencies—do not abandon us. Women *and* men are counting on you to become who you are meant to be: teachers of the truth. And the truths expressed here are not merely the dreaded abstractions you seem to fear. They begin in the lived experience of women everywhere. They were just waiting to be expressed, finally, in the language of our time.

Population Control[*]

Obianuju Ekeocha

Population-Explosion Alarmism

The United Nations Department of Economic and Social Affairs (UN DESA) has projected Africa's share of global population to grow to 25 percent in 2050 and to 39 percent in 2100.[1] Much of this growth would be the result of the phenomenal fertility of women in sub-Saharan Africa. This population boom could, under the right conditions, form the base of a formidable workforce and tax base that, if well managed and leveraged, could make Africa the world's largest market and a dominant player in the global economy.

On the other hand, the same forecast shows that, from 2010 through 2015, eighty-three countries, including some of the most powerful nations in the world—China, Germany, and Russia—had below-replacement fertility.[2] Yet the most publicized Western demographers, and the policy leaders who listen to them, have chosen to sound the alarm with their vision of an African population bomb instead of a population *boom*, which could help to grow African economies and to lift many Africans out of poverty. They are instilling fear in African leaders by painting a vivid picture of their countries at the sharp edge of

---

[*] This essay was originally published in *Target Africa: Ideological Neocolonialism in the Twenty-First Century* (San Francisco: Ignatius Press, 2018), pp. 31–57.

[1] United Nations Department of Economic and Social Affairs, Population Division, *World Population Prospects: The 2015 Revision, Key Findings and Advance Tables* (New York: United Nations, 2015), p. 3, https://esa.un.org/unpd/wpp/Publications/Files/Key_Findings_WPP_2015.pdf.

[2] Ibid., p. 10.

environmental destruction, natural-resource depletion, hunger, poverty, pandemic, and disorder. In their narration of the fate of Africa, they bring back to life every debunked Malthusian prediction.

Malthusian scholars and thinkers, such as Paul Ehrlich, renowned author of the 1968 book *The Population Bomb*, are still consulted for their thoughts and recommendations regarding world demographics, particularly in Africa, and their opinions resound in the statements of leading scholars on the issue. In an article about the high birth rate in Niger, John May, with the Population Reference Bureau, was quoted as saying: "This is a time bomb, because all the Sahel is in this situation, and especially with climate change, the food supply will be less abundant than before. It's a huge crisis."[3] It is with this Malthusian mind-set that solutions are being formed and proposed for Africa.

These solutions rely heavily on a single-minded strategy that entails removing or drastically reducing the source of the population growth in Africa—female fertility. Thus, Western nations, organizations, and foundations wage war against the bodies of African women. The first weapon in their arsenal is contraceptive drugs and devices, usually referred to as "family planning". According to the UN DESA: "To realize the substantial reductions in fertility projected in medium variant, it is essential to invest in reproductive health and family planning, particularly in the least developed countries."[4] Jagdish Upadhyay, an executive at the United Nations Population Fund (UNFPA), described contraception as a human right: "If all actors can work together to provide women in every country with the means, which is their right, to voluntarily exercise yet another right to freely determine their family size, then we are likely to see a significant slowing of global population growth."[5]

An interview with a well-known British television personality published in the *Telegraph* in 2013 displays this population-explosion

[3] Quoted in Jill Filipovic, "Why Have Four Children When You Could Have Seven? Family Planning in Niger", *Guardian*, March 15, 2017, https://www.theguardian.com /global-development-professionals-network/2017/mar/15/why-have-four-children-when -you-could-have-seven-contraception-niger?CMP.

[4] United Nations Department of Economic and Social Affairs, *World Population Prospects*, p. 5.

[5] Quoted in Liz Ford, "Rise in Use of Contraception Offers Hope for Containing Global Population", *Guardian*, March 8, 2016, https://www.theguardian.com/global-development /2016/mar/08/rise-use-contraception-global-population-growth-family-planning.

alarmism.[6] Unless more population-control efforts are made, he said, the world is "heading for disaster". Also evident in the interview is the Englishman's condescension toward the people of Africa and his lack of understanding of the situation in Africa. Many of his comments were predicated on falsehoods and prejudices, not on facts. For example, he stated that the famines in Ethiopia are caused by too many people living on too little land. Yet the population density of Ethiopia is 82.6 per square kilometer, whereas the population density of Great Britain is 302 per square kilometer. With more than three times the population density of Ethiopia, Britain has more than enough food to feed its population. So how can anyone living there tell the Ethiopians to control their "wild" reproduction rate or forever face the scourge of famine? The reporter did not ask questions along these lines, of course, but simply passed along the Englishman's ominous warning that if we do not act soon, with greater population-control efforts, "the natural world will do something."

The Englishman's view is neither new nor fresh; it is the same theory that many before him have promoted—the theory of the bogus menace of the ticking population time bomb, which is bound to explode if the fertility rate in the developing world is not reduced right away.

According to many experts, a big problem in much of the world is not that too many people are being born but that too few are. For them, the concern is not a population explosion brought on by high birth rates but a population implosion caused by low birth rates. Some are calling the phenomenon a "demographic winter". Science writer Fred Pearce reported that "half the world's nations have fertility rates below replacement level, of just over two children per woman. Countries across Europe and the Far East are teetering on a demographic cliff, with rates below 1.5. On recent trends, Germany and Italy could see their populations halved within the next 60 years." He added that "many demographers expect a global crash to be under way by 2076."[7]

---

[6] Quoted in Hannah Furness, "If We Do Not Control the Population the Natural World Will", *Telegraph*, September 18, 2013, http://www.telegraph.co.uk/culture/tvandradio/10316271/Sir-David-Attenborough-If-we-do-not-control-population-the-natural-world-will.html.

[7] Fred Pearce, "The World in 2076: The Population Bomb Has Imploded", *New Scientist*, November 16, 2016, https://www.newscientist.com/article/mg23231001-400-the-world-in-2076-the-population-bomb-did-go-off-but-were-ok/?utm_campaign=Echobox&utm_medium=Social&utm_source=Twitter#link_time=1499341645.

The demographic decline now occurring in developed countries, where the fertility rate has dropped below the replacement rate, is creating all sorts of challenges associated with an aging population: labor shortages, loss of tax revenue and the resulting increase in public debt, unsustainable social health and welfare systems, and countless old people without anyone to care for them. A case in point is Japan, "a nation with an unprecedented rapidly aging and declining population".[8] For the past twenty years or so, Japan has been suffering from a declining birth rate and, as a consequence, has seen little or no economic growth.[9] In 2015 about 1 million babies were born, a slight increase over the previous year, but 1.3 million people died, amounting to a net loss of almost 300,000 people.[10]

The shrinking population has adversely affected Japanese society. Many young adults have moved to the cities for jobs, leaving the elderly behind in economically declining towns with fewer and fewer resources and services, including health-care providers. For this reason, the Japanese government has been attempting to entice working people back to the villages by shoring up lagging fisheries and farms, while trying to figure out ways to relocate some of the elderly to more populous areas. In the effort to reverse the fertility trend, boosting the birth rate has become one of the goals of Prime Minister Shinzō Abe's administration, which has declared that it will raise the fertility rate from the current 1.4 to 1.8 by 2025 or so. The government hopes to encourage more births by making it easier for families to raise children, such as by increasing the places available in nursery schools.[11]

[8] "Japan's Depopulation Time Bomb", *Japan Times*, April 17, 2013, http://www.japan times.co.jp/opinion/2013/04/17/editorials/japans-depopulation-time-bomb/# .WLiZOPnyvIV.

[9] "The Japanese Solution", *Economist*, November 5, 2015, https://www.economist.com news/finance-and-economics/21677648-despite-shinzo-abes-best-efforts-japans-economic -future-will-be-leap.

[10] Kyodo, "Slightly More Babies Born Last Year in Japan, but Population Suffers Net Loss of Almost 300,000 People", *Japan Times*, January 1, 2016, https://www.japantimes.co.jp /news/2016/01/01/national/slightly-babies-born-last-year-japan-population-suffers-net-loss -almost-300000-people/#.WbrGXkHTWEd.

[11] Mizuho Aoki, "In Sexless Japan, Almost Half of Single Young Men and Women Are Virgins: Survey", *Japan Times*, September 16, 2016, https://www.japantimes.co.jp/news /2016/09/16/national/social-issues/sexless-japan-almost-half-young-men-women-virgins -survey/#.WbrB-EHTWEc.

Although population size is not as much of a concern in Europe and the United States because of immigration, which Japan does not want to increase, these places too are experiencing the so-called graying of their populations. Upside-down family trees, with more elderly people than young people, are commonplace. As a result, the unavoidable fate of many old people is the nursing home, where loneliness, neglect, and even abuse are rampant. In contrast, in the developing world, there are enough children and grandchildren to care for the elderly in warm, loving multigenerational households. For many Africans, children and grandchildren are a sure and steady source of tender loving care in old age, although population-control enthusiasts may see them as nothing more than a sure and steady source of pollution and carbon dioxide emission. Even among the poorest in the developing world, a child is considered not just a mouth to feed but a gift to the family and the community.

With regard to population, Africa's problem has more to do with uncontrolled urbanization. Most African governments invest most of their development funds in a few strategic cities, which has caused mass migration into these areas by people searching for jobs and basic amenities such as electricity, health-care facilities, and schools. A striking example is Lagos, the commercial center of Nigeria. The megacity of 16 million people is in the smallest state of Nigeria, also called Lagos. The state has less than 0.5 percent of the country's landmass, yet 10 percent of the Nigerian population lives in the Lagos metropolitan area, which takes up about a fourth of the state. Lagos has been a magnet because it is the financial center of the country and a major economic hub in West Africa. Similar urban sprawl can be seen in other key African cities such as Douala, Nairobi, and Kampala. Migration to these cities has placed a strain on the existing infrastructure and has resulted in the growth of huge slums, where many people end up when they cannot afford better housing. These slums are usually horrible places with hazardous living conditions. The solution to the slums is not depopulation but rather investment in rural Africa, in its agricultural sector, so that people can make a living wherever they are. If development were more even, severe and unsustainable urbanization would be reduced because people would return to or remain in the regions they are from. Then Africa's growing working-age population would become an economic asset rather than an economic liability.

Ignoring the Desire for Children

For world leaders, the plan of action is very clear—a dedicated effort in population control in developing countries. But in their single-minded obsession to reduce the fertility rate of women in sub-Saharan Africa, the one important consideration the experts have omitted is the desired fertility rate of the women in question.

In 2010, the United States Agency for International Development (USAID) released a report on the number of children desired by people in various parts of the world. It was quite revelatory, as it showed that the desired number of children is highest among people in western and middle Africa, ranging from 4.8 in Ghana to 9.1 in Niger and 9.2 in Chad, with an average of 6.1 children for the region.[12] In all the regions and countries surveyed, the level of unwanted births is also remarkably lowest, at 6 percent, in eighteen west and middle African countries. In fact, the report shows that in a country such as Niger, there is hardly any indication of unwanted fertility. In other words, women in Niger consider all their babies as wanted (even when pregnancy is unplanned).[13]

These facts call into question the much-lamented crisis of "unmet need" for family planning. "Unmet need" has become the phrase used within Western elite circles to speak about the "appallingly low" prevalence of contraception use in developing countries. It has become the core of their case for multibillion-dollar contraception projects, the scaffold for their most important policies, and their first and last talking points at every population-themed event. They have even come up with an estimated number of women with an unmet need for family-planning services—220 million. They assume that these millions of women fail to contracept because they lack contraceptives, but in reality most of these women desire to have children—in fact, many children. There is a big difference between the invented unmet need and the real unmet needs of African women.

In the article "Why Have Four Children When You Could Have Seven? Family Planning in Niger", Western journalist Jill Filipovic reported on the strong desire for children in Niger:

---

[12] Charles F. Westhoff, *Desired Number of Children, 2000–2008*, DHS Comparative Reports No. 25 (Calverton, MD: ICF Macro, 2010), p. 3, http://www.dhsprogram.com/pubs/pdf/CR25/CR25.pdf.
[13] Ibid., p. 21.

Despite having the highest fertility rate in the world, women and men alike in Niger say they want more children than they actually have—women want an average of nine, while men say they want 11. . . .

Mariama Hassan, who has lived in Darey Maliki village her whole life, got married at 18, late by village standards. As she breastfeeds her daughter, Ramatou, she says she wants to see her baby girl finish school, and eventually get married as well—but not until she's 25. "I want her to be a doctor," Hassan says. "I say 25 because I want her to be mature before getting married, and I want her to finish her studies."

Her hopes for her own life are different. "In my lifetime, I want to have what God decides for me," she says. What does that mean in terms of children? She smiles and laughs. "I hope God gives me 12."[14]

Hassan's sentiments match those of many women in Africa who firmly believe that children are good and precious gifts from God.

I am the sixth child of my parents, and in my childhood I was surrounded (both in my neighborhood and in my school) by children from large families that looked much like mine. And even though we were not wealthy at all, our parents were comfortable in their role of welcoming, raising, feeding, and forming many children. Whether we were planned or unplanned, we were certainly precious to our parents, and it was obvious that they thought of us as God's gifts to them.

Africans are the most philoprogenitive people in the world. This reality is perhaps the single most inconvenient truth behind the resistance to population control in various African communities. It is the unvarnished truth that refutes every fragile project or policy built upon the claim of "unmet need". It is the disruptive truth that population-control experts, ruling elites, and enthusiasts have chosen to ignore as they wage war against the fertility of African women.

In the town I come from, a new baby is always welcomed with much joy. In fact, we have a special song reserved for births, a sort of "Gloria in Excelsis Deo". The day a baby is born, the entire village celebrates by singing this song, clapping their hands, and dancing. I can say with certainty that Africans love babies.

With all the challenges and the difficulties of life in Africa, there is much to complain about, and Africans, like many other people, lament their problems openly. Throughout my life I have heard people complain

[14] Filipovic, "Why Have Four Children?"

of many things, yet I have never heard a woman complain about her baby (born or unborn).

Even with substandard medical care in most places, women are valiant in pregnancy. And once their babies arrive, they gracefully and heroically embrace their maternal responsibilities. I worked for almost five years in a medical setting in Africa, yet I never heard the clinical term "postpartum depression" until I came to live in Europe. The condition might have been underdiagnosed or hidden, but I never witnessed it, even with the relatively high birth rate around me. (I estimate that I had at least one family member or close friend give birth every single month, so I saw at least a dozen new babies per year.) Amid all our African afflictions and difficulties, amid all the socioeconomic and political instabilities, our children are always a firm symbol of hope, a promise of life continuing, a reason to strive for a bright future.

The War against Our Fertility

In 2012 I stumbled upon Melinda Gates' plan to collect pledges for almost $5 billion to ensure that the African woman would be less fertile, less encumbered, and, yes, more "liberated". With her incredible wealth she wanted to replace the legacy of an African woman (which is her child) with the legacy of "child-free sex". I was so outraged that I wrote a public letter to Melinda Gates, which went viral on the Internet and is now posted on the webpage of the Vatican's Pontifical Council for the Laity.[15]

In that letter, I explained to Gates, a Catholic, that many of the sixty-nine countries she was targeting for her contraceptive campaign had large Catholic populations, with millions of Catholic women of child-bearing age. Unlike Gates and other Catholic women in the developed Western world, African Catholic women tend to regard highly Pope Paul VI's encyclical *Humanae vitae*. African women, in all humility, have heard, understood, and accepted the precious words of the prophetic pope. Women with little education and material wealth have embraced

---

[15] Obianuju Ekeocha, "An African Woman's Open Letter to Melinda Gates", Pontifical Council for the Laity, 2012, www.laici.va/content/laici/en/sezioni/donna/notizie/an-african-woman-s-open-letter-to-melinda.gates.html.

what the average *Vogue-* and *Cosmo*-reading woman in the United States has refused to understand: that when sex and marriage and children are separated, promiscuity, divorce, abortion, prostitution, and pornography spread as never before. Contraception brings about not greater respect and freedom for women, said Pope Paul VI, but less.

With most African women faithfully practicing and adhering to a faith (mainly Christian or, in some cases, Muslim), there is a high regard for the sexual act as a sacred and private trust between a husband and a wife. The trivialization of sex common in the West is simply not an acceptable part of African society, at least not yet. But the moment huge amounts of contraceptive drugs and devices are injected into our society, they will undoubtedly start to erode the sexual ethics that have been woven into our culture by our faith, not unlike the erosion that befell the Western world after the mass distribution of the birth control pill that began in the 1960s.

As we have seen in the West, the easy availability of contraceptives increases sexual promiscuity and infidelity, especially since sex is presented by the promoters of contraception as a casual pleasure sport that can come with no strings—or babies—attached. I shudder to think of the exponential spread of HIV and other STDs in Africa, as men and women with abundant access to contraceptives take up multiple, concurrent sex partners.

And, of course, there are bound to be inconsistencies and failures in the use of these drugs and devices, so naturally, there will be many more unplanned pregnancies as well. How convenient, then, that the West has been pressuring African governments to loosen their abortion laws.

As if this were not enough, I sadly realized that the pro-contraceptive media blitz that will accompany these drugs and devices will not tell Africans the whole truth about them. They will not be told about failure rates, adverse side effects, and the increased risks of cancer and heart disease. They will not be told that promiscuity itself is the leading cause of sexually transmitted diseases, which hormonal contraceptives such as the Pill and the patch do nothing to prevent. Given that women in Western societies are left in the dark about these things, the chances that African women will be respected enough to be given all the facts are rather slim. But unlike most Western women, African women tend not to have regular doctor visits; if African women suffer from negative consequences of contraceptive use, they will suffer from them without follow-up care.

In short, I concluded in my letter to Melinda Gates, I saw her billions of dollars as buying Africans not the real health care that they need but only misery. Needless to say, my letter did nothing to stop the Gates Foundation's full-speed-ahead push for contraceptives. Indeed, two years later, in November 2014, the foundation sponsored a huge family-planning conference in Abuja, the capital of Nigeria.

The Abuja Family Planning Conference had immediate results in my country. A month later, the Federal Ministry of Health launched its Nigeria Family Planning Blueprint to raise contraceptive use among Nigerian married women from 15 to 36 percent.[16] The cost of the program? Six hundred million dollars. After all, it takes a lot of money to change the behavior of millions of women. The urgent reason given for this huge expense, which will require massive amounts of foreign aid? To avert 1.6 million unintended pregnancies as well as 400,000 infant and 700,000 child deaths by 2018. The conference leaders argued that increasing contraceptive use is essential for "sustainable national development and security" for "maternal and child health and overall quality of life".[17] They also called for "increased funding commitments for family planning and a rights-based approach to reproductive health".

The Ministry of Health and those with vested interests in promoting contraception are perpetuating the cruel deception that high maternal mortality rates are the result of high birth rates. It is true that if fewer children were born in a given year, fewer mothers would die because of complications during childbirth. Deaths due to childbirth, however, could also be prevented by better health care. For example, both Maldives and Tanzania have a contraception prevalence rate of 35 percent. Yet Maldives has a maternal mortality rate of 68, while Tanzania's is 398. Why do so many more Tanzanian women die during and shortly after childbirth? Poor health care. Let's look at another comparison: Ghana has a very low contraception prevalence rate (19 percent), yet it has a

---

[16] Nigeria Federal Ministry of Health, *Nigeria Family Planning Blueprint (Scale-Up Plan)*, October 2014, https://www.healthpolicyproject.com/ns/docs/CIP_Nigeria.pdf.

[17] Health Policy Project, "Federal Ministry of Health of Nigeria Launces the Nigeria Family Planning Blueprint (Scale-Up Plan)", December 11, 2014, http://www.healthpolicy project.com/index.cfm?ID=NigeriaCIP.

lower maternal mortality rate (319) than Zimbabwe's (443), even though Zimbabwe has a high contraception prevalence rate (58 percent).[18]

In other words, the availability of contraception does not necessarily mean that a country has adequate maternity care. What African nations need is not a massive infusion of contraceptives into their communities but a renewed commitment to building up the various branches of the dilapidated health-care systems across the continent. Imagine if billions of dollars were invested in that!

Congregating in the Mighty Name of Contraception

There are increasing numbers of gatherings around the world for the sole purpose of moving Africa toward the Western standard of low fertility rates and high contraception prevalence. The Gates Foundation has taken a leadership role in this project, which on its surface is about women but at its core is about population control.

In their 2014 Abuja Family Planning Conference, the Gates Foundation was joined by other Western sponsors, including Britain's Department for International Development, the United States Agency for International Development (USAID), the MacArthur Foundation, and the United Nations Population Fund (UNFPA). Any one of these organizations could have single-handedly sponsored a conference in any part of the world, but their reason for having it in Nigeria is worth careful examination. Listed alongside these sponsors as the conference's "corporate partners/planning committee" were about twenty-five powerful organizations, some well known in Europe and America for their promotion of contraception and abortion: International Planned Parenthood Federation (IPPF), Marie Stopes International (MSI), Ipas, Pathfinder, and others. Yes, they all gathered in Abuja to nudge and prod Nigeria toward their ideal of family planning.

The term "family planning" is (or should be) self-explanatory. It should mean the planning of one's family. It should point to married

---

[18] Central Intelligence Agency, *The World Factbook* (Washington, DC: Central Intelligence Agency, 2017), "Contraceptive Prevalence Rate", https://www.cia.gov/library/publications /the-world-factbook/fields/2258.html; and "Maternal Mortality Rate", https://www.cia .gov/library/publications/the-world-factbook/fields/2223.html.

couples who have a family to plan. It should be family centered and should connote self-discipline (for every good plan should be under-girded by discipline). Family planning should be a good, healthy, pure, and beautiful concept. A couple, guided by the spirit of openness to love and life, can plan their family together while understanding that any life conceived by their union is a gift of enormous value. Family planning should be natural and healthy for both husband and wife. It should not be destructive or detrimental to the health of soul and body, as is contraception.

Family planning should entail much love, understanding, generosity of spirit, humility, patience, self-control, fidelity, communication, care, and cooperation. All of these enrich the marital bond and strengthen the family-oriented culture of Nigeria. However, the family-planning conference in Abuja had very little, if anything, to do with self-control or fidelity or patience or even marriage! On the contrary, it promoted a hedonistic, individualistic, selfish view of sex.

In spite of the government's stated goal to focus attention on married women, the conference focused on normalizing sexual activities among Nigerian youth outside of marriage. The conference included highly eroticized campaigns targeting the young and presentations on topics such as "Addressing the Family Planning Service Needs of Youth". What need do youth have for family planning? What is so dire about the family-planning needs of our adolescents to warrant eleven powerful sponsors and twenty-five corporate partners?

The truth is, the listed organizers, sponsors, and planners of this con-ference are very much in tune with the goals of Family Planning 2020, which are to generate global commitments to make high-quality, volun-tary family-planning services, information, and supplies more available, acceptable, and affordable for "an additional 120 million women and girls in the world's poorest countries ... by 2020".[19] These wealthy, prestigious organizations gathered in our capital with their conference in order to disparage our widely held cultural and religious views on life, love, marriage, and family. Their campaigns represented nothing less than an attack on the natural modesty and innocence of our vulnerable and impressionable young people.

[19] "Financial", Family Planning 2020, July 11, 2017, www.familyplanning2020.org /entities/66/commitments.

This conference was not convened out of great necessity in our country, and it was not conceived in Nigeria. Rather, it was convened at the behest of the cultural imperialists who consider themselves our "betters". It was conceived in the hearts of powerful Western interests who are committed to and profit from spreading the sexual revolution, in spite of the fact that it has resulted in higher-than-ever rates of divorce, illegitimacy, abortion, and STDs in the nations where it originated. They are the same people who are promoting abortion throughout the world. They are the same ones who are pushing the movement to normalize lesbian, gay, bisexual, and transgender (LGBT) identity and behavior. They are the same ones implicated in various draconian population-control programs around the globe in the name of saving the world. And they favor more long-acting contraceptive methods, yet are deafeningly silent about the significant medical side effects associated with some, if not all, of these drugs. These have, in many documented cases, proved detrimental and dangerous to women's health and well-being.

The Dangers Undisclosed

Blood clots, sinusitis, nausea, migraines, cardiovascular diseases (notably stroke and heart attack), ovarian cysts, heavier periods, depression, anxiety, weight gain, hair loss, uterine perforation, pelvic inflammatory disease, osteoporosis, breast cancer, and death are among the side effects disclosed by pharmaceutical manufacturers in the fine-print inserts that come with the most familiar contraceptive drugs and devices—oral contraceptives, NuvaRing, intrauterine devices, implants, and injectables. Yet these side effects are rarely discussed by the promoters of contraception or even by the doctors who prescribe them.

When Norplant made its market debut in 1992, it was hailed as a breakthrough for women: they could have a mere ten-minute procedure to insert the contraceptive and then not worry about getting pregnant for years. Because of Norplant's adverse side effects, however, it was withdrawn from the United Kingdom in 1999. Also in 1999, after years of litigation in the United States, Norplant's manufacturer offered cash settlements to thirty-six thousand American women who claimed that the drug had caused side effects that they had not been adequately warned about, such as excessive menstrual bleeding, headaches, nausea, dizziness, and depression. The parent company, American Home Products, offered each of the plaintiffs $1,500. Three years later, Norplant distribution ended in the United States.[20]

The distribution of Norplant was not discontinued globally until 2008, after it had been widely administered to women in a number of African countries: Egypt, Ghana, Kenya, Nigeria, Zambia, Zaire (now the Democratic Republic of the Congo), Rwanda, Malawi, Madagascar, Tanzania, South Africa, Zimbabwe, and Burkina Faso.[21] Surely at least some African women have experienced adverse side effects, but they will likely never receive any compensation for their suffering, because there will likely be no class action suit filed on their behalf.

In a more recent case, nearly twenty thousand lawsuits have been filed in the United States against Bayer for alleged harm done by their Yaz and Yasmin birth control pills. The plaintiffs are seeking both compensatory and punitive damages for blood clots, heart attacks, strokes, and gall bladder injuries. Some of these potential side effects have been linked with one hundred deaths. The suits claim that Bayer failed to heed warnings about the dangers posed by the synthetic hormone drospirenone, an active ingredient in the pills, and to disclose the information to the public. Bayer says that the hormone is safe and continues to sell Yaz and Yasmin, although the company has already settled thousands of cases for billions of dollars and as of 2017 was expecting further lawsuits. Legal challenges are cropping up in other countries as well.[22]

Several years ago, critics began urging the United States Food and Drug Administration (FDA) to recall birth control pills with drospirenone, and in 2012 the FDA issued the following safety announcement:

---

[20] David J. Morrow, "Maker of Norplant Offers a Settlement in Suit over Effects", *New York Times*, August 27, 1999, https://nytimes.com/1999/08/27/us/maker-of-norplant -offers-a-settlement-in-suit-over-effects.html?pagewanted=all&referer=.

[21] Irving Sivin, Harold Nash, and Sandra Waldman, *Jadelle Levonorgestrel, Rod Implants: A Summary of Scientific Data and Lessons Learned from Programmatic Experience* (New York: Population Council, 2002), p. 5, http://www.respond-project.org/pages/files/4_result_areas /Result_1_Global_Learning/LA_PM_CoP/june2009-launch/Jadelle-Levonorgestrel-Rod -Implants.pdf.

[22] "Yaz Lawsuits and Litigation", DrugWatch.com, accessed April 20, 2018, https://www .drugwatch.com/yaz/lawsuits/.

The U.S. Food and Drug Administration (FDA) has completed its review of recent observational (epidemiologic) studies regarding the risk of blood clots in women taking drospirenone-containing birth control pills. Drospirenone is a synthetic version of the female hormone, progesterone, also referred to as a progestin. Based on this review, FDA has concluded that drospirenone-containing birth control pills may be associated with a higher risk for blood clots than other progestin-containing pills. FDA is adding information about the studies to the labels of drospirenone-containing birth control pills.[23]

The notification came on the heels of some scientific studies that demonstrated a sixfold increased risk of blood clots in users of combined pills with desogestrel, gestodene, drospirenone, or cyproterone acetate, compared with nonusers.[24]

Given the limited reporting on the adverse side effects of oral contraceptives and the assurances from medical professionals and pharmaceutical companies that their benefits outweigh their risks, the global distribution of the more dangerous pills is not exactly clear. Africa has been flooded in recent years with various oral contraceptives. In 2014 alone, 77,225,741 units of unspecified birth control pills were collectively donated to African countries by the UNFPA, USAID, the IPPF, MSI, Population Services International, the German-government development bank Kreditanstalt für Wiederaufbau, and the British Department for International Development.[25] African health-care providers and leaders must find out which pills are being distributed and what their side effects could be and then share this information with African women.

Another Bayer contraceptive that has recently stirred controversy is Essure, a nonsurgical, permanent method of sterilizing women. It

---

[23] "FDA Drug Safety Communication: Updated Information about the Risk of Blood Clots in Women Taking Birth Control Pills Containing Drospirenone", U.S. Food and Drug Administration, April 10, 2012, https://www.fda.gov/Drugs/DrugSafety/ucm299305.htm.

[24] Ø. Lidegaard et al., "Hormonal Contraception and Venous Thromboembolism", *Acta Obstetricia et Gynecologica Scandinavica* 91, no. 7 (July 2012): 769–78.

[25] Dr. Kabir Ahmed et al., *Contraceptives and Condoms for Family Planning and STI and HIV Prevention: External Procurement Support Report 2014* (New York: UNFPA, 2014), pp. 102–3, http://www.unfpa.org/sites/default/files/pub-pdf/UNFPA_External_Procurement_Support_Report.pdf.

involves inserting tiny coils into the fallopian tubes. Tissue then builds up around the coils and blocks sperm from reaching eggs. Essure was hailed as an affordable, less-invasive alternative to surgical sterilization procedures that block, cut, or seal the fallopian tubes.[26]

Beginning around 2013, however, the FDA began receiving many adverse-event reports related to this device:

> Reported adverse events include persistent pain, perforation of the uterus and/or fallopian tubes, intra-abdominal or pelvic device migration, abnormal or irregular bleeding, and allergy or hypersensitivity reactions. Some women have had surgical procedures to remove the device. In addition, Essure failure, and, in some cases, incomplete patient follow-up, have resulted in unintended pregnancies.[27]

In 2015 the FDA consulted with doctors and patients about Essure, issued some statements about the possible need for labeling changes, and continued its approval of the product. That same year, an important study of Essure was published by the *BMJ* (formerly *British Medical Journal*). It found that this form of sterilization carried a more than tenfold higher risk of reoperation than laparoscopic sterilization.[28]

The following year, the FDA decided that Essure labeling should henceforth include the addition of the following boxed warning:

> WARNING: Some patients implanted with the Essure System for Permanent Birth Control have experienced and/or reported adverse events, including perforation of the uterus and/or fallopian tubes, identification of inserts in the abdominal or pelvic cavity, persistent pain, and suspected allergic or hypersensitivity reactions. If the device needs to be removed to address such an adverse event, a surgical procedure will be required. This information should be shared with patients considering sterilization with

[26]Julie Deardorff, "Women Report Complications from Essure Birth Control", *Chicago Tribune*, December 22, 2013, http://articles.chicagotribune.com/2013-12-22/health/ct -essure-safety-met-20131222_1_essure-conceptus-fallopian-tubes.

[27]"Essure Permanent Birth Control", U.S. Food and Drug Administration, last modified August 23, 2017, https://www.fda.gov/MedicalDevices/ProductsandMedicalProcedures /ImplantsandProsthetics/EssurePermanentBirthControl/default.htm.

[28]Jialin Mao et al., "Safety and Efficacy of Hysteroscopic Sterilization Compared with Laparoscopic Sterilization: An Observational Cohort Study", *BMJ* 351 (October 13, 2015), http://www.bmj.com/content/351/bmj.h5162.

the Essure System for Permanent Birth Control during discussion of the benefits and risks of the device.[29]

Bayer complied with the decision and added the FDA warning to its product.[30]

Women claiming to have been harmed by Essure cannot sue Bayer because of a law that indemnifies manufacturers of medical devices. But thousands of them have joined support groups on social media to discuss the debilitating side effects and the baffling medical problems that they have associated with Essure. In 2014 the famous consumer-rights advocate Erin Brockovich, whom Julia Roberts played in an Oscar-winning film, began championing their efforts to convince Bayer to stop manufacturing Essure. In response, Bayer Healthcare, which purchased Essure manufacturer Conceptus in 2013, said that the device was "overwhelmingly safe" and had been placed in 750,000 women worldwide.[31]

WomanCare Global announced in 2011 that it was going to distribute Essure in Ghana, Kenya, Mexico, Puerto Rico, and Turkey. According to its press release, which has been deleted from the organization's website but is published elsewhere, additional countries will be added.[32] Who will advocate for the women in these countries if they experience negative side effects from Essure?

Although American women with grievances against pharmaceutical companies can take action through appeals to the FDA, the media, and the judicial system, the typical African woman has no such means of recourse if she suffers adverse effects from the contraceptives she is being pressured to use. Between the launch of Melinda Gates' contraception campaign in 2012 and 2016, there were 30.2 million additional

[29] U.S. Food and Drug Administration, *Labeling for Permanent Hysteroscopically-Placed Tubal Implants Intended for Sterilization: Guidance for Industry and Food and Drug Administration Staff*, October 31, 2016, https://www.fda.gov/downloads/MedicalDevices/DeviceRegulationand Guidance/GuidanceDocuments/UCM488020.pdf.

[30] See Essure website: http://www.essure.com/.

[31] Regan Morris, "Erin Brockovich Calls for End to Bayer's Essure", BBC News, June 24, 2014, http://www.bbc.co.uk/news/business-27871265.

[32] "WomanCare Global to Distribute Essure in 5 Countries", Reproductive Health Supplies Coalition, January 11, 2011, https://www.rhsupplies.org/news-events/news/article /womancare-global-to-distribute-essure-r-in-5-countries-1283/.

users of contraception in the "focus countries", and 13 million of these were in Africa.[33]

The contraceptive that has been most assiduously pushed among African populations recently is injectable depot medroxyprogesterone acetate (DMPA), which is commonly known as Depo Provera or simply the Depo shot. The latest form of this shot can be administered under the skin (subcutaneously) once every three months. A 2014 UNFPA report recommended the use of DMPA in the developing world:

> It is hoped that the introduction of sub-cutaneous DMPA will address the unmet need for family planning through: (i) attracting new users; (ii) method switching from traditional and other temporary methods; and (iii) reduction of discontinuation rate of injectable contraceptives. Potential advantages of sub-cutaneous DMPA include increased convenience and ease of administration and the potential to contribute to system-level logistics benefits in terms of storage, transport, and distribution.
>
> Sub-cutaneous DMPA is recommended as an addition to the family planning method mix, serving to extend access and increase use in resource-constrained settings, potentially also in humanitarian situations.[34]

According to the same report, as of 2014 Western donor nations and organizations had contributed more than 102 million injectable contraceptives, and 50 percent of them had been given to African countries.

An example of the injectable-birth-control trend is the agreement between Pfizer Inc., the Bill and Melinda Gates Foundation, and the Children's Investment Fund Foundation to expand access to Pfizer's injectable contraceptive, Sayana Press, for women in the world's poorest countries.[35] Some of the countries targeted for contraception injections are Burkina Faso, Kenya, Niger, Senegal, Uganda, and Nigeria. The announcement of this project was immediately picked up and praised

---

[33] Family Planning 2020, "Additional Users and mCPR", chap. 3 in *FP2020 Momentum at the Midpoint, 2015–2016*, http://2015-2016progress.familyplanning2020.org/page/measurement/additional-users-mcpr-indicator-1-2.

[34] Ahmed et al., *Contraceptives and Condoms*, p. 60.

[35] Pfizer, "Novel Agreement Expands Access to Pfizer's Contraceptive, Sayana® Press, for Women Most in Need in the World's Poorest Countries", press release, November 13, 2014, http://press.pfizer.com/press-release/novel-agreement-expands-access-pfizers-contraceptive-sayana-press-women-most-need-worl.

by many news agencies in the Western world, including the British Broadcasting Corporation (BBC), which described the shot as the "one dollar contraceptive set to make family planning easier".[36] Easier for whom? For Ugandan, Kenyan, and Nigerian women? For the multibillionaire foundations spearheading the campaign? Or for the pharmaceutical company that just got a dream deal?

How does practically sterilizing the poorest women in the world give them control over famine, draught, disease, and poverty? It does not make them more educated or more employable. It does not provide food or safe drinking water. It does not make African women happier or more satisfied in their marriages. No. This extensive contraception project will only make them sterile at the cheapest rate possible. This is certainly not what we African women have asked for. It is not the help that our hearts crave amid the trials and difficulties of Africa. But in a world of shocking cultural imperialism, it is what our "betters" have chosen for us.

What makes the massive exportation of injectable contraception downright insidious is that while it is being pushed on African women, it is being questioned in the developed world after having been shown in various studies to carry dangerous and even lethal side effects.

In October 2011 the New York Times published the article "Contraceptive Used in Africa May Double Risk of H.I.V.", based on a cohort study by the prestigious medical research journal Lancet that showed that "the risk of HIV-1 acquisition doubled with the use of hormonal contraception, especially the injectable methods."[37] This study was partly funded by the Bill and Melinda Gates Foundation, and yet, following these findings, they still launched this high-risk product in the targeted countries of their choice (Uganda, Kenya, Niger, Nigeria, and many others), where the women may not be able to raise their voices when the lethal effects set in.

---

[36] Jane Dreaper, "The One Dollar Contraceptive Set to Make Family Planning Easier", BBC News, November 16, 2014, http://www.bbc.com/news/health-30026001.

[37] Renee Heffron et al., "Use of Hormonal Contraceptives and Risk of HIV-1 Transmission: A Prospective Cohort Study", Lancet 12, no. 1 (January 2012): 19–26, http://www.thelancet.com/journals/laninf/article/PIIS1473-3099(11)70247-X/fulltext#article_upsell. See also Pam Belluck, "Contraceptive Used in Africa May Double Risk of H.I.V.", New York Times, October 3, 2011, http://www.nytimes.com/2011/10/04/health/04hiv.html?pagewanted=all&_r=0.

In addition to the HIV-related effects of injectable contraception, there is also the doubled risk of breast cancer demonstrated by various studies, such as that done by the Fred Hutchinson Cancer Research Center in Seattle and published by the National Institutes of Health in 2013. The research team found that "recent DMPA use for 12 months or longer was associated with a 2.2-fold increased risk of invasive breast cancer."[38]

Furthermore, this same product has been linked to permanent bone-density loss, and regarding this health issue, Pfizer has had a staggering number of prosecutions, class action lawsuits, and out-of-court settlements with millions of dollars in payouts.[39] As a direct result of these cases, the FDA issued the following compulsory warning for the product Depo Provera:

> Use of Depo-Provera CI reduces serum estrogen levels and is associated with significant loss of bone mineral density (BMD). This loss of BMD is of particular concern during adolescence and early adulthood, a critical period of bone accretion. It is unknown if use of Depo-Provera CI by younger women will reduce peak bone mass and increase the risk for osteoporotic fracture in later life.... Depo-Provera CI should not be used as a long-term birth control method (i.e., longer than 2 years) unless other birth control methods are considered inadequate.[40]

How does a product shown to be flawed, dangerous, and in some cases even lethal become what the BBC refers to as the "contraceptive set to make family planning easier"?

The push for use of DMPA in Africa proves that the Western proponents of population control willfully ignore the glaring reality of the hazardous side effects of contraceptives so that they can impose their views and their dangerous products on Africans. In their campaign, conference,

---

[38] Christopher I. Li et al., "Effect of Depo-Medroxyprogesterone Acetate on Breast Cancer Risk among Women 20–44 Years of Age", NIH Public Access, April 15, 2012, https://aleteiaen.files.wordpress.com/2014/11/nihms359669.pdf.

[39] "Depo-Provera Birth Control and Osteoporosis", BigClassAction.com, June 27, 2005, https://www.bigclassaction.com/lawsuit/depo_provera_contraceptive_osteoporosis_class_action.php.

[40] Food and Drug Administration, Black Box Warning for Depo-Provera CI, revised October 2010, https://www.accessdata.fda.gov/drugsatfda_docs/label/2010/020246s036lbl.pdf.

and summit speeches, I have never heard any serious mention of these side effects or of the inadequacy of the health-care systems in Africa to deal with the health problems that are sure to follow widespread use of injectable contraceptives. The insistence on reducing the population of Africa, no matter what the cost to the Africans themselves, is racism, imperialism, and colonialism disguised as philanthropy.

Come, and Become One Who Sees

Humanae vitae, *Theology of the Body, and the Triumph of the Immaculate Heart*

Christopher West

> If then your whole body is full of light, having no part dark, it will be wholly bright, as when a lamp with its rays gives you light.
>
> —Luke 11:36

In our postsexual revolution world, we are experiencing a total eclipse of the meaning of sex, gender, marriage, and the family. Something is blocking the light, and we simply no longer *see* the fundamental significance of the human body to human identity and human relationships.

For most of man's history, an eclipse of the sun was an ominous event. Before astronomers understood the phenomenon, inexplicable blackness in the middle of the day spelled the end of the world, until, of course, after a few minutes of sheer terror, the sun reappeared. What has passed in front of the light blocking the body's meaning? Are there any "astronomers" out there who can explain this phenomenon, who can help us understand why this has happened and if, when, and how the darkness will pass? In this essay, I will point to three: Our Lady of Fatima, Pope Blessed Paul VI, and Pope Saint John Paul II.

Our Lady of Fatima and the Errors of Russia

As most Catholics know, between May 13 and October 13, 1917, Mary appeared to three peasant children in Fatima, Portugal, delivering a three-part message—the "three secrets" of Fatima. The first presented a horrifying vision of hell. The second involved a prophecy of World War II and the warning that "Russia would spread her errors throughout the world". However, Mary assured the children that "in the end" her Immaculate Heart would triumph and an "era of peace" would be granted to the world. Mary also told the children that "the Holy Father will have much to suffer." This brings us to the "third secret" of Fatima, which we will revisit at the end of the essay.

When we hear of the errors of Russia, we rightly think of the spread of Communism, the atheistic ideology based on Marxist economic theory. As most of us learned in school, Karl Marx considered class struggle to be the defining factor of history. But less known is that Marx also believed that the fundamental "class struggle" was found in marriage and, indeed, in the sexual difference itself. "The first division of labor," Marx co-wrote with Frederick Engels, "is that between man and woman for the propagation of children." In turn, Engels affirmed that Marxist theory "demands the abolition of the monogamous family as the economic unit of society".[1]

It seems that the deeper revolution—and the deeper "error of Russia"—is the one aimed at destroying marriage and the family. In fact, much later in her life, Sister Lucia (the only of the three visionaries of Fatima to live beyond childhood; she died in 2005) wrote that "a time will come when the decisive battle between the kingdom of Christ and Satan will be over marriage and the family."[2] The modern agenda to deconstruct gender, marriage, and family life often draws straight from Marx. As feminist author Shulamith Firestone wrote in her 1970 manifesto *The Dialectic of Sex*: "Just as the end goal of socialist revolution was ... the elimination of the ... economic class distinction itself, so the end goal of feminist revolution must be ... the elimination of ... the

---

[1] Frederick Engels, *The Origin of the Family, Private Property, and the State* (New York: William Morrow, 1970), p. 11.

[2] Sister Lucia wrote these words in a letter to the late Carlo Cardinal Caffarra when he served as president of the John Paul II Institute for Studies on Marriage and Family. Caffarra has given sworn testimony that these were in fact her words. See Diane Montagna, "(Exclusive) Cardinal Caffarra: 'What Sr. Lucia Wrote to Me Is Being Fulfilled Today'", Aleteia.org, May 19, 2017, https://aleteia.org/2017/05/19/exclusive-cardinal-caffarra-what-sr-lucia-wrote-to-me-is-being-fulfilled-today/.

sex distinction itself [so that] genital differences between human beings would no longer matter culturally."[3]

Rendering the Genital Difference Meaningless

What kind of revolution would be needed to render the genital difference meaningless? To answer that question, we must call to mind the fundamental purpose of the genital difference. It used to be obvious to everyone: genitals are meant to generate. We called it "the facts of life". But today those facts are entirely up for grabs, thanks to the collective impact of modern contraceptive technology. Based on its Greek root, the very word "gender" means "the manner in which one generates" (we see the same root in words like "genesis", "generous", "genitals", "progeny", "genes", and "genealogy"). We no longer see the gender-generation connection today because we are viewing ourselves through condom-colored glasses: erase the manner in which one generates from the sexual equation, and the very meaning of gender is eventually eclipsed.

Few today realize that, until 1930, all Christian denominations were unanimous in their firm opposition to any attempt to render our genitals unable to generate. That year, the Anglican church was the first to change its teaching. In the years that followed, every major Protestant denomination followed suit, and unimaginable global pressure was being put on the Catholic Church to do the same. In the early 1960s, the Fathers of the Second Vatican Council stated that they reserved judgment on "certain questions which need further and more careful investigation". These "have been handed over ... to a commission ... in order that, after it fulfills its function, the Supreme Pontiff may pass judgment."[4]

The point in question was the Pill, a new technology that seemed to some not to qualify under the traditional teaching against contraception. The Council's tacit admission of uncertainty on this point gave people the impression that a papal blessing on the Pill was forthcoming.

---

[3] Shulamith Firestone, *The Dialectic of Sex* (New York: Bantam Books, 1972), pp. 10–11.

[4] Vatican Council II, Pastoral Constitution on the Church in the Modern World *Gaudium et spes* (December 7, 1965), no. 51, note 14, http://www.vatican.va/archive/hist_councils /ii_vatican_council/documents/vat-ii_cons_19651207_gaudium-et-spes_en.html.

In fact, the majority of the commission (the Pontifical Commission on Birth Control) advised Paul VI not only to accept the Pill, but other forms of contraception as well. When the "Majority Report" was leaked to the press in early May 1967, there was a sense of certainty that a change was imminent. One week later, Paul VI visited Fatima. He came on her feast (May 13) and prayed specifically against "new ideologies" that were threatening the Church by introducing a "profane mentality" and "worldly morals".[5]

Over a year later, Paul VI shocked the world when he issued *Humanae vitae*, reaffirming the immorality of *all* forms of contraception.[6] In doing so, he showed himself to be an "astronomer" who understood the power of contraception to eclipse the meaning of the body, casting a dark shadow over the meaning of the gender difference itself, and, hence, the meaning of marriage and the family. He warned that a contracepting world becomes a world of rampant infidelity—a world where women and childbearing are degraded, a world in which governments trample on the rights and needs of the family, and a world in which human beings believe they can manipulate their bodies at will.[7] Who can deny that this is the world we live in today?

Paul VI also observed in *Humanae vitae* that, in order to understand the Church's teaching on sex and procreation, we need to consider "the whole [vision of] man and the whole mission to which he is called".[8] This is what his successor set out to do in the first major teaching project of his pontificate—provide this vision of man that would enable us to understand and live joyfully the Church's vision of the meaning and purpose *of human life (humanae vitae)*.

John Paul II's Theology of the Body

The operative term here is "vision". John Paul II understood that, while the people of the modern world were obsessed with looking at the

---

[5] See Paul VI, homily at Fatima, May 13, 1967, my translation.
[6] Paul VI, encyclical letter *Humanae vitae* (July 25, 1968) (hereafter cited as *HV*), http://w2.vatican.va/content/paul-vi/en/encyclicals/documents/hf_p-vi_enc_25071968_humanae-vitae.html.
[7] See *HV* 17.
[8] *HV* 7.

human body, "they look but do not see" (Mt 13:13 NAB). Over the course of 129 Wednesday audience addresses delivered between 1979 and 1984,[9] the Polish pope invited every human being to "come, and become one who sees" (see Jn 1:39).[10] If we allow Christ to heal our blindness, we come to see that the human body, precisely in the mystery of the genital difference, is a sign—in fact, a sacramental sign—that's meant to reveal the divine mystery. We come to see that the human body is not only biological; it's theological. Hence the working title John Paul II gave his project: Theology of the Body.

We cannot see God. As pure Spirit, he is invisible. And yet, the invisible God has made himself visible. How so? This brings us to the thesis statement of John Paul II's Theology of the Body, the brush with which he paints his entire vision:

> The body, in fact, and only the body, is capable of making visible what is invisible: the spiritual and divine. It has been created to transfer into the visible reality of the world the mystery hidden from eternity in God, and thus to be a sign of it.[11]

Through the profound unity of body and soul, the human body *reveals* or makes visible, so to speak, the invisible reality of the spiritual soul. But, because we are made in the image and likeness of God, the human body also makes visible something of God's own mystery.

The body is not divine, of course. But it *is* the most powerful sign of the divine mystery in all creation. The divine mystery always remains infinitely "beyond"; it cannot be reduced to its sign. Yet the sign is indispensable, paradoxically, in making visible the invisible mystery. As

---

[9] John Paul II actually divided his manuscript into 135 talks. However, some of the content of his reflections on the Song of Songs was considered too "delicate" for the Wednesday audience format, so he condensed 10 talks in that section to 4, thus delivering only 129. For an extended treatment of the undelivered talks, see my book *Heaven's Song: Sexual Love as It Was Meant to Be* (West Chester, PA: Ascension Press, 2008).

[10] John 1:39 is typically rendered "Come and see." As I once learned in my biblical studies (from those much more learned than I on such matters), the more accurate rendering of Christ's words is "Come, and become one who sees."

[11] John Paul II, *Man and Woman He Created Them: A Theology of the Body*, trans. Michael Waldstein (Boston: Pauline Books and Media, 2006), 19:4. References are to the audience number and paragraph number. Hereafter, all Theology of the Body references will be cited as TOB.

the *Catechism of the Catholic Church* (*CCC*) says, "Man needs signs and symbols to communicate.... The same holds true for his relationship with God."[12]

Tragically, because of sin, the "body loses its character as a sign"[13]—not objectively, but subjectively. In other words, in itself, the body retains its character as a sign of the spiritual and divine, but we've been blinded to it; "seeing [we] do not see" (Mt 13:13). As a result, we tend to consider the human body merely as a physical "thing" entirely separated from the spiritual and the divine. And this is why the very expression "theology of the body" seems so odd to people today, even to many Christians. It shouldn't, if we believe in the Incarnation. As John Paul II put it, "Through the fact that the Word of God became flesh, the body entered theology ... through the main door."[14]

Everything in Christianity hinges on the Incarnation. God's mystery has been revealed in human flesh rendering the human body a study of God, a *theology*. Theology of the Body, therefore, is not merely the title of a series of papal talks on sex and marriage; theology of the body is fundamental to the very logic of Christianity. For "in the body of Jesus 'we see our God made visible and so are caught up in love of the God we cannot see.'"[15]

The Divine Mystery

Several times already we have spoken of the divine mystery or the "mystery hidden for ages in God" (see Eph 3:9). What does this mean? In the Christian sense, "mystery" does not refer to some unsolvable puzzle. It refers to the innermost "secret" of God and to his eternal plan for mankind. These realities are so far beyond anything we can comprehend that it can seem as if all we can really utter is the word "mystery". And yet God's secret is knowable—not based on our ability to decipher some divine puzzle, but because God has made it known.

As the *Catechism* says, "God has revealed his innermost secret: God himself is an eternal exchange of love, Father, Son, and Holy Spirit, and

---

[12] *CCC* 1146.
[13] TOB 40:4.
[14] TOB 23:4.
[15] *CCC* 477, quoting *Roman Missal*, Preface of Christmas I.

he has destined us to share in that exchange."[16] God is an infinite com-munion of Persons experiencing eternal love-bliss. And he created us for one reason: to share that eternal love and bliss with us. This is what makes the Gospel *good news*—there is a banquet of love that corresponds to the hungry cry of our hearts, and it is God's free gift to us! We needn't climb some high mountain to find it. We needn't cross the sea. The "great mystery" of God's love is very close to us, intimately part of us. Indeed, God inscribed an image of this "great mystery" in the very form of our bodies by making us "male and female" (Gen 1:27) and calling the two to "become one flesh" (Gen 2:24).

The Spousal Analogy

Scripture uses many images to help us understand God's love. Each has its own valuable place. But, as John Paul II wrote, the gift of Christ's body on the Cross gives "definitive prominence to the spousal meaning of God's love."[17] In fact, from beginning to end, in the mysteries of our creation, fall, and redemption, the Bible tells a nuptial or marital story.

It begins in Genesis with the marriage of the first man and woman, and it ends in Revelation with the marriage of Christ and the Church. Right in the middle we find the erotic poetry of the Song of Songs. These bookends and this centerpiece provide the key for reading the whole story. Indeed, one way we can summarize God's purpose as pre-sented in Scripture is with five simple, yet astounding, words: *God wants to marry us*—"For as a young man marries a virgin, so shall your sons marry you" (Is 62:5).

In the midst of unfolding the biblical analogy of spousal love, it's very important to understand the bounds within which we're using such language and imagery. "It is obvious," writes John Paul II, "that the analogy of ... human spousal love, cannot offer an adequate and complete understanding of ... the divine mystery." God's "*mystery remains transcendent with respect to this analogy* as with respect to any other

---

[16] *CCC* 221.

[17] John Paul II, apostolic letter *Mulieris dignitatem* (August 15, 1988), no. 26, https://w2 .vatican.va/content/john-paul-ii/en/apost_letters/1988/documents/hf_jp-ii_apl_19880815 _mulieris-dignitatem.html.

analogy."[18] At the same time, however, John Paul II maintains that the spousal analogy allows a certain "penetration" into the very essence of the mystery.[19] And no biblical author reaches more deeply into this essence than Saint Paul in his Letter to the Ephesians. Quoting directly from Genesis, Paul states: "'For this reason a man shall leave his father and mother and be joined to his wife, and the two shall become one flesh'" (Eph 5:31, quoting Gen 2:24). Then, linking the original marriage with the ultimate marriage, he adds: "This is a great mystery, and I mean in reference to Christ and the Church" (Eph 5:32).

We can hardly overstate the importance of this passage for John Paul II and the whole theological tradition of the Church. He calls it, in some sense, the "summa" of Christian teaching about who God is and who we are.[20] He says this passage contains the "crowning" of all the themes in Sacred Scripture and expresses the "central reality" of the whole of divine revelation.[21] The mystery spoken of in this passage "is 'great' indeed," he says. "It is what God ... wishes above all to transmit to mankind in his Word."[22] Thus, "one can say that [this] passage ... 'reveals—in a particular way—*man to man himself* and makes *his supreme vocation* clear'."[23]

So what is this "supreme vocation" we have as human beings that Ephesians 5 makes clear? Stammering for words to describe the ineffable, the mystics call it "nuptial union"—*with the Infinite*.[24] Christ is the New Adam, who left his Father in heaven. He also left the home of his mother on earth. Why? To mount "the marriage bed of the cross", as Saint Augustine had it[25]—that is, to unite himself with the Church and consummate the union forever. "On the Cross, God's eros for us is made manifest," proclaims Pope Benedict XVI. "Eros is indeed ... that force which 'does not allow the lover to remain in himself but moves him to become one with the beloved' (*De Divinis Nominibus*, IV, 13: PG 3,

---

[18] TOB 95b:1, emphasis in original.

[19] Ibid.

[20] See John Paul II, *Letter to Families* (February 2, 1994), no. 19, https://w2.vatican.va/content/john-paul-ii/en/letters/1994/documents/hf_jp-ii_let_02021994_families.html.

[21] TOB 87:3.

[22] TOB 87:6, emphasis in original.

[23] TOB 93:2, emphasis in original.

[24] See, for example, John Paul II, apostolic letter *Novo millennio ineunte* (January 6, 2001), no. 33, https://w2.vatican.va/content/john-paul-ii/en/apost_letters/2001/documents/hf_jp-ii_apl_20010106_novo-millennio-ineunte.html.

[25] St. Augustine, *Sermo Suppositus*, 120:3.

712). Is there more 'mad eros' (N. Cabasilas, *Vita in Cristo*, 648) than that which led the Son of God to make himself one with us even to the point of suffering as his own the consequences of our offences?" he asks.[26]

The more we allow the brilliant rays of Christ's "mad eros" to illuminate our vision, the more we come to understand, as the *Catechism* observes, how the "entire Christian life bears the mark of the spousal love of Christ and the Church. Already Baptism ... is a nuptial mystery; it is so to speak the nuptial bath which precedes the wedding feast, the Eucharist."[27] In the Eucharist, "Christ is united with his 'body' as the bridegroom with the bride," John Paul II tells us.[28] And this is why only males can be ordained to the sacramental priesthood. Priesthood is not a career choice; it's a call to spiritual fatherhood. A female cannot be ordained a priest, because she is not ordained by God to be a father; she is ordained by God to be a mother. This is where the sexual difference matters—in the call to holy communion and generation. If a female were to attempt to confer the Eucharist, the relationship would be bride to bride. There would be no possibility of Holy Communion and no possibility of generating new life.

Assuming we have a proper understanding of what it means that the priest acts in *persona Christi*, the above is all readily apparent—*unless* we have eclipsed the meaning of gender with a contraceptive mentality. Rob the genitals of their ability to generate, and the natural purpose of the gender distinction is lost. In turn, since grace builds on nature, when we're confused about the natural reality, we're also confused about the supernatural reality: "If I have told you earthly things and you do not believe," asks Jesus, "how can you believe if I tell you heavenly things?" (Jn 3:12).

Ethics of the Sign

We can argue against contraception without any appeal to faith or the Bible. But John Paul II's project was to show the deepest *theological* reason for the immorality of contraception. Here it is: Rendering the one-flesh

[26] Message of His Holiness Benedict XVI for Lent 2007 (November 21, 2006), http://w2.vatican.va/content/benedict-xvi/en/messages/lent/documents/hf_ben-xvi_mes_20061121_lent-2007.html.

[27] *CCC* 1617.

[28] *Mulieris dignitatem*, no. 26.

union sterile falsifies the sacramental sign of married love. It violates what we call, based on John Paul II's teaching, the ethics of the sign.[29]

As a sacrament, marriage not only signifies God's life and love; it *really participates* in God's life and love—or, at least, it's meant to do so. For sacraments to convey grace, the sacramental sign must accurately signify the spiritual mystery. For example, as a physical sign of cleansing, the waters of Baptism really and truly bring about a spiritual cleansing from sin. But if you were to baptize someone with tar, no spiritual cleansing would take place because the physical sign no longer conveys the spiritual reality.

All of married life is a sacrament. All of married life is meant to be a sign of God's life and love. But this sacrament has a consummate expression. Sexual intercourse is the full-bodied sign language of God's love. Here, like no other moment in married life, spouses are invited to participate in the "great mystery" of God's creative and redemptive love. But this will only happen if their sexual union accurately *signifies* God's love. Therefore, as John Paul II concludes, we can speak of moral good and evil in the sexual relationship based on whether the couple gives to their union "the character of a truthful sign".[30]

As John Paul II brilliantly illuminates, the human body has a "prophetic" language inasmuch as it's meant to proclaim the truth of God's love. However, we must be careful to distinguish true and false prophets. If we can speak the truth with our bodies, we can also speak lies. Insert contraception into the language of the body, and (knowingly or unknowingly) the couple engages in a *countersign* of the "great mystery". Rather than proclaiming, "God is life-giving love," the language of contracepted intercourse says, "God is *not* life-giving love." In this way spouses (knowingly or unknowingly) become "false prophets". They blaspheme. Their bodies are still proclaiming a theology, but it's a theology that falsifies divine love.

Natural Family Planning

Assuming a couple has a serious reason to avoid a child, what could they do that would not violate the consummate expression of their

---

[29] See TOB 36:7.
[30] TOB 37:6.

sacrament? In other words, what could they do to avoid conceiving a child that would not render them false prophets? Everyone does it nearly all the time! They could *abstain* from sex. If we understand the dignity of the human being and the astounding meaning of becoming one flesh, we will logically conclude, as the Church always has, that the only method of "birth control" in keeping with human dignity is self-control.

A further question arises: Would a couple be doing anything to falsify their sexual union if they engaged in the marital embrace during a time of natural infertility? Take, for example, a couple past childbearing years. They know their union will not result in a child. Are they violating the sacramental sign of their marriage if they engage in intercourse with this knowledge? Are they contracepting? No. Contraception, by definition, is the choice to engage in an act of intercourse, but then do something to *render* it sterile. This is by using various devices, hormones, surgical procedures, and the age-old method of withdrawal (*coitus interruptus*).

Couples who use natural family planning (NFP)[31] when they have a just reason to avoid pregnancy never *render* their sexual acts sterile; they never contracept. They track their fertility, abstain when they are fertile and, if they so desire, engage in the marital embrace when they are naturally infertile. Modern NFP methods are 97–99 percent effective at avoiding pregnancy when used properly. Furthermore, any woman, regardless of the regularity of her cycles, can use NFP successfully.[32] This is not the outdated and much less precise "rhythm method".

To some people this seems like splitting hairs. "What's the big difference," they ask, "between rendering the union sterile yourself and just *waiting* until it's naturally infertile? The end result is the same thing: both couples avoid children." To which I respond, "What's the big difference between killing Grandma and just *waiting* until she dies naturally? The end result is the same thing: dead Grandma." Yes, the end result is the same thing, but one case involves a serious sin called murder, while in the other case, Grandma dies, but there's no sin involved whatsoever. Give it some thought: those who can understand the significant moral difference between euthanasia and natural death can understand

<hr />

[31] See "Benefits of NFP", Couple to Couple League, accessed April 23, 2018, https://ccli .org/what-is-nfp/benefits/.

[32] See "NFP and Effectiveness", United States Conference of Catholic Bishops, accessed April 23, 2018, http://www.usccb.org/issues-and-action/marriage-and-family/natural-family -planning/what-is-nfp/science/nfp-and-effectiveness.cfm.

the significant moral difference between contraception and natural family planning. As John Paul II rightly maintained: the difference between contraception and periodic abstinence "is much wider and deeper than is usually thought, one which involves in the final analysis two irreconcilable concepts of the human person and of human sexuality."[33]

Most couples who use contraception simply have no idea what they are doing or saying with their bodies. They haven't ever heard or understood the "great mystery" of their sexuality. Hence, the conclusions we're drawing here about the objective seriousness of contraception is not a matter of assigning culpability: "Father, forgive them; for they know not what they do" (Lk 23:34). The good news is that Christ came into the world not to condemn but to save (see Jn 3:17). It doesn't matter how "dyslexic" or even "illiterate" a person has been in reading the divine language of the body. As John Paul II boldly proclaims, through the gift of God's mercy "there is always the possibility of passing from 'error' to the 'truth'."[34]

Conclusion

The Third Secret of Fatima

The "third secret" of Fatima was shrouded in mystery for eighty-three years. In the year 2000, at the beatification ceremony of two of the young visionaries to whom Mary appeared (Francesco and Jacinta), John Paul II finally unveiled it. In 1917, the three children had seen a vision of bullets and arrows fired at "a bishop dressed in white".[35]

Sixty-four years later, while driving through the crowd in Saint Peter's Square, a "bishop dressed in white" was gunned down by Turkish assassin Ali Agca—*on the memorial of Our Lady of Fatima*: May 13, 1981. Thankfully, while the bishop in the vision fell dead, John Paul II

[33] John Paul II, apostolic exhortation *Familiaris consortio* (November 22, 1981), no. 32, http://w2.vatican.va/content/john-paul-ii/en/apost_exhortations/documents/hf_jp-ii_exh_19811122_familiaris-consortio.html.

[34] TOB 107:3.

[35] Congregation for the Doctrine of the Faith, *The Message of Fatima* (June 26, 2000), http://www.vatican.va/roman_curia/congregations/cfaith/documents/rc_con_cfaith_doc_20000626_message-fatima_en.html.

miraculously survived. Many years later the pope himself reflected: "Agca knew how to shoot, and he certainly shot to kill. Yet it was as if someone was guiding and deflecting that bullet." That "someone", John Paul believed, was Our Lady of Fatima. "Could I forget that the event in Saint Peter's Square took place on the day and at the hour when the first appearance of the Mother of Christ ... has been remembered ... at Fatima in Portugal? For in everything that happened to me on that very day, I felt that extraordinary motherly protection and care, which turned out to be stronger than the deadly bullet."[36]

The fact that John Paul was shot on the memorial of Fatima is well known. What few people realize is that the pope was planning to announce the establishment of his Pontifical Institute for Studies on Marriage and Family on that fateful afternoon. This was to be his main arm for disseminating his Theology of the Body around the globe. Could it be that there were forces at work that didn't want John Paul II's teaching to spread around the world? (In fact, by May 13, 1981, John Paul II was only about halfway through delivering the 129 addresses of his Theology of the Body. Had he died, obviously, the full teaching never would have been presented.) And could it be that, by saving his life, Our Lady of Fatima was pointing to the importance of his teaching reaching the world?

It would be over a year later that John Paul II officially established his institute (of which I'm a proud graduate). On that day, October 7, 1982—not coincidentally the Feast of Our Lady of the Rosary—John Paul II entrusted the Pontifical Institute for Studies on Marriage and Family[37] to the care and protection of Our Lady of Fatima. By doing so, he himself was drawing a connection between his miraculous survival and the importance of the Theology of the Body. "Precisely because the family is threatened, the family is being attacked, so the Pope must be attacked," he would write some years later. "The Pope must suffer, so that the world may see that there is a higher gospel, as it were, the gospel of suffering, by which the future is prepared, the third millennium of families."[38]

---

[36] John Paul II, *Memory and Identity* (New York: Rizzoli International, 2005), p. 163.

[37] In 2017, Pope Francis changed the institute's name to the John Paul II Pontifical Theological Institute for Marriage and Family Sciences.

[38] Angelus (May 29, 1994), as cited in Jason Evert, *Saint John Paul the Great: His Five Great Loves* (Lakewood, CO: Totus Tuus Press and Lighthouse Media, 2014), p. 194. My thanks to Jason Evert for pointing this out to me.

If the third millennium is to be the "millennium of families", it's an understatement to say we're not off to a very good start. It was Father Carlo Caffarra, in his role as president of the John Paul II Institute for Studies on Marriage and Family, to whom Sister Lucia had written in the early 1980s, saying: "Father, a time will come when the decisive battle between the kingdom of Christ and Satan will be over marriage and the family." She added, however, that there was no need to be afraid, "because Our Lady has already crushed his head."[39] In May 2017, just a few months before his own death, Caffarra stated: "What Sr. Lucia wrote to me is being fulfilled today."[40]

The Triumph of Purity of Heart

At the start of this essay, we learned that the errors of Russia go deeper than Communism: at the heart of the Marxist worldview is a calculated attempt to eliminate the purpose of gender—that of generating children—so that the male-female distinction itself becomes culturally irrelevant. There is no doubt that this error has taken hold of much of the world and continues to spread today at rampant speed. But here's the good news: just as John Paul II's vision of the human person inaugurated a revolution that led to the fall of Communism, that same vision has the potential to topple today's sexual ideology (or, shall we say, a-sexual ideology) as well. It's called the Theology of the Body, and it has already started a growing movement that is spreading from heart to heart around the world.

In a 2005 interview, Lech Wałęsa, who led the movement in Poland against Communism, reflected on the revolution of conscience that John Paul II ignited: "For twenty years I could only find ten people who wanted to fight [the Communist regime], from a nation of forty million. Nobody, I repeat, nobody thought that communism would end. Then, this incredible thing happened—a Pole became ... the Pope. And within a year after his visit to Poland [in June 1979]—in one year—it went from ten people to a movement of ten million."[41]

---

[39] Montagna, "Caffarra: 'What Sr. Lucia Wrote to Me'".
[40] Ibid.
[41] *John Paul II: Ambassador of Peace* (Discovery Channel, 2005).

The political philosopher Zbigniew Stawrowski reflects on the experience of the Polish people after John Paul II's historic visit to his homeland as follows:

> When we are talking about a revolution of conscience, we are talking about people who suddenly asked themselves: "Who am I? What am I doing here? What is the purpose of my life?" We lived within something that was permeated by the feeling of nonsense. We fully realized that it was false, that it was a lie, one huge lie. However, you were trapped in it. And suddenly someone arrives who says, "No! There's no need to lie any longer."[42]

In the same way, today's gender ideology (more aptly, genderless ideology) is based on a lie. And lies eventually collapse on themselves, doomed from the start by their own falsity. We are now in the umbra of the eclipse of the body, but the light of truth will emerge, perhaps sooner than we think. In the Book of Revelation the sexual distortion of the nations—symbolized by the "whore of Babylon" (see chap. 17), that mysterious feminine figure who mocks the Bride of the Lamb and seduces the world with her harlotry—is brought to ruin in "one hour" (see 18:10–17). And then comes the triumph of the New Jerusalem, the Bride who has "made herself ready" (19:7) for her Bridegroom. She is dressed in "fine linen, bright and *pure*" (19:8; emphasis added). She is "clothed with the sun" (12:1).

This radiant Bride, in other words, magnifies the light of the sun rather than eclipsing it. And let us not overlook this illuminating detail: the Bride in the Book of Revelation is *pregnant* (see 12:2). John Paul II pointed out the difference between the Bride and "the hostile and furious presence"[43] of Babylon as follows: the woman clothed with the sun "is endowed with an inner fruitfulness by which she constantly brings forth children of God".[44] In contrast, Babylon embodies "death and inner barrenness".[45] In fact, this feminine figure *prefers* barrenness. She

---

[42] *Liberating a Continent: John Paul II and the Fall of Communism*, documentary, directed by David Naglieri (Public Broadcasting Service, 2016).

[43] John Paul II, General Audience, "The Church: A Bride Adorned for Her Husband" (February 7, 2001), no. 5, http://w2.vatican.va/content/john-paul-ii/en/audiences/2001/documents/hf_jp-ii_aud_20010207.html.

[44] Ibid., no. 4.

[45] Ibid.

chooses it and seduces the nations with the promise of sexual pleasure without sacrifice (which is to say, without divine love).

The pregnant Bride in the Book of Revelation, of course, is person-ified in Mary, the same woman who promised the children of Fatima: "In the end, my Immaculate Heart will triumph." What does this mean? In short, it means that *purity of heart* will triumph. As Cardinal Ratzinger explained in his official commentary on the third secret: "According to Matthew 5:8 ['Blessed are the pure of heart, for they shall see God'], the 'immaculate heart' is a heart which, with God's grace, has come to perfect interior unity and therefore 'sees God'. To be 'devoted' to the Immaculate Heart of Mary means therefore to embrace this attitude of heart, which makes the *fiat*—'your will be done'—the defining centre of one's whole life."[46]

Purity is not prudishness or fear of the body and its genital func-tions. Purity, says John Paul II, "is the glory of the human body before God. It is the glory of God in the human body, through which mas-culinity and femininity are manifested."[47] Those who are pure of heart are those who have followed Christ's invitation to come, and become one who sees (see Jn 1:39). And what they *see* is the fact that human sexuality "bears in itself the sign of the divine mystery of creation and redemption".[48] What they see is the fact that the "body, in fact, and only the body, is capable of making visible what is invisible: the spir-itual and divine. It has been created to transfer into the visible reality of the world the mystery hidden from eternity in God, and thus to be a sign of it."[49]

The Era of Peace Will Come through the Cross

At the top of page 1 of the original handwritten manuscript of John Paul II's Theology of the Body is the dedication "tota pulchra es Maria" (Mary, you are all beautiful), and below that is the date he started writ-ing it: December 8, 1974. Is it merely a coincidence that John Paul II

---

[46] Congregation for the Doctrine of the Faith, *The Message of Fatima*.
[47] TOB 57:3.
[48] TOB 131:5.
[49] TOB 19:4.

began writing his Theology of the Body on the Feast of the Immaculate Conception? Right from the start, it seems, John Paul II's Theology of the Body is mysteriously connected with the triumph of Mary's Immaculate Heart.

Of course, we know not the day nor the hour of the fulfillment of these prophecies, be they biblical or the Church-approved prophesies of Fatima. But John Paul himself wrote already in 1994 that the latter "seem to be close to their fulfillment".[50] This much is certain: since the family is the fundamental cell of society, if an "era of peace" is to be granted the world, that peace can only come if there is peace in the marital relationship—in the womb; in the family. And this will only happen if we are reconciled to the truth of our own greatness as men and women who bear in our bodies the sacramental sign of the divine plan—a plan that inevitably leads us to the nuptial mystery of the Cross.

As the icon of divine love, marriage has been under attack since the beginning. In fact, as John Paul II observed, "Sin and death have entered into man's history *in some way through the very heart of that unity that had from the 'beginning' been formed by man and woman*, created and called to become 'one flesh' (Gen 2:24)."[51] But if the enemy entered the sanctuary of married life from the beginning to sow seeds of death and destruction, let us never forget where Christ performed his first miracle: "On *the third day* there was a marriage at Cana" (Jn 2:1; emphasis added). And let us also remember that that wedding was a foreshadowing of the "hour" of Christ's death (Jn 2:4). Unfathomable as it is to human wisdom, this is God's method of victory: the death and Resurrection of the Bridegroom is the gift that assures the triumph of the Bride.

We must ponder this anew if we are to understand what is happening in our world today: marriage is going the way of its exemplar. It's already been put on trial, condemned, mocked, rejected, spat upon, scourged, and it's now being crucified. Significantly, on the day of Christ's Crucifixion, Luke reports that "darkness [came] over the whole land ... while the sun's light failed" (Lk 23:44–45). Thereafter, Christ's body—the light that illuminates the meaning of our bodies—was placed in the darkness of the tomb.

[50] John Paul II, *Crossing the Threshold of Hope* (New York: Random House, 1995), p. 211.
[51] TOB 20:1, emphasis in original.

Many in the Church today are understandably fearful and anxious because of the darkness that is descending upon us. Three "astronomers"—Our Lady of Fatima, Pope Blessed Paul VI, and Pope Saint John Paul II—have enabled us to understand what's happening. As with every eclipse, the eclipse of the body is sure to get darker before it gets lighter. The truth proclaimed by Paul VI in *Humanae vitae* and explained so compellingly by John Paul II in his Theology of the Body remains a sign of contradiction fiercely resisted not only by the world at large, but also by strong forces within the Church. A new wave of attacks against this truth may well bring fresh defeats for the Body of Christ and for mankind.

None of this should be surprising. For the Church must "follow her Lord in his death and Resurrection" in order to enter her glory, as the *Catechism* observes.[52] We know not the day nor the hour of Christ's return, but this we do know: "Before Christ's second coming the Church must pass through a final trial that will shake the faith of many believers. The persecution that accompanies her pilgrimage on earth will unveil the 'mystery of iniquity' in the form of a religious deception offering men an apparent solution to their problems at the price of apostasy from the truth."[53]

While we can't conclude with any certainty that we are now facing this final trial (after all, *all* previous predictions that we are facing the final trial have been wrong!), it is eerily curious how precisely contraception fits the bill of this "religious deception". With all the forces of darkness arrayed against her teaching, we should not expect "a historic triumph of the Church" and her teaching. Rather, by accepting "the way" of death and resurrection, we will witness "God's victory over the final unleashing of evil, which will cause his Bride to come down from heaven."[54]

As the eclipse of the body continues to cast its dark shadow over the world, let us take courage: *Sun*-day is not far off. When "the third day" dawns, the body will be rebirthed from the darkness of the tomb (or, shall we say, womb) and there will be a miraculous wedding: "He has set a tent for the sun, which comes forth like a bridegroom leaving his chamber ... and there is nothing hidden from its heat" (Ps 19: 4–6);

[52] CCC 677.
[53] CCC 675.
[54] CCC 677.

and another great sign will appear in the sky, the Immaculate Woman, clothed with the sun, showing the world what it means to *open bodily* to the divine fire of life-giving love. Then "the glory of the LORD shall be revealed, and all flesh shall see it together" (Is 40:5).

Let it be, Lord, according to your word. Amen.

The Argument about Contraception in the Theology of the Body

Michael Waldstein, Ph.D., Th.D.

"What" Anything Is Flows from the Good

At the very center of Saint John Paul's argument about contraception stands a link between "what" a being is and the good it aims at from within itself. When one asks, what is it? about anything—that is, when one asks, what is its essence or nature?—one needs to turn to the good from which that essence or nature flows. In each case, there is some specific good that is first. What a thing is comes second as the root of inclination and movement toward that good.

For example, when one asks, what are eyes? one needs to look primarily at the act of seeing, which is the good to which the eyes are oriented as eyes. The act of seeing is the good that belongs to the eyes as their very own good or purpose, in contrast to the good of the ears or nose. It is impossible to understand "what" eyes are without grasping their own specific purpose, which is what makes them eyes—namely, seeing.

One can raise the same question about the act of seeing—that is, what is it? It is impossible to understand *what* the act of seeing is without understanding the good that makes that act be what it is. The defining good of seeing is the object of sight, colors, shapes, and the expression of life in living beings. Without this object, which is the good embraced by the act of seeing, seeing could not and would not be what it is. On every level of a being, from the most fundamental through its powers and acts, there is some good that shapes the specific nature.

The customary name for that good is "the specifying good" or "primary end"—primary in the sense of being the source of *what* any given being, power, or activity is. Understanding a being's specifying good

103

or primary end is to understand that being, its powers, and its acts. The intelligibility flows from the goodness of the end. The specific good is most intimate to the being, to its powers, and to its acts—more intimate than these are to themselves, because *what* they are flows from that good.

What is the human mind? One can answer this question only by grasping the good that specifically shapes what the mind is. The act of knowing is the mind's primary end. It is the mind's defining act. It is the good that makes the mind be what it is.

When one goes one step further and asks what it is to know, one needs to turn to truth as the good that makes knowledge be what it is. Our knowledge as expressed in statements reaches its own end when we grasp that what we think corresponds to what is the case. Knowing could not exist without truth as its own good. If understanding truth (the correspondence between what is and what we think) were impossible, knowing could not exist at all as a specific kind of activity.

The Difficulty of Understanding Sex in Our Culture

Similarly, to answer the question about what sex is, and the closely related question about what marriage is, one needs to look at the good that makes them be what they are. It is only from the vantage point of the primary end or specifying good that one can understand them.

The culture in which we live makes it difficult for us to look at sex in this way. A fish is unavoidably wet, both outside and inside. And yet, as the proverb has it, a fish is the last to realize that it is swimming in water. It takes the water for granted. In a similar way, the scientific-technological image of the world that is dominant in our culture seeps into us without our noticing it. As a deep habit of the mind, it tends to take on the appearance of what is self-evidently true and does not need to be critically examined.

Much of the scientific picture is indeed true; it is confirmed by observation and experiment. Falsity and error enters mainly by the exclusion of some aspects that are clearly present in our ordinary experience, but nevertheless denied by the dominant picture of the world. These denials are imposed by will, not discovered by reason and observation.

What is it that man and woman do when they unite sexually? The "scientific" answer tends to be that sex is cells touching cells, sexual organs touching sexual organs, while neurons fire from tissues rich in nerve cells. The brain, activated by sexual hormones, coordinates these impulses. The whole sexual mechanism took millions of years to evolve. It is the result of random mutation and natural selection by survival of the fittest. Sex is a randomly selected process in a bio-chemical machine. The real facts of sex can only be stated in the value-free language of natural science.

The experienced meaning of sex—that is, the goods or values embodied and expressed in it—is not objectively in the act. As an objective event in the world of matter, sex is meaningless. We choose what it shall mean for us. We can desire this or that. We are not free to choose our own scientific facts, but we are free to choose our own values.

There is much truth in this "scientific" answer, but it is a partial truth. If one sees it as the whole truth, one blinds oneself to the reality of sex and refuses to address the question about what it is. To overcome this blindness, one needs to examine the historical roots of the violent exclusions. How did our culture arrive at this point of a separation between objective events in the world of matter and the meaning or value we attach to them?

Descartes gave classical expression to the philosophical principles that blind us to the role of goodness in nature. Following Francis Bacon, Descartes chose power over nature as the primary purpose of knowledge.

> It is possible to reach knowledge that will be very useful to life and instead of the theoretical philosophy which is now taught in the schools [Aristotelian philosophy] we can find a practical one, by which, knowing the force and the actions of fire, water, air, stars, the heavens, and all the other bodies that surround us as distinctly as we know the various skills of our artisans we can employ them in the same way for all the uses for which they are fit, and so make ourselves masters and possessors of nature.[1]

Since Descartes seeks a "practical philosophy", he chooses mathematical mechanics as the queen of sciences. It is the science that promises to make us "masters and possessors of nature". Descartes views everything in the material world through the lens of this science. It is useful as a lens,

---

[1] Descartes, *Discourse on Method* 6.61–62, in *Oeuvres de Descartes*, vol. 6, ed. Charles Adam and Paul Tannery (Paris: Léopold Cerf, 1897–1909).

if one seeks power over nature. It is less useful if one simply attempts to understand the world with all the resources at one's disposal. Mathematics studies only one aspect of reality. It does not—and cannot—make judgments about what is good or bad.

The privileging of mechanics leads to canceling the question, what is it? It is a pointless question, given the choice of what knowledge counts as relevant. As heirs of the Cartesian way of looking at nature, we have increasingly made ourselves blind to the fact that material things and the material actions characteristic of those things are constituted in their very being by ordering to specifying goods—goods that define their nature. Yet, we cannot succeed in blinding ourselves totally to that role of the good. Our ordinary experience inevitably brings it to our attention. We inevitably understand eyes by reference to seeing and minds by reference to knowing. In our own actions, we cannot escape being motivated by the good. Our minds are divided between seeing the world as Cartesians and seeing it as human beings, as personal bodies. The divided state of our minds is better, of course, than having our minds totally colonized by the Cartesian way of seeing.

Nothing prevents us from taking decisive steps to overcome this division. We can agree that the mathematical form of natural science grasps an important aspect of nature—we learn much from weighing and measuring. Yet, the totalitarian claim that mathematically oriented empirical science covers the full breadth of reality should be unmasked as a violent ideology.

The first requirement for a reasonable use of reason is that we remain open to all that comes to meet us in our experience. Censoring some aspects of experience simply because they do not fit the ambition for power over nature is an irrational use of reason.

Paul VI's Argument

Paul VI expresses the argument against contraception in the following four sentences of his encyclical *Humanae vitae.*

> The Church ... teaches that it is necessary that each and every conjugal act remain through itself [or of itself] ordered to the end of the procreating of human life.

This doctrine, which the Magisterium of the Church has often explained, rests on the unbreakable connection established by God, which man on his own initiative may not break, between the unitive meaning and the procreative meaning, both of which are inherent in the conjugal act.

For, because of its intrinsic account [ratio, logos], the conjugal act, when it unites husband and wife with the closest of bonds, also makes them capable of bringing forth new life, according to the laws written into the very nature of man and woman. If, then, each such essential account, namely that of unity and of procreation, is preserved, the conjugal act fully keeps the sense of mutual and true love and its order to the most high mission of parenthood, to which man is called.[2]

The most widely used English translation of the first sentence differs from the one given above. The normative Latin text reads "ad vitam humanam procreandam per se destinatus permaneat" (must remain through itself [or of itself] ordered to the procreating human life).[3] The most widely used English translation follows the defective Italian translation and replaces "per se destinatus" with "open to the transmission of life".

"Openness to new life" has become, at least in the English-speaking world, the central term in the debate about Humanae vitae. "Open" is not false. Particularly when one applies it to the conjugal act, rather than to an attitude in man and woman, it is open to being read as "per se destinatus", but does not of itself express the ordering of an act to its specifying good or primary destination and end.

As a phrase joined to "destinatus", "per se" can be translated as "through itself", to bring out that the ordering to procreation belongs to the conjugal act through itself, through what it is. It can also be translated as "of itself" or "as far as it itself is concerned" in the context of "must remain" to bring out that its constitutive relation to its specifying good should not be destroyed, as far as lies in the act.

In the *first* sentence, Paul VI understands the conjugal act as an act defined by a specific good—namely, procreation. It is an act through

---

[2] Paul VI, encyclical letter *Humanae vitae* (July 25, 1968), nos. 11–12, trans. Janet E. Smith, in *Humanae Vitae: A Challenge to Love* (New Hope, KY: New Hope Publications, 2006) (hereafter cited as *HV*).

[3] Ibid., no. 11.

itself ordained to procreation—that is, ordained to procreation by what the act is. "Per se destinatus" expresses the idea of a destination or purpose deeply within a being (*per se*). *Destinatus* does not imply "destiny"—that is, procreation as an inescapably realized end—but as the end that makes the act be what it is. The first sentence also states the moral norm that the act should remain what it is rather than being changed in its nature.

The *second* sentence gives a reason for this moral norm: two meanings—that is, two experienced goods, two words from man and woman to each other—are found in the act. It is both unitive and pro-creative. These two goods, ends, or meanings cannot be separated. If one of them is destroyed, the other is destroyed as well. To seek one is to seek the other; to violate one is to violate the other.

The *third* sentence makes explicit that both goods or meanings shape the "nature" of the conjugal act. What man and woman do flows from these two goods.

The *fourth* sentence underlines that the two meanings are preserved only together. In his Theology of the Body, John Paul II points out on this basis that the two meanings come to be through each other.

John Paul II's Argument

The central point of the argument in the Theology of the Body is, as in *Humanae vitae*, the indissolubility of the link between the unitive and the procreative meanings or ends of the conjugal act.

> In the conjugal act, it is not licit to separate artificially the meaning of love from the meaning (that is, sign) of potential parenthood, because the one as well as the other belongs to the innermost truth of the conjugal act. The one is realized together with the other and, in a certain way, the one through the other. This is what the encyclical teaches (see *Humanae vitae*, 12). Thus, in such a case, when the conjugal act is deprived of its inner truth, because it is deprived artificially of potential parenthood, it also ceases to be an act of love. The meaning of the act of love—"unitive meaning" as we read in *Humanae vitae*, 12—belongs to it in an "indissol-uble link" (ibid.) with the other meaning, namely, potential parenthood.
>
> One can say that in the case of an artificial separation of these two meanings, a real bodily union is brought about in the conjugal act, but

it does not correspond to the inner truth and dignity of personal union, *"communio personarum."* This union demands that the "speech of the body" be expressed reciprocally in the integral truth of its meaning. If this truth is lacking, one can speak neither of the truth of possessing oneself nor of the truth of the reciprocal gift of self and of the reciprocal acceptance of oneself by the persons. Such a violation of the inner order of conjugal union, a union that plunges its roots into the very order of the person, constitutes the essential evil of contraception.[4]

John Paul brings out a capital truth by using the word "through" to explain the indissolubility of the two meanings: "The one is realized together with the other and, in a certain way, *the one through the other."* Just as each of the two meanings comes to be through the other, so each perishes by the destruction of the other. One can look at this indissolubility from both sides. The conjugal act is by its very nature—by "what" it is—procreative *through* being unitive (unitively procreative) and unitive *through* being procreative (procreatively unitive).

Luke Timothy Johnson objects against both sides of "through". His objections help to clarify what is at stake in the argument.

[Objection against "unitive through being procreative":] John Paul II recognizes, from one side of his mouth, two ends of sexual love, namely unitive intimacy and procreation. But from the other side of the mouth, he declares that if, in an act of intercourse, procreation is blocked, not only that end has been cancelled, but the end of unitive intimacy has as well. He has thereby, despite his protestations to the contrary, simply reduced the two ends to one.

[Objection against "being procreative through being unitive":] This can be demonstrated by applying his logic in reverse: Would we insist that an act of sexual intercourse that did not manifest unitive intimacy also cancels the procreative end of the act? The papal position could actually be read as approving as moral an act of intercourse within marriage that was coerced, even violently, so long as a contraceptive was not used.[5]

---

[4]John Paul II, *Man and Woman He Created Them: A Theology of the Body*, trans. Michael Waldstein (Boston: Pauline Books and Media, 2006), 123:6–7. References are to the audience number and paragraph number. Hereafter, all Theology of the Body references will be cited as TOB.

[5]Luke Timothy Johnson, *The Revelatory Body: Theology as Inductive Art* (Grand Rapids: Eerdmans, 2015), Kindle edition, locations 808–14.

Procreative by Being Unitive (Unitively Procreative)

Let us look at the second objection first. When a husband coerces his wife violently into sex, he destroys the act's unitive meaning, but a child can still be conceived. Johnson is obviously right on that point. In this case, sex seems to be nonunitively procreative. The link between the two meanings cannot, therefore, be indissoluble.

The response lies in the sense of "procreative" that is at stake in the argument. "Procreative" does not have the merely factual sense of pointing to the outcome, a new life. "Procreate" has a specifically human sense. Irrational animals *reproduce*, but do not *procreate*, just as they *eat*, but do not *dine*. "Procreating" is the act of a person and implies a definite moral profile. It implies that the child is welcomed and can grow within the intimate space created by the love between its parents. John Paul's Theology of the Body usually uses the phrase "the conjugal act" to refer to the act that is by nature procreative. (The word "conjugal" comes from Latin *coniugi*, spouses.) "Conjugal act" is not a euphemism or an antiquated way of saying "sex", but a name for sex between spouses (Latin, *conjugi*) in its full human nature as a personal act.[6] "Sex" is to "conjugal act" as "eating" is to "dining".

Homer's *Odyssey* offers a striking illustration of the fully human and personal nature of the union between husband and wife presupposed by this understanding of "procreation". Odysseus, king of Ithaca, has come home from the Trojan War after twenty years. On his return, he finds his wife, Penelope, faithful to him despite a large crowd of suitors who have been occupying the royal palace. Her faithfulness reaches a paradoxical extreme when she refuses to recognize him, despite strong proofs of his identity.

Late in the night, they stand at the door of their bedroom and she uses a final test. He has her permission, she says, to sleep in the marriage bed, but alone, outside the bridal chamber, in the hall, where their son, Telemachus, is sleeping. She instructs the servants to carry the bed out. She herself will be sleeping on the floor of the bedroom. Odysseus responds angrily.

> Oh woman, this word you speak stings my heart. Who has moved my bed? Hard it would be for one, even very skilled, unless a god were to

---

[6] See the brilliantly clear explanation of this point in Donald Asci, *The Conjugal Act as Personal Act* (San Francisco: Ignatius Press, 2002), esp. chap. 3.

come who might easily set it in another place, if he wanted. But of men there is none living, however strong in his youth, who could force it with a crowbar, for a great sign [μέγα σῆμα] is wrought in the well-fashioned bed. It was I who made it and nobody else.

A bushy olive with thick foliage was growing in the inner court, mature and thriving, the trunk massive as a pillar. Around this I built the bridal chamber until I reached the end [ὄφρ' ἐτέλεσσα: the verb contains the noun *telos*, end] with close-fitting stones, covered it well with a roof, setting firmly glued doors, closing tight, then sheared off the rich-leafed olive branches, shortened the trunk above the roots, worked all around it with a plane, smooth and exact, straight to the plumb-line, fashioning it into a bedpost, and drilled it all with a drill.

Beginning with this, I built the bed until I reached the end [ὄφρ' ἐτέλεσσα: again *telos*, end], decorating it beautifully with inlaid gold and silver and ivory. Then I fastened a web of ox hide strips, shining purple.

Thus I show you this sign [τόδε σῆμα]. I know nothing, whether the bed is still firmly set in the ground, woman, or some man has cut away the trunk of the olive and moved the bed elsewhere.[7]

It is fascinating to observe the parallels between Homer's language and John Paul's account of the sexual gift of self as sacramental sign. The "great sign [μέγα σῆμα]" built by Odysseus is similar to John Paul's phrase "great sign",[8] which in turn unfolds the Pauline phrase "great mystery [μυστήριον ... μέγα]" (Eph 5:32) of marriage.

Odysseus did not touch the living olive tree, ancient symbol of fruitfulness, until he had reached the end (ἐτέλεσσα), the end of building the bridal chamber around it. Only then did he cut off the tree's branches and transform its trunk into a bedpost.

It is part of the archetypal power of this scene that the marriage bed itself serves as the "great sign" of recognition between husband and wife after their separation, just as it had been the "great sign" of their union twenty years earlier. The center post of the bed, a living olive tree with roots deeply anchored in the earth, expresses the stability of the interior space created by love. Odysseus built the bed with his own hands so that it could not be moved. The tree eventually died, but the fruitful life it symbolized continued where its leaves and branches used to be.

The wedding chamber in the *Odyssey* is part of a large house, the royal palace of Ithaca, which has room for many people. The good of

---

[7] *Odyssey*, bk. 23, lines 183–202.
[8] TOB 95b:7; 97:2.

hospitality, a great and central good in Homer and the whole tradition of the West, belongs to the very nature of spousal love. By its innermost nature, the space that love creates for itself is not a space for the spouses alone. From the very center of this space, from the marriage bed and the conjugal act, a larger space is built, in which there is room for the most important guests, children, and for other guests besides.

This power of the conjugal act in building a room of love seems to be the reason for a curious way of speaking in the Catholic tradition. Thomas Aquinas, for example, writes, "The end which nature intends from within sex [*ex concubitu*] is the procreation *and education* of children."[9] How does sex *educate* children? Surely not as an educational display. The point is, rather, the power of the conjugal act in building an intimate space as the core of a larger home, in which children can be welcomed as guests, a space in which they can grow and be educated.

It is in this way that sex is unitively procreative. The union it produces is an open union that leads of itself to hospitality for children.

One can see this essential role of union for procreation both from the side of the children and from the side of the parents. From the side of the children, the wider space of a home that is built up from the more intimate space created by the love of their parents is exactly the space children need. They need it to be conceived in a way fitting for bodily persons. A person, created by the trinitarian God of love, out of love, and for love, should be conceived in love. Children also need it to grow and receive their education in the right setting, in a house animated by a spirit of love. From the side of the parents, the gift of children completes and fulfills the space of union that their love creates. The pain of couples who are unable to have children is a testimony to the greatness and joy of this fulfillment, despite the labors and difficulties that come with it.

The unitively procreative meaning of the conjugal act is the basis on which one can see the moral problems of in vitro fertilization and embryo transfer. "The act of conjugal love is considered in the teaching of the Church as the only setting worthy of human procreation [unicum locum dignum procreationis humanae]."[10] In vitro fertilization is one

---

[9] Thomas Aquinas, *Super Sent.*, lib. 4, d. 33, q. 1, a. 3, qc. 1 co, emphasis added.

[10] Congregation for the Doctrine of the Faith, Instruction on Respect for Human Life in Its Origin and on the Dignity of Procreation *Donum vitae*—Replies to Certain Questions of the Day (February 22, 1987), II, 5, http://www.vatican.va/roman_curia/congregations/cfaith/documents/rc_con_cfaith_doc_19870222_respect-for-human-life_en.html.

side of the coin. It compromises the act's "unitively procreative" meaning. Contraception is the other side of the same coin. It compromises the act's "procreatively unitive" meaning.

Unitive by Being Procreative (Procreatively Unitive)

While the unitively procreative nature of sex is easy to see, its procreatively unitive nature is more difficult to grasp. John Paul formulates it in sharp terms. "When the conjugal act is deprived of its inner truth because it is deprived artificially of potential parenthood, it also ceases to be an act of love".[11] Johnson objects with great vehemence against this side of the argument.

His objection contains an important truth. Contraception does not turn off the love of a couple. It does not flick the main power switch in their house of love to extinguish all the lights at once. The main reason why couples use contraceptives is that they want to express their love for each other sexually even when the conception of a child should for various reasons be avoided.

The response to Johnson's objection lies in focusing on the form of unity that is at stake in "procreatively unitive". It is, as Asci puts it, the unity of those who do what men and women do to become parents. It is the unity called marriage.

This is the point at which the full precision of meaning in the phrase "[through itself] ordered to the end of the procreating of human life [ad vitam humanam procreandam per se destinatus]"[12] becomes important. Just as the ovum, semen, and genitals of men and women are by their nature generative or procreative, even when they are not brought into play in a procreative act, so a procreative act is procreative in its very nature, even when no child is conceived. The nature, which is specified as this and no other nature by its interior ordering to a specific good, remains the same on a deep level, whatever the effect of a particular act may be.

It is easy for us to dismiss this claim as a mere construct—something that human beings have made up rather than something that describes nature. The reason is that we are under the thrall of the intellectual

[11] TOB 123:6.
[12] HV 11.

custom, rooted in a Cartesian view of nature, of refusing to recognize what is naturally good in things. The only good that Descartes finds in things is the good to which we put them. If we choose to see the procreative possibility of sex as a good, then it is one, but if we choose not to, if it is not of value to us, then there is no good in nature, and therefore no specifying good.

By performing an act that is in its nature procreative, a man and a woman say definite words of the body to each other. They say them "according to laws written into the very nature of man and woman".[13] "You are the one with whom I want to have children." "I want our children to be both from you and from me together, to be formed by our bodies and minds together, because I love you." "I want to share the lot of life with you totally." "I want a home hospitable to children, suited to their education, shaped by our common life." Even if in a particular case a man and a woman are unable to have children, their bodies speak this procreatively unitive language.

By its procreative nature, the conjugal act brings about a particular form of the unity of love between a man and a woman. It is a form of unity brought about only by this act. It cannot be brought about by holding hands or kissing, not even by mutual masturbation. It is brought about by what men and women do, if they are to have children. This kind of act and no other is through itself ordered to the good of new human life. This kind of act and no other expresses a procreative form of the unity of love. It expresses and actualizes the distinctively conjugal union, the union that constitutes marriage as marriage. This is what John Paul has in mind when he writes, as previously mentioned, "When the conjugal act is deprived of its inner truth because it is deprived artificially of potential parenthood, it also ceases to be an act of love".[14] It ceases to be an act of love *as distinctively conjugal* love. Some aspects of a unity of love, of course, can remain in contracepted sex, just as they remain in mutual masturbation. Contracepted sex can remain lovemaking in expressing and fulfilling a couple's feelings of emotional closeness. What such lovemaking cannot be, however, is *conjugal* lovemaking. This defect deeply undermines the other elements of unitive meaning that might still be present.

---

[13] Ibid., no. 12.
[14] TOB 123:6.

The Common Logic of Gift in the Two Meanings

The two meanings are closely united by the logic of gift. By its very nature, the conjugal act expresses and accomplishes a radical gift of self: "I am yours, you are mine"; for "man ... cannot fully find himself except through a sincere gift of himself."[15] The ordering of this sexual gift of self to the good of procreation, which shapes its very nature, completes this trajectory of the gift.

> In its most profound reality, love is essentially a gift; and conjugal love, while leading the spouses to the reciprocal "knowledge" which makes them "one flesh" (cf. Gen. 2:24), does not end with the couple, because it makes them capable of the greatest possible gift, the gift by which they become cooperators with God for giving life to a new human person. Thus the couple, while giving themselves to one another, give not just themselves but also the reality of children, who are a living reflection of their love, a permanent sign of conjugal unity and a living and inseparable synthesis of their being a father and a mother.[16]

[15] Vatican Council II, Pastoral Constitution on the Church in the Modern World *Gaudium et spes* (December 7, 1965), no. 24, http://www.vatican.va/archive/hist_councils/ii_vatican_council/documents/vat-ii_cons_19651207_gaudium-et-spes_en.html.

[16] John Paul II, apostolic exhortation *Familiaris consortio* (November 22, 1981), no. 14, http://w2.vatican.va/content/john-paul-ii/en/apost_exhortations/documents/hf_jp-ii_exh_19811122_familiaris-consortio.html.

The One-Flesh Union and the Holiness of God

Biblical Foundations of Humanae vitae[*]

Joseph Atkinson, S.T.D.

Introduction

Biblically speaking, in a fallen world, the starting point in the evaluation of the morality of a human act is not the specific human act itself, but rather the divine acts that have initiated, constituted, and provide the ground for human nature and all actions that follow therefrom. These divine acts (of both creation and redemption) provide a framework, a matrix, that reveals the objective criteria for the evaluation of any specific human action. This theocentric analysis situates each human person and each human act within the context of a covenant. The finality of the person and his actions is coherence with the holiness of God. Within this covenantal context, the divine nature and holiness become the criteria by which the intrinsic meaning of acts is revealed and by which they can be evaluated. Scripturally, participation in holiness is the telos (the purpose for which something was made) of both the human person and of all specific actions done in freedom that are constitutive of man's existence.[1] All must be ordered to, and cohere with, the holiness of God.

If moral analysis does not hold this finality of holiness as determinative of human action, or rejects it as irrelevant to the moral structure of

---

[*] This is a revised version of an essay contained in *Five Perspectives on Sex, Life, and Love in Defense of Humanae Vitae* (San Diego, CA: Catholic Answers, 2018).

[1] We are to "become partakers in the divine nature" (2 Pet 1:4).

an act, then the creatureliness of the human person (which includes the givenness of his nature and his freedom) no longer serves as the key to revealing the intrinsic meaning of willed human action. When this happens, the analysis moves out of a biblical worldview and utilizes some other system of values to evaluate the human act. Scripturally, this is not the way of wisdom. Wisdom in Scripture is a way of life predicated on knowing one's end and the way to get there.

While there are strong currents within *Humanae vitae* that reference the supernatural and eternal dimensions of man,[2] perhaps those dimensions do not figure enough in the encyclical. Indeed, when the encyclical was released, then-Cardinal Ratzinger found that while the teaching was essentially correct, the encyclical relied too much on natural law and was not anthropologically comprehensive. In 2016, as pope emeritus, Benedict XVI wrote: "The reasoning, for us at that time, and for me too, was not satisfactory. I was looking out for a comprehensive anthropological viewpoint."[3]

Speaking about contraception in an address to moral theologians in February 1999, John Paul II perceptively touched upon the key anthropological principle that grounds moral analysis and that proceeds from God's own nature, manifested in his act of creation and redemption.

> Here one touches upon a central point of the Christian doctrine concerning God and man. On close inspection what is brought into question in rejecting that teaching is the very idea of God's holiness.... *[T]hose moral norms are simply the demand*, from which no historical circumstance can dispense, *of the holiness of God* who participates in the concrete, and indeed not in the abstract, in the individual human person.... In dying for our sins, *he re-created us in the original holiness that must express itself in our everyday intra-worldly activity.*[4]

---

[2] See Paul VI, encyclical letter *Humanae vitae* (July 25, 1968), no. 7, http://w2.vatican.va/content/paul-vi/en/encyclicals/documents/hf_p-vi_enc_25071968_humanae-vitae.html.

[3] Pope Benedict XVI, *Last Testament: In His Own Words*, with Peter Seewald, trans. Jacob Phillips (New York: Bloomsbury, 2016), p. 157.

[4] Address of John Paul II to the Participants at the Second International Congress on Moral Theology (November 12, 1988) (emphasis added), quoted in Sandro Magister, "'Humanae Vitae' under Seige: But It Will Have to Go over Wojtyla and Caffarra's Dead Bodies", *L'Espresso*, February 2, 2018, English translation by Matthew Sherry, http://magister.blogautore.espresso.repubblica.it/2018/02/02/humanae-vitae-under-siege-but-it-will-have-to-go-over-wojtyla-and-caffarras-dead-bodies/.

John Paul II realizes that the *holiness of God* is the determinative factor in the evaluation of any human act. Yet, although John Paul II's writings are profoundly undergirded by his sense of the holiness of God, this holiness does not emerge thematically in his writings. This essay will present the biblical evidence for the claim that the holiness of God (which is evidenced in the order of creation and the economy of salvation) is the underlying criterion by which human actions are ultimately evaluated and purposes that only in the light of God's nature and holiness (which are in fact one and the same) can the interior meaning and moral structure of a human act be adequately evaluated.

The Created Order

The overriding concern of many modern Christian ethicists is the place of human subjectivity and freedom in the moral evaluation of an act. Previous understandings of the human person and the structure and meanings of human acts (especially those of biblical origin) are often dismissed as primitively physicalistic. The views developed within the "outdated" Judeo-Christian framework are exchanged for the enlightened views of the modern age. The radicalness of this approach is rarely appreciated. It purposes the exchange of an anthropology derived from the revelation of God that has endured throughout the whole of Jewish and Christian history with an anthropology that is based on modern categories of thought, having little or no historical testing, and seemingly in constant flux.[5]

Modern secularism with its emphasis on experience rejects the concept of revelation. With its devotion to social science data, it rejects the concept of a created order with a given human nature that has a telos. Nature is essentially rendered mute in the name of personal freedom. Scripturally, there is irony here because this view leads to man actually losing the very foundation of his freedom. In the Gospel of John, Jesus taught that to be free one had to know the truth, but he qualified that truth as being in his Word (8:32), thereby showing that man's freedom

---

[5] In fact, that often seems to be the criterion of many modern anthropological propositions: man can only exercise his freedom when he is no longer bound to either his biology or history.

is derived from God. Paul, in his Letter to the Romans, showed that our freedom depends on our acknowledgment of the truth that there is a Creator and that we should be worshiping him alone (1:25–26). By rejecting the truth of creation and believing "the lie" of self-worship, we are separated from truth and given up to the bondage of our disordered passion. Freedom, as we shall see, is found in being obedient to the truth of God's divinely willed order of creation and our experience of this within our own bodies and souls.

Foundational Evidence from Ancient Israel

As mentioned, the starting point for any moral analysis is the creative act of God because it gives us the clues we need to understand his nature and will. Consequently, we need to examine the first three chapters of Genesis, which provide the narrative of creation and the *principles* for a biblical anthropology. It is these principles, taken as a whole, that will enable the Christian to understand the interior meaning and moral structure of any contraceptive act within the act of marital intercourse.

History as Escape into Meaning

The first words of the revelation to Israel, "In the beginning God created" (Gen 1:1), uprooted the foundations of the pagan and mythological thought and thus by positing an absolute beginning point in creation implied there was also an end, a telos.[6] This was revolutionary because in the surrounding pagan societies, the meaning of life and the sense of time was derived from the religious cults that were tied to the endless cyclical agricultural seasons. There was also a pantheon of gendered gods forever involved in violence and immoral sexual acts and who were subject to impersonal fates whose power was even greater than that of the gods. In fact, the gods were not self-existent but were themselves

---

[6] Cf. Walther Eichrodt, "In the Beginning", in *Israel's Prophetic Heritage* (New York: Harper and Brothers, 1962), p. 9. See Bernhard Anderson, *Creation vs. Chaos* (New York: Association Press, 1967), pp. 111–12.

created.[7] Man existed only as a pawn among these divine powers.[8] Human acts had little value or meaning in such an endlessly cyclical system, and man had little sense of agency.

The Hebraic revelation supplanted the cyclic concept of time tied to nature with the concept of linear time tied to God and his covenant, which had a beginning and thus moved toward an implicit end.

Events, which before were conceived as embedded in an enclosed cyclical framework, could now be evaluated in relationship to their final purpose. This revolutionary biblical concept of history is predicated on (1) the will of God, which inscribes a telos in every creature, and (2) the implication that human acts carry meaning by either fulfilling or deforming the will of God—that is, individual human acts matter and are integrally part of the salvific will of God for creation.[9]

Creator and Process

The absolute divide between that which creates and that which is created, while impossible within the pagan conceptual framework,[10] is foundational for Israelite thought. This division is grounded in the Hebraic text by the use of verb *bārā'* (meaning "to create"), which is something God can do. Secondly, there is not any preexistent material out of which God creates. Thus, God's Word alone brings entities into existence. Every created thing is contingent upon this Lord of creation. God's Word, as the agent of creation, makes each thing what it is, gives each thing its nature, and orders each thing to the whole. Hence, it is only in this Word (i.e., the Logos revealed in John's Prologue [vv. 1–18]) that *the final intelligibility of the created order* can be found.

Besides the agency of God, the second notable principle of the creation narrative is the process. It is critical to note that things are not

---

[7] See James Prichard, *Ancient Near Eastern Text*, 2nd ed. (Princeton, NJ: Princeton University Press, 1955), pp. 61, 120. See Joseph Atkinson, *Biblical and Theological Foundations of the Family* (Washington, DC: CUA Press, 2014), pp. 33–78.

[8] E.g., the creation story of *Enuma 'Elish*, where man is a slave of the gods. See Alexander Heidel, *The Babylonian Genesis* (Chicago: University of Chicago Press, 1963), p. 52.

[9] As Claus Westermann claims, history is salvific. See Claus Westermann, *Genesis 1–11*, trans. John J. Scullion (Minneapolis, MN: Fortress Press, 1994), p. 65.

[10] This is because the pagan gods, while powerful, are still part of the created order, which is evidenced by their being gendered.

created in isolation and then brought together. Rather, there is a beginning point of earthly reality when God creates the initial inchoate and formless mass (Gen 1:2). As God speaks his Word successively into it, the various earthly entities (plants, trees, animals, etc.) emerge from it (Gen 1:11, 20–21, 24–25). This is a concrete example of the principle at work in creation: the multitude of particularities (i.e., the many earthly entities) are grounded in an original preceding unity. What is important for us is that the specificities of the masculine and the feminine are grounded in, and find their identity in, an original unity. As we shall see, this ontological *unity* is critical for understanding the nature of both God and man. Understood properly, this dynamic of unity becomes the fundamental criterion for the moral evaluation of actions. Ultimately, the creature is not understandable without reference to God and his creative act.[11]

Man qua Man

It can be argued that a fundamental anthropology is discernible in the narrative of creation, the first two chapters of Genesis. Biblically, man is created on the sixth day, being the final complement of the animal kingdom. This leads to the inevitable question of whether man is simply the highest form of animal life or if he possesses qualities that also transcend his animal nature. In this narrative are several indications that point to the uniqueness to man, his nature, and the vocation he has in the created order. First, man's creation is heralded by the first and only dramatic pause in the creative process. God stops the process before creating man and announces his intention, and does so by having a dialogue within himself. "Then God said, 'Let us make man in our image'" (Gen 1:26). He desires to create a being who carries a form of transcendence within his nature, and so he makes man in his own image. The magnitude of this is hard to comprehend.

Since man is created in God's image, to know the nature of the human person requires a knowledge of the nature of God, a key to which is

---

[11] "The truth is that only in the mystery of the incarnate Word does the mystery of man take on light ... Christ the Lord. Christ ... fully reveals man to man himself." Vatican Council II, Pastoral Constitution on the Church in the Modern World *Gaudium et spes* (December 7, 1965), no. 22, http://www.vatican.va/archive/hist_councils/ii_vatican_council/documents /vat-ii_cons_19651207_gaudium-et-spes_en.html.

revealed in the divine inner dialogue that prefaces man's creation. "Let *us* make man in *our* image" bears witness to some form of inner communion within God. This form of plurality would seem to threaten the oneness of God, but this sense has already been prepared for. These pronouns show the Creator to have both the sense of one (unity) and also to have some sense of more within himself.

In several key places, the word *'echad* is used to express a diversity possessed of a unity. In these instances, *'echad* does not have a monadic sense of an undifferentiated unity. Genesis 1:5 reads, "There was evening and there was morning, one day." Here, two parts (evening and morning) make up the one (*'echād*) day. Similarly, in Genesis 2:24, the man and the woman become "one flesh". Again, the two genders, coming together, form one unity. In these cases, "one" has the sense of differences held together in a unity, or conversely, it is a unity of differences. This understanding of "one" provides the opening for the possibility of a communion of differences that exists within God. If God is characterized by the reality of communion, then man, made in his image, is also so ordered.

This is further reinforced by Genesis 1:27: "God created man in his own image, in the image of God he created him; male and female he created them." What should be noted is not only the mention of the bipolarity (gender distinction) of the human race in the context of the image of God, but also that this is the first mention of gender itself—even though gender is required for the animal reproduction mentioned in Genesis 1:22. This suggests that gender functions in man at a much higher level than in the animals, for gender in human beings not only enables procreation but at the same time images forth the inner nature of God and his internal communion.

Man alone of all the animals has the capacity (via the *imago*) to represent God iconically in his creation.

Be Fruitful and Multiply

A foundational principle of the created order is found in the first command of God: "God blessed them.... 'Be fruitful and multiply'" (Gen 1:28). Blessing in the Hebrew mind referred to the abundance of something. To be blessed was to have an abundance of lands, cattle, children, wealth, and so forth. A blessing is especially tied to procreation for those faithful to the covenant: "He will love you, bless you, and multiply you; he will also bless the fruit of your body" (Deut 7:13). The opposite of fecundity, sterility, could be overcome by returning to God.

> And because you listen to these ordinances, and keep and do them, the LORD your God will keep with you the covenant.... He will also bless the fruit of your body.... There shall not be male or female barren among you. (Deut 7:12–14)

Covenant blessings such as fecundity follow from walking in obedience, whereas sterility is a deformation of creation's orientation to life. Michael Kaufman concludes: "In Judaism procreation is a major—if not *the* major—purpose of the sexual act; the reproductive organs were created for generation."[12] Since the sexual nature of our bodies has a telos inscribed in them, this becomes one of the major principles that emerge in Judaism that determine the morality of sexual acts: the duty to procreate. Rabbinical commentary has confirmed this teaching over the centuries, which is well captured in the words of the *Shulchan Aruch* (1563), arguably the primary Code book in Judaism: "Every man is obliged to marry in order to fulfill the duty of procreation, and whoever does not is as if he had shed blood, diminished the image of God and caused the holy presence to depart from Israel."[13] It is important to note here the link between willful nonprocreation and the loss of a future generation and of the presence of God.

One Flesh

One of the earliest mysteries of God (see Eph 5:32) is the concept of the marital union of man and woman described in terms of being one flesh. This becomes the central concept upon which Jesus gives his teaching on the indissolubility of marriage in Matthew 19 (and, as we shall see, is foundational to the Church's teaching on contraception as well). It

---

[12] Michael Kaufman, *Love, Marriage, and Family in Jewish Law and Tradition* (Northvale, NJ: Jason Aronson, 1992), p. 139, emphasis in original.

[13] *Shulchan Aruch, Even HaEzer* 1:1, cited in ibid., p. 5.

is also the concept that links and identifies the union within human marriage with the union of Christ with the Church. The term "one flesh" (*bāsār 'echād*) is explicitly mentioned in Genesis 2:24, where the primordial man and woman "become one flesh". But the foundation for this one-flesh unity can be found in Genesis 1:27: "In the image of God he created *him*; male and female he created *them*" (emphasis added). This text functions in two ways. First, it announces human masculinity and femininity in the context of the image of God; this would seem to indicate that human-gendered existence and the finality of gender (fecundity/communion) are somehow reflective of the inner life—in the wholeness, the oneness—of God.[14] Second, Genesis 1:27 expresses the Semitic principle of corporate personality. This means that the personal, specific dimensions of our being (i.e., our individual, personal existence) are always grounded in a larger organic whole, such as the family or the covenantal community. This idea is succinctly expressed in this African proverb: "I am because we are." Thus, the human person exists as a particular (the person) within, and expressive of, a whole (the family line) and as a whole (the family line), which is concretized in this particular individual.[15]

In Genesis 1:27, God creates the singular *him* in the divine image, and only after that does he create the plural (*them*). But the plural is not the mere physical replication of the same (i.e., the masculine), but the creation of another who is "other" and yet similar to (identifiable with) the male. By their nature they are ordered to each other, forming the one-flesh union that is further ordered to the procreation of a third.[16] Genesis 1 reveals the single-plural dimension of humanity, but does not explain it. This only comes in Genesis 2.

In chapter 2, we see that the oneness of the first man, the undifferentiated existence of *'adam*, is not the oneness-of-unity of God's

---

[14] As we will see, this is resolved not by importing gender into God (which would, after all, be a return to paganism); but, rather, the reality of communion-existence in the divine economy takes the form of trinitarian life (Father, Son, and Holy Spirit), while in the human economy, it takes the form of the one-flesh unity of man and woman.

[15] See Johannes Pedersen, *Israel: Its Life and Culture*, vols. 1 and 2 (London: Oxford Press, 1973), and H. W. Robinson, *Corporate Personality in Ancient Israel* (Bloomsbury: T&T Clark, 1999).

[16] Note the critical difference between the two chapters. Genesis 1 only knows of procreation; Genesis 2 only knows of communion. Hence, both chapters are essential movements in a single narrative of creation that presents a full anthropology of gender.

internal being. Adam is alone and "it is not good" (Gen 2:18). Astonishingly, although the first man's communion with God in Eden was not broken (since there was no sin), something constitutive of the man *was* missing: he is alone. Man is created to image forth in this world God's nature of *communion-in-being*, and so the man cannot be fulfilled until he experiences the *oneness-of-flesh* with the other whose gender capacitates them for such union. But notice that this union is not merely instrumental. The other is not created as an autonomous creature whose sexual union with the man is merely an instrumental unity. Rather, the "building" (*bānah*) of the woman follows the same process as the rest of creation. In Genesis 1, an original unity (*tohu vevohu*) was further differentiated. Here, in Genesis 2, there is the original unity in the first *'adam*, the substance from whom the woman is formed (2:21–22). The "rib" (v. 22) plays a key theological role: it symbolizes the prior ontological unity before differentiation. Furthermore, this identification is strengthened by the exclamation of the man when God presents the woman to him and he says: "This at last is bone of my bones and flesh of my flesh" (2:23).

It is precisely the manner in which the human creature is brought forth that provides us with the hermeneutical key to understanding the nature of man in his historical, bodily, and sexual existence—and of the importance of procreation to his nature.

The detailed process in Genesis 2 resolves the mysterious singular-plural tension of Genesis 1:27. There is an original one (the unity) from whom comes the other (forming the plurality). This process provides the constitutive structure of the *one-flesh union*. The differentiation of male and female is predicated at some level on an original primordial unity that existed before the distinctions were made. Because of that original unity, the one-flesh union is indissoluble. Christ, in restoring the fallen world to its originally created order, provides a midrash on this process and reveals that (1) God is the agent who created this particular *one-flesh union* and, therefore (2) being willed by God, the one-flesh union is indissoluble (Mt 19:6). Hence, the one-flesh union is not a contractual arrangement between separate, independent individuals, but flows from the given structure of the person (as originally having diversity within himself from which the other is created). The marital embrace, which is the privileged expression of the *one-flesh union*, is an iconic participation in the original primordial unity—a union that, like the unity of God, is ordained to overflowing—"the good is diffusive of itself."[17]

Theologically, the one-flesh union of man reflects, in the economy of creation, the *'echad*/unity of God in the divine economy—that is, the intracommunion (the oneness) of God's own life. At this seminal point in Genesis, the oneness of flesh of the male-female union is associated with the image of God.[18] As a reflective image, man, in the psychosomatic unity of his gendered being, has the vocation to be a concrete expression of the intracommunion of God. In this way, gender in the human person has a dimension that transcends animal sexuality. As such, the meaning and form of the sexual embrace are grounded in the oneness (the inner communion) of God. It is this framework that provides adequate criteria by which sexual acts can be morally evaluated.[19] Clearly, one principle has emerged at this point. If the unity of the sexual act, in terms of its nature and its own integral structure (which is simultaneously ordered to communion and life), is intentionally attacked, then the ability to image forth and participate in the inner communion of God is damaged and put at great risk.

Conception and the Child

A critical moment in the establishment of the covenant comes when God reveals his covenantal name to Moses in Exodus 3:14: "God said to Moses, 'I AM WHO I AM.'"[20] The root of the divine name is *hayah*, which is the verb "to be". Clearly mysterious, the name seems to refer to the fact that only God is the source of all being, that he is the "I AM" from which all other being derives. He is being; he is life. As such, he brings life into being; all that he creates is ordered to life. Death in all its forms is the opposite of life and is antithetical to God. Creation teems

---

[17] St. Thomas Aquinas, *Summa theologiae* I–II, q. 2, a. 3, obj. 2.

[18] These are two different orders, and so there is no reading back of sexuality into the Godhead. Also, this iconic function is in embryonic form in these texts but develops organically throughout history.

[19] Without knowing the end (telos) of a human act, no proper moral evaluation can be made.

[20] See Roland de Vaux, "The Revelation of the Divine Name YHWH", in *Proclamation and Presence*, ed. John Durham and J.R. Porter (Richmond, VA: John Knox Press, 1970), pp. 38–75.

with life (Gen 1:20); all animate things are created to reproduce their own kind, of which the seed is already within them (Gen 1:11–12). There is only life; death only emerges as a result of the turning away from God (1 Cor 15:21).

Besides the commandment to procreate, there are also the covenantal promises that show the immediate agency of God in human conception and birth. Scripture witnesses to God being the agent (initiator) who opens the womb, sustains the growth, and predestines the future of the child. The child is thus a blessing and gift, another person in the *imago Dei* and another actor in history.

When Cain was born, Eve declares: "I have gotten a man with the help of the LORD" (Gen 4:1). Jacob, as a frustrated husband, complains to his wife Rachel: "Am I in the place of God, who has withheld from you the fruit of the womb?" (Gen 30:2). In Isaiah, Yahweh says: "*Shall I, who cause to bring forth*, shut the womb?" (Is 66:9; emphasis added). From these Scriptures it is clear that man is not the sole agent to bring forth a child but rather is meant to *cooperate with God*.

In secular culture, we claim technological dominance over all things, including the meaning and structure of the one-flesh union, willing to eliminate the agency of God positively from the procreative process. This is to reject man's role, which, while contingent, is also to be the steward of creation. It is to reject the call to genuine cooperation, and to reject God. We no longer are the steward of the mysteries of God (especially concerning the transmission of life), and instead become their masters.

Holiness as Criterion

The criterion that determines the very existence of the covenantal people is that of holiness. To ensure this holiness, God provides extensive laws given to the priests and tells Israel, "Be holy ... for I the LORD am holy" (Lev 20:26), to ensure that human actions do not contradict the holiness of God.[21] To act contrary to the holiness of God is to act

---

[21] "You shall be holy to me; for I the LORD am holy, and have separated you from the peoples, that you should be mine" (Lev 20:26). At the core of the meaning of holiness is the concept of separation. His people must become holy; otherwise, they would live in opposition to him.

contrary to one's own identity. For man, holiness is a derived reality. For the Hebrews, only God is holy. In Christ, one becomes holy only by identifying with and participating in the divine holiness.[22] We see the danger of rejecting this holiness in God's condemnation of the unholy behavior of Israel. Through Hosea, after years of apostasy and injustice, God finally announces that Israel is *lō' 'ammi* ("not my people") (Hos 1:9). Without holiness, Israel ceases to exist.

The laws of the Torah especially linked human sexual behavior with holiness, determining which actions were connatural with and those which were antithetical to God's holiness. Jewish texts such as the Berachot and Leviticus Rabbah (fourth to sixth centuries A.D.) show ancient rabbinic Judaism's concern with human sexual behavior and the maintenance of the covenant.

A specific section found in the law code of Israel (Lev 17–26) is called the Holiness Code. In a highly unusual move, the Old Testament announces the rationale for the laws of that section, something that the Old Testament rarely does. The Lord commands, "You shall be holy to me; for I the LORD am holy, and have separated you from the peoples" (Lev 20:26). This rationale is given five times throughout the text. The value of human action is determined by its relationship to God's holiness. What is further noteworthy is the fact that a large number of these laws concern sexual behavior. To be holy, to be ordered properly to God, one's willed actions cannot contradict the inherent nature of holiness.

The Symbolic Function of Holiness

To understand the unique function of holiness as a criterion of human action, we need to understand that Scripture conceives of human existence as having two stages. The narrative of creation shows that, before sin, the paradisal state of man was characterized by the tangible nearness of God and the total transparency of human-divine relationships. This was the state of shalom, of total integration in justice, in which *the body was fully under the control of the spirit* of man in communion with God. The rejection of God, *caused by the desire to become like God*, effects a

---

[22] See Samson Hirsch, *The Pentateuch: Leviticus (Part II)*, 2nd ed., trans. Isaac Levy (Gateshead, England: Judaica Press, 1976), p. 584.

disintegration of this communion. The result is that man now lives, not in an integrated state of unity, but in a state of disintegration. His existence is one of separation from God, yielding disintegrated relationships and interior brokenness, characterized by fear. This conflictual situation is reflected not only in man's fractured interior but also in the fracturing of the world he inhabits. It is upon this newly disintegrated fallen reality that the cult of Israel is predicated. This is shown in the Mosaic priest whose role was specified by the ability "to distinguish between the holy and the common, and between the unclean and the clean" (Lev 10:10).

Because the preternatural communion with God was broken, the covenant with Israel was instituted by God to show the way back to holiness, the precondition for renewed communion. It primarily served as a way to negotiate between these different spheres of reality, enabling Israel to avoid or deal with being in a state of existence that was inimical to God.[23] Whenever an Israelite was impure (which was antithetical to holiness), he could not enter the Temple where the Presence of God resided. When a woman had an issue of blood because of menstruation, a person had a skin disease, a man released semen, and so forth, the person became unclean and remained so until a specific amount of time passed or when the blood, flux, or disease stopped; then often the person would go through a water ritual (see Lev 12–15). When we look for a unifying link to these causes of impurity, we see that they are somehow linked to death. Blood is a primary symbol of death; gametic material dies in menstruation and when seed is wasted; and disease is a form of bodily disintegration.

For the Jews, one place holiness existed was within their homes. This is clearly seen in the many laws that regulated behavior in the home, to make it cohere with divine holiness. After the fall of the Temple in A.D. 70 the attributes of the Temple were transferred to the synagogue and home. The home of the covenant was seen as parallel to the Temple and was considered a small temple (*mishkan katan*). The holiness of the Temple, which in the Torah was already related to behavior in the home (especially sexual behavior), was seen to exist in the home. This relationship continued to be explored in rabbinical writings; we see a high point of this development in the work of Samuel Hirsh (d. 1889). Hirsch draws the parallel between the ritual bath (*mikveh*) of

---

[23] See Jacob Milgrom, *Leviticus 1–16* (New York: Doubleday, 1991), pp. 615ff. and 730ff.

the High Priest, who is readying himself to enter the Holy of Holies on Yom Kippur, with the water ritual of the wife preparing for the marital embrace with her husband after her menstrual cycle. Both must go through the *mikveh* (purifying bath) to be able to participate in holy activities.[24] Hirsch "compares the married woman's immersion in ... waters of the *mikvah* prior to resuming marital relations to the *kohen's* [priest's] immersion in the *mikvah* prior to entering the Sanctuary for the Temple service in Jerusalem. On Yom Kippur, the climax of the Temple ritual was the entry of ... the High Priest, into ... the Holy of Holies. Five times during the day, before each major service, he would immerse himself in a *mikvah*. The immersions were symbolic acts of purification which had the effect of raising his spiritual status."[25]

Hirsch is not afraid to compare the preparation ritual for the most sacred act of the high priest with the ritual preparations for sexual union. This is not surprising because marriage was understood as a form of holiness. In fact, the tractate (i.e., a major section of the Talmud) that deals with marriages and betrothals is entitled Kiddushin, meaning "Sanctification". Hirsch, in his work, shows the similarity between the dynamic that is at work in the Temple and that which is in the home: both are ordered to, and participate in, the holiness of God.

Ancient Israel: Behavior and Holiness

Holiness in ancient Israel was not an abstract notion but was tied concretely to behaviors. We have already seen above that the first commandment given to man was the commandment concerning the transmission of life. This law was written into the very nature of the whole creation, such that created things had within themselves the seeds of future life (Gen 1:12) and were meant to replicate themselves. Death, barrenness, and sterility were not part of the intended order of creation but only emerged after the Fall.[26] This orientation of the creation to life is linked

---

[24] In Judaism, the *mikveh* is a pool or container of water that a person totally immerses in for ritual reasons, often to make the impure pure. See Aryeh Kaplan, *Waters of Eden* (New York: Orthodox Union, NCYS, 1993).

[25] Kaufman, *Love, Marriage, and Family*, p. 197.

[26] "Therefore as sin came into the world through one man and death through sin, and so death spread to all men because all men sinned" (Rom 5:12).

to the revelation to Moses of the Divine Name (i.e., nature) in Exodus
3:14. The covenantal name "I AM" gives the essence of God's nature as
he who is the ground and source of all life, of all being, of all existence.
The prologue of John reveals that it is the Word through whom all
comes into existence, and that "in him [the Word] was life" (Jn 1:4).
Constitutively, holiness is ordered to life. Any willed human action that is
ordered to death contradicts the essence of life and holiness. Any willed
action that violates the ordination of the sexual act contradicts the connection between life-giving and holiness.

The second text that deals with procreation and holiness is Genesis
38, the Onan incident. The text deals with Semitic custom, later called
the law of levirate. Judah has two sons, Er and Onan. Er marries Tamar,
but because he is wicked, the Lord kills him. According to the custom
of the time, Judah orders the younger son, Onan, to go into Tamar to
have sexual relations so Er's family line would continue. Onan goes in
to her but intervenes to prevent the natural conclusion of the sexual act
by spilling his seed on the ground. "But Onan knew that the offspring
would not be his; so when he went in to his brother's wife he spilled the
semen on the ground" (Gen 38:9).

There has been a consistent strain of interpretation by Jewish and
Christian commentators that sees Onan's action as a form of *coitus
interruptus*. Tractate Niddah 13a of the Talmud (written in the fourth
to fifth centuries A.D.) provides rabbinical teaching grounded in this
text: "Whosoever emits semen in vain deserves death, for it is said
in Scripture. And the thing which he did was evil in the sight of the
Lord, and He slew him also.... He is as though he shed blood."[27]
This within the procreative act (which becomes known as the *wasting of seed*) is evil. Second, it is so grave as to constitute a capital
offense. Third, the gravity of the sin is great because this unnatural
act is compared to murder. This linking of the wasting of seed with
murder (of the next generation) is well established in the rabbinic tradition. This concept results from the biblical principle of corporate
personality that sees the individual as the specific concretization of
the continuum of the family, which comprises the past, present, and
future. Thus, in a real sense, one carries within one's body the future

---

[27] All Talmudic references are taken from the *William Davidson Talmud*, Sefaria, accessed
May 2, 2018, https://www.sefaria.org/william-davidson-talmud.

generations.[28] This principle underlies the Pauline doctrine of original sin ("in Adam all die" 1 Cor 15:22).

Yebamoth 34b, another part of the Talmud, states: "After a woman gives birth, her husband penetrates inside and spills his semen outside ... so that his wife not become pregnant.... These acts are nothing other than acts similar to those of Er and Onan, which are prohibited." This time, the rabbinical authorities produce an alternative interpretation. Onan's actions are seen as a form of anal intercourse.[29] In both interpretations, spilling seed is strictly prohibited and seen as a grave moral evil.

There have been attempts, particularly recently, which try to move the focus away from the physical act of wasting seed (which is embedded in the Jewish tradition) and which understand the refusal to perform the act of levirate marriage as the grave sin. However, this is not plausible, because the law on levirate marriage specifically provides the punishment for noncompliance with the levirate law: public shaming.[30] This type of reasoning, separating as it does the emission of semen from its teleological function, becomes at times a way to de-legitimize the Onan story as supporting the teaching of *Humanae vitae*. But biblically this attempt is not sustainable exegetically.[31] The gravity of Onan's sin lies in frustrating the natural function of semen, thereby perverting the natural processes of sexual intercourse—through an act of the will that closes off the sexual act to the future generations. Surely this passage supports the teaching of *Humanae vitae*.

---

[28] A fuller explanation is found in Johannes Pedersen, *Israel*, p. 109. See Atkinson, *Biblical and Theological Foundations*, pp. 161–96.

[29] "Er and Onan engaged in sexual intercourse in an atypical manner, i.e., anal intercourse" (Yebamoth 34b).

[30] "Then his brother's wife shall go up to him in the presence of the elders, and pull his sandal off his foot, and spit in his face; and she shall answer and say, 'So shall it be done to the man who does not build up his brother's house'" (Deut 25:9).

[31] It is interesting to note the foundations for sexual ethics in rabbinic Judaism. The rulings on male contraceptive behavior are based on the commandment to procreate and on the Onan incident of Genesis 38, both biblical. The rulings on female contraceptive actions are not based on Scripture but on a story found in the Talmud, *Beraita of the Three Women* (see Yebamoth 12b). The Babylonian Talmud deals with the biblical-rabbinic divide and says, "Real holiness comes from rabbinic law, not biblical law" (Naomi Koltun-Fromm, *Hermeneutics of Holiness: Ancient Jewish and Christian Notions of Sexuality* [New York: Oxford University Press, 2010], p. 225). We are concerned only with the biblical foundations dealing with contraceptive behavior. See also Charles D. Provan, *The Bible and Birth Control* (Monongahela, PA: Zimmer, 1989).

The key biblical texts that underlie the Jewish teaching on sexual morality are these two texts: Genesis 1:28 ("be fruitful and multiply"), which commands procreation, and Genesis 38 (the Onan incident), which prohibits the wasting and ruining of male seed.[32] To act against these laws is to act against the nature of God, who is life. The constant teaching of the Catholic Church is that all willed actions that prevent the created capacity for the transmission of life within the sexual act are as gravely immoral, for they are antithetical to the life of God, who is holiness.

Christ: Logos and Revelation

The Christ Event

The Incarnation and revelation of Christ initiates God's last movement in man's redemption, which takes the form of a "new creation" (2 Cor 5:17). Often overlooked is the fact that Christ is the Logos; that is, he *is* the intelligibility of creation. At the heart of Christ's mission is his task of fulfillment that shows that in him there is both a radical continuity with all that has gone on before in salvation history and a fundamental radical discontinuity. In the Sermon on the Mount, Jesus says to the crowd, "Do not think that I have come to abolish the law and the prophets; I have come not to abolish them but to fulfil them" (Mt 5:17). But at the same time, he links the fulfillment of the law and change: "For truly, I say to you ... not an iota, not a dot, will pass from the law *until* all is accomplished" (Mt 5:18; emphasis added). When Jesus utters his last words, "It is finished" (Jn 19:30), all is accomplished. His death opens the way for man to receive the gift of the Spirit of God, who re-creates us in Christ and who now begins to live within us (Gal 2:20). Fulfilled, now the law is lived not within its external form, but from its interiority, which Christ, as Logos, is alone able to reveal:

You have heard that it was said to the men of old, "You shall not kill."
... But I say to you that every one who is angry with his brother shall
be liable to judgment.... You have heard that it was said, "You shall not

---

[32] See *Shulchan Aruch, Even HaEzer* 23:5.

commit adultery." But I say to you that every one who looks at a woman lustfully has already committed adultery with her in his heart. (Mt 5:21, 27–28)

In fulfillment of Jeremiah 31:31 ("I will make a new covenant"), Christ, through his Passion, gives man a new heart that is able to perceive the interior meaning of the law hidden by sin. During his ministry, Jesus showed the transformation that was needed for salvation. More was needed than the "righteousness" of the Pharisees that was achieved through strict ritual observance (Mt 5:20). Reading the external words of Moses, they failed to grasp the interiority of the law that the Logos, standing in their midst, was revealing to them. Typologically in the Sermon on the Mount, Jesus becomes the new Moses and authoritatively teaches that man must cohere to the holiness of God not only in his outward actions but also in his interior being. It is union with this Logos that enables man to live as the new creation, not in external obedience only, but from an interiority that is one with God. As Saint Paul showed, the law, while good in itself, could not effect salvation but served to show the separation of man from God's holiness (cf. Gal 3:23–24).

This newness in Christ's ministry is found in his encounter with the Pharisees over his teaching on marriage:

He said to them, "For your hardness of heart Moses allowed you to divorce your wives, but from the beginning it was not so. And I say to you: whoever divorces his wife, except for unchastity,[33] and marries another, commits adultery." (Mt 19:8–9)

Here, Jesus shows that divorce (a form of death) was, in fact, contrary to God's will for creation, resulting as it did from hardness of heart. In Christ's new reality, divorce and remarriage are not possible, because they are forms of adultery and hence mitigate against the

---

[33] Some biblical versions read *porneia*, rather than "unchastity"; but the meaning of *porneia* has been controversial. However, it is clear from the passage itself that it cannot simply refer to adultery, for that was already part of Jewish law. If it meant adultery, why would the apostles be astonished? Joseph Fitzmyer's work on the Dead Sea Scrolls has shown that *porneia* is the Greek word for the Hebrew *zenut*, which in the scrolls refers to unlawful marriage. See Joseph Fitzmyer, "The Matthean Divorce Texts and Some New Palestinian Evidence", *Theological Studies* 37, no. 2 (1976): 197–226.

holiness of God. Even in the old law there was a foreshadowing of this in the laws governing the marriage of priests. Priests were not allowed to marry a divorced woman because "the priest is holy to his God" (Lev 21:7). In restoring the original intention of the created order by taking away the distorting effects of the Fall, Christ opens up a new way of living: "What therefore God has joined together, let no man put asunder" (Mt 19:6). This work of restoring and securing the indissoluble bond of the one-flesh union is achieved only in the Cross. In Matthew, we get the first intimations of the radicalized interiority of the law, which Jesus is revealing to mankind. In his redemption, he effects a new creation that overcomes the hardness of heart (the rejection of the design of God). Thus, to introduce separation or division into the divinely willed structure of one-flesh union is to reject the salvific work of the Cross.

Paul's Appropriation of the Law

Saint Paul is an example of the transformative effect of Jesus. Mentored by Gamaliel, a renowned rabbi of that era (Phil 3:1–8; Act 23:3), Paul would have had an authoritative knowledge of Scripture and rabbinical writings.

Because Jesus was the fulfillment of the Torah, Paul had to reevaluate all his beliefs in the christological light. Interestingly, even though trained in rabbinical teaching that had been influenced by Greek thought and dualism, Paul derived his anthropology directly from the biblical witness. Jesus, as risen Logos, enabled Paul to grasp the theological meaning of such things as creation, the new creation, and the one-flesh union, which become fundamental to his thought. In particular, his framework for moral evaluation relates God as Creator, the divinely willed structure of creatures, and the intrinsic relationship between worship and human sexuality:

> For what can be known about God is plain to them [the wicked], because God has shown it to them.... His invisible nature ... has been clearly perceived in the things that have been made. So they are without excuse; for although they knew God they did not honor him as God ... and their senseless minds were darkened.... Therefore God gave them

... to impurity, to the dishonoring of their bodies among themselves, *because they exchanged the truth about God for a lie.* ... For this reason God gave them up to dishonorable passions. ... Though they know God's decree that those who do such things deserve to die, they not only do them but approve those who practice them. (Rom 1:19–21, 24–26, 32; emphasis added)

Paul grasped the christological foundation to creation. In Colossians, Paul states that in Christ "all things were created. ... And in him all things hold together" (1:16–17). Thus, creation reflects in some way the nature of God, which is clearly shown in the passages from Romans above. For Paul, the truth of God is encoded in the physical structure of reality. Consequently, the rejection of the created order is a rejection of God, which inevitably leads to a form of self-worship and sexual immorality. For Paul, the rebellion against God is iconically situated in the body, its functional life-oriented structure in which the natural use of the body is perverted. "Their women exchanged natural relations for unnatural, and the men likewise gave up natural relations with women and were consumed with passion for one another" (Rom 1:26–27). To reject the created structures and teleological sexual functions of our persons is to accept "the lie" that fundamentally separates man from God.[34] It would not be forcing things to infer that not only were sexual relationships of female with female and male with male wrong, but so was sexual intercourse that did not honor the procreative power inherent in it.

What is of particular interest to us here is how Paul's understanding of morality is founded on a deeper understanding of the order of creation. In the Torah, while male homosexual acts are condemned, no mention is made of female same-sex activity. For the rabbis, any act that wasted male seed was condemned (Onan) because it was *contra* procreation. In female-female sexual acts, however, no seed was wasted. Now, in Christ the full meaning of the created order becomes clear and all human action that is antithetical to the divinely given structure and meaning of the human body (especially the act of one-flesh union) is a rejection of God. Paul's moral framework is derived from the functioning of the redeemed body within the salvific order of creation. From this are derived the

---

[34] The literal translation of Romans 1:26–27 reads: "They exchanged the truth about God for the lie" (tw/ yeu,dei). This appears to be a midrash on Genesis 3 and the Fall.

criteria that determine whether or not an act coheres with the holiness of God.

1. Integral Unity of Body and Soul

The Incarnation demonstrates that flesh can cohere with the holiness of God. The narrative of creation in Genesis 2:7, when "the Lord God formed man of dust from the ground, and breathed into his nostrils the breath of life", shows that man qua man is a composite unity (body and soul)[35] in which human actions, both of body and soul, interpenetrate each other. Consequently, willed acts involving the body affect the person's spiritual life and vice versa. No dualism between these two spheres is possible in the biblical vision of man.

2. Bodily Acts Not Indifferent

All Christians are called to holiness, which means that one's bodily acts have to conform to the holiness (integrity) of the body given by God. Salvation is not a mental or even theological construct but is lived out through the willed acts of our bodies.

3. Agency and Salvation

In the Pauline vision of salvation, there is an initial act of justification that only Christ can effect. Being separated by God through sin, there was nothing we could do to bring about salvation. Once we are justified (put in right relationship to God) in Baptism, this salvific gift has to be worked out in and through the daily willed bodily acts of the human person. In Philippians, Paul reveals the interplay between the divine and human agency in salvation: "Work out your own salvation with fear and trembling; for God is at work in you, both to will and to work for his good pleasure" (2:12–13). Salvation is the coherence of man's nature with the holiness of God. God restores sanctifying grace to man in the act of justification; man is in-dwelt by the Holy Spirit and called to bring all his actions into conformity with the divine holiness, not in his own strength but in cooperation with the Holy Spirit living within him.

---

[35] See Pedersen, *Israel*, p. 99; Robinson H. Wheeler, "The Hebrew Conception of Corporate Personality", in *Werden und Wesen des Alten Testament*, B.Z.A.W. 66, ed. Paul Volz, Friedrich Stummer, and Johannes Hempel (Berlin: Alfred Topelman, 1936), pp. 49–62.

The freedom of the human person is deeply respected. Man's bodily acts are not indifferent but are an intrinsic part of the salvific process, either helping or deterring one's communion with God.

Theological Form of Marriage in Ephesians[36]

To evaluate the meaning of a specific phenomenon in a culture we have to understand the overarching symbolic structure of that culture.[37] In our case, we now come to examine the overarching meaning and symbolic function of marriage within the Judeo-Christian view of reality. This will then lead us to evaluate the value and meaning of contraceptive behavior. The sense of the nuptial meaning of God's relationship with his covenantal people Israel became most explicit during the prophetic period. Hosea describes Yahweh as the husband of his people (Hos 1–3; Is 54:5). Later on, the Lord says, "I will espouse you for ever; I will espouse you in righteousness and ... steadfast love" (Hos 2:19). Much later, it is John the Baptist who announces the arrival of the Divine Bridegroom (Jn 3:29). But it is with Paul that there is a systematic development of the nuptial theme. He tells the Corinthians, "I betrothed you to Christ to present you as a pure bride to her one husband" (2 Cor 11:2). Then, in Ephesians, this theme reaches its greatest depth. Here marriage takes on its theological form as a form of participation in Christ's salvific love for the Church. Paul applies cultic Temple language of purity, holiness, and sacrifice to the one-flesh union of man and woman. Most astonishingly, he then makes the two realities of man-woman and Christ-Church convertible.

Temple Imagery and Sacrificial Language

Ephesians is thematically structured around the concept of "unity", which finds its center in Paul's expansive opening, focused on a Greek word that means "to gather together under one head":

---

[36] Harold Hoehner in his *Ephesians: An Exegetical Commentary* (Grand Rapids: Baker, 2002) discusses the authorship question and writes that Ephesians is the earliest attested book of the New Testament canon as well as the first one to be called Scripture (by Polycarp); it was listed as one of Paul's letters in the Muratorian Canon; and both Marion and Tertullian considered Paul to be its author. There are varied opinions within the scholarly community today.

[37] Mary Douglas, *Purity and Danger* (New York: Routledge, 2003), p. 42.

The mystery of his will ... a plan for the fullness of time, [is] to unite all things in him [Christ], things in heaven and things on earth. (1:9–10)

1. In chapter 4, Paul emphasizes unity once more: "There is one body and one Spirit ... one hope ... one Lord, one faith, one baptism, one God and Father of us all" (4:4–6). Then, as a culmination to this theme, Paul expounds on the final theme of unity, that of the marital embrace. In his conclusion, Paul identifies the marital unity with the unity between Christ and the Church: "This is a great mystery, and I mean in reference to Christ and the Church" (5:32). The profundity of this declaration is easy to miss. Paul is here articulating the *theological norm* that is constitutive of the authentic form of marriage.[38] With insight, Paul presents the essential reciprocal nature of the man–woman relationship with the Christ–Church relationship. This reciprocal relationship becomes the evaluative norm for any willed act that is inserted into the process of sexual union because it affects the meaning or unity of the one-flesh union of man and woman.

2. Pauline exegesis brings into relief the organic *unity* of the somatic embrace. Von Balthasar notes that Paul "does not mean here that the two partners, as individual Christians, must each follow Christ, he makes it very clear that their marriage itself is to be a reflection of the relationship between Christ and the church".[39] Here, Ephesians' theme of unity reaches its dramatic conclusion: one Lord, one faith, one God and Father, one-flesh union of man and woman participating in the oneness of Christ and the Church.[40]

3. Most importantly, Paul presents the relationship between Christ and the Church as the archetypical ground for marriage. There is a theological paralleling going on. He discloses that "the husband is the head of the wife *as* Christ is the head of the Church" (5:23; emphasis added). But this headship is qualified by Christ's sacrificial love. The husband is

---

[38] Hans Urs von Balthasar, "A Word on *Humanae Vitae*", in *Christian Married Love*, ed. R. Dennehy (San Francisco, CA: Ignatius Press, 1986), p. 63.

[39] Ibid., p. 56.

[40] Andre Villeneuve's excellent book on nuptial symbolism expresses something similarly: "Yet unity finds its fullest and strongest expression in the language of love ... and most especially in the metaphor of the 'one flesh' union in marriage. This theme regroups together all of the aforementioned ones, namely, the consecration of the Church/Temple/bride for the purpose of sanctification, rooted in a permanent covenantal bond of love, and fully expressed in humble self-sacrifice." Andre Villeneuve, *Nuptial Symbolism in Second Temple Writing, the New Testament, and Rabbinic Writings* (Boston, MA: Brill, 2016), p. 220.

to love his wife *as* "Christ loved the Church and gave himself for her" (5:25). This relational symmetry is unprecedented. The human marital communion is perfected when it takes on its own teleological form: its ecclesial identity. God wills the marital union to be the dramatic icon of God's redemptive love. The one-flesh union of man and woman is an *imitatio Christi*, as it is based on Christ-like humility (submission) and Christ-like sacrifice (laying down one's life).

It is also important to account for the cultic language found in Ephesians 5:26–27. The Lord sanctifies the Church, cleansing her so she is holy and without spot. These are terms related to the Temple sacrifice where *purity* was essential. Now the husband has to be concerned about his wife in the same way. We see here that the Old Testament cultic terms have not been overcome but are rather *fulfilled* in Christ and become constitutive of a marriage in Christ. This is the paradox of the Gospel. Only by living in a sacrificial manner and by offering ourselves and bodies do we open up to life. Sacrifice in Christ never ends in death but in life, life in abundance. As Jesus taught, only when the seed dies can it bring forth fruit (Jn 12:24). By learning to live within the sacrificial form of marriage, we are then opened to embracing life and becoming fruitful. In this way, Christocentric marriage functions as a *participatory icon* in Christ's sacrificial love. Like Christ, marriage becomes an offering to the Lord *through* the mutual sacrificial living of each spouse. This new *form* of marriage reveals that any willed action, contrary to the purposes of the sacrificial form (including its orientation to redemption and life), can only be antithetical to the meaning of both the one-flesh union of man and woman and the union between Christ and the Church. It would be impossible to envision any contraceptive measures between Christ and his Church.

4. In Ephesians 5:28–32, Paul reveals that it is the bodily sacrifice of Christ that is the ground of marriage. But even more, the dramatic love within marriage between the gender-differentiated spouses is a reflection, in the order of salvation, of Christ's own love for the Church. One reality penetrates the other. The ontological bond that exists between Christ and his Church (his own Body) is somehow reflected in the man and woman becoming one flesh. In making the comparison, Paul refers to them as a "great mystery" (5:32), both the man-woman and Christ-Church unity. This is not an analogy *per se*, but posits a form of reciprocal identification between the two

unities.[41] It is precisely because human marriage participates in Christ's love for the Church that the latter becomes ground for the former. Remember that this divine sacrificial love of the Lamb existed before the founding of the world. Andre Villeneuve, in his *Nuptial Symbolism in Second Temple Writing*, remarks: "This is the type of sacrificial love that husbands should imitate for the sake of their brides. It would presumably involve a long and arduous process of 'practicing death' in self-denial, self-mortification and kenosis (self-emptying) in imitation of Christ."[42]

If Paul's identification of these two realities is mere metaphor, while illuminating on some level, it would not yield for us any useful biblical criteria by which to evaluate contraceptive acts affecting the marital embrace. If, on the other hand, Paul's teaching here provides us with the overarching meaning of marriage (that marriage is the iconic participation in the union of Christ with the Church), then specific criteria do emerge. Specific willed acts, which purpose to enter in and redefine the meaning of the sexual act, can be assessed in terms of whether they express or obscure the overarching meaning that grounds marriage. The inner and theological meaning of marriage is a transcendent one: *in and through the unity of the one-flesh unity of man and woman* Christ's union with his own Body, the Church, is to be manifested in the created order. Thus, the body, the acts we carry out with it, and the interventions we employ to redirect both its structure and purpose become a form of theological expression in the marital embrace. *We are "doing theology" with our bodies when we contracept.* What we do with and in our bodies manifests the inner beliefs that we are committed to, much more effectively than our words.

Christ's union with the Church is an indissoluble unity of love. It is a love that flows from the holiness of God himself; that is, it expresses the nature of God. As such, it is a love that coheres with divine holiness that is sacrificial, taking on the form of self-denial, as it bears the cross. It is a love that is predicated on humility and obedience to the Father in order to accomplish the will of the Father. It is a love that lays down its life,

[41] Andrew Lincoln in his commentary shows the depth of this comparison. It is both "the standard and *prototype* for the writer's instructions about human marriage", and "the *archetype* for human marriage, the one-flesh relationship between husband and wife". Andrew Lincoln, *Ephesians* (Nashville, TX: Thomas Nelson, 1990), pp. 352, 362.

[42] Villeneuve, *Nuptial Symbolism in Second Temple Writing*, p. 232.

even to the point of giving totally of its self. The purpose of this divine love is always to bring forth life so that many can live. This love is the antithesis of death and its very enemy. As Paul says, *this is a great mystery*.

From this overarching meaning of marriage emerges a criterion that helps us to assess the meaning and value of contraception. The criterion by which contraception will be evaluated is whether or not it coheres with or attacks the theological norm revealed in Ephesians. The union of the one reflects and lives within the unity of the other. Therefore, one has to evaluate whether or not an intervention inserted into the sexual embrace (1) seeks to redefine the meaning of the act and its telos of the bodily or its constitutive elements (e.g., gametic material if it is involved), (2) attacks in any way the various *unitive processes* and meanings inherent in the sexual act by way of separating that which God intended to be one, or (3) evacuates the ordination to life and union *ontologically inherent* in the sexual act and in bodily products associated with intercourse. If any part of the theological norm that safeguards the deepest meaning and ground of the sexual act is attacked or rendered mute by a specific act, that act cannot be authentic, because it does not cohere with the nature, the intention, and the holiness of God, which are all one.

By way of a simple practical analysis, extrapolating from this theological framework of Ephesians 5, we can ask if an act of contraceptive behavior attacks the sacrificial values that flow from any genuine act that participates in Christ's Cross. Does a specific intervention enable the practice of humility, promote self-denial, or help the couple to learn how to bear their cross as a couple? Alternatively, does a specific act circumvent or damage some or all of these Christ-like values? These are critical questions because an attack on the unity of the one-flesh union, on its given structure, its meaning, or its telos, is also an attack on the union between Christ and his Church. This is why Paul reveals the identification between these two realities and says *it is a great mystery*.

Criteria from a Biblical Anthropology

While cultural appropriation of contraceptive behaviors has varied greatly over the millennia, the witness of the Church has been unified, comprehensive, and unanimous. Primarily, this has been because creation has not been viewed as neutral data that man controls but was seen as an organic gift reflective of God's will and nature. The modern worldview has replaced the organic understanding of creation with the paradigm of creation-as-machine, which has led to the response of control and domination.[43]

Creation points first and foremost to the Creator, the one to whom worship and obedience is due. Secular modernity, with its distorted understanding of human freedom, rejects this; we make ourselves. Obedience requires the acceptance of what is God-given and working within the boundaries of that given. *Domination rejects the gift.* The drama of creation is precisely over the use of human freedom, and in that drama man fails. In Genesis, sexual differentiation is the reality of being ordered to the other, of which the privileged expression is the one-flesh union. This unity is not only the unity of the two complementarily gendered people, but also the indissoluble unity of procreation and communion. In the unitive act, genetic material is released whose sole teleological purpose is the continuation of the human race. The bodily communion of the spousal embrace is the divinely willed matrix for the process of procreation. The unity of the two produces the third.

But at the beginning of biblical revelation, the one-flesh union, which differentiates man from the animal kingdom—precisely because of its meaning—is revealed for the first time within the context replete with covenantal and Temple imagery. When unpacked, this imagery shows that the meaning of the sexual act within the created order is intended to be a reflection and imaging forth of the communion and unity within God. Thus, (1) to will sexual union (which by its nature produces gametic material that by its very nature is ordained to new life) and (2) simultaneously to will an act that prevents the union and life-giving power of the gametic cells (which by nature is the telos of those cells) *is to try to attack one divinely willed unity at the expense of the other* on the bodily level, thereby deforming both unities. At an even more radical (i.e., *radax* = roots) level, a technological intervention that attacks the

---

[43] See introduction to "Majority Report of the Papal Commission for the Study of Problems of the Family, Population, and Birth Rate"; the emphasis on technology is a central point in the papal Majority Report, which evaluated contraceptive behavior: "The story of God and of man, therefore, should be seen that man's tremendous progress in control of matter by technical means ... correspond perfectly to the divine decrees". BostonLeader shipBuilders.com, accessed May 2, 2018, http://www.bostonleadershipbuilders.com/0church /birth-control-majority.htm.

meaning inscribed in nature is also an attack on the communion within, and the unity of, God at the theological level. *Again, we do theology with our bodies.*

The New Testament shows us that the one-flesh union is to be identified with the love of Christ for the Church. The marital union is an iconic participation in, and reflection of, the unity between Christ and his Body. The great mystery of the sexual embrace where two become one and that procreates a further image of God is grounded in the Christ-Church relationship.[44] If there is a genuine ontological interplay between these two relationships, then how we live out the one affects the other. To intervene in the processes of sexual union intentionally, intended and created by God, so as to prevent, pervert, or destroy the ability to conceive life, which is inherently tied to this act, is to reject God's design of creation and, at the same time, to affect our salvific relationship with Christ gravely through this act.

In modernity's attempt to make an absolute value of personal freedom and our subjective experience, the voice of creation, as a criterion for determining moral behavior, has been muted and rejected. We have distanced ourselves from the evident interpretation of Onan's act as a contraceptive or antilife act. But this view must ultimately be deconstructed if contraceptive behavior is to be accepted—the reason being that the Onan incident witnesses to *the integrity and indissoluble union* of the sexual act and all that it initiates. The structure of the act (the sexual union of male-female bodies) and the processes it begins (the journey toward union of the gametic cells) must be respected and allowed their full development. The act cannot be defrauded of its purpose or its meaning. *Humanae vitae* reflects this in its condemnation of "any action which either before, at the moment of, or after sexual intercourse, is specifically intended to prevent procreation—whether as an end or as a means."[45]

A high point in revelation was reached when Paul identified the union of man and woman with the union of Christ and his Body, the Church. The clear intimations of the covenantal and cultic purpose of marriage in Genesis 2 are fulfilled on the Cross when Christ, the Bridegroom, gives his life for his beloved Bride, the Church. Paul then reveals the inner

---

[44] See Claude Chavasse, *The Bride of Christ: An Enquiry into the Nuptial Element in Early Christianity* (London: Faber and Faber, 1940).

[45] *Humanae vitae*, no. 14.

meaning of human marriage when he announces that the sacrificial love of Jesus for his Church is nuptial.

Astonishingly, the marital sexual union participates in the holiness of Christ and in the total self-offering he makes on the Cross for his Bride. As in Genesis 2, the cultic language in Ephesians 5 alerts us to the sacramental and covenantal dimension of Christian marriage. For spouses to encounter one another in the one-flesh sexual union is also to effect, at some level, an encounter with the Lord. This encounter can be compared to the High Priest entering the Holy of the Holies. To enter, the priest needs to be in a state of holiness; otherwise, the encounter between the holy and the unholy would be deadly. Similarly, there can nothing in our sexual embrace as Christians that is antithetical to the holiness of God, or it would be deadly to us.

Conclusion

Contraception wills the separation of the inherent procreative dimension from sexual union, thus reducing the conjugal act to an experience without a form or a natural telos. Contraceptive sexual union partakes of an illusion. The bodies of the spouses *appear* to function in a manner that coheres with their created design, and the subjective experience of sexual communion *appears* to have been attained. However, when inscribed meanings of the body and its processes are denied, then those appearances are emptied of their integral meaning and no longer serve as a way to experience the holiness of God or to image forth his communion and love in our bodies and in this created world.

Humanae vitae: What If?[*]

George Weigel

Carlo Cardinal Caffarra of Bologna has long been a vocal supporter of *Humanae vitae*'s teaching on the morally appropriate means of family planning. So it was noteworthy that Cardinal Caffarra conceded that, while *Humanae vitae*'s conclusions were true, its presentation of those truths left something to be desired. As the cardinal put it, "No one today would dispute that, at the time it was published, *Humanae Vitae* rested on the foundations of a fragile anthropology, and that there was a certain 'biologism' in its argumentation."[1]

Which put me in mind of a document I discovered in 1997 in a dusty Cracovian library while ingesting copious amounts of antihistamines: "The Foundations of the Church's Doctrine on the Principles of Conjugal Life".[2] Its somewhat academic title notwithstanding, that document represents one of the great "what if" moments in modern Catholic history.

The document was the final report of a theological commission established in 1966 by the archbishop of Cracow, Karol Wojtyła, to help him in his work on the Papal Commission for the Study of Problems of the Family, Population, and Birth Rate, inevitably dubbed the "Birth Control Commission" by the world media. According to one of the document's authors, Father Andrzej Bardecki, the Polish theologians on Wojtyła's commission had seen two drafts of an encyclical on conjugal

[*] This essay was previously published in *First Things*, May 7, 2014.

[1] Carlo Cardinal Caffarra, "From Bologna with Love: Hold on a Moment!", *Il Foglio*, March 14, 2014, at https://zenit.org/articles/cardinal-caffarra-expresses-serious-concerns-about-family-synod-debates/.

[2] See pp. 149–89 of this volume.

morality and fertility regulation. One had been prepared by the Holy Office (now the Congregation for the Doctrine of the Faith); it strung together various papal statements on the issue without even mentioning Pius XII's endorsement of natural family planning. And that, Bardecki told me, struck the Cracow theologians as "stupid conservatism".[3] The other draft had been sponsored by German cardinal Julius Doepfner;[4] it represented a grave misreading of what God had inscribed in human sexuality "in the beginning", the Cracovians believed, and did so in a way that emptied individual choices and acts of their moral significance.

So, were the only options "stupid conservatism" or the deconstruction of Catholic moral theology?

The Cracovians didn't think so. They thought that the truth of the Church's teaching about conjugal morality and fertility regulation could be presented in a humane and personalistic way—one that acknowledged both the moral duty to plan one's family and the demands of self-sacrifice in conjugal life; one that affirmed the methods of fertility regulation that respected the body's dignity and its built-in moral "grammar"; one that recognized the moral equality and equal moral responsibility of men and women, rather than leaving the entire burden of fertility regulation on the wife. In proposing this fresh presentation of classic moral truths in a delicate area of pastoral care, the Cracovian theologians drew on the pioneering work done by their archbishop, Karol Wojtyła, in his 1960 *Love and Responsibility*[5]—work that Wojtyła, as John Paul II, would later develop in the Theology of the Body.

And so, what if? What if Paul VI had adopted the Cracovian approach to presenting the truths he taught in *Humanae vitae*? What if the encyclical had been built upon a less formalistic, even abstract, view of the human person and human sexuality? What if *Humanae vitae* had deployed a richly textured and humanistic anthropology that was not susceptible to the charge of "biologism"?

---

[3] George Weigel, *Witness to Hope: The Biography of Pope John Paul II* (New York: Harper-Collins, 1999), p. 208.

[4] Ibid.

[5] Karol Wojtyła, *Love and Responsibility*, English ed. (1981; repr., San Francisco: Ignatius Press, 1993); updated version: Karol Wojtyła, *Love and Responsibility: A New Translation of John Paul II's Classic Work*, trans. Grzegorz Ignatik (Boston: Pauline Books and Media, 2013).

The year 1968 being what it was, and the theological politics of the moment being what they were, there would still have been an uproar, I expect. But had the Cracovian report provided the framework for *Humanae vitae*, the Church would have been better positioned to respond to that uproar.

The Catholic Church now has ample materials with which to make sense of, teach, and apply her settled convictions on the morality of marital love and procreation: the Theology of the Body; John Paul II's magnificent 1981 apostolic exhortation, *Familiaris consortio*; and the pastorally sensitive 1997 document by the Pontifical Council for the Family, *Vademecum for Confessors concerning Some Aspects of Conjugal Life*. And anyone in need of information on the harms of contraception should consult Mary Eberstadt's *Adam and Eve after the Pill*.

Still, I wonder, what if?

The Foundations of the Church's Doctrine concerning the Principles of Conjugal Life

A Memorandum Composed by a Group of Moral Theologians from Kraków*

Karol Cardinal Wojtyła et al.

I. The Natural Law as Foundation for the Condemnation of Contraception by the Magisterium of the Church

A. Current Views

1. Three Preliminary Questions

The Magisterium is opposed to contraception, on the basis of natural morality. The reports of the papal commission mention the declarations

---

*This essay originally appeared in "Les Fondements de la doctrine de l'église concernant les principes de la vie conjugale", *Analecta Cracoviensia* (1969): 194–230. The English edition of this essay is from *Nova et Vetera* 10, no. 2 (2012): 321–59. [Note to the English version: The document has been translated from the French by Thérèse Scarpelli Cory, with the collaboration of Janet E. Smith. Janet Smith's commentary on this essay was published in "The Krakow Document", *Nova et Vetera* 10, no. 2 (2012): 361–81.] In 1966, at the initiative of Karol Cardinal Wojtyła, the Metropolitan Archbishop of Kraków, a group of Krakovian moral theologians—Rev. Stanislas Smolenski, Rev. Thadeus Slipko, S.J., and Rev. Jules Turowicz, professors of theology in the Great Seminary of Kraków; Rev. Georges Bajda, professor at the Seminary of Tarnów; and Rev. Charles Meissner, O.S.B., physician—took up the task of examining the problem of the theological grounds for the Christian ethical norms of conjugal life. Cardinal Wojtyła himself directed the research, taking active part in the discussions and suggesting numerous ideas. Research continued until February 1968. The present redaction, prepared for publication by Adam Kubiś, presents their definitive conclusions.

of the Magisterium while proposing for discussion a set of more general problems related to these declarations. The questions to be discussed are as follows:

1. Does the Church have the right to make authoritative pronouncements on matters of morality and natural law?
2. Is her teaching on this subject infallible or not?
3. Can this teaching change?

The response to these questions provides a doctrinal context that allows us to explain the precise place of natural law in the Church's teaching.

2. Moral Theologians Who Defend Contraception

In the report released to the public, the supporters of contraception do not articulate a clear answer to the first of these questions. On the other hand, it is evident from the statement submitted by their opponents that at least some of those who endorse contraception challenge the Church's right to define the norms of natural law. In fact, they argue that the Church is competent solely in the realm of revealed law; alternatively, they limit the Church's authority to "the relation of men to God and each other",[1] taken in the broadest possible way. This amounts to denying the Church the right to propose detailed norms in the domain of natural law.

---

[1] *Status*, II.B.I, p. 174. The documents presented to Pope Paul VI by the members of the pontifical commission regarding the problems of population, family, and birth rate are the following: (1) *Documentum syntheticum de moralitate regulationis nativitatum* [General document concerning the morality of birth regulation]; (2) *Status quaestionis: Doctrina Ecclesiae eiusque auctoritas* [Status of the question, the teaching of the Church, and its authority]; (3) *Schema documenti de responsabili paternitate* [Draft of a document concerning responsible parenthood]. They are here cited according to the Latin text published in *Contrôle des naissance et théologie: Le dossier de Rome*, trans. Jean-Marie Paupert, with notes (Paris: Seuil, 1967). The pagination refers to this edition. [Editor's note: These reports were published in *The Birth Control Debate*, ed. Robert G. Hoyt (Kansas City, MO: National Catholic Reporter, 1968). The *Status quaestionis* was a statement of the minority, those who supported the Church's teaching; the *Documentum syntheticum* was the reply to the *Status quaestionis* by members of the majority, who argued the Church should change its teaching on contraception; the *Schema* was a portion of the final report of the commission, a report that argued the Church should change her teaching. Many of these documents are now available online at www.twotlj.org /BCCommission.html.]

The supporters of contraception respond to the second question in the negative. In defense of their position, they point out that although the Church and the popes have unanimously taught throughout the centuries that the use of marriage is only licit for the sake of procreation, or that it is at least permissible as a remedy for concupiscence, the Church and theologians distance themselves from these positions today.[2] The same historical fact also provides them with a justification for giving a positive answer to the third question.

Regarding the moral judgment concerning contraception, the supporters of the liceity of contraception say that the present-day notions of nature and of the natural law have changed in meaning. The teaching of the Church recognizes this fact and therefore changes.[3]

3. Moral Theologians Who Uphold the Traditional Position

In their statement, the opponents of contraception examine all these arguments and critique them. Providing substantial documentation, they argue that the Church's doctrine on contraception has never varied throughout its entire history, and that it remains negative.[4] The texts to which they appeal in support of their position, especially the declarations of the Magisterium, emphasize the fact that in the realm of conjugal and familial life, as in the realm of contraceptives and their use, the Church relies primarily on natural law, from which she also draws her ethical norms.

With respect to the problem of the Church's right to interpret natural law and establish specific norms that are binding in conscience, the opponents of contraception do not analyze this right in detail, apparently considering the matter to be clear enough already. Instead they simply appeal to the declarations on this point by Pius XII, John XIII, and the Second Vatican Council,[5] in which this right was clearly affirmed.[6]

The opponents of contraception vigorously defend the Church's infallibility in moral matters, particularly regarding the present question. They repeatedly emphasize that, on this point, a change in the future

[2] *Documentum*, I.5, p. 158.
[3] Ibid., I.3, p. 157.
[4] *Status*, I.B, pp. 163–66.
[5] Ibid., I.F.2, p. 170.
[6] Ibid., II.B.1, p. 174, and II.B.4.a and c, pp. 174–76.

teaching of the Magisterium would amount to a self-repudiation, with disastrous consequences for the Church.[7]

The same authors also address the question of evolution in the Church's teaching, though solely with respect to conjugal morality. While recognizing that the doctrine in this area has been increasingly enriched, they note that this is not the case with respect to contraception: on this subject, the teaching is of surprising immutability and continuity, despite differences of vocabulary and varying explanations of the doctrine.[8]

Finally, the opponents of contraception note certain naturalistic or evolutionary overtones in the way in which the proponents of contraception understand natural law and human nature. Against this naturalism, they emphasize that the immutability of human nature provides an objective foundation [to natural law].[9]

4. Some Conclusions

This brief exposition, to the degree that it is accurate, shows that the moral theologians who oppose contraception have provided a rather in-depth treatment of the question of natural law as the foundation for the Church's condemnation of contraception in her official teaching. Our present essay does not, therefore, introduce the notion of natural law as a new element in the argument against contraception, as though moral theologians had been previously unaware of it. We simply wish to reexamine the matter in greater depth and to suggest some additional considerations that we believe could lend more weight to the argument.

From section I.E.3 of their statement,[10] it seems that for those moral theologians who uphold the traditional position, the whole problem of the competence and infallibility of the Church's Magisterium in matters of natural law is a topic for academic debate that only serves as a distraction from the main controversy. In our opinion, this view is entirely inaccurate. If one abstracts from the points of dispute, the issue may well appear to be clear and decided. But taking into consideration the

---

[7] Ibid., III, pp. 176–78.
[8] Ibid., I.B.3, p. 165.
[9] Ibid., II.B.2 and 3, p. 174.
[10] Ibid., p. 169.

mindset of the opposite side, this issue proves to be of considerable weight in the conflict between these two opposing parties and consequently must be properly explicated. Its significance is most evident in the fact that the proponents of the traditional view were in fact obliged to appeal to these foundational notions and to point out once more the corresponding principles.

Moreover, it seems that the Church's right to teach infallibly in matters of natural law (including conjugal morality) ought to be granted the same role in arguments for the rejection of contraception that it retains in arguments for the objective hierarchy of norms—namely, the role of a fundamental premise. This premise indicates a direction for our present inquiry—namely, to lend the support of solid theological reasoning to the solution of this problem. In their statement, the proponents of the traditional position seem to relegate this viewpoint to the background; in any case, they treat it only as a side issue, mentioned only in polemics against the proponents of contraception.

Our work here is aimed at providing a more comprehensive line of argumentation for the traditional position. The Church's teaching concerning natural law inasmuch as it is the foundation of the condemnation of contraception—a theme currently dispersed across various parts of the report—will here be assembled into a coherent, logical, and clearly presented whole. In this way, natural law will be clearly revealed as not only a philosophical but also a theological category, since, in addition to its philosophical and even prephilosophical content, it includes formally theological elements—namely, the authority of the Magisterium. We believe that in this way we will bring to light an accurate understanding of natural law and of human nature, on which this law rests. For, in fact, the proponents of contraception understand these notions in a way that significantly departs from their authentic and traditional meaning in philosophy and theology.

B. Principles Governing the Development of a Theological Thesis on the Question of Contraception

The condemnation of contraception in Church teaching constitutes the application, in this particular case, of certain more general principles.

Since these principles are an integral part of the Church's doctrine, they must be addressed here.

1. The Church has the right and the duty to pronounce on the subject of morality and natural law, to define corresponding norms, to interpret them, and to apply them to the conditions of human life. Indeed, the observation of the precepts of natural law, which constitutes an integral part of the moral law, is one of the elements of "the life of faith", by which man strives toward his ultimate end. Scripture, the unchanging doctrinal tradition, and the practice of the Church in the last century [nineteenth century], beginning with Pius IX, provide particularly abundant proof of this point.[11] The Church's doctrine on natural law, outlined in these documents, sees in the natural law an objective moral order, inscribed in the rational nature of man. Consequently, this order is independent of positive law, decreed by the State. It is stable and immutable; it is binding for all human beings, since all share the same human nature and are called to attain ethical ends. It contains not only the most general notions and ethical principles, but also a whole set of detailed moral norms. In its fullest meaning, natural law therefore constitutes the moral law, which must be carefully distinguished from "law of nature" in the sense used by the natural sciences today.

2. With a few exceptions, the Church's doctrine concerning natural law and its particular norms has not taken the form of solemn

---

[11] Pius IX, *Qui pluribus*, in *Pii IX Pontificis Acta* (Rome, 1854), pars prima, I, 4–24; *Quanto conficiamur moerore*, in *Pii IX Pontificis Maximi Acta* (Rome, 1865), pars prima, III, 609–21. Leo XIII, *Arcanum divinae sapientiae*, in *Leonis XIII Pontificis Maximi Acta* (Rome, 1882), II, 10–40; *Diuturnum illud*, ASS 14 (1881/82): 3–14; *Immortale Dei*, ASS 18 (1885/86): 161–80; *Libertas praestantissimum*, ASS 20 (1887/88): 593–613; *Pastoralis officii*, ASS 24 (1891/92): 203–7; *Quod apostolici muneris*, ASS 11 (1877/78): 369–76; *Rerum novarum*, ASS 23 (1890/91): 641–70. Pius X, *Singulari quadam*, AAS 4 (1912): 657–62. Pius XI, *Casti connubii*, AAS 22 (1930): 539–92; *Divini illius Magistra*, AAS 22 (1930): 49–86; *Divini Redemptoris*, AAS 29 (1937): 65–106; *Mit brennender Sorge*, AAS 29 (1937): 145–67; *Quadragesimo anno*, AAS 23 (1931): 177–228. Pius XII, *Allocution to the Tribunal of the Roman Rota*, October 3, 1941, AAS 33 (1941): 421–26; *Allocution to the Italian Catholic Union of Midwives*, October 29, 1951, AAS 43 (1951): 835–54; *Allocution to the Fourth International Congress of Catholic Doctors*, September 29, 1949, AAS, 41 (1949): 557–61; *Allocution to the Seventh Hematological Congress*, September 12, 1958, AAS 50 (1958): 732–40; *Allocution to the Second World Congress on Fertility and Human Sterility*, May 19, 1956, AAS 48 (1956): 467–74. John XXIII, *Mater et Magistra*, AAS 53 (1961): 401–64; *Pacem in terris*, AAS 55 (1963): 257–304. Paul VI, *Populorum progressio*, AAS 59 (1967): 257–99. Cf. Favara Fidelis, *De iure naturali in doctrina Pii Papae XII* (Rome: Desclée, 1966).

pronouncements by the Extraordinary Magisterium. Rather, it is found in the Ordinary Magisterium of the Church, and in its teaching—primarily in the teaching of the sovereign pontiffs, as well as in the teaching of the bishops in union with the See of Rome. This doctrine, then, has an authoritative character and is consequently owed obedience and respect.

3. Similarly, the Ordinary Magisterium of the Church is infallible also with respect to natural morality. Nevertheless, it should be remembered that the doctrinal statements of an individual pope do not constitute the Ordinary Magisterium. These are merely acts distinct from the Ordinary Magisterium, to which the faithful owe obedience in view of the supreme authority of the teaching Church, even though some acts, lacking infallibility in and of themselves, may include errors and may be only provisional. All this applies likewise to the principles of morality.

The Ordinary Magisterium, however, is infallible only when it is continued over an extended period of time, stretching through an entire line of sovereign pontiffs, and when it concerns a sufficiently grounded doctrinal tradition regarding a specific point of doctrine—in the present case, a principle of morality.

4. The evolution of the Ordinary Magisterium, in the realm of morality and natural law, consists in developing certain moral norms and becoming more profoundly conscious of, or extending its doctrine to, related elements of morality. A change in the teaching of the Ordinary Magisterium can occur only with respect to objects that are changeable (for example, in the case of charging interest on a loan), and not with respect to objects that are fixed by their very natures, conditioned by the fundamental relations of human nature.

5. Concluding remarks: It is in light of the principles outlined above that one must examine the theological aspects of the moral judgment regarding contraception. In the first place we must consider the official declarations of the Church. These are Pius XI's encyclical *Casti connubii*, Pius XII's allocution to midwives, and a whole series of other related documents, including John XXIII's encyclical *Mater et Magistra*[12] and the declarations of numerous bishops.[13]

[12] See note 11.
[13] See *Status*, I.B.2, p. 165.

The following conclusions may be drawn from these documents:

1. First, the Church, in her official teaching, condemns contraception as being morally evil and impermissible.
2. Second, the teaching on this subject is consistent from Pius XI to Paul VI, the latter having neither revoked nor questioned it.
3. Third, the condemnation of contraception, from the point of view of morality, is considered by the Church as a norm of natural law, and therefore an objective norm flowing from nature, immutable and obligatory for all, and not only for Catholics.

Should this teaching of the Church on contraception thus be taken as the expression of the Ordinary Magisterium in the sense outlined above? It seems that, up until now, this has not been the case, especially if one considers the fact that Paul VI has named a special commission to study the problem again. Nevertheless, one cannot deny that the constant doctrine of the Church in this area, confirmed by well-known declarations of Paul VI on this subject, is close to reaching the point of full development and maturity when it will be able to be recognized as part of the Ordinary Magisterium of the Church. A future doctrinal declaration on the part of Paul VI, promulgated to the whole Church and bearing an obligatory character, would be of incomparable importance in this respect.

But independently of this fact, the Church's present teaching on contraception already constitutes a doctrinal norm, binding on the moral theologian in research and all the more on pastors in the confessional and in ministry. From a theological point of view, this teaching is objectively certain on account of the authority of the teaching Church, despite the opposition of certain moral theologians, and notwithstanding certain practices in various Catholic (and especially non-Catholic) environments. On the other hand, the reasoning that underlies the doctrine, taking into consideration the axiological aspects of contraception, is an entirely different problem. From this point of view, a set of factors, some philosophical, ought to be mentioned; we will examine them below. We merely note here that from the point of view of Christian philosophy, all theories must be rejected that conceal the seeds of relativism and of situation ethics, because they undermine the objective and immutable foundations of morality and ultimately lead to subjectivism and anarchy in the understanding of principles and in behavior. In place of an authentic morality, then, we would have the destruction of the moral sense in human action and of the moral dignity of man.

II. Justification of the Church's Condemnation of Contraception

1. The Human Person, His Dignity, and His Flourishing

a. The human person, his value, and the laws of his development provide the foundation for the principles of morality. In order to discuss the person, it is first necessary to have a clear notion of what a person is. But the notion of the person as understood by psychology—that is, the purely subjective notion, in which the person is conceived as subject or even as a substratum of experience— provides an insufficient foundation for an objective moral norm and leads to the danger of situation ethics.

It is necessary, therefore, to begin with the ontological concept of the person, understood as substantial subject of conscious and free actions. In order to answer the question "What is man?" the Constitution *Gaudium et spes*[14] refers to the Book of Genesis (1:26), where it is said that man is created in the image of God. This is why the ontological definition of the person must take into consideration his relation to God and to the world. Man is not an absolute nor a supreme value, but he is a creature of God. Thus, his relation to God includes not only a creaturely dependence on God, but also the human faculty of consciously recognizing this dependence and of collaborating responsibly with God.

This structure of the person also includes his relation to the world. Man belongs to the world, but he is distinguished from other creatures by the ability to follow with full consciousness the

---

[14] See Vatican Council II, Pastoral Constitution on the Church in the Modern World *Gaudium et spes* (December 7, 1965), no. 12 (hereafter cited as *GS*). English citations for all Vatican II references are taken from *Vatican Council II: The Conciliar and Post Conciliar Documents*, ed. Austin Flannery (Collegeville, MN: Liturgical Press, 1984).

truth and goodness that he knows—the ability to have a moral life.[15] Man can read in the world the order of nature and its finality with respect to himself and his good. Set amid this order of things, man can recognize the normative force based on this order.[16] Moreover, the world is ordered to the man, because he is, in the words of *Gaudium et spes*, "set by [God] over all earthly creatures that he might rule them, and make use of them, while glorifying God."[17] With his intelligence and in full responsibility, he must collaborate in the creative and salvific plan of God. This consists, among other things, in recognizing and guarding the limits of his dominion over the world, limits that are fixed by the very nature of the faculties that he has received from the hands of his Creator.

b. The power of transmitting life is a gift of God, and it forms part of the totality of the human person. It is precisely in terms of this nature, taken as a whole, that man must reckon with this power and its specific structure.

Therein his intellect discovers a biological law, which, although biological, is related to the human person as a unity of body and soul. This law cannot be conceived as deriving solely from nature understood in the broadest sense. It follows that it is one thing to act on the surrounding environment to transform it (including the animal world), and another thing to intervene in the biological laws of the human person.[18]

---

[15] Ibid., no. 14.

[16] Cf. *Status*, I.B.2, pp. 165–66.

[17] GS 12.

[18] It seems that some theologians commit the fundamental error of viewing the human body as belonging to "nature"—by which they mean the realm of subhuman beings that humans can manipulate as they please, as though the body were an entity inferior to and dependent on the person. But soul and body together form the unity of the person. To treat the body is to treat oneself, to direct oneself. The human body participates in the dignity and rights of the person. In our opinion, the *Documentum*, in certain passages—I.1, p. 156; 1.4, p. 157; II.1, pp. 158–59; II.2, p. 159—exemplifies a lack of comprehension of the relation between the human body and the person, even though the same document says, "Processus biologicus ... personalitatem hominis" (II.3, p. 153). [Editor's note: The passage in question reads: "The biological process in man is not some separated part (animality) but is integrated into the total personality of man" (Hoyt, *Birth Control Debate*, p. 70), a text from which the authors fail to draw the necessary conclusions. The same lack of comprehension of this relation is also evident in *Schema*, I.II.2, p. 182; I.III, pp. 183–84.]

The use of contraceptives constitutes an active intervention into the structure of the sexual act, and therefore of the action of the person; in this way, it is a violation of the person as a being gifted by sexuality, and of his biological laws. This is therefore not a case of employing a means that is in itself indifferent (such as a weapon, for instance) and that can be used well or badly, depending on the intention of the acting subject.

c. Moreover, the structure of the person includes his relations to others—namely, relations between persons and relations between the individual and society.[19] In all these relations there is a binding obligation to respect the rights and dignity of the person.[20]

When discussing the dignity of the human person, we must distinguish carefully the empirical or psychological use of the term "dignity" from its philosophical meaning and even more from that meaning based on revelation. The philosophical sense, which takes into consideration the specific properties of the person—reason and freedom—alone can have a normative character. In other words, only this dignity, taken in the philosophical sense, can serve as the foundation and justification for the demands and obligations of which the person is the object. This is especially relevant when one benefits at the expense of one or more persons. A person should never be treated as an object used for one's own ends; rather, we are obliged to manifest to others a benevolent love that protects the person's true good (including moral good) and the fulfillment of his vocation.

The dignity of the person also includes certain obligations toward oneself, particularly the obligations to act rationally, freely, and responsibly. "Man's dignity therefore requires him to act out of conscious and free choice, as moved and drawn in a personal way from within, and not by blind impulses in himself or by mere external constraint."[21]

d. The person is called to develop and perfect himself. This development consists, among other things, in perfecting one's acts, which ought to become ever more free and conformed to reason. All

[19] See GS 12.
[20] Cf. note 29.
[21] GS 17.

one's tendencies must be progressively and wisely integrated into the responsible fulfillment of one's vocation. This is why a person's flourishing and perfection does not consist in totally satisfying his instincts, but consists in ruling them with full awareness and integrating them into the totality of his moral life. In this way, the Christian, aided by grace, restores and strengthens the harmony of his interior being, disturbed by sin.[22] The progressive recovering of this balance makes it possible to overcome selfish tendencies effectively and to grow strong in true love.

2. Conjugal Love and the Good of the Family

The virtues of justice and love govern relations among persons, and, what is more, the New Covenant places emphasis on love. It is the new commandment; it is a participation in divine life, in the love with which the Persons of the Trinity love each other.[23] But if love rules all interpersonal relations, it clearly must also be normative in the life of the couple, which enjoys such unity and communion. Similarly, it is just as clear that only love as virtue, love as charity, can be the moral norm. The human person's love is an incarnate love. It is manifested in goodwill, thoughtfulness, dialogue, and the common sharing of goals, as well as in mutual affection and likewise in the sexual act, as long as the latter is accomplished in a way that corresponds to the true dignity of the human person[24] and to the objective criteria defined by his nature and natural activities. These criteria safeguard the full meaning of the spouses' mutual gift of self and of the transmission of life, accomplished in the manner worthy of man; but this requires the cultivation of the virtue of chastity.[25]

For this reason, conjugal love can be manifested not only in the fertile act but also just as much in a normally completed but naturally infertile act. It can also be manifested in abstinence from the conjugal act, when prudence counsels to abstain from procreation. On the other hand, conjugal love cannot be manifested by an act that is voluntarily deprived of

---

[22] Cf. ibid., no. 13.

[23] The Lord Jesus implies "that there is a certain parallel between the union existing among the divine persons and the union of the sons of God in truth and love" (ibid., no. 24).

[24] Ibid., no. 49.

[25] Ibid., no. 51. See note 39 below.

fertility, because active intervention in the sexual act or in the organic functions of the human person contrary to their purpose, solely for the sake of pleasure or sensual love, is equivalent to using one's partner for one's own ends. Such use is opposed to the dignity of the person[26] and to conjugal chastity (in that one seeks sexual satisfaction in a way contrary to reason); and it is certainly not in the image of the fruitful union of Christ and the Church, nor in the image of the fully disinterested union of the Divine Persons in the heart of the Trinity. Rather, it involves egoism and self-seeking on the part of one of the spouses—or sometimes of both, which is nonetheless always egoistic. The elements essential to all virtues—self-mastery, self-gift, and disinterestedness—are eliminated for the sake of pleasurable experience, satisfaction of the senses, or emotion.[27] Such acts not only do not constitute true love, but, when repeated, necessarily lead to the destruction of love, for they are contrary to it.

Moreover, such acts do not contribute to creating in the home an atmosphere of love, the indispensable climate for the spiritual and fully human formation of children. Parents who cannot master themselves, who cannot sacrifice their egoism to the good of their spouse, will likewise lack generosity, patience, serenity, and calm assurance in their relations with their children. They will love their children to the degree to which their children bring them joy—that is, selfishly and not for their own sakes; they will cajole them and teach them self-indulgence and self-love. Instead of the peace given by self-mastery, unrest will reign in the family, because the state of tension created by a truncated sexual act surrounded by precautions, an act that is not an unreserved gift of self, must in the long term be communicated to the children. It seems that the increasing prevalence of anxiety and even certain neuroses results in large part from contraceptive practices. The good of the family therefore requires true love—namely, the love that is able to master itself for the good of the

---

[26] See above, II.1.b.

[27] "A love like that ... is actually developed and increased by the exercise of it. This is a far cry from mere erotic attraction, which is pursued in selfishness and soon fades away in wretchedness" (GS 49). "Married people should realize that in their behavior they may not simply follow their own fancy.... Whenever Christian spouses in a spirit of sacrifice and trust in divine providence carry out their duties of procreation with generous human and Christian responsibility, they glorify the Creator and perfect themselves in Christ" (ibid., no. 50).

loved one. And this is nothing other than to love God in the person of one's spouse.

3. The Equality of Man and Woman in Marriage

   a. Following are the universally accepted principles:

- Man and woman are equal in their nature (metaphysically), in their dignity as persons, and in their final vocation.[28]
- They are likewise equal as to the right of contracting marriage, in the choice of a spouse, and in the activity proper to spouses in everything concerning the essence of marriage.
- Nevertheless, their parity as human persons, in their life as spouses, is marked by the difference of the sexes.

   b. Man and woman both have an equal right to the full flourishing of their own (individual and unique) vocations, in which their different sexes must be taken into consideration. The fact of being one sex or the other does not in itself determine the vocation of the person, since this vocation essentially transcends sexuality as such; it only determines the manner in which this vocation is accomplished. The person is sexual, but sexuality, in itself, does not define the person. The vocation of a person is accomplished not through sexuality but through an encounter between persons of different sex (referring here to the vocation to marriage). This is why

---

[28] "All men are endowed with a rational soul and are created in God's image; they have the same nature and origin and, being redeemed by Christ, they enjoy the same divine calling and destiny; there is here a basic equality between all men and it must be given ever greater recognition" (ibid., no. 29). "Any human society, if it is to be well-ordered and productive, must lay down as a foundation this principle, namely, that every human being is a person, that is, his nature is endowed with intelligence and free will. Indeed, precisely because he is a person he has rights and obligations flowing directly and simultaneously from his very nature. And as these rights and obligations are universal and inviolable, so they cannot in any way be surrendered" (John XXIII, *Pacem in terris*, no. 9, in *Catholic Social Thought: The Documentary Heritage*, ed. David J. O'Brien and Thomas A. Shannon [New York: Orbis Books, 1992], p. 132). The equality of human persons in their human dignity is, according to the teaching of the Second Vatican Council, the source of the unity of marriage: "The unity of marriage, distinctly recognized by our Lord, is made clear in the equal personal dignity which must be accorded to man and wife in mutual and unreserved affection" (*GS* 49).

relationships between persons are never fulfilled solely at the sexual level; rather, in beings endowed with reason, the sexual relationship can be forged only at the level of the person.

c. Sex differentiates man and woman, but this differentiation is not merely in service of the personal and exclusive good of the individual. Moreover, this differentiation does not justify burdening one of the two spouses with a greater responsibility. Marriage consists in community and not only in reciprocity, and it is only with respect to the common, objective end that transcends them both that one can define the roles belonging to the man and the woman as spouses and determine the proper reciprocal relationship in the actions of the spouses. The matrimonial right is not the "sum of individual rights" and does not consist exclusively in the "reciprocal gift". The "reciprocity" of marriage is truly accomplished only when it is based objectively and essentially on what is genuinely communal and transindividual, and not only on the purely subjective "intention". True community between the two exists solely in its relation *ad Tertium* (a communal, interior, transcendent relation).

d. Man and woman, equal in human dignity, differ nevertheless in their sex, a property that inheres in the human body and therefore in the human person. Sex constitutes a biological fact that correlates to, and remains in the service of, the power of transmitting life. But the biological participation in the sexual act and in the labors of parenting is not the same for the man and for the woman. The sexual act is accomplished within the body of the woman, who, unlike the man, can be violated. Moreover, pregnancy and childbirth are uniquely a burden for the woman. The education of the child, especially in the first years of life, also falls primarily to her. Moreover, under normal conditions the man is always fertile; in contrast, the woman is only periodically fertile, for very short, though relatively frequent, stretches of time. Furthermore, it is the man who generally takes the initiative for seeking sexual encounter.

All these biological inequalities between the man and the woman, in the sexual act and in the labors of parenting, and in the obligations of the woman resulting from sexual activities (incomparably heavier than those of the man)—all this imposes on the man a correspondingly greater responsibility. When the man eschews his responsibilities, the woman's equality in human dignity is no longer being respected. Her elementary human rights will not be protected.[29]

e. Contraception makes no contribution to the woman's personal rights. Since it is a process that makes it possible to satisfy the "needs of the sexual instinct" without taking on any responsibility for the consequences of sexual activity, it primarily benefits the man. This is why, once accepted, contraception leads to sanctioning his erotic hedonist behavior. In this situation, inevitably, the man benefits at the expense of the woman. He ceases to regard the woman in the context of transmitting life. She becomes for him simply the occasion for enjoying pleasure. If one adds to this the fact that it is inscribed in the very structure of man to take initiative in the sexual realm and that the danger of being violated is a threat primarily to the woman, then one must admit that the moral condition of the woman appears grim indeed. Therefore, when contraception is used, the woman faces not only inequality, but also sexual slavery.[30]

4. The Consequences of Original Sin

The claims of those who defend a practically limitless freedom in the regulation of births seem to be anchored in a belief in the innate goodness

---

[29] "It also follows that in human society to one man's right there corresponds a duty in all other persons: the duty, namely, of acknowledging and respecting the right in question. For every fundamental human right draws its indestructible moral force from the natural law, which in granting it imposes a corresponding obligation. Those, therefore, who claim their own rights, yet altogether forget or neglect to carry out their respective duties, are people who build with one hand and destroy with the other" (John XXIII, *Pacem in terris*, no. 30, in *Catholic Social Thought*, p. 135); "A civic society is to be considered well-ordered, beneficial and in keeping with human dignity if it is grounded on truth. As the Apostle Paul exhorts us: 'Away with falsehood then; let everyone speak out the truth to his neighbor; membership of the body binds us to one another' [Eph 4:25]. This will be accomplished when each one duly recognizes both his rights and his obligations toward others" (ibid., no. 35, p. 136).

[30] "If the positions of the contracting parties are too unequal, the consent of the parties does not suffice to guarantee the justice of their contract, and the rule of free agreement remains subservient to the demands of the natural law" (Paul VI, *Populorum progressio*, no. 59, in *Catholic Social Thought*, p. 254).

of man and the absolute integrity of his nature. Unfortunately, this optimism does not find any confirmation in Holy Scripture, or in the doctrinal tradition and practice of the Church, or, finally, in the history and daily experience of humanity.

In our view, man is not only far from this ideal, but he presents in certain respects such a tragic face that even those observers who reject the doctrine of original sin tend to recognize an inexplicable deterioration in human nature, which is responsible for his current disharmony and inclination to evil. The whole human person bears the mark of this interior disorder, but it is most strikingly evident in the realm of sexual instinct, which is without doubt one of the strongest human instincts.

The Old and New Testaments concur in pointing out an innate human inclination to sin, together with the concrete reality of his sins.[31] But if the Old Testament remains perplexed by this, awaiting divine assistance and unsure of how the story will end, the New Testament, in contrast, shows us the powerful sources of strength flowing from Christ and his salvific work, which are capable of destroying sin in us, since they are infinitely more powerful than sin.

This does not mean, however, that the redemption has radically changed human nature for the better, or that it has totally extinguished therein the embers of sin. These embers continue to smolder, and we must always reckon with their destructive power. It is necessary to remain on guard, especially where concupiscence and sin ally with the *sarx* (flesh), the enemy of the spirit. Vigilance thus is one of the essential elements in the conversion of man to God.

III. Responsible Parenthood

1. The couple fulfills their duty of transmitting life and raising children in the context of the concrete conditions of their state of life. In desiring to carry out this duty effectively and in accordance with the divine plan, the spouses must weigh all circumstances and consider all the requirements imposed by these circumstances, with prudence and conscious

---

[31] Cf. Sir 25:24; Song 2:23–24; Jer 1:14–15; 1 Jn 2:16; Rom 1:24–32; 7:18–24; Gal 5:16–26.

of their responsibility.[32] This is why the number of children called into existence cannot be left to chance. On the contrary, because of all the human values that are involved here, the number of children must be decided by the spouses in full consciousness. They therefore undertake this work as persons, and the decision itself must be an act of human responsibility.

All of this has been recognized by the bishops in the Second Vatican Council[33] and by Paul VI in his encyclical *Populorum progressio*.[34]

---

[32] The conception and birth of the child has a considerable impact on the organic functions of the mother. One must therefore consider her health. The education of the child requires many years of work on the part of the parents. Moreover, the child has the right to health and life: from the moment of his conception, he is the subject of the rights belonging to the person. Once born, he has the right to be raised in conditions that are appropriate to his dignity as a human person. Moreover, other circumstances must be taken into consideration. The child must be a member of society, which is composed of other persons who also have rights. In short, the transmission of life is an act of great significance, not only for those who are intimately affected by this event, but also for society; it therefore necessarily demands a strong sense of responsibility. The obligation to bear and raise children is certainly incumbent on the parents—an obligation that used to be called the duty of "preserving the human race" or more simply of assuring its continuation. But "the general principles can now be stated that the fulfillment of a positive duty may be withheld should grave reasons, independent of the good will of those obliged to it, show that such fulfillment is untimely, or make it evident that it cannot equitably be demanded by that which requires the fulfillment—in this case, the human race" (Pius XII, "Allocution to Midwives", in *The Human Body: Papal Teachings*, ed. Monks of Solesmes [Boston: St. Paul Editions, 1979], p. 164).

[33] "Married couples should regard it as their proper mission to transmit human life and to educate their children; they should realize that they are thereby cooperating with the love of God the Creator and are, in a certain sense, its interpreters. This involves the fulfillment of their role with a sense of human and Christian responsibility and the formation of correct judgments through docile respect for God and common reflection and effort; it also involves a consideration of their own good and the good of their children already born or yet to come, an ability to read the signs of the times and of their own situation on the material and spiritual level, and, finally, an estimation of the good of the family, of society, and of the Church. It is the married couple themselves who must in the last analysis arrive at these judgments before God.... Whenever Christian spouses in a spirit of sacrifice and trust in divine providence carry out their duties of procreation with generous human and Christian responsibility, they glorify the Creator and perfect themselves in Christ" (*GS* 50). "Because in virtue of man's inalienable right to marriage and the procreation of children, the decision regarding the number of children depends on the judgment of the parents and is in no way to be left to the decrees of public authority. Now, since the parents' judgment presupposes a properly formed conscience, it is of great importance that all should have an opportunity to cultivate a genuinely human sense of responsibility which will take account of the circumstances of time and situation and will respect the divine law" (ibid., no. 87).

[34] "Finally, it is for the parents to decide, with full knowledge of the matter, on the number of their children, taking into account their responsibilities toward God, themselves, the

Consequently, the spouses' consideration of the number of children that they undertake to bear and raise necessitates a decision regarding the responsible regulation of births and involves the following factors:

- an attitude of faith and trust in God;[35]
- a serene magnanimity and a willingness to undergo renunciation and sacrifice;[36]

---

children they have already brought into the world, and the community to which they belong. In all this they must follow the demands of their own conscience enlightened by God's law authentically interpreted, and sustained by confidence in him." Paul VI, *Populorum progressio*, no. 37, in *Catholic Social Thought*, p. 249.

[35] In contracting marriage, Christian spouses receive from God a specific duty to fulfill in his creative and salvific plan. Conjugal life is a vocation. The first question that every Christian must ask in order to be able to respond to other problems of his life to the best of his ability is, how does God view the fulfillment of my duties in the concrete situation of my life? As Christians, we believe in the love that God has for us. This is the reason for our unshakeable confidence in divine assistance in the fulfillment of the duties dictated by conscience.

Moreover, parents must be conscious of the fact that "human life and its transmission are realities whose meaning is not limited by the horizons of this life only: their true evaluation and full meaning can only be understood in reference to man's eternal destiny" (*GS* 51).

[36] The education of children is certainly the source of many joys, but nevertheless the fulfillment of this duty often involves much labor, disappointment, and suffering. The same applies to the other obligations that life brings. But it is precisely the attitude toward suffering and the labors of life, more than anything else, that constitutes the essential difference to those who believe in the Son of God, Jesus Christ the man, who by his Passion and Cross has redeemed the world and called all to salvation. As Christians we must be conscious that the Son of God lives, is present, and acts in his Body the Church—the People of God of the New Covenant. The sufferings of this People and of each of its members participate in the work of salvation. Christ himself says: "If any man would come after me, let him deny himself and take up his cross daily and follow me" (Lk 9:23), and, "Whoever does not bear his own cross and come after me, cannot be my disciple" (Lk 14:27).

Moreover, we are conscious that Christ accompanies us in our daily labors: "Come to me, all who labor and are heavy laden, and I will give you rest. Take my yoke upon you, and learn from me; for I am gentle and lowly in heart, and you will find rest for your souls. For my yoke is easy, and my burden is light" (Mt 11:28-30). Cf. Vatican Council II, Dogmatic Constitution on the Church *Lumen gentium* (November 21, 1964), chap. 5 (hereafter cited as *LG*).

It would be good for parents, in deciding how many children they wish to have, to meditate on the following exchange between Christ and his apostles in this scene from the Gospel of Mark: "And he took a child, and put him in the midst of them; and taking him in his arms, he said to them, 'Whoever receives one such child in my name receives me; and whoever receives me, receives not me but him who sent me'" (9:36-37).

The Magisterium of the Church respects the magnanimity of parents: "Therefore, since the primary office of matrimony is to be at the service of life, Our special regard and Our paternal gratitude go to those generous husbands and wives who, for the love of God and trusting in Him, courageously raise a numerous family" (Pius XII, *Allocution to the National Congress of the Italian Family Front and the Associations of Large Families*, in *Papal Teachings:*

- a consciousness of their community, the fruit of conjugal life (this decision regarding the regulation of births ought to be reached within a dialogue of love between husband and wife);[37]
- justified motives;[38]
- the behavior of the spouses in undertaking the regulation of births must be in accord with the divine law expressed by the Magisterium of the Church.[39]

The last two factors require a deeper analysis.

2. The documents of the Second Vatican Council and of Paul VI outline a deeper and more detailed teaching on the motives for responsible parenthood than that of Pius XII. The spouses must consider

---

Matrimony, trans. Michael J. Byrnes [Boston: The Daughters of St. Paul, 1963], no. 616, p. 416). "Among the married couples who thus fulfill their God-given mission, special mention should be made of those who after prudent reflection and common decision courageously undertake the proper upbringing of a large number of children" (*GS* 50).

[37] The parity of the man and the woman in their dignity as persons, the character of the matrimonial contract, which imposes on them a similar obligation to respect mutually the person of the other spouse, and the demands of reciprocal respect, as well as common duties entailing common responsibilities—all this results in that the spouses must, "with common accord and common effort", make a well-considered judgment regarding the regulation of births. Parents bear a common responsibility toward the child; in the same way, the regulation of births must be the fruit of a common discernment of the duties that both bear together.

[38] Pius XII was the first to discuss the moral requirements in this area. He enumerated "medical, eugenic, economic, and social indicators" as motives for a morally justified regulation of births (Pius XII, "Allocution to Midwives", in *Human Body*, p. 153), http://w2.vatican .va/content/pius-xii/it/speeches/1951/documents/hf_p-xii_spe_19511029_ostetriche.html. See note 32 for the citation from "Allocution to Midwives".

[39] "Married people should realize that in their behavior they may not simply follow their own fancy but must be ruled by conscience—and conscience ought to be conformed to the law of God in the light of the teaching authority of the Church, which is the authentic interpreter of divine law. For the divine law throws light on the meaning of married love, protects it and leads it to truly human fulfillment" (*GS* 50).

"Man's sexuality and the faculty of reproduction wondrously surpass the endowments of lower forms of life; therefore the acts proper to married life are to be ordered according to authentic human dignity and must be honored with the greatest reverence. When it is a question of harmonizing married love with the responsible transmission of life, it is not enough to take only the good intention and the evaluation of motives into account; the objective criteria must be used, criteria drawn from the nature of the human person and human action, criteria which respect the total meaning of mutual self-giving and human procreation in the context of true love; all this is possible only if the virtue of married chastity is seriously practiced. In questions of birth regulation the sons of the Church, faithful to these principles, are forbidden to use methods disapproved of by the teaching authority of the Church in its interpretation of the divine law" (ibid., no. 51).

- the vocation to which God calls them in his creative and salvific plan;
- their own good and their own responsibility toward themselves (here one must add the care for their health—namely, the motives that Pius XII designated as the medical indicator for the regulation of births);
- the good of the children already born or yet to be born, and responsibilities toward them (to this group of motives belong Pius XII's "eugenic indicators");
- the good of the community to which the spouses belong: family, temporal society, and Church;
- the temporal circumstances;
- material as well as spiritual conditions (here one would include the economic and social indicators mentioned by Pius XII).[40]

Present-day catechesis recognizes the importance of appealing to the responsibility that Christians have for their life and journey toward God. The various motives listed above, which must prevail in a decision so important to the lives of the spouses, can not only motivate them to abstain from procreation but even encourage them to procreate consciously and voluntarily.

[40] These motives must be evaluated with the utmost probity. The spouses must have a "well-formed conscience". For instance, it is often said that the fewer children one has, the better they can be raised. Experience teaches us that this generalized and unqualified statement is without basis in actual fact. It is difficult to educate an only child normally. Often someone who has been raised without the company of brothers and sisters remains unhappy throughout his life, experiences difficulties in developing his personality, and is less able to adapt to others (cf. Charles Combalusier, *L'enfant seul* [Paris: P. Letheilleux, 1955]). Moreover, the child has the right to receive formation in a normal situation, such as one finds in a family environment that includes other children. To deprive the child of these surroundings is a decision that could affect him for life, and consequently it can be motivated only by truly serious considerations.

The same applies to the judgment concerning the concrete situation of the spouses. It is evidently often the case that the income of the spouses is modest, and that their living arrangements are not what they should be. Still, it is not unusual for egoism to exaggerate these difficulties; what is identified as an economic difficulty is in this case often simply a hidden desire for an easier life. All this creates serious educational problems. Material well-being, the goal for which the parents strive throughout most of their lives, is accepted by children as normal and owed to them. Consequently, they do not take care of their belongings, do not value the parents' labor or respect their work, and finally have only disdain and distrust for the less fortunate. It is this desire for an easier life that is the cause of the contemporary shift toward bourgeois life.

3. The intention with which we act clearly bears moral weight. But in order for an act to be morally good, further conditions must also be met. "We concede that God wants always and first of all a right intention; but this is not enough. He also wants the act to be good."[41] The act of a person must itself correspond to the divine plan, which is inscribed in the concretely existing structure of the human being, as well as in the action that is properly human. The Second Vatican Council merely restates the Church's unchanging teaching on this point.

It is therefore necessary to formulate the fundamental moral requirements governing the means that the spouses employ in regulating births, so that their actions may conform to the dignity of the human person. In order to preserve rectitude, these means must take into account the inherent meaning of human sexual life. This is the goal of divine law in this realm.

a. The first of these postulates follows from the equality between man and woman because they both are human persons; in short, there must be equality and proportionality between the contribution of the man and the woman in the work of regulating births.[42] This principle must be kept in mind when examining the morality of women's use of oral contraceptives (ovulation inhibitors) or intrauterine devices (IUDs). To cause biological changes in the woman that make fertility impossible, which at the same time frees the man of his responsibility in the sexual act, is to do violence to the person of the woman and to transgress against justice.[43]

b. The place that sexuality occupies in the structure of the person and in his actions provides the foundation for other postulates. In the life of the human person, sexuality fulfills several functions:

- the biological function of procreation;
- a transindividual, interpersonal, and social function;
- a sign-function, an element in the communication between people in the formation of social bonds.

---

[41] Pius XII, *Allocution to the Congress of the World Union of Young Catholic Women*, April 18, 1952, English translation in *Discorsi e radiomessagi di Sua Santità Pio XII* (Tipografia Poligotta Vaticana), vol. 12, pp. 69–78.

[42] See above, section II.3.

[43] Cf. note 30.

From a biological point of view, sex is essentially linked with procreation. We have already emphasized that the body participates in the dignity of the person: together with the soul, it forms one single human being.[44] This is why sex, a property of the body, is a property of the person; likewise, sexual activity, an essentially bodily event, participates in human activity.

Indeed, man is a social being.[45] The reproductive system is the only organic system that requires the cooperation of two persons in its normal operation. The sexual act involves the human body, but through the body it reaches the person, who by this bodily bonding-gesture (which is essentially a function of the *vis generativa* [the generative power]) enters into a special personal bond with another person.

The sexual instinct therefore is the essential factor that gives rise to the basic interpersonal and social bonds—those of marriage and family. This is why the sexual instinct, impelling one to physical union with an individual of the opposite sex, is a kind of instrumental dynamism serving the person's social needs.

The transindividual function of sexuality is not limited to the formation of interpersonal bonds. Sexual life, intimately linked to the power of procreation, is therefore an essential factor in the existence of society.[46] The mature desire for a child properly belongs to interpersonal sexual love.[47] The documents of the Second Vatican

[44] It is doubtless that all theologians are aware of this, but not all draw therefrom the consequences that logically follow from it. See *Schema*, I.II.2, p. 182, and *Documentum*, II.3, p. 159, and IV.2 b, p. 161.

[45] "Man by his very nature stands completely in need of life in society.... Life in society is not something accessory to man himself: through his dealings with others, through mutual service, and through fraternal dialogue, man develops all his talents and becomes able to rise to his destiny. Among the social ties necessary for man's development some correspond more immediately to his innermost nature—the family, for instance, and the political community; others flow rather from his free choice" (*GS* 25).

[46] For a more detailed philosophical-moral analysis of the problem, see Karol Wojtyła, *Love and Responsibility* (San Francisco: Ignatius Press, 1981), pp. 216–23. See also Helmut Schelsky, *Les formes sociales des relations sexuelles*, in Hans Giese et al., *Seksuologia* (Warsaw: Państwowy Zakład Wydawnictw Lekarskich, 1959), translated from the German: *Die Sexualität des Menschen* (Stuttgart: Enke, 1955).

[47] In its teaching, the Second Vatican Council never separates the ends of marriage as institution from the love of the persons who engage in it. In fact, there is not and cannot be any opposition between these two realities. According to *Gaudium et spes*, "Marriage and married love are by nature ordered to the procreation and education of children. Indeed children are the supreme gift of marriage and greatly contribute to the good of the parents

Council articulate precisely what is required for the parental attitude of the spouses and do not merely affirm that marriage as an
institution is ordained to procreation.[48]

As for sexuality as a sign, it offers the possibility of communicating with one's fellows. It is therefore not only a need proper
to the human being as a "social being" but also a condition sine
qua non of the existence of society. Indeed, the sexual life of man
belongs to the order of signs by which one subject expresses something to another, manifesting the realm of the spirit that cannot be
directly grasped. Sexuality attracts individuals to each other. This
is why its manifestations are a very appropriate means of expressing that which unites human beings—namely, a recognition that
the other possesses a value by which one is drawn toward common union for the sake of the ends proper to human persons. It is
in this that love consists. The sexual life, in its expressions, is therefore a very appropriate way of showing one's love.[49] And since this
body-soul conjunct constitutes, in this life, the undivided unity of
the person, the love that is expressed through sex—that is, through

---

themselves.... Without intending to underestimate the other ends of marriage, it must be
said that true married love and the whole structure of family life which results from it are
directed to disposing the spouses to cooperate valiantly with the love of the Creator and Sav-
iour, who through them will increase and enrich his family from day to day. Married couples
should regard it as their proper mission to transmit human life and to educate their children;
they should realize that they are thereby cooperating with the love of God the Creator and
are, in a certain sense, its interpreters" (GS 50). And, "By its very nature the institution of
marriage and married love is ordered to the procreation and education of the offspring and it
is in them that it finds its crowning glory" (ibid., no. 48).

[48] Among other texts already cited above, one reads in the Constitution *Lumen gentium*:
"Christian married couples help one another to attain holiness in their married life and in
the rearing of their children. Hence by reason of their state in life and of their position they
have their own gifts in the People of God (cf. 1 Cor 7:7). From the marriage of Christians
there comes the family in which new citizens of human society are born and, by the grace
of the Holy Spirit in Baptism, those are made children of God so that the People of God may
be perpetuated throughout the centuries" (*LG* 11).

[49] "Thus the man and woman, who 'are no longer two but one' (Mt 19:6), help and serve
each other by their marriage partnership; they become conscious of their unity and experience
it more deeply from day to day. The intimate union of marriage, as a mutual giving of two
persons" (GS 48).

"Married love is an eminently human love because it is an affection between two persons
rooted in the will and it embraces the good of the whole person; it can enrich the sentiments
of the spirit and their physical expression with a unique dignity and ennoble them as the
special elements and signs of the friendship proper to marriage.... Married love is uniquely
expressed and perfected by the exercise of the acts proper to marriage. Hence the acts in
marriage by which the intimate and chaste union of the spouses takes place are noble and

THE FOUNDATIONS OF THE CHURCH'S DOCTRINE 173

the genital organs—is clearly defined in its genus by the sexuality of the body. As a consequence of the unity of the person, who is simultaneously body and spirit, the sexuality of the body and therefore the sexuality of the person creates special requirements for the personal love that is marked by sex.

Every sexual act between spouses ought therefore to be "mutual self-bestowal",[50] a bodily expression of their mutual love. Because this love "by its very nature ... is ordered to the procreation and education of offspring",[51] it should also express their parental attitude.

The multiple functions of the human sexual act are safeguarded only in the act that retains its proper relation to procreation—in other words, when its sexual structure (as an act of the *vis generativa* [generative power]) is willingly preserved. Because procreation can and must be directed by man, and because this act has other functions besides the purely biological, it follows that man can engage in acts that do not result in fertilization,[52] as long

---

honorable; the truly human performance of these acts fosters the self-giving they signify and enriches the spouses in joy and gratitude" (ibid., no. 49).

"But marriage is not merely for the procreation of children: its nature as an indissoluble compact between two people and the good of the children demand that the mutual love of the partners be properly shown, that it should grow and mature" (ibid., no. 50).

Besides the text cited above, which concerned "the truly human performance of acts", the Council elsewhere uses the following expression: "the acts proper to married life are to be ordered according to authentic human dignity and must be honored with the greatest reverence" (ibid., no. 51). This whole passage is cited in note 39 above. See also the very important passage cited in note 53 below.

[50] Ibid., no. 48. Cf. also the following text: "A love like that, bringing together the human and the divine, leads the partners to a free and mutual giving of self, experienced in tenderness and action, and permeates their whole lives; besides, this love is actually developed and increased by the exercise of it" (ibid., no. 49).

[51] Ibid., no. 48. See also the following text: "When it is a question of harmonizing married love with the responsible transmission of life ... the objective criteria must be used ... criteria which respect the total meaning of mutual self-giving and human procreation in the context of true love" (ibid., no. 51).

[52] "But marriage is not merely for the procreation of children" (ibid., no. 50). This has been, in fact, always the Church's conviction. The exercise of the conjugal right by sterile or elderly spouses has never been considered illicit.

The memorandum *Schema documenti de responsabili paternitate* [Scheme of the document concerning responsible parenthood], the report of the majority of the special commission on birth regulation—to which this document is a response—includes the following passage: "Moralitas ergo actuum sexualium inter coniuges imprimis et specifice significationem sumit ab ordinatione eorum actuum in vita coniugali fecunda ... et non pendet proinde a fecunditate directa uniuscuisque actus particularis" (I, II.2, pp. 182–83). ["Therefore the morality of sexual acts among married people takes its meaning first of all and specifically from the ordering

as the purpose and meaning of their biological structure remain intact. This requirement results from the fact that the sexual act of the person is one act, though polyvalent and structured. It is a biological act of the person: all the personal values are signified in it precisely through its biological orientation. Active intervention in the structure of the act results in its truncation, which does violence to its value as a sign [means of communication]. It is marked by a disintegration of instinct and love. In such circumstances, the sexual act is impelled by autoeroticism and does not fully constitute the revelation of a love encompassing the entirety of affections and instincts.

A complete sexual act that is nevertheless preceded by an intervention into the woman's organic functions in order to prevent fertilization (the "Pill", IUDs)—independently of the violence done to the rights of the person—expresses the same disorder as intervention into the act itself.

This analysis of the role of sexual life in the structure of the person and his actions makes it possible to formulate the postulates of morality governing the responsible regulation of fertility, as follows:

---

of their actions in a fruitful married life.... It does not then depend on the direct fecundity of each and every particular act" (Hoyt, *Birth Control Debate*, p. 87).] The same thought is expressed by the authors of the *Documentum syntheticum*: "Actus coniugales quae ex intentione infoecundi sunt (seu infoecundi redduntur) ordinantur ad expressionem unionis amoris: ille amor autem suum culmen attingit in ipsa foecunditate cum responsabilitate accepta et propterea alii actus unionis quodammodo incompleti sunt et eorum plenam moralitatem cum ordinatione ad actum foecundum recipiunt.... Actus coniugales infecundi cum actu foecundo unam totalitatem constituunt et unicam specificationem moralem accipiunt" (III, p. 160). ["Conjugal acts which by intention are infertile (or which are rendered infertile) are ordered to the expression of the union of love; that love, however, reaches its culmination in fertility responsibly accepted. For that reason, other acts of union in a certain sense are incomplete and they receive their full moral quality with ordination toward the fertile act.... Infertile conjugal acts constitute a totality with fertile acts and have a single moral specification" (Hoyt, *Birth Control Debate*, p. 72).]

It is difficult to agree with this opinion, which argues that sexual relations of sterile couples or of those who for grave reasons are dispensed from the obligation of procreating should be considered to be deprived of their positive moral value. This would amount to rigorism and would not conform to the teaching of the Church.

On the other hand, a participation of the infertile acts in the fertile acts, or even the moral unity of both, requires some sort of grounding. But this grounding is found only in the biological relation of the sexual act to procreation and therefore in the structure of the act, which is essentially procreative (*actus potentiae generativae* [acts of generative power]) and sexual.

- Sexual life must always signify and express, in full truth, the spouses' mutual gift of self and a love that is attentive to the good of the person.
- Every sexual act must express the "parental" character of conjugal love and of married life.
- The sexual integrity of conjugal relations must be preserved.

In light of these principles, all contraceptive procedures displaying antiparental behavior must be excluded from sexual activity. Contracepted relations cannot constitute the expression of the parental attitude, since they are not an unrestricted gift of self, a total communion with the other, regardless of whether this fact is veiled by various illusions.

These requirements demand from us a great ascetic effort, self-mastery, and full consciousness of our actions.[53]

c. Other postulates dictated by morality, to which methods of regulating births must conform, flow from each person's call to seek maturity and growth toward perfection.[54]

Personal development consists, among other things, in perfecting one's actions, which ought to become ever more rational and free. The obstacle [to this goal] will be the tendency to disorder that results from original sin. This tendency is similarly manifested in the realm of sexuality, and personal development and perfection is no less necessary here than in other areas of life.[55] Contemporary discussions of marital morality do not adequately recognize a point of which every pastor is aware—namely, that the mere fact of entering into marriage does not cure the spouses of their tendency

---

[53] The moral requirements clearly also show the importance of a proper formation for young people.

[54] "In the design of God, every man is called upon to develop and fulfill himself, for every life is a vocation. At birth, everyone is granted, in germ, a set of aptitudes and qualities for him to bring to fruition. Their coming to maturity, which will be the result of education received from the environment and personal efforts, will allow each man to direct himself toward the destiny intended for him by his Creator. Endowed with intelligence and freedom, he is responsible for his fulfillment as he is for his salvation. He is aided, or sometimes impeded, by those who educate him and those with whom he lives, but each one remains, whatever be these influences affecting him, the principal agent of his own success or failure. By the unaided effort of his own intelligence and his will, each man can grow in humanity, can enhance his personal worthy, can become more a person." Paul VI, *Populorum progressio*, no. 15, in *Catholic Social Thought*, p. 243.

[55] Cf. GS 8, 13.

to moral disorder.[56] The teaching of the Second Vatican Council manifests a considerable effort to highlight the positive aspect of marriage and its dignity. Yet it also offers a very lucid assessment of corrupted human nature: "Outstanding courage is required for the constant fulfillment of the duties of this Christian calling: spouses, therefore, will need grace for leading a holy life: they will eagerly practice a love that is firm, generous, and prompt to sacrifice and will ask for it in their prayers."[57]

The conciliar Constitution *Lumen gentium* repeatedly emphasizes the revealed doctrine of the universal call to perfection and imitation of God.[58]

We cannot fail to note the tendency to sexual disorder, together with the fact that "the gate is narrow and the way is hard, that leads to life" (Mt 7:14).[59] Opinions that blame the difficult moral situation of today's couples (and is this really a uniquely contemporary problem?) on the unsuitability of the Church's moral teachings [to the contemporary situation] are quite simply naïve. On the one hand, they manifest a completely unjustified optimism according

---

[56] Cf. *Documentum*, II, p. 159; III, p. 160, and especially the following phrase: "Copula etiam cum interventu est oblativa" (IV.4.d, p. 162). ["Intercourse even with intervention is self-offering" (Hoyt, *Birth Control Debate*, p. 77)]. Although certain theologians appeal to the "progress of sexology" (*Documentum*, I.4, p. 157; *Schema*, I.III, p. 183), they do not seem to notice the existence of a psycho-sexual infantilism that is often found especially in men (cf. A.C. Kinsey, *Sexual Behaviour in the Human Male* [Philadelphia: W.B. Saunders, 1948]). One must reckon with the case of autoerotic fixation that appears precisely, among other things, in a contraceptive choice (see, among others, M. Oraison, *Vie chrétienne et problèmes de la sexualité* [Paris: P. Lethielleux, 1952], and M. de Wilmars, *Psychopathologie de l'anticonception* [Paris: P. Lethielleux, 1955]).

[57] GS 49.

[58] The words of Christ: "You, therefore, must be perfect, as your heavenly Father is perfect" (Mt 5:48), so often repeated by the apostle Paul, e.g., "Therefore be imitators of God, as beloved children" (Eph 5:1), are broadly developed in *Lumen gentium*: "It is therefore quite clear that all Christians in any state or walk of life are called to the fullness of Christian life and to the perfection of love" (*LG* 40); "The forms and tasks of life are many but holiness is one— that sanctity which is cultivated by all who act under God's Spirit and, obeying the Father's voice and adoring God the Father in spirit and in truth, follow Christ, poor, humble and cross-bearing, that they may deserve to be partakers of his glory" (ibid., no. 41). "Therefore all the faithful are invited and obliged to holiness and the perfection of their own state of life. Accordingly let all of them see that they direct their affections rightly, lest they be hindered in their pursuit of perfect love by the use of worldly things and by an adherence to riches which is contrary to the spirit of evangelical poverty, following the apostle's advice: Let those who use this world not fix their abode in it, for the form of this world is passing away (cf. 1 Cor 7:31)" (ibid., no. 42).

[59] See Mt 19:8–9; Mk 10:5; Rom 1:24, 26–27; 7:14–25; 1 Cor 5:1, 6:9, 13–20.

to which every desire for the sexual act is solely a yearning of love.[60] On the other hand, these same opinions are grounded in a theological pessimism according to which man, the subject of disordered tendencies, is practically incapable of ordering his own actions. Finally, these opinions exhibit moral legalism, which manifests itself in the barely concealed belief that reason is unable to discern what is morally ordered or disordered in marriage,[61] and that thus the requirements of the natural law are neither knowable nor definable. Consequently, in order for man to stop sinning, it suffices to change the "law"—namely, the principles proclaimed by the Church.

In this domain of sexual life, there is tension between man's sensations in the sexual act and the interpersonal and social values of this act. Sexual activity becomes morally disordered every time that these interpersonal values are subordinated to the sensory dimension of carnal intercourse. Rational sexual behavior therefore requires, by the very nature of things, abstinence from the act whenever love demands it. This willed abstinence from the sexual act can

---

[60] This is why one encounters the simplistic affirmation that spouses who use contraceptives only do it to solidify their love. See note 56 and *Documentum*, I.3, p. 157, and II.4, p. 159. The memoranda *Schema* and *Documentum* include statements that imply that their authors are taking into account the sexual disorder within marriage. But they attribute it solely to an interior attitude, and not to the exterior manifestations of sexual life in marriage. See *Schema*, I.II.2, p. 183, and *Documentum*, III, p. 160.

[61] Cf. *Documentum*, I.1, p. 156; I.2, p. 157; II.1, p. 158; *Status*, I.D, p. 167. This memorandum, however, also includes a very detailed critique of the thesis that upholds the relativity of reason's principles in relation to the present subject (the whole second part).

The *Schema* frequently invokes the natural law, which the authors seem to consider to be evident: "Ceterum vero, ipsa naturalis lex, atque ratio fide christiana illuminata, dictant ut coniuges in eligendis mediis non pro arbitrio, sed secundum criteria obiectiva procedant." ["Moreover, the natural law and reason illuminated by Christian faith dictate that a couple proceed in choosing means not arbitrarily but according to objective criteria" (Hoyt, *Birth Control Debate*, p. 93).] The first of these criteria, according to the authors, is "ut actio correspondeat naturae personae eiusdemque actuum, ita ut integer sensus mutuae donationis ac humanae procreationis in contextu veri amoris observetur." ["The action must correspond to the nature of the person and of his acts so that the whole meaning of the mutual giving and of human procreation is kept in a context of true love" (Hoyt, *Birth Control Debate*, p. 94).] Unfortunately, the authors say nothing of the conditions that the sexual act must fulfill in order to comply with this fundamental requirement (*Schema*, I.IV.2, p. 185). We also find the following statement: "Non ergo arbitrarie, sed,—lege naturae et Dei sic iubente,—coniuges omnibus criteriis simul consideratis iudicium obiective fundatum sibi formant" (ibid., p. 186). ["Therefore not arbitrarily, but as the law of nature and of God commands, let couples form a judgment which is objectively founded, with all the criteria considered" (Hoyt, *Birth Control Debate*, p. 94).]

even express a greater love than the act itself.[62] To strive toward perfection in the conjugal life thus requires on the one hand, being able to express love in abstaining from the conjugal act, and on the other, subordinating one's own pleasure in the sexual act to the interpersonal and social values of the act.

It should also be noted that there is an essential difference between rational behavior that is conscious of its consequences and the precautions prudently taken to avoid the results of undisciplined behavior. Striving for perfection necessitates that one's activity become ever more rational, for it is here that the integration of the person becomes apparent. This is why instinctive impulses must be integrated into behavior that is governed by reason. This is the path to the true maturation of the person. On the other hand, this should not be taken to include calculated foresight into the undesirable results of thoughtless and disintegrated action.

On the basis of these observations, we can now formulate the two last moral postulates to which the regulation of births must conform:

- It must be the expression of growth in Christian perfection, toward the full maturing of the person.
- The sensory dimension of sexual life must always be subordinated to the interpersonal values of this life: each must also be able to express his or her love by abstinence from the sexual act.

In light of these principles, no contraceptive method can be reconciled with the human vocation to full maturation through ever more perfect actions. These methods most often result from entirely subjective difficulties experienced by man in the realm of sexual instinct.

IV. Responsible Parenthood: The Sketch of a Solution

The condemnation of contraception as a method of regulating births in no way leaves today's couples without resources for resolving this problem efficaciously and morally. Leaving aside total continence, which

---

[62] The authors of the *Schema*, I.II.1, p. 182, note this fact; the authors of the *Status*, p. 176 (toward the end), express the same thought with more circumspection.

more than one couple, loving each other deeply, has undertaken due to circumstances, and of which every human being must be capable (for it is absolutely required of celibates and guarantees marital fidelity when one of the spouses is absent), there is also another path opened by contemporary science. In fact, it is possible to regulate births by abstaining from fertile conjugal acts.

1. Medical Summary

Under normal conditions, the male human being constantly produces sperm in large quantities. In contrast, the woman is fertile only at intervals. In principle, the ovaries release eggs one at a time, at relatively fixed points in time.[63] Moreover, the woman is fertile only when an egg has

---

[63] In 1827 K. E. Baer published the results of his research on female gametes in mammals and man (*Epistola de ovi mammalium et hominis genesi* [Leipzig: Leopoldi Vossii, 1827]), and from that moment, reproductive science entered new paths. Soon the relation between the woman's visible sexual cycle and the preparation in her reproductive system of a gamete for release was recognized. Shortly thereafter, theories began to surface concerning the woman's periodic fertility. In 1853, the Holy See was questioned for the first time regarding the morality of engaging in matrimonial relations while aware of their infertility, given the woman's physiological infertility.

For some years, medical opinions on the woman's periodic infertility were contradictory, due to imperfections in methods of research. In 1924, Kyusaku Ogino published in Japan the results of his studies of the fertility of the woman, relying on a considerable number of observations. His work was published in German ("Ovulationstermin und Konzeptionstermin", *Zentralblatt für Gynäkologie* 54 [1930]: 464) in the same journal, and almost simultaneously with that of Herman Knaus ("Eine neue Methode zur Bestimmung des ovulationstermines," *Zentralblatt für Gynäkologie* 53 [1929]: 193), who had arrived at the same results independent of Ogino. The results of their research can be summarized as followed: gametes are released into the female reproductive tract in cyclical cycles in the defined phase of the sexual cycle. The woman can be fertilized only when the ovum has been released from the ovary. This is why, taking into consideration the limited vitality of the ovum and variations in the length of sexual cycles, one can statistically pinpoint a woman's fertile period and therefore her infertile period. The research effected by Ogino and by Knaus gave rise to two different methods of calculating the woman's periods of fertility and infertility (called "calendar methods"). We note in passing that it is unfortunate that the names of these two scientists are paired, as though there were only one method. The above methods rely on statistical observations, which makes them fairly easy to use in practice.

In Europe, H. Stieve attempted to cast doubt on Knaus' thesis by arguing that there is a paracyclical ovulation (*Der Einfluss des Nervensytems auf Bau und Tätigkeit der weiblichen Geschlechtsorganen* [Stuttgart: Thieme, 1952], pp. 85–111). This would mean that, contrary to the claims of Ogino and Knaus, the woman can become pregnant at any moment because a number of stimuli can cause the release from the ovary of a second ovum within the same sexual cycle.

Medical opinion too hastily agreed with Stieve's conclusions, with the consequence that Ogino's and Knaus' conclusions were treated with hesitation. Finally, H. Rauscher showed

been released into her reproductive tract. In these conditions, it is possible to regulate births efficaciously by abstaining from sexual relations, as long as one has sufficiently certain knowledge of the functional state of the woman's reproductive system. Observations recorded for more than sixty years (1904–1967) by numerous doctors have made it possible to understand the functional changes in the woman's reproductive system that accompany the various phases of the menstrual cycle. Among all the methods that have precisely, methodically, and systematically examined the functional state of the woman's reproductive system, the method of body temperature taken at rest is the simplest. It is, moreover, accessible enough that anyone can practice it, and verified by meticulous studies undertaken by several researchers.[64] The temperature curve makes

---

in 1963 that Stieve's theses were incorrect ("Ovulation [Morphology]", *Archiv für Gynäkologie* [1965]: 202, 121–31. See also W. Fijałkowski, "Zagadnienie paracyklicznej owulacji w świelte obserwazji własnych [The problem of paracyclical ovulation in light of proper observations]", *Ginekologia Polska* 38 [1967]: 501, summarized in English). Medical science today agrees that

- the release of the ovum or ova occurs in the woman at a specific stage in the sexual cycle;
- in the rare event that there is more than one ovum, they are all released at the same time;
- one phase of preparation in the reproductive system precedes the release, and after this, the system remains prepared for the implantation of the ovum when fertilized;
- after releasing the ovum, the reproductive system undergoes a transformation that inhibits the expulsion of the next ovum;
- because the ovum, once released, lives only for a short time after ovulation, a phase of physiological infertility begins for the woman;
- the release of the ova and the changes connected to the sexual cycle depend on hormonal changes that provoke different symptoms, making it possible to verify the functional state of a woman's reproductive system;
- the term of ovulation can fluctuate (these physiological variations never surpass five days), which depends on several factors and can be noted by observing accompanying symptoms. Subsequent ovulation of two or more ova in the course of one and the same cycle does not occur.

From these observations, we can conclude that, from the medical point of view, abstinence from sexual relations during the fertile part of the cycle (i.e., during the phase of ovulation, taking into consideration the period of the ovum's vitality and that of the sperm in the female body) is a sure method of regulating births.

[64] T. H. van der Welde, *Über den Zusammenhang zwischen Ovarialfunktion, Wellenbewegung und Menstrualblutung* (Harlem: De Erven F. Bohn, 1904); "Basal Body Temperature in Disorders of Ovarial Function and Pregnancy", *Surgery, Gynaecology and Obstetrics* 75 (1924): 768. R. Palmer, "Basal Body Temperature of the Woman", *American Journal of Obstetrics and Gynaecology* (1950): 551, 155ff. M. Chartier, "Fécondité et continence périodique", *Cahiers Laennec* 14, no. 4 (1954): 2–34; "Interprétation de la courbe thermique pour le diagnostic de l'ovulation et des périodes dites fécondes du cycle menstruel", *Journal des sciences de Lille* 83 (1965): 515–32. J. G. H. Holt, *Het getij. Het verband tussen vruchtbaarheid en temperatuur bij de vrouw* (Bilthoven: Dekker & Van de Vegt, 1956). K. G. Döring, *Die Bestimmung der*

it possible to determine precisely the periods of the woman's physiological fertility and infertility. The interpretation of this curve is quite
simple, and any interested person who receives proper instruction can
use it.[65] Difficulties of interpretation are rare.[66] The application of the
method almost never disappoints: the failure rate varies from 0.8 to 1.3
of unplanned pregnancies per one hundred users of the method.[67] A
serious and well-informed expert observes, "The exact observation of
the thermal method yields no negative results due to the method itself.
No fertilization has been noted from the third day of the hyperthermal
phase, among women who were following the rules. The few pregnancies that occurred despite the practice of the method were almost all due
to errors made by those involved."[68]

Concluding, we have at our disposal today a method of regulating
births that is "absolutely unobjectionable and voluntarily practiced".[69] It
is sufficiently certain, simple, and low-cost so that every family of goodwill, with adequate instruction, can use it. It consists in abstaining from
conjugal relations during the fertile period of the woman's menstrual
cycle. This phase can be recognized by using an empirical method. In

---

fruchtbaren und unfruchtbaren Tage der Frau mit Hilfe der Körpertemperatur (Stuttgart: Thieme,
1957); *Empfängnisverhütung, ein Leitfaden für Ärtze und Studenten* (Stuttgart: Thieme, 1966),
with a substantial bibliography; "Über die Zuverlässigkeit der Temperaturmethode zur Empfängnisverhütung", *Deutsche medizinische Wochenschrift* 92 (1967): 23, 1055–61. S. Geller, *La
courbe thérmique, guide de la femme* (Paris, 1960); *La courbe thermique, guide du practicien en endocri-
nologie féminine* (Paris: Masson et Cie, 1961). J. Marshall, *The Infertile Period* (London: Darton,
Longman & Todd, 1965). G. van der Stappen, *Précis de la méthode des temperatures* (Paris:
Editions ouvrières, 1961). C. Rendeau, "La régulation des naissances dans le cadre familial et
chrétien", *NRTh* 87 (1965): 606–31. C. G. Hartmann, *Science and the Safe Period* (Baltimore:
Williams & Wilkins, 1962). J. Rötzer, *Kinderzahl und Liebesehe* (Vienna: Herder, 1966). A.
Vincent and B. Vincent, "Valeur de l'abstention periodique comme méthode de regulation
des naissances", *Journal des sciences de Lille* 83 (1965): 643–92. C. S. Keefer, *Human Ovulation*
(London: J & A Churchill, 1965).

At a conference of the International Planned Parenthood Federation in April 1967, periodic continence was presented as the first among the birth-planning methods (Rhythm
Method—The Use of Basal Body Temperature). Cf. *International Planned Parenthood News*
157 (March 1967).

[65] Instruction does not need to be given by a doctor. Pastoral experience in Poland shows
that those best suited are women instructors who have been properly trained, i.e., young
mothers who have personal experience of this practice in their married lives.

[66] See Chartier, "Fécondité", p. 24.

[67] See Döring, "Über die Zuverlässigkeit", table 2.

[68] Ibid. [This and the following quote are translated from the French translation given in
the original text of the memorandum.]

[69] Ibid.

order to make it available to everyone, however, appropriate individual instruction is required—publicity alone is not enough.[70] It is therefore crucial to train instructors in this method, both men and women, who can give assistance to those who need it.

2. Some Remarks Relating to the Moral Analysis of the Problem

a. Some people believe that methods involving periodic continence are merely another way of practicing contraception. The difference, they say, consists solely in a use of different secondary factors— namely, time (for those who employ periodic continence) and place (for those who employ contraceptives)—for the sake of the same goal: rendering a sexual encounter sterile. According to these authors, the method of periodic continence consists in choosing infertile days for sexual relations, which they consider to be equivalent to an active sterilization of this relation (or of the woman).[71]

1. This opinion could perhaps be justified if the spouses were faced with the alternative of engaging in sexual relations either solely on infertile days, or solely on fertile days. One could therefore speak of choosing the period of infertility for sexual relations. But this is not the case.[72] Consequently, the regulation of births by means of periodic continence essentially consists in abstaining from sexual relations during the fertile phase, while engaging in these relations at other times according to the norms of conjugal life. It is thus a matter of giving up an action whose results would be undesirable. By using contraceptives, the subject demonstrates unwillingness to give up this action; this is why he intervenes actively to obstruct the inherent consequences of the act. It seems to us that this is an essential difference.

2. Because sexual relations on infertile days are normal and willed as such, they maintain the respect due to the hierarchy of values and the full meaning of sexual life. Thus they can fittingly

---

[70] This is the experience of parish counseling in the dioceses of Poland.

[71] L. Janssens, *Mariage et fécondité* (Paris: P. Lethielleux, 1967).

[72] According to Pius XII, "The right deriving from the marriage contract is a permanent [right], uninterrupted and not intermittent, of each of the partners, in respect of the other" ("Allocution to Midwives", in *Human Body*, p. 163).

express the "parental" character of conjugal life and of the love uniting the spouses. This is entirely the opposite of the conscious sterilization of the relation, which, actively deprived of its proper role, cannot be the sexual expression of the love uniting two persons.[73]

For example, consider the case of oral contraceptives. A practice such as periodic continence, that takes into consideration the sexuality of the woman and consequently her dignity as person, is entirely opposed to the inhibitive intervention into her sexual biological functions, which amounts to an intrusion into the private domain of the person. It is necessary to recall that the body is not distinct from the person, nor "subject" to it; rather, with the soul, it constitutes one single unique person, and it participates in the rights and dignity of the person.[74]

b. In examining the moral aspect of the problem, we must point out the essential difference between that which is permissible to will (that which may be willed) (*volitum*) and that for which one is free to strive (*voluntarium*).[75] All agree that in certain cases, the choice not to transmit life does not necessitate total abstinence from the sexual act, since in man, that act is not solely limited to the function of procreation.[76] But it is wrong to conclude therefrom that it is morally justifiable to deprive sexual relations of their procreative function actively, and that one can knowingly engage in such behavior. In light of what has just been said, we see no possibility of rationally or theologically justifying such a conclusion.

c. Abstinence from sexual relations during the fertile time, together with the safeguarding of the sexual character of relations outside this phase, can be a manifestation of respect for the hierarchy of values. But although it *can* manifest such respect, it does not do so necessarily, for the practice of periodic continence for the sake of not transmitting life without sufficient rational motives (for example, an aversion to children, pleasure alone, aesthetic considerations,

---

[73] See above, III.3.b.

[74] See above, II.1; III.3.b.

[75] See P. Böckle, "Pour un débat Chrétien sur la regulation des naissances", *Concilum* 5 (1965): 111.

[76] See above, III.3.b.

etc.) bears witness to a disorder within one's psycho-sexual behavior. But this possibility in no way changes the fact that periodic continence, practiced for reasonable motives, is the only morally good way of regulating births.

d. Nearly every couple undergoes periods of continence in their sexual life. A number of factors are involved.[77]

For instance, there are some days on which spouses are constrained by the very nature of things to renounce sexual encounters (for example, in the case of illness, or in the weeks before and after childbirth). To take some additional—and very important—factors into consideration is normal and ordinary.[78]

e. Intentional abstinence from the sexual act is clearly the common project of both spouses.[79] Here there is no danger of one spouse subordinating the other to his or her own sexual pleasure. On the contrary, abstinence can be the appropriate expression of the respect due to the person as a sexual being.

To the objection that in this case the male is placed at a disadvantage because it is harder for him to master his instinct and because his desire for sexual relations is generally stronger than the woman's, it must be replied that, precisely on account of his constant power to fertilize, the male must recognize that he bears a correspondingly greater responsibility.[80] In the realm of sexual

---

[77] Sexologists have even sought to define frequency of sexual intercourse as the test of abnormal sexual life. See S. Liebhart and B. Trebicka-Kwiatkowska, *Zagadnienia życia seksualnego kobiety* (The problems of the sexual life of the woman) (Warsaw: Państ: Zakład Wydawnictw Lekarskich, 1964), pp. 34–55; and R. von Urban, *Sex Perfection* (London: Rider, 1964), pp. 96–97.

[78] It is in [such consideration] that the "humanization of the intellect" consists. Man does not and should not "spontaneously" satisfy any of his instinctive needs. That would not be a human way of acting.

It is relevant to note here that the Old Testament prohibited sexual relations during menstruation and the following week (Lev 15:19–24, 28; 13:19; 20:18; Ezek 18:5–6) as well as after childbirth (Lev 12:1–5). Similarly, soldiers in time of war were forbidden to approach a woman, even if they had the occasion to spend some time at home (1 Sam 21:6; 2 Sam 11:11). Although these prohibitions were of a ritual order, they nevertheless show that abstaining is possible within marriage and that it does not destroy the essence of conjugal love. St. Paul even foresees the possibility of abstaining from conjugal relations within marriage (1 Cor 7:5–6). The example of the Holy Family also implies that sexual continence in itself does not weaken the bond of marriage.

[79] See above, II.3.a.

[80] See above, II.3.

THE FOUNDATIONS OF THE CHURCH'S DOCTRINE

life, there is no biological parity between the male and the woman. The just proportion of their common contribution to the regulation of births can only be found, therefore, when the male is able to integrate the dynamism of his instinct into the totality of his reason-dominated life, and to express his love by the sexual act in a reflective manner. Otherwise, the woman would be excessively burdened by sexual life and its consequences, or would simply become—at least to a certain extent—an object that her husband uses to satisfy his lust.

Moreover, the difficulties experienced by the male in the realm of sexual instinct most often derive (setting aside pathological cases) from a lack of effort to master himself.

It has been objected more than once that the woman experiences a stronger desire for sexual encounter in the fertile phases. Studies on this subject, however, have shown that this is not the case.[81]

f. Human sexual life is to a certain degree, by its very nature, the sign of love.[82] One might therefore ask whether abstinence from sexual relations does not weaken this love.

The response to this question is that not only the consciously willed sexual act, but also abstention from the sexual act, can be a sign of love.[83] This naturally occurs during the course of an engagement, when the engaged couple must abstain from sexual relations; this is, for them, a sign of mutual love. The necessity [for abstinence] likewise arises occasionally for married couples, and when it is practiced out of respect for higher values, it can manifest an even greater love than the sexual act on its own.[84] Abstaining from the sexual act can help spouses live the sexual act more deeply, precisely inasmuch as it is an act of love, and continence is often counseled for sterile couples, inasmuch as it is a way of deepening mutual love.[85]

g. Recourse to contraceptive practices is often the result of an inability to overcome impulses.[86] Lacking the strength to oppose them,

[81] See Liebhart and Trebicka-Kwiatkowska, *Zagadnienia zyčia seksualnego kobiety*, pp. 34–35, and the bibliography cited; Urban, *Sex Perfection*, pp. 193–94.

[82] See *GS* 49, and above, II.3.b.

[83] See above, II.2 and III.3.c.

[84] Analogous to silence, which in some cases can be more eloquent than speech.

[85] See above, III.3.c.

[86] See above, II.2, II.3, and III.3.

the individual also wishes to avoid the possible consequences of this disordered behavior. This results in a situation of conflict. Literature on this subject also refers to the psycho-pathological character of contraception.[87] In those who practice contraception, the fear of children, a significant source for neuroses, is well known. Serious medical and pastoral observations show that when spouses adopt periodic continence as a method of regulating births after having practiced contraception during a more or less extended period of time, they experience a deepening of their mutual bond and the disappearance of neuroses and the fear of children—indeed, they often begin to desire a child, even if their state in life prevents them from having one. But all these symptoms are unknown to couples who voluntarily sterilize their sexual relations.

Without a doubt, there are no couples who would not like to have normal sexual relations. Thus every intervention into sexual relations by means of a contraceptive element entails a frustration that weighs on the psyche of the spouses.

h. From what has been said earlier,[88] it clearly follows that the regulation of births by means of periodic continence fully conforms to the Christian vocation to strive for perfection.

i. It seems that there is a link between inadequate theological appreciation of celibacy and the defense of contraception. It must be clearly recognized that the regulation of births by means of periodic continence presupposes

1. that such continence is not only possible, but a condition of psycho-sexual maturity;
2. that abstinence from the sexual act can be a sign of truly mature love.

Those who do not understand the meaning of periodic continence in the life of the couple will not be able to understand the meaning of celibacy, in which these two presuppositions are fully expressed.[89]

---

[87] Among others, see de Wilmars, *Psychopathologie de l'anticonception.*

[88] See above, III.3.c.

[89] One gets the impression that the intensive propaganda in favor of contraception conceals other motives than that of research into theological and moral truth and the good of humanity. In our own country, we are aware of the efforts made in this respect by the institutions

V. Pastoral Problems

1. Education

New obligations facing today's families require that the faithful be adequately prepared for conjugal life. This is why education must be informed by a respect for the other, respect for the body, and respect for the realities of sex. It is necessary to speak straightforwardly to young people about family life, its bonds and its laws; about conjugal life, its values and qualities, its joys, duties, and difficulties. It is necessary to make clear to them that men and women have equal rights as well as psychological and biological differences that make enormous demands for mutual responsibility. It is necessary to emphasize the special value of a life that takes its origin from the body of the parents, but whose human personality is called into existence by the creative act of God alone.

The formation appropriate to family life is at the same time a formation for the choice of celibacy, for those who have a calling to that state. The choice of either vocation requires equal maturity in men and women. Education cannot neglect this aspect of the Christian call to perfection.

All the problems that young people encounter on their road and that may cause them distress must be discussed and resolved in a fraternal dialogue full of understanding. In addition to catechesis properly speaking, it is advisable to organize classes for young people to discuss the problems of family and marriage and to provide a psycho-sexual formation. The problem of regulating births must also be treated. A responsible approach to this problem requires long preparation for young men and women.

Classes for marriage preparation, introduced by numerous pastors, are extremely important and should include the participation of doctors, psychologists, teachers, married couples, and parents.

Finally, we must always remember that pastors have an obligation to provide immediate marriage preparation for engaged couples. A suitable catechesis, directly preceding the marriage itself, is likewise necessary.

---

responsible for the secularization of life and for atheism. In capitalist countries, one must doubtless take into consideration the interest of capital, which gains a considerable source of revenue from the manufacture of contraceptives, particularly chemical ones. This manufacture is clearly profitable, if every couple has to use these products throughout the entirety of their fertile years, i.e., for at least twenty years.

2. Pastoral Matters

It is essential to the present problem that all those who have the care of souls throughout the world be unanimous in explaining the principles of morality as taught by the Church, and in applying the directives of the Magisterium in the same way. The ministers of the Church must not only inform the faithful about the principles of morality but also make available to them all the means of facilitating moral behavior in life. Neglect in this area is, unfortunately, considerable. Our contemporaries are greatly confused about the principles of morality governing the regulation of births; the source of this confusion is, among other things, a lack of energy and determination in efforts to help people to benefit from scientific discoveries that make it possible to regulate births in conformity with divine law. This is why, wherever the need is manifested, pastors should provide services through the parish by means of which lay professionals from various disciplines can counsel couples and families, not only concerning all the problems relating to responsible parenthood, but also in other areas related to family life (education, conflict management, etc.). The faithful must be guaranteed free, professional, and responsible counseling that is faithful to Christian doctrine. Without this endeavor, it is useless to speak of forming consciences. The pastor who neglects to organize this aid for the good of his flock will be gravely culpable and co-responsible for the moral disorder that destroys the domestic and religious life of contemporary families.

3. The Laity

In providing formation for marriage and assistance to Christian couples, the laity has a primary and irreplaceable role in introducing a regulation of births worthy of the human person. No one can provide better assistance to spouses experiencing difficulties than other informed Christian couples who are faithful to the directives of the Church.

A special role belongs to doctors, nurses, and midwives. People have the right to expect from them appropriate assistance in everything concerning the regulation of births, in conformity to the demands of morality. Responsible parenthood is a grave duty and, at the same time, a weighty issue for today's couples. Abandoned to their own devices, married couples will have no way out of their difficulties. Without

competent help, they risk turning away from God and becoming impris-
oned in inextricable and desperate moral conflicts. Doctors, nurses, and
midwives ought therefore to follow attentively the progress of medicine
in this area and to draw their knowledge from dependable sources.
Already in 1951, Pius XII exhorted them to do so.[90] The Second Vatican Council directs a similar appeal to all those who are competent in
this area. "People should be discreetly informed of scientific advances in
research into methods of birth regulation, whenever the value of these
methods has been thoroughly proved and their conformity with the
moral order established."[91]

[90] According to Pius XII, "You are rightly expected to be well informed, from the medical
point of view, of this well-known theory and of the progress which can still be foreseen in this
matter; and moreover, your advice and help are expected to be based, not on simple, popular
publications, but on scientific facts and the authoritative judgment of conscientious specialists
in medicine and biology." "Allocution to Midwives", in *Human Body*, p. 162.

[91] *GS* 87. Or: "Some men nowadays are gravely disturbed by this problem [of population];
it is to be hoped that there will be Catholic experts in these matters, particularly in universities, who will diligently study the problems and pursue their researches further" (ibid.).
"Experts in other sciences, particularly biology, medicine, social science and psychology, can
be of service to the welfare of marriage and the family and the peace of mind of people, if
by pooling their findings they try to clarify thoroughly the different conditions favoring the
proper regulation of births" (ibid., no. 52).

Only Union Plus Fruit Equals Love

A Personalist Explains the Teaching
of Humanae vitae[*]

Maria Fedoryka, Ph.D.

Introduction

The fiftieth anniversary of *Humanae vitae* gives us the opportunity to meditate once again on the Church's teaching on the generation of new human life, and on the magnificent articulation of this teaching in recent decades, coming from both magisterial documents and from the writings of many religious and lay faithful. While the Catholic Church's stance on contraception is perennial, over the last century an entirely new light has been shed that illuminates aspects of marriage and the marital act previously remaining in the shadows. Perhaps one could cautiously suggest that this new light might even constitute a development of doctrine in the Church's moral teaching.[1]

---

[*] This is a modified version of an article originally published as "The Centrality of Love to the Teaching of *Humanae vitae*", *Homiletic and Pastoral Review*, July 21, 2017, https://www .hprweb.com/2017/07/the-centrality-of-love-to-the-teaching-of-humanae-vitae/.

[1] Some examples of norms brought into focus in a new way in the course of recent reflection: see how *Donum vitae*, the document giving the Church's teaching on in vitro fertilization, illuminates the child's right to be conceived in an individual, the concrete act of love of the spouses for each other (Congregation for the Doctrine of the Faith, Instruction on Respect for Human Life in Its Origin and on the Dignity of Procreation *Donum vitae*—Replies to Certain Questions of the Day [February 22, 1987], http://www.vatican.va/roman_curia /congregations/cfaith/documents/rc_con_cfaith_doc_19870222_respect-for-human-life _en.html). See also the way in which Karol Wojtyła's *Love and Responsibility* shows with new clarity the absolute demand that each spouse approach the other as an end in himself or herself in the conjugal act; and see the way in which the Theology of the Body gives a deep grounding to the need for chastity within marriage—and we could give many more examples.

The new reflections on this old subject arose in the face of unprecedented challenges from the modern world, challenges that included the accusation that the Catholic teaching poses a threat to the love between the spouses. In response, the Church sought to pronounce more clearly on the dimension of love proper to marriage. The result was a great deposit of writings yielding a breathtaking depiction of the grandeur and sublimity of spousal love, which yielded, paradoxically, a new and deeper grounding of the essential fruitfulness of marriage, and of the marital act.

In spite of the countless resources now available on the topic, objectors to the Church's teaching continue to misunderstand and misrepresent it.[2] Just like the early dissenters, they interpret the prohibition against contraception as having its foundation in the person's biological dimension, as forbidding a disruption of the physical end of the act—a position that they label as "biologistic". Dissenters charge that the Church subordinates the love of the spouses to the physical, animal structures beneath them as persons, and thus denies the great scope it would otherwise have if the life of the spirit were allowed free play. But recent orthodox writing on the issue makes clear that the prohibition against contraceptive acts derives from the nature of love itself—the very thing the dissenters are so anxious to guard—rather than from the mere biological structure of the sexual act.

The central point of the teaching's new cast is found in a more precise interpretation of the traditional "two ends" of the marital act, the unitive and the procreative: firstly, they are both together affirmed as making up marital love, and secondly, they are declared to be inseparably united "meanings" of the sexual act,[3] and more precisely, as co-implying each other—such that rejecting the procreative dimension is not merely to deny a possible consequence of the marital act, but would amount to a dismantling of the act as an act of love. What the Church, up to this point, had referred to as the two ends of marriage—without speaking of

---

[2] A secondary impetus for the writing of this article is a recent statement put out by the Wijngaards Institute, which repeats many of these misinterpretations: Wijngaards Institute, "Catholic Scholars' Statement on the Ethics of Using Contraceptives", August 2016, http://wijngaardsinstitute.com/statement-on-contraceptives/.

[3] See Paul VI, encyclical letter *Humanae Vitae* (July 25, 1968), no. 12, trans. Janet E. Smith, in Humanae Vitae: *A Challenge to Love* (New Hope, KY: New Hope Publications, 2006) (hereafter cited as *HV*).

the organic connection between them—turns out to be more precisely two dimensions of one and the same reality: the reality of love.

What I offer here is not a technical philosophical analysis, but a philosopher's meditation on the centrality of love in this new vision reflected in recent Church instruction on the procreation of new human life. Since so many of the misunderstandings of the teaching on contraception center on a misunderstanding of the place of the bodily dimension in that teaching, I will focus on showing the particular way that the body has moral significance in the equation, thereby demonstrating that the Church's view is in no way biologistic. On the contrary, it is not merely because of the natural biological end of the act, but because of the law of love that contraception goes against the truth about sexuality. I will show that it is because the bodily act is formed and shaped by the spiritual reality of love, and therefore in some mysterious, but real way, participates in it, that the bodily act of marital union is subject to its laws. This "law of love", as we will see, protects the essential fruitfulness of the marital act.

The picture of sexuality presented here will be very different from the one found in our present culture. Sex is generally taken as not having much inherent meaning; rather, it is something into which one may enter casually. But the contrary is the case: because sex is related to the most intense kind of human love that exists in the depth of our being, and because it is related to the creation of new human life, sex is in fact inherently and deeply meaningful. As a bodily expression of marital love, and as the source of human life, sex will turn out to be as deep as these two realities, and to occupy a central place within the human person.

As a final point by way of introduction, some readers may notice that my defense here of *Humanae vitae* is not the traditional one. The traditional philosophical defense focuses on the natural teleology (goal-directedness) of the marital act toward the coming into existence of new human life. Since the goal of an act determines its nature, this position holds, the act is by its nature procreative, and so to contracept is to destroy the nature of the act. This position defends itself against biologism by adding that the workings of nature in this case belong to a personal being and so are not merely biological. I believe that something is missing in this traditional defense, which still leaves it vulnerable to the biologistic objection. Without contradicting the traditional position, I seek to ground it more deeply by unearthing one more anthropological layer underlying the teaching of *Humanae vitae*, according to which the physical structure of the act is not as such binding, or even binding simply by virtue of existing within a personal being, but only because it is in its *metaphysical*[4] structure an embodiment of *love*, and therefore governed by the law of love which prohibits the separation of union from its proper fruit.

Initial Overview

We begin, then, by noting some essential truths about the nature of love. Firstly, love is made up of two dimensions: union—brought about through the mutual self-giving and receiving of two persons—and fruitfulness. That fruitfulness is part of love can easily be seen by anyone who has experienced love, and especially romantic love—this close union of persons gives rise to a new life within the souls of those who love, a kind of new way of being. But secondly, there is an inherent generosity to love, whereby it seeks to go beyond itself, to bestow good on others. In fact, going back to Plato, many authors have observed that new life has its source in love. John Paul II notes that only a being who loves goes outside itself to give the gift of existence to another being for its own sake. He writes about this essential connection between love and creation in the following passage:

> The Creator is he who "calls to existence from nothingness," and who establishes the world in existence and man in the world, *because he "is love"* (1 Jn 4:8). We admittedly do not find this word love (God is love) in the creation account; nevertheless, that account often repeats: "God saw everything that he had made, and indeed, it was very good" (Gen 1:31). Through these words we are led to glimpse in love the divine motive of creation, the source, as it were, from which it springs: *only love, in fact, gives rise to the good and is well pleased with the good* (see 1 Cor 13).[5]

---

[4] For the reader who may not be familiar with this technical philosophical term, it refers to elements in a thing that make up its deep structure.

[5] John Paul II, *Man and Woman He Created Them: A Theology of the Body*, trans. Michael Waldstein (Boston: Pauline Books and Media, 2006), 13:3, emphasis in original. References are to the audience number and paragraph number. Hereafter, all Theology of the Body references will be cited as TOB.

This dimension of love becomes clearer when we consider how impossible it is to associate love with destruction, diminishment, negation, or even a self-directed, self-enclosed sufficiency. No, love is by its very nature superabundant, paradoxically always greater than itself.

Moreover, the giving of love is not merely a giving of something, but is always simultaneously—and even more centrally—a giving of self to the beneficiary. In a beautiful passage in *Dives in misericordia*, John Paul II refers to this essential, self-giving character of love, particularly in the gift of man's creation. There he tells us that the concept of "fatherhood" captures the sense of a creative act that is much more than simply an act of bringing a new person into existence, but an act that places the creature in a love relation with the one who creates:

> God, as Christ has revealed him, does not merely remain closely linked with the world as the Creator and the ultimate source of existence. He is also Father: he is linked to man, whom he called to existence in the visible world, by a bond still more intimate than that of creation. It is love which not only creates the good but also grants participation in the very life of God: Father, Son and Holy Spirit. For he who loves desires to give himself.[6]

Even more, in *Donum vitae*—the Church's document on in vitro fertilization—the Church makes clear that because of the great dignity of the human person, the coming into existence of new human life in strict justice requires a love origin.

We have laid the groundwork for considering the creation of new human life. Now, we know that God is always faithful to these laws governing creation in love. But by a free decision, God does not bring about each new human life in the fullness of its being directly. He does make each human soul individual out of nothing, but he does not directly make the body which that soul will animate. Rather, he involves human agents in his creative act; in fact, parents are "co-creators" with God. How can this be? How can all the above conditions apply in the case of a creature?

[6] John Paul II, encyclical letter *Dives in misericordia* (November 30, 1980), no. 7, w2.vatican .va/content/john-paul-ii/en/encyclicals/documents/hf_jp-ii_enc_30111980_dives-in -misericordia.html.

The first question is about the love origin of human life: How is it to be preserved, considering the cooperation of human agents? Firstly, God has ordained that a child comes into existence in an act of loving union between two persons, an act in which the child then is the fruitful dimension of the parents' love. Coming into existence as the fruit flowing from the parents' union, the child is truly incorporated into a real act of love.

The second question is how it should be possible for a creature to bring a new being into existence, for only an omnipotent God can bring something out of nothing. It is here that we begin to see the significance of the human body. If a mere human person is somehow to take part in the creation of a new person, since he cannot bring it into existence out of nothing, his creativity would be about sharing something he already has. An angel, as pure spirit, does not have anything of himself to give away. But the human person, who has a body, does: he can share some of his own bodily existence with another.

But thirdly, the love origin of human creation would require one more element, as we have seen: a love origin requires self-giving to the one created, and not merely the giving of existence. How can this occur since a creature cannot give the life of his soul to another, as can God the Creator? The answer lies in the special nature of the personal body: since the human person's body is, in some important sense, truly identical with his being as person, in giving a share of his own body to another, the person does not just give the "stuff" of his body, but truly makes a gift of himself. And thus do the human progenitors truly participate in God's Fatherhood, truly becoming "parents" (and not just "efficient causes", to use philosophical language) of the child, making a gift of themselves to the child in and through their bodies.

In the creature that is the human person, then, we find that matter gives love a new power; because of the body, the fruitfulness of spousal love can take on a new dimension. A mere human person is incapable of creating a new being, much less a personal being. And yet, man is truly incorporated into the creative act of God, by virtue of the intrinsic generosity of love itself, which acquires a new ability in the life-generating capacity of the body.

The point at which we find the highest expression of love between human persons, we find the most profound meaning of the human body, in the sense of its "reason for being"—because of the body, the human spouses' spiritual act of love is able to participate in bringing a new person into existence. As we have said, no angel can co-create. And while it would only be speculation, we might be able to go even further, and guess that the vast cosmos, the whole expanse of material reality as such, was created for one reason: so that some bits of this matter could become integrated into a personal being so that this bodily person could enter into a way of loving that grants him a participation in God's Fatherhood.

From all of this it becomes clear that to reject the coming-to-be of a child would be to compromise deeply the love itself between the spouses, for a child is the embodiment of one of the two essential dimensions of that love, as found in the particular embodied expression of marital lovemaking. In what follows, I offer a deeper explanation of these truths about love and procreation.

Deeper Reflection on Love and Procreation

John Paul II's illumination of the special nature of the body-soul unity, and his bringing to light the body's centrality in issues surrounding marriage, sexual morality, and bioethics, is to my mind one of the most important philosophical contributions of his pontificate. In his *Man and Woman He Created Them: A Theology of the Body*, he makes it clear that the human body is more than matter inhabited by a soul, but is rather a personal soul having *become* "enfleshed". This reality is difficult to put into language, but here are some of the ways that John Paul speaks about it: the body is "penetrable and transparent ... in such a way as to make it clear who man is";[7] it alone "makes visible the invisible".[8] In his *Letter to Families*, he speaks of the soul as "embodied", and of the human body as "spiritualized".[9] All of these ideas are meant to express that the human body is, as it were, the very incursion of a personal soul into the realm of matter, in such a way that the body truly is the person. We could say that the human person is one being existing in two dimensions.

---

[7] TOB 7:2.

[8] Ibid., 19:4.

[9] John Paul II, *Letter to Families* (February 2, 1994), no. 19, https://w2.vatican.va/content/john-paul-ii/en/letters/1994/documents/hf_jp-ii_let_02021994_families.html.

Since the body is an extension of the person himself, John Paul emphasized that the body participates in the human person's subjectivity—and
is not merely an "object" or instrument that he uses.[10] It is "co-subject"
with the person in his performance of bodily acts. This is already a hint
that the spouses do not give "merely" of their bodies in the creation of a
child; rather, they give themselves to the child because of their presence
in their bodies.

However, this mutual "indwelling" of body and soul, found in the
embodied person's way of being, is not all that underlies the gift of self
in the case of the spousal act. According to Dietrich von Hildebrand,
there is a uniquely deep intersection of body and soul in the sexual
sphere. Sex is inseparably bound up with the center of the person.
Because of this, the bodily act of sex is never merely bodily, but is,
firstly, by its very nature, connected with deep spiritual and psychological experiences in the human person; secondly, it allows the spouses to
make a gift of their very selves in the deepest part of their being.[11] Sex,
he says, occupies a most deep and intimate place within the person, so
that "when [sex] speaks, it is no mere *obiter dictum* (casual expression),
but a voice from the depth, the utterance of something central, and of
the utmost significance."[12]

Now, based on this unique character of sexuality, the marital act itself
is a special kind of bodily act: it is a bodily act with an "interior space",
fashioned to be "animated" from within by a spiritual reality, specifically by the reality of spousal love.[13] Compare this with other bodily
actions—such as, for example, a wave of the hand. This bodily behavior
has no "inner side" and, therefore, has no intrinsic meaning. Its meaning is given to it from the outside, by convention, and can therefore

[10] "Man is a subject not only by his self-consciousness and by self-determination, but also
based on his own body. The structure of this body is such that it permits him to be the author
of genuinely human activity. In this activity, the body expresses the person; it is thus, in all
its materiality ... penetrable and transparent as it were, in such a way as to make it clear who
man is" (TOB 7:2).

[11] Dietrich von Hildebrand, *In Defense of Purity* (Steubenville, OH: Hildebrand Press,
2017), p. 3. This is why the Church has always taught that the union of marriage is not complete until the spouses enter into the marital act: the act "consummates" the marriage.

[12] Ibid. This depth of sexuality explains the privacy that surrounds the sexual sphere, as well
as the salutary shame associated with it.

[13] "In virtue of its profound centrality and intimacy, as also of its mystery, sex is capable
of a particular relationship with love, the most spiritual and the deepest of all experiences"
(ibid., p. 5).

legitimately be changed, and the act used to mean something different. The bodily act of sex, by contrast, because it has an interior that is filled out with love, "speaks" the language of spousal love in unison with the soul, as a kind of "second dimension" of the act of love. The depth at which this act takes place—based on the unique structure of sexuality described above—means that a unique degree of reciprocal self-giving is accomplished, which is often referred to as a "consummation" of spousal love. Because of the inherent love meaning of this bodily act, it cannot be separated from this interior dimension without suffering violence.

All love is, at its heart, self-donation. Spousal self-donation takes on a particular, concrete nature or form, insofar as it incorporates the bodily dimension of the human person. But we must go further: the body augments the human act of love, adding something that it would otherwise not possess. Thus, we must say that the body "acts on" the soul, deepening both the reality and the experience of communion between the spouses. Benedict XVI refers to this marvelous exchange in *Deus caritas est*: "Christian faith ... has always considered man a unity in duality, a reality in which spirit and matter compenetrate, and in which each is brought to a new nobility."[14] The body also augments the fruitful dimension of the spouses' love, by allowing it to take the form of an entirely new being, a new human person.

We must note the significance of the fact that it is by means of just such an act that the human person is created. We are so accustomed to this that it no longer makes us pause. But it is not something that should be taken for granted—since God could have arranged for the creation of the human person to happen in any number of ways. In fact, however, a child is conceived in an act of love that takes place between the spouses, such that sex is not a "procreative faculty" in a straightforward manner, as it is in the animal world; rather, it is "spousal" by its very structure. John Paul writes:

> The human body, with its sex—its masculinity and femininity—seen in the very mystery of creation, is not only a source of fruitfulness and of procreation, as in the whole natural order, but contains "from the beginning" the "spousal" attribute, that is, the power to express love: precisely

---

[14] Benedict XVI, encyclical letter *Deus caritas est* (December 25, 2005), no. 5, http://w2.vatican.va/content/benedict-xvi/en/encyclicals/documents/hf_ben-xvi_enc_20051225_deus-caritas-est.html.

that love in which the human person becomes a gift and—through this gift—fulfills the very meaning of his being and existence.[15]　.

As spousal, the sexual act is an act of tremendous depth and significance for the spouses themselves, involving their most intimate being—it is the consummation of the longing for union to which their spousal love for one another has impelled them; it is an act in which it is imperative that the spouses be truly conscious and aware, and focused on one another in mutual self-giving. The full meaning of marriage is achieved in the family—that is, in the coming-to-be of a child; but what we are seeing here is that the whole situation is deeply defined by the fact that it is just such an act that is at the origin of the child's being. In the case of human generation, quite unlike animal generation, the coming-to-be of the child is the "outflow" of an act distinct from the event of its creation: an act between the spouses of mutual self-donation.[16]

In this concrete instantiation of love in its two dimensions, the mutual self-donation of the spouses that occurs in the marital act ends up simultaneously effecting the spouses' gift of self to the child—as the overflow of their union. And so the coming into being of the child is also the completion of the union between the spouses, insofar as the child is the highest instance of the fruitful dimension of their love. The union of the spouses flowers into a new being that is a "living reflection of their love, a permanent sign of conjugal unity".[17] As a new agent of love, drawn into and expanding the already existing circle of love between the spouses, the child is truly the "ultimate crown" of their union.[18] Having discovered this ultimate fruitfulness of the spousal act, we see that even if conception does not result from every act of intercourse, the full

---

[15] TOB 15:1.

[16] This is perhaps one of the reasons that the Church has never to my knowledge spoken of the parents as being required to aim at the coming into existence of the child, but only of the requirement for them to be open to its coming into existence. The argument of *Donum vitae* rests wholly on this dimension of procreation: that the conception of the child is not something that the parents "do", but a reality of which they are the recipients. See William May's insistence on this same point in "Begetting vs. Making Babies", Christendom Awake, November 14, 2004, christendom-awake.org/pages/may/begetting.htm#_ednref8.

[17] John Paul II, apostolic exhortation *Familiaris consortio* (November 22, 1981), no. 14, http://www.vatican.va/holy_father/john_paul_ii/apost_exhortations/documents/hf_jp-ii _exh_19811122_familiaris-consortio_en.html.

[18] Vatican Council II, Pastoral Constitution on the Church in the Modern World *Gaudium et spes* (December 7, 1965), no. 48, http://www.vatican.va/archive/hist_councils/ii_vatican _council/documents/vat-ii_cons_19651207_gaudium-et-spes_en.html.

meaning of the spousal exchange is found in the concept of parenthood. At the same time, we see how the spousal act, understood in this way, safeguards the love origin (required in justice) of the child.[19] The child is truly incorporated into the equation of love, as a kind of "incarnation" of the fruitfulness of the spouses' union with one another.

Here, in the fruitful dimension of love, as in the case of union, the body gives the spirit a new power: through it, the spouses can be co-creators with God the Father. The spirit is indeed "brought to a new nobility" through the human person's bodily being.

We said above that the love origin of the child is safeguarded by the fact that the act in which it is conceived is an act of love between the parents. Now we can add, it is this fact that is one important reason why the Church does not allow contraception. The coming into being of a child is organically connected to the union of the spouses: the child is the concrete embodiment of the fruitfulness of spousal love in this particular manifestation—that is, in its deepest, embodied manifestation. Just like all love, the marital act "embodies" both dimensions of love, the unitive and the fruitful. And it does so in an extraordinary fashion: the total self-giving found in the union between the spouses is absolutely unsurpassed by any other human relationship of love, and the fruitfulness characteristic of love is, in this case, the coming into being of an individual person with an immortal soul, a person in his own right. Even though God could have arranged matters differently, it is clear that there is a deep correlation between the kind of union of persons taking place in and through the bodily spousal act, and the kind of fruitfulness into which it flowers.

Once we have discovered the connection between spousal self-giving and its specific fruit in this particular incarnation of love, we see that to directly make impossible the overflowing of this expression of love into physical fruitfulness is to rend love asunder, and thus (to one degree or another) to destroy it. We have seen that union and fruitfulness are

---

[19] Safeguarding the love origin of the child is one of the main concerns expressed in *Donum vitae*: "In his unique and irrepeatable origin, the child must be respected and recognized as equal in personal dignity to those who give him life. The human person must be accepted in his parents' act of union and love; the generation of a child must therefore be the fruit of that mutual giving which is realized in the conjugal act wherein the spouses cooperate as servants and not as masters in the work of the Creator who is Love. In reality, the origin of a human person is the result of an act of giving. The one conceived must be the fruit of his parents' love" (II.B.4.c).

inseparably intertwined to make up the single reality of love. We have seen how embodied spousal love is a particular expression of this law of love: just as this act of union is wholly specific and concrete—in virtue of its bodily nature, of the special faculties employed, of its specific gestures, of its specific dynamism, of the specific spiritual and psychological experiences, of its tremendous depth—so also is the highest fruitfulness flowing from this union of a wholly specific nature. And so now we understand why the two cannot be directly separated from one another without both being undermined and destroyed. This is why earlier in the very same sentence in *Humanae vitae* in which the Church says that spouses *may not* on their own attempt to separate the union from the fruit, it first says that the connection between the two *cannot* be broken:

> The doctrine that the Magisterium of the Church has often explained is this: there is an unbreakable connection [*nexu indissolubili*] between the unitive meaning and the procreative meaning [of the conjugal act], and both are inherent in the conjugal act. This connection was established by God, and Man is not permitted to break it through his own volition.[20]

This implies that removing the fruitfulness is not to retain the union on its own, but it is also to destroy the union: because the two are organically connected, to remove one is to undo the whole.

Let us pause over this. Both dimensions of union and fruit are deeply related to the body: the body in its sexuality provides a new totality and depth of union, and the body in its fertility provides the possibility of a new person, a new immortal soul. Just as any union that rejects its specific fruit is by definition corrupted, so to make the marital act directly infertile is to give an infallible witness that the act was not entered into as an act of spousal union—that is, that the act was vacated of its intrinsic meaning. For this *particular* expression of love has tied to it this *particular* expression of fruitfulness, at least as its highest possibility. To attempt to separate the fruitfulness from the union is to witness that the bodily act, now vacated of its soul, was used as an instrument for the achievement of some end external to the act itself—perhaps pleasure or some other end.

The fact that the act is not in every individual instance fruitful in the highest possible way does not change things. Its "occasional" fruitfulness

---

[20] *HV*, no. 12, in Smith, Humanae Vitae: *A Challenge to Love*, p. 550.

in this particular way has to do with the particular conditions of human fertility—one of them being the direct action of God in creating the soul; another is the bodily rhythms that God put in place by his free decision, or even the fact that some people's reproductive faculties do not function well or at all because of a defect, disease, or age. But the fact that the conditions of fertility make it so that not every act culminates in conception in no way obscures the deep connection between the union, and the fruitfulness, and its moral implications.

Conclusion

While *Humanae vitae* reaffirmed the age-old doctrine of the Church on the generation of human life, it offered something new in casting the teaching in terms of the inseparable connection between the marital act in its two dimensions of union and fruitfulness. What I have done in these reflections is to bring out the personalist metaphysics of the marital act underlying this new cast of the old doctrine, and in doing so, have offered a strong defense against the charge that this teaching is biologistic. While participating in some way in the rhythms of the natural world, the internal form of human sexuality is not that of animal nature; rather, insofar as human sexuality is just that—*human*—it is structured from within to be an embodiment of the personal reality of spousal love. The marital act, then, "repeats" in an incarnated way the reality of love, and as such, it is governed by the law of love. So while the specific fruitfulness of the act certainly depends on the contribution of the body, the marital act is far from being merely biological; it is spousal love become incarnate. This means, firstly, that its procreative capacity follows from its unitive character, and secondly, that the moral norms surrounding it arise from the moral norms proper to love itself. When the Church forbids contraception, it is not on the grounds of the marital act's sheer biological ordination to generation, but on the grounds that this ordination is an expression of a spiritual reality—the reality of love—that may not be rent asunder. And so Paul VI writes in *Humanae vitae* that only "if both essential meanings [*ratio*] are preserved, that of union and procreation, the marital act fully maintains its capacity for [fostering] true mutual love".[21]

[21] Ibid.

Why Natural Sex Is Best[*]

Janet E. Smith, Ph.D.

Mankind has always used a variety of expressions for the act of sexual intercourse—some technical, some romantic, some euphemistic, some crude. The documents of the Catholic Church rarely speak of "having sex" or "sexual intercourse"; they speak of "conjugal acts", and perhaps a more modern translation would speak of "marital acts". Certainly the Church knows that couples have sex outside of marriage, but clearly for the Church the act of sexual intercourse is properly understood as an act belonging within marriage and thus has its name or designation from its proper context. Our culture no longer thinks of sex as properly confined to marriage and thus finds the phrases "conjugal acts" or "marital acts" peculiar and antiquated.

In the not-so-distant past, society employed the euphemism "making love" for "having sex". How sad that it has disappeared, for clearly it discloses another element that properly belongs to the act of having sex also forgotten by our culture—that the act of having sex ought to be an expression of love, not just an act that satisfies a physical desire. But, in fact, the signification of the phrase "making love" for "having sex" was in itself a diminution of its meaning; in Victorian novels the phrase referred to the sweet talk engaged in by a young man who was wooing a young woman. Indeed, it was not so long ago that we spoke of the relationships of those who were unmarried but "having sex" as a "free love relationship", a phrase one no longer hears, I suspect, since we now know very well that most such relationships have a fairly tenuous relationship with love.

[*] This essay was originally delivered as "Why Aquinas Thinks Natural Sex Is Best" (lecture, Center for Thomistic Studies' Aquinas Lecture, University of St. Thomas, Houston, January 2003); it was adapted for the Aquinas-Luther Conference at Lenoir-Rhyne College, October 2004.

And isn't it sad that we no longer speak of wooing or courting! The scenarios in Victorian novels that have a young man desperately trying to get a private moment with the object of his affection in a busy parlor room, or on a stroll in the countryside in the midst of a whole party of individuals, evoke a time when individuals were expected to get to know each other as persons—to discover their characters and commitments— long before the sexual relations began, which was supposed to be after the marriage vows were spoken. Persons were supposed to be relating to persons rather than bodies to bodies. And thus they made love in the conversational sense before they made love in the physical sense. Now people have sex before they know each other's last names! Teenagers speak of "friends with benefits"[1]—sexual partners for whom they do not have and do not want any emotional attachment, so far are they from associating sex from love.

There seem to be fewer and fewer boundaries in respect to sexuality in the modern age; a wide variety of kinds of sex are freely discussed nearly everywhere and portrayed in various degrees of explicitness in the media. Our age prides itself on its liberation about sexual matters, but there is considerable evidence that personal happiness has not been much advanced through the sexual license we now permit ourselves. There is one kind of sex that receives less and less attention, and that is what I want to call natural sex—that is, sex between a male and female who believe that sexual intercourse belongs only within marriage, is an expression of committed and unconditional love, and welcomes the natural outcome of children. I am going to argue that this is the best sex, certainly in terms of morality but also, perhaps surprisingly to some, the best sex in terms of the most satisfying sex. Since the procreative meaning is particularly rejected in our contraceptive age, I am going to emphasize that meaning but will show its centrality to the full human meaning of the act of sexual intercourse.

And to speak to a very hot topic: our disregard for the procreative meaning of sexual intercourse greatly contributes to the movement in our culture to make marriage a possibility between homosexuals. I sus- pect that until we begin to give greater respect to the procreative mean- ing of sexual intercourse, those of us who want to defend the claim that

[1] Benoit Denizet-Lewis, "Friends, Friends with Benefits and the Benefits of the Local Mall", *New York Times Magazine*, May 30, 2004.

marriage is properly only between one man and one woman will not be successful—if sex is primarily for pleasure or for overcoming loneliness and experiencing intimacy, an argument can be made that the procreative element is irrelevant and not defining of the sexual relationship, and thus heterosexuality is not essential for marriage. Here I am going to explore some thoughts of Aquinas and Luther on the subject of the importance of the procreative meaning of the sexual act.

So why turn to Aquinas and Luther for a way out of this morass? Although there were significant theological differences between them, they were certainly united in their view that the procreative meaning of the sexual act is central to its meaning and to its moral assessment. The primary emphasis here will be on Aquinas, since I know his work best, but I shall make reference to some writings of Luther as well, to hear from another influential Christian voice. Luther was a happily married man, father of six children, and thus lived out the message he taught—so did Aquinas, but as a virtuous celibate. The one story from Aquinas' life that bears upon his sexual behavior is that of his brothers trying to destroy his vocation by sending a prostitute to his room. Aquinas is reported to have chased her from the room with a torch. I heard one individual interpret this story as indicating that Aquinas was a homosexual—that otherwise he surely would have given into the temptation. I think it proves he was not a homosexual but rather a man of healthy heterosexual desires; otherwise, he would have invited her to sit down and have a glass of wine. But why would a healthy heterosexual not take advantage of the situation? A man seeking to be moral would know such an encounter was not true to the natural purpose and meaning of human sexual intercourse; that he would be exploiting the prostitute; that he would not be acting in a loving fashion; that the act was neither in accord with his dignity nor hers; that he would be harming any child conceived through the action; that he would be violating God's will; that he would be sinning.

Aquinas discussed sexual ethics almost entirely in the context of marriage;[2] all sexual sins are essentially sins against the good of marriage. Momentarily we shall focus on Aquinas' insistence that for sexual intercourse to be moral, full respect must be given to the procreative meaning

---

[2] He has fairly lengthy discussion of marriage in *Summa theologica* III, suppl., qq. 41–68; and in the *Summa contra gentiles* 3.122–26. Hereafter the *Summa theologica* will be cited as *ST*; *Summa contra gentiles*, *SCG*.

of the sexual act. Here let us briefly consider the other two goods that
Aquinas believes are the goods of marriage. Aquinas spoke of fidelity
as an end and good of marriage—which means that one man and one
woman remain faithful to each other throughout the marriage, a good
that both enables them to develop fully as persons and that enables them
to fulfill well the duties of parenthood. The other good of marriage is
that it is a sacramental sign; it images the union of Christ and his Church
in its indissolubility—marriage is an act of committed and unconditional
love. In fact, although Aquinas speaks of children as the *essential* end of
marriage, he identifies the sacrament as the most important and most
excellent end of marriage.[3]

Aquinas defines marriage in this way: "Matrimony consists in a certain inseparable union of souls, by which husband and wife are pledged
by a bond of mutual affection that cannot be sundered."[4] He states:
"The union of husband and wife by matrimony is the greatest of all
unions, since it is a union of soul and body, wherefore it is called a
conjugal union."[5] While Aquinas accepts the dictum of Scripture that
the husband should be the head of the household, he repeatedly speaks
of a kind of natural equity in marriage, and even more importantly he
speaks of the loving relationship between the spouses. He uses the word
amicitia, customarily translated as "friendship". *Amicitia*, however, should
perhaps, in many contexts, be translated as "loving relationship", for it
has the word *amor* or "love" at its base. *Amicitia* can be a very elevated
relationship—it is precisely the relationship that man seeks to have with
God. About the spousal *amicitia*, Aquinas states:

> The greater the loving relationship [*amicitia*], the more need for it to be
> firm and lasting. But the loving relationship [*amicitia*] of man and woman
> is the greatest of all; seeing that they are united, not only in the sexual
> act, which even among beasts makes a sweet partnership, but also for the
> sharing in common of all domestic life, as a sign whereof a man leaves
> even father and mother for the sake of his wife (Gen. 2:24). It is fitting
> therefore for marriage to be completely indissoluble.[6]

---

[3] *ST* III, suppl., q. 49, a. 3, resp.

[4] *ST* III, q. 29, a. 2, resp, in St. Thomas Aquinas, *Summa theologica*, trans. Fathers of the
English Dominican Province (New York: Benziger, 1948).

[5] *ST* III, suppl., q. 44, a. 2, ad. 3, my translation.

[6] *SCG* 3.123, my translation.

Aquinas believes that nature, the nature of human relationships that includes the need for lifetime companionship, requires that marriage be indissoluble. But Aquinas also notes, of course, that divine law, or revelation, also dictates that marriage should be indissoluble, because it images Christ's indissoluble union with his Church:

> But since it is necessary that all other things be ordered to that which is best in man, the union of male and female should be ordered according to law not only because it is right from the view of offspring, just as among other animals, but also it must ordered for the sake of good morals [mores], which right reason orders either to the individual man or to man insofar as he is a part of a household or a part of civil society.[7]

What he is saying here is that the indissolubility of marriage not only benefits the children; it also benefits the spouses, the family, and society at large. And in speaking about indissolubility, he reveals that, for a monk quite cloistered in the academy, he had a surprising understanding of some of the practical dimensions of marriage. He states:

> The indissolubility of the union of male and female pertains to good morals since the love they will have for one another will be more faithful since they will know that they are indissolubly united. Each partner will be more solicitous for household matters, since they will remain in the possession of these things. The sources of discord between a man and his wife's relatives are removed, which might arise if a husband should divorce his wife; rather a stronger love grows between the relatives. Also, the occasions for adultery are removed, which would happen if a man were able to divorce his wife or she him.[8]

In fact, Aquinas evinces sensitivity to the needs of women. In speaking against polygamy, he states:

> Friendship [amicitia] consists in a certain equality. Therefore if it is not permitted to a woman to have many husbands because this makes paternity uncertain, it should not be permitted to a man to have many wives for then the friendship [amicitia] would not be of a free woman with her

[7] Ibid.
[8] Ibid.

husband, but rather like that of a slave. Reason and experience agree on this point; that when men have many wives, the wives are treated like servants. And furthermore, intense friendship [*intensa amicitia*] towards many is not possible.... If therefore a wife has only one husband, and her husband has many wives, there will not be an equal friendship [*amicitia*] between them. It will not be a free friendship [*amiticia*] but will in some respect be servile.[9]

He goes on to say that there will also be discord in society if a man has many wives.

Aquinas did not think it right that a wife be a menial servant to her husband; she is a free person as well as he and deserves his respect. In fact, Aquinas views marriage, in a sense, as designed to meet the needs of a mother; when answering the question whether matrimony is fittingly named, he speculates, among other possibilities, that it may be derived from "*matris munium*" or the munus or mission of a mother or from "*matrem muniens*", which would refer to the husband's obligation to provide for and protect the mother.[10]

When speaking of the spouses responding to the request for love-making, he notes that it is more in the nature of the male to initiate, and thus wives need not try to anticipate their husband's desires but may wait for a request to be made. On the other hand, he says it is more difficult for women to make the request and that the husband should be attentive to his wife, and make love to her when he understands that that is what she so desires, even though she does not ask.[11] He also speaks against too vehement lovemaking by the husband, whereby the husband treats his wife more as a concubine than a wife.[12]

Nor, of course, does Aquinas ignore the pleasure-giving power of sexual intercourse; largely, he worries about it because after the Fall it is so disordered that it is likely to lead us to sin and irrational behavior, but he does not think that sexual intercourse in itself is sinful in spite of the fact that those participating in it generally do lose use of their reason![13] In fact, Aquinas thinks God attached pleasure to sexual intercourse so

[9] Ibid., 3.124, my translation.
[10] *ST* III, suppl., q. 44, a. 2, resp.
[11] Ibid., q. 64, a. 5, ad. 2.
[12] Ibid., q. 49, a. 6, resp., and ad 1 and 3.
[13] *SCG* 3.126; *ST* III, suppl., q. 49, a. 1.

that we would be enticed to marry,[14] and that Adam and Eve would have had sublimely pleasurable sex because it would have been without any disordered elements.[15] These nuggets are interspersed throughout his writings—writings, again, that contain no in-depth treatment of all the dimensions of marriage.

Now let us see how Aquinas understands responsibility toward children to be a fundamental criterion for determining the morality of sexual behavior and the meaning of marriage. Anyone reading Aquinas' writings on sex and marriage will be struck by the emphasis that he puts on the good of children—indeed, he referenced the procreative meaning of sexuality in every discussion on sexual morality; he found it foundational for condemning such actions as masturbation, fornication, acts of homosexual intercourse, and adultery as well. As Aquinas states repeatedly: "In relation to marriage a thing is said to be contrary to the natural law if it prevents marriage from reaching the end for which it was instituted. Now the essential and primary end of marriage is the good of the offspring."[16] In Aquinas' view, respecting the procreative meaning of sexual intercourse would save one from almost every other sexual sin.

Some critics of Aquinas' view of marriage argue that he depended too much upon the likeness of human sex with animal sex to explain the purposes of marriage. They believe that Aquinas held Ulpian's view of nature—that nature is what human beings share with animals, and that since animal sex is for reproduction of the species, human sex is also for the reproduction of the species. Aquinas certainly evoked that principle numerous times, but he made it his own. He emphatically distinguished the purpose of human sexual intercourse from animal sexual intercourse, and he repeatedly stated that nature disposes each animal to its proper work in accord with its species or nature.[17] As Aquinas himself notes, obviously the numerical reproduction of the human species could take place outside of the institution of marriage; yet for human beings that would not be fitting, since a child needs the attention and guidance of

[14] *ST* III, suppl., q. 49, a. 1, ad 1.

[15] *ST* I, q. 98, ad 3.

[16] *ST* III, suppl., q. 54, a. 3, resp.

[17] See, for instance, *ST* III, suppl., q. 54, a. 3, ad 3 and 65; *SCG* 124; Aquinas, *Quaestiones disputatae de malo*, q. 15.

both his parents—thus only marriage protects the good of the child.[18] Thus, what nature teaches human beings about sexuality would be different from what it teaches other animals.

Aquinas establishes the end of *human* sexual intercourse precisely by *distinguishing* it from animal intercourse; the initial point of contrast is that human offspring require a much different upbringing than offspring of other species. In the *Summa contra gentiles* he notes that

> we must take into consideration that among animals in which the female alone suffices for the education of the offspring, male and female do not remain together after the sexual act, as is evident among dogs. Among animals in which the female does not suffice for the education of the offspring, male and female remain together after the sexual act as long as is necessary for the education and instruction of the offspring, as is the case among certain birds.[19]

He notes that male birds have a natural instinct to provide food for the young while the female keeps them warm. He then states, "It is clear that in the human species the female alone does not suffice for the education of the offspring, since the necessities of human life requires many things which are not able to be supplied through one person alone. Therefore it is fitting for human nature that the husband remain with his wife after the sexual act and that he not immediately depart, connecting up with anyone he meets, as happens with fornicators."[20]

He goes on: "And further we must take into account that in the human species, offspring not only need nutrition for the body, as do other animals, but also needs instruction for the soul. For other animals naturally have their own 'wisdom' [*suas prudentias*] by which they provide for themselves, man however lives through reason, which in order to achieve wisdom [*prudentiam*] needs experience over a long time; thus it is necessary that children be instructed by their parents, as by experts."[21] Moreover, "because of the impulses of the passions, by which the judgment of prudence is corrupted, there is need not only of instruction, but also of discipline. For this, the female alone does not

---

[18] *ST* III, suppl., q. 54, a. 3, ad. 3 and 65.
[19] *SCG* 3.122.6, my translation.
[20] Ibid.
[21] Ibid., 3.122.8.

suffice, but at this point especially the work of the male is necessary, in whom there is reason more perfect for instruction and more powerful strength for chastisement."[22] Nor is the education that is to be provided simply an education that enables the children to be successful in this world; rather, he states: "The chief good of marriage is the offspring to be brought up to the worship of God.... Education is the work of father and mother in common."[23]

Now we may not like the claim that men have "reason more perfect to instruct" (though we must note that he speaks of *both* the father and the mother providing religious instruction); in fact, there are several statements in Aquinas that would offend modern sensibilities concerning women, and I am neither going to try to excuse them nor justify them, since that would be too burdensome for my narrative. Thus I will sidestep these challenging passages, most of them, by the way, based on Scripture.

There is a hidden premise in Aquinas' insistence that the chief good of marriage is children. Remember that Aquinas holds that every human being has an immortal soul individually created by God;[24] spouses are, as various Church documents state, co-creators with God.[25] Surely that is a lofty task and not one at all on the animal level. Human parents are not just breeders of the next generation; they are partners with God in bringing forth creatures made in the image and likeness of God and destined for eternal union with God.

So Aquinas might be right to justify various features of sexual morality and marriage by reference to what will benefit children—fornication and adultery are wrong because children are not benefited by being born out of wedlock; polygamy is wrong because children are not benefited by being the children of a man with many wives, for those relationships won't be harmonious; children are not benefited by divorce because they are deprived of the instruction of both parents (we can easily show that poverty and psychological instability and even crime are increased by divorce); children are not benefited by coerced marriages for these lead

[22] Ibid.

[23] *ST* III, suppl., q. 59.

[24] See, for instance, *SCG* 4.82.

[25] See, for instance, John Paul II, *Evangelium vitae* (March 25, 1995), no. 43, http:// w2.vatican.va/content/john-paul-ii/en/encyclicals/documents/hf_jp-ii_enc_25031995 _evangelium-vitae.html.

to unstable marriages; mixed marriages are problematic because children are not benefited by parents who do not share the same faith. While modern social sciences abundantly verify Aquinas' belief that children benefit enormously from stable monogamous marriages,[26] the principle is so widely violated in our culture that it sometimes seems children are of minimal concern to those having sex. I now work in the astonishing city of Detroit, Michigan, where 76 percent of all babies are born out of wedlock.[27] And, of course, fatherless homes are the greatest predicators of children being involved in premarital sex, drugs, and crime, as well as of being sexually abused, living in poverty, and suffering from depression and other psychological disorders.

Aquinas is known as a natural law ethicist—and while the essential core of natural law is that man must live in accord with his being a rational creature, part of being a natural law ethicist is believing that our natural inclinations, the bodily ones as well as the spiritual ones, are basically good—that it is wise for us to seek to satisfy our natural desires but that we must do so in accord with right reason, that is, in accord with the full or integral human good. In fact, he believes that we have a natural inclination to order all of our desires, even our sexual desires, and that is undoubtedly true; for absolutely no one acts on every sexual desire—otherwise, elevators would be very unsafe places.

Students sometimes ask how we know what the purpose of sex is. That question has always struck me as strange: Aquinas did not just sit in some remote room pondering abstract concepts in his mind and thus arbitrarily assign procreation to sex as its purpose or even simply deduce it to be so from some predetermined principles! Generally we learn what something is by what it does. We know that a match ignites gasoline because we have seen it happen. As Aquinas says, operation

---

[26] For modern verification of these claims see "The Moynihan Report 50 Years Later: Why Marriage More than Even Promotes Opportunity for All", Heritage Foundation, March 27, 2018, https://www.heritage.org/marriage-and-family/report/the-moynihan-report-50-years-later-why-marriage-more-ever-promotes; and William J. Bennett, *The Index of Leading Cultural Indicators: American Society at the End of the 20th Century*, updated and expanded ed. (New York: Broadway Books; Colorado Springs: WaterBrook Press, 1999). For an online source of professional studies, see Marripedia, http://marri.us/.

[27] Julie Mack, "Which Michigan County Ranks No. 1 in Births to Unmarried Women?", MLive, November 28, 2017, http://www.mlive.com/news/index.ssf/2017/11/which_michigan_counties_have_h.html.

follows being; or we might say function follows form. If an animal barks, it is likely a dog; if a plant produces a tomato, it is a tomato plant; babies are conceived as a result of sexual intercourse; ergo, that is one of the purposes of sexual intercourse. It has other purposes as well, but the casual disregard that our culture has for the procreative meaning of sex and indeed its hostility to the good of children has many wanting to dismiss or ignore or eliminate the procreative power from sexual intercourse. Those who might have an enthusiastic response to such a power are considered somewhat bizarre—they seem to be expected to respond to the question "Sure, have your one or two children, but why should the possibility of children be the defining feature of sex, the one that makes marriage a necessary arrangement for responsible sexual intercourse, that should guide one's selection of a spouse and that necessitates one remaining married to the same person for a lifetime?" If those are the requirements of marriage, it is thought, surely they must have a basis other than the good of children, for that simply is not a sufficiently important good to justify the restraint of human sexual desires. Again, let us note that Aquinas was not focused on simply raising a human child to adulthood so that the species could be further propagated. Rather, he understood each human being to be destined for eternal union with God, and the role of parents was to advance their children on that journey, not just to raise them successfully to adulthood.

In fact, Aquinas raises the question whether a marriage can dissolve once the children are grown, and his answer to that question discloses another feature of marriage of constant interest to him, as he explains the need for indissolubility for marriage. Some of these statements may seem a bit outrageous, but they are proffered in a context where a whole list of reasons is being given for the indissolubility of marriage, so we should not take any one reason as *the* reason. He states: "Woman is taken into partnership with man for the need of childbearing: therefore when the fertility and beauty of woman ceases, there is a bar against her being taken up by another man. If then a man, taking a woman to wife in the time of her youth, when beauty and fertility wait upon her, could send her away when she was advanced in years, he would do the woman harm, contrary to natural equity," and further, "if the man were allowed to desert the woman, the partnership of man and woman would not be on fair terms, but would be a sort of slavery on the woman's side."[28] Aquinas is definitely against a husband abandoning the wife that put him through law school for a "trophy bride" in middle age.

Several centuries later, Luther, in his "Estate of Marriage", repeatedly extols the centrality of children to marriage. For instance, in part 3, he states:

> But the greatest good in married life, that which makes all suffering and labour worth while, is that God grants offspring and commands that they be brought up to worship and serve him. In all the world this is the noblest and most precious work, because to God there can be nothing dearer than the salvation of souls.[29]

Elsewhere he states:

> You will find many to whom a large number of children is unwelcome, as though marriage had been instituted only for bestial pleasures and not also for the very valuable work by which we serve God and men when we train and educate the children whom God has given us. They do not appreciate the most pleasant feature of marriage. For what exceeds the love of children?[30]

> The purpose of marriage is not to have pleasure and to be idle but to procreate and bring up children, to support a household ... those who have no love for children are swine, stocks, and logs unworthy of being

---

[28] "The reason why a wife is not allowed more than one husband at a time is because otherwise paternity would be uncertain. If then while the wife has one husband only, the husband has more than one wife, there will not be a friendship of equality on both sides, friendship consisting in a certain equality. There will not be the friendship of a free man with a free woman, but a sort of friendship of a slave with her master. The husband might well be allowed a plurality of wives, if the understanding were allowable, that the friendship of each with him was not to be that of a free woman with a free man but of a slave with her master. And this is borne out by experience: for among men that keep many wives the wives are counted as menials" (*SCG* 3.124).

[29] Martin Luther, "The Estate of Marriage", in *Luther's Works: The Christian in Society II*, vol. 45, trans. Walther I. Brandt (1522; Philadelphia: Fortress Press, 1962), https://www.1215 .org/lawnotes/misc/marriage/martin-luther-estate-of-marriage.pdf, p. 14.

[30] From Ewald M. Plass, *What Luther Says: An Anthology*, 2 vols. (St. Louis: Concordia Publishing House, 1959), 2:2834.

called men and women; for they despise the blessing of God, the Creator and Author of marriage[31]

(Luther has rightly earned his reputation for rhetorical flare!) There are some delicious nuggets in Luther's treatment of marriage as well. While he denied that marriage was a sacrament, he thought it was clearly instituted by God for divine purposes. There are some passages in his "Estate of Marriage" that indicate he had a marvelous notion of the mutuality and equality between husband and wife. He rebukes the husband who chafes at rocking the baby, washing its diapers, making its bed, smelling its stench, staying up nights with it, taking care of it when it cries, healing its rashes and sores, and on top of that caring for his wife and making a living.[32] He then provides a rendition of what someone with faith would say:

> O God, because I am certain that thou hast created me as a man and hast from my body begotten this child, I also know for a certainty that it meets with thy perfect pleasure. I confess to thee that I am not worthy to rock the little babe or wash its diapers. or to be entrusted with the care of the child and its mother. How is it that I, without any merit, have come to this distinction of being certain that I am serving thy creature and thy most precious will? O how gladly will I do so, though the duties should be even more insignificant and despised. Neither frost nor heat, neither drudgery nor labour, will distress or dissuade me, for I am certain that it is thus pleasing in thy sight.[33]

Lest we think Luther is not serious, he makes the point again:

> Now you tell me, when a father goes ahead and washes diapers or performs some other mean task for his child, and someone ridicules him as an effeminate fool, though that father is acting in the spirit just described and in Christian faith, my dear fellow you tell me, which of the two is most keenly ridiculing the other? God, with all his angels and creatures, is smiling, not because that father is washing diapers, but because he is

---

[31] *Lectures on Genesis: Chapters 26–30*; V, 325–28; vol. 28, 279; commentary on the birth of Joseph to Jacob and Rachel; vol. 45, 39–40, in *Luther's Works*, American edition, ed. Jaroslav Pelikan (vols. 1–30) and Helmut T. Lehmann (vols. 31–55) (St. Louis: Concordia Publishing House [vols. 1–30]; Philadelphia: Fortress Press [vols. 31–55], 1955). V, 325–28; vol. 28, 279.

[32] Luther, "Estate of Marriage", online.

[33] Ibid.

doing so in Christian faith. Those who sneer at him and see only the task but not the faith are ridiculing God with all his creatures, as the biggest fool on earth. Indeed, they are only ridiculing themselves; with all their cleverness they are nothing but devil's fools.[34]

Luther also admonishes a man whose wife becomes an invalid to care for her as if she were the Lord himself.[35] Thus, we see that Luther, in addition to valuing the inestimable good of children, evinces a portrait of marriage that resembles a wonderful friendship wherein the duties of child-rearing are shared.

What we are exploring here is the concern that those engaging in sexual intercourse must look to what is good for offspring. So how do we know what is good for offspring? In nearly every culture in the history of mankind, it has been believed, on the basis of experience, observation, the collected wisdom of the culture, and good common sense, that children are served best when raised by a mother and a father. There certainly are times and places where other arrangements have been pursued, and significant evidence that when that happens considerable damage has been done to children; one might think of boarding schools in England or some use of daycare centers in the United States.

We in the modern age have ways of studying the world called the "social sciences" and "psychological sciences", which indeed do help us have a fuller understanding, usually a quantitative measuring, of what we might learn by other means as well. It is not difficult to find nearly daily in the media reports of studies that quite massively support many of the conclusions that Aquinas draws. Failing to respect the procreative power of sexual intercourse has led to sex outside of marriage that in turn has led to unwed pregnancy; abortion; sexually transmitted diseases; one out of three children born out of wedlock; the poverty and social chaos resulting from single parenthood; the heartbreak and alienation of failed relationships and divorce; increased infertility; recourse to artificial means of reproduction with the consequence of "excess embryos" that are presenting a fierce temptation to research scientists—I could go on and on.[36]

---

[34] Ibid.

[35] Ibid.

[36] For good data and good analysis of the data on these issues, see Janet Smith's talk "Contraception: Cracking the Myths", Augustine Institute, accessed June 5, 2018, https://www.lighthousecatholicmedia.org/store/title/contraception-cracking-the-myths.

Those who have lived the morality of sex that the procreative meaning requires generally fare fairly well. We learn that teenagers who refrain from sex have a better chance of completing high school and going to college; couples who abstain before marriage have longer lasting and happier marriages than those who do not; couples who do not cohabit before marriage have longer lasting and happier marriages than those who do; couples who are faithful in marriage have longer lasting and happier marriages than those who are not; couples who share a faith commitment and practice it have long-lasting and happier marriages than those who do not;[37] couples who use natural family planning almost never divorce[38]—I could go on and on but you get the picture. Living by the morals that Aquinas and Luther discovered in fact turns out to be the surest predictor of a long-lasting and happy marriage. What is good for the children turns out to be good for the spouses.

Aquinas himself would likely have found the social and psychological sciences very useful, for, as I stated, he did not deduce moral teachings from some abstract notion of human nature; rather, he thought we needed to be attentive to our natural inclinations, our reflection on experience, and accumulated wisdom. Perhaps he would have found of some special interest the recent work of Lionel Tiger, the Charles Darwin Professor of Anthropology at Rutgers, who has written the fascinating book *The Decline of Males*. Tiger is aptly named for the line of work that he is in—that is, anthropological studies that involve the study of animal behavior as a way of understanding human behavior. The *Decline of Males* seeks to explain the increased withdrawal of men from the family; Tiger identifies contraception as one of the chief culprits. Likely not

---

[37] Support for these claims can be found in Edward O. Laumann et al., *The Social Organization of Sexuality: Sexual Practices in the United States* (Chicago: University of Chicago Press, 1994). For instance, it states, "For both genders, we find that the virgins have dramatically more stable first marriages" (p. 503). "Those who frequently attend religious services are only about half as likely to separate" (p. 501). "If the couple differed by religious preference, they were more than twice as likely to separate" (p. 502). "Those who have vaginal intercourse relatively early or have sex before a marriage are those who enter a partnership at an early age, are more likely to enter an informal cohabitational partnership, and are more likely to separate or divorce" (p. 505). For some interesting statistics on divorce, see "U.S. Divorce Statistics: Divorce and Marriage Rates in the U.S. for 2002", DivorceMagazine.com, updated July 13, 2015, http://www.divorcemag.com/statistics/statsUS.shtml.

[38] See Mercedes Arzu Wilson, "The Practice of Natural Family Planning versus the Use of Artificial Birth Control: Family, Sexual and Moral Issues", *Catholic Social Science Review* 7 (November 2002): 185–211.

an avowed Aristotelian-Thomist, Tiger employs Aristotelian-Thomistic principles, one of which is that our bodies are reliable readers of reality. Tiger notes that our hormones actually help us respond well to reality and thus reasons that the use of hormonal contraceptives may well skew our responses to reality. He believes that males are more attracted and attached to females who are fertile, and he used as one of his justifications for this claim a study that was done on monkeys. He reports of a tribe of monkeys where the lead monkey, dubbed Austin, had his pick of the females.[39] Austin chose three females to be exclusively his sexual partners. The researchers noted that he had a grand time with these three. After months of observing Austin have abundant sexual activity with the chosen ones, the researchers injected the favored females with Depo-Provera, a chemical contraceptive given by injection. Austin was no longer interested in sexual intercourse with them but chose new sexual partners who had not been contracepted. When the first group of selected females came off the Depo-Provera, Austin resumed interest in his original choices. Three months later the researchers put all the females on contraception, and Austin began "to attempt rape, masturbate, and behave in a turbulent and confused manner".[40] When the contraceptives wore off, Austin resumed normal sexual relations with the female. Might some of the hunger for pornography and perverse sexual behavior be at least partially traced to the fact that few men are having sexual intercourse with fertile females and thus are not truly having their sexual desires satisfied? Might the phenomenal success of natural family planning marriages be explained in part, at least, by the fact that males are in the presence of females with their fertile hormones intact and thus may be having more satisfying sexual relations?

Consider another study Tiger cites. He tells of women not using contraceptives who "ranked the desirability of an anonymous array of smells taken from male clothing. They preferred the scents of men socially regarded as desirable potential mates."[41] A group of women using contraceptives, however, "reversed their preferences and chose inappropriate partners."[42] Tiger concludes, "In a sense there was no point for them

---

[39] Lionel Tiger, *The Decline of Males* (New York: Golden Books, 1999), pp. 37ff.
[40] Ibid., p. 40.
[41] Ibid., p. 42.
[42] Ibid., p. 43.

to select promising progenitors because they were already pregnant. The subtle system of selection had shut down. New rules prevailed."[43] Might this evidence help explain why so many good men say they have trouble attracting women and so many women seem to prefer losers? Women with their fertile hormones repressed are impaired in their judgments of males.

I think contraception diminishes the pleasure of sex not only for physiological reasons but also for psychological reasons. Since most individuals engage in sex before marriage, the meaning and importance of sexual intercourse has been diminished—especially for those who were promiscuous, sex was something that was done casually and without commitment—how now can it be a sign of commitment? Furthermore, one of the justifications for the use of contraception is that it would increase the pleasure of sex if the anxiety concerning a possible unwelcome pregnancy were removed. I think there is evidence that removing the procreative power of the sexual act diminishes the meaning of the act and reduces the pleasure. In fact, I suspect too few modern Americans have an extended experience of what Aquinas would call "natural sex"—again, that is, sex between a male and female who are committed to each other and who are open to children, and would welcome many children as a gift from God. There is much evidence that indicates that for most people nearly all the sex they have had has been contracepted (or sterilized) sex—people contracept before marriage and after marriage; they stop for a short period of time to conceive a child; they contracept again, then they stop for another short period of time to conceive another child, and then they get sterilized. Now, it is worth pondering that possibly the sex that they had during the times they were trying to conceive was in fact the sex that they experienced as the most meaningful and even most pleasurable. Making babies enhances making love. At least anecdotally, I have heard that such is the case.

That such is the most pleasurable sex might seem counterintuitive to many who believe the procreative power of sex to be a cruel appendage to the act of sexual intercourse. They may argue that the contraceptive sex they have is terrifically pleasurable. But they have nothing against which to test this claim. Much like those who have not cultivated a taste for wine may not appreciate fine wine, or those who have eaten only

43 Ibid.

hothouse tomatoes may not know the incredible taste of a vine-ripened tomato, those who have had their understanding and appreciation of sex shaped by the concept that contraception is beneficial to sex simply have no basis for comparison.

At any rate, there seems to be some interesting modern evidence that disregard of the procreative power of sexual intercourse impacts relationships negatively between the sexes, something that Aquinas would expect.

Luther, too, was a strong opponent of contracepted sex. Luther is known for the perhaps excessive fervor of his views, and we find some true fervor in his evaluation of Onan, who spilled his seed rather than father a child by his dead brother's wife, as he was obliged to do under Jewish law (Gen 38:8–10). Luther asserts that "surely ... the order of nature established by God in procreation should be followed." In fact, Luther claimed that what Onan did "was a sin far greater than adultery or incest, and it provoked God to such fierce wrath that he destroyed him immediately".[44] In fact, Luther was so enthusiastic about the act of bringing forth children that he seems to be what in Catholic circles is called a providentialist—this means that spouses should not in any way attempt to control or limit their family size; rather, they should just let the babies come, even if this means great financial worry or threatens a woman's life or health.[45] Luther did not think that babies being a threat to one's health or life was reason to limit childbearing; he stated: "Those who are fruitful, however, are healthier, cleanlier, and happier. And even if they bear themselves weary, or ultimately bear themselves out that does not hurt. Let them bear themselves out. This is the purpose for which they exist. It is better to have a brief life with good health than a long life in ill health."[46] Nor did he think fear of financial worries sufficient reason to limit family: "A young man should marry at the age of twenty at the latest, a young woman at fifteen to eighteen; that's when they are still in good health and best suited for marriage. Let God worry about how they and their children are to be fed. God makes children; he will surely also feed them."[47] I doubt that Luther was truly indifferent to the physical and financial hardships that having children can present;

---

[44] Martin Luther, *Letters on Genesis, Chapters 38–44* (1544), in *Luther's Works*, vol. 7, 20–22.
[45] Luther, "The Estate of Marriage", online.
[46] Ibid.
[47] Ibid.

rather, I think his purpose here is to stress the goodness of having children and the sometimes great demands of being radically committed to doing God's will.

Now let's move to the question of marriages for homosexual couples. Aquinas' condemnation of homosexual sexual intercourse was also based upon his understanding of sex as being ordained to procreation. He certainly would have agreed with the shorthand, sound-bite evaluation of homosexuality: the claim that "the parts don't fit". That would be many parts—surely the genitals, but also that the sperm does not meet its natural mate, the egg, and males who cannot provide psychological complementarity with males or females with females.

Some want to argue that since many advocates of marriage allow the infertile and those past childbearing age to marry, that means that the procreative meaning of sexual intercourse is not in fact essential to it. How is homosexual sex different from the sex of heterosexuals who are infertile? They will also argue that because Aquinas respected nature, he should have allowed for homosexual relations since some people are born with homosexual tendencies, and, in fact, homosexual sexual intercourse exists in the world of nature—some animals evidently engage in homosexual sexual intercourse.[48]

Such claims misunderstand Aquinas' understanding of nature. When Aquinas speaks of human nature, as indicated above, he does not mean simply human biology or what human beings share with animals or even all of what is inborn. Rather, he refers to the human essence, the fact that human beings are thinking, feeling, relating entities, who have an innate drive to govern themselves. What is natural to human beings are those inclinations that are written into their being that direct them to what is good. Sometimes our physiology does not permit us to actualize the potencies that are in us—we are defective in the ability to manifest all human abilities, but we still possess them as part of our nature. Those who are born blind, for instance, still have the potency to see written deep into their being—they are "seeing-kinds" of creature, and the whole of their lives will be governed by that reality; attempts will be made to help them "see" in various ways. Those who are infertile because of some physical defect are still procreative creatures—we shall

[48] Dinitia Smith, "Love That Dare Not Squeak Its Name", *New York Times*, February 7, 2004, https://www.nytimes.com/2004/02/07/arts/love-that-dare-not-squeak-its-name.html.

try to help restore their fertility, but their acts of sexual intercourse still retain the procreative ordination, even though they may not be able to attain the procreative possibility; their acts are still defined by that possibility. Infertile heterosexual couples are able to actualize and enjoy the other purposes of marriage—fidelity and indissolubility. The lived reality of couples who are infertile does not in the least match that of homosexual couples. The amount of promiscuity and infidelity among practicing homosexuals suggests that it would be extremely difficult for homosexuals, for whom the procreative end of marriage is no kind of possibility at all, to meet the other ends of marriage: fidelity and indissolubility.[49]

Nor would Aquinas be swayed by the claim that some individuals might be born with a homosexual orientation. In this fallen world we are born with all sorts of orientations or acquire those orientations that are not in accord with what is good for us. Some of us are congenitally irritable; some acquire various addictions.

Aquinas speaks of acts of homosexual sexual intercourse as acts that are "contrary to nature".[50] Let me hasten to note that Aquinas speaks of all immoral acts as being contrary to nature since all immoral acts violate human nature; they are not in accord with human nature that is rational; in short, they are unnatural because they are not in accord with reason. Yet some immoral actions retain some degree of naturalness. For instance, acts of fornication are unnatural because they violate reason; they do so because provision for offspring has not been made. Yet, since acts of fornication can fulfill the purpose of sexual intercourse in generating offspring, they are still natural insofar as they allow the semen and ovum to fulfill their natures partially; on a psychological level, the acts are able in some way to express the complementarity of male and female. Homosexual acts of sexual intercourse do not achieve these levels of naturalness.

---

[49] For a summary of the health risks and other aspects of the homosexual lifestyle, see John R. Diggs, "The Health Risks of Gay Sex", Corporate Resource Council, 2002, available online at https://www.catholiceducation.org/en/marriage-and-family/sexuality/the-health-risks-of-gay-sex.html; see also A. W. Richard Sipe, *Sipe Report: Preliminary Expert Report*, BishopAccountability.org, accessed April 27, 2018, http://www.bishop-accountability.org/tx-dallas/resource-files/sipe-report.htm.

[50] *SCG* 3.122.5; *ST* I–II, q. 94, a. 3, reply 2. Some of this portion on Aquinas and homosexuality was published as part of my article "Aquinas's Natural Law Theory and Homosexuality", in *Homosexuality and American Public Life*, ed. Christopher Wolfe (Dallas: Spence, 1999), pp. 129–40.

That homosexuality appears in nature would not have challenged Aquinas' position. Again, he does not think that "nature" is what we share with the animals—human nature is our rational nature. As we saw above, in his discussion of monogamy, Aquinas argues that humans should not imitate the many species of animals that are promiscuous; rather, since humans, like birds, need both a male and female for the successful raising of offspring to adulthood, monogamy is appropriate for humans. Aquinas did not object to or approve of specific behavior because it is or is not found in the animal kingdom; rather, Aquinas used behavior in the animal kingdom to help him discover what about certain animals would make certain behavior deleterious or beneficial; if humans are like those animals in that respect (such as needing parents of both sexes), he would use that information to help him determine what is fitting behavior for humans.

In discussing the unnaturalness of acts of homosexual sexual intercourse, Aquinas does not make reference to the unitive purpose of the sexual act and how homosexual sexual intercourse is also incompatible with the unitive meaning. Yet, an indication that he shares the understanding that homosexual acts are not truly unitive can be found in the fact that Aquinas includes homosexual acts as sins against the sixth commandment, the commandment against adultery. All sins that misuse the sexual faculties are considered to be sins of unfaithfulness—one is using one's sexual powers outside of the marital relationship or not in accord with the goods of the marital relationship; in other words, one is not sharing one's sexuality with one's spouse, or one is not sharing one's sexuality with one's spouse properly (as in contracepted sexual intercourse). In Aquinas' view there is a sense in which one's sexual powers belong to one's spouse, for they exist to strengthen the spousal relationship and to create a family. Homosexual sexual intercourse bestows one's sexual favors on someone other than a spouse, the proper individual with whom to unite and procreate.

The Homosexual Condition

To this point we have been considering Aquinas' evaluation of homosexual acts. He also makes some remarks that indicate his views about the source of the homosexual condition. Let us first note that while

Aquinas speaks of homosexual acts as being particularly objectionable, he does not make that claim about the homosexual condition. And we must recall that when he speaks of homosexual acts as being particularly objectionable, he is comparing them to other sins of intemperance. Sins of intemperance are not the most serious sins; sins of pride and sins against charity are much worse. As for all human action, Aquinas maintains that one cannot judge the moral value of an action apart from a consideration of the state, character, and intention of the agent. There is ample evidence that Aquinas shared in the modern understanding that the homosexual condition may not be one that an individual has chosen; he allows that it may be the result of a bodily temperament, of a psychological disease, or of bad conditioning.[51]

In an article entitled "Whether Any Pleasure Is Not Natural?" Aquinas quotes Aristotle in maintaining that "some things are pleasant not from nature but from some defect of man's nature."[52] He speaks of "some pleasures that are not natural speaking absolutely, and yet connatural in some respect."[53] Those with defects in their system find what is unpleasant to humans as a species to be pleasant to them as individuals. Aquinas speaks of defects of both the body and the soul. As an example of a defect of the body that would distort natural pleasures, he gives a man with a fever to whom bitter things seem sweet. As examples of defect of the soul, he speaks of a man who through custom takes some pleasure in unnatural intercourse, bestiality, or cannibalism.

One reader of Aquinas, John Boswell, argues that this reasoning should lead Aquinas to see that homosexuality is natural; he believes that Aquinas should concede that homosexuality is natural in some individuals since Aquinas holds that some individuals take a connatural delight in pleasures that are not pleasant to humans as a species.[54] But Aquinas finds the origin of the "connaturality" to be some defect and thus would not understand the condition to be natural.

[51] Anthony C. Daly, S.J., "Aquinas on Disordered Pleasures and Conditions", *Thomist* 56, no. 4 (October 1992): 583–612, gives an excellent review of the relevant texts on this issue.

[52] *ST* I–II, q. 31, a. 7.

[53] See my article "Are Natural and Unnatural Appetites Equally Controllable? A Response to Jensen's 'Is Continence Enough?'", *Christian Bioethics* 10, nos. 2–3 (August–December 2004): 177–88.

[54] John Boswell, *Christianity, Social Tolerance, and Homosexuality: Gay People in Western Europe from the Beginning of the Christian Era to the Fourteenth Century* (Chicago: University of Chicago Press, 1980), pp. 326–28.

Boswell also argues that although Aquinas speaks of homosexuality coming about through some defect, Aquinas may not necessarily mean some moral defect. And Boswell is certainly correct in this observation.[55] The text upon which Aquinas draws here is a text from Aristotle wherein Aristotle uses the desire for one's own sex as an example of a perverse desire that may have been fostered by childhood sexual abuse.[56] Indeed it is significant that studies show that approximately 50 percent of males with a homosexual orientation were sexually abused.[57] Certainly, if abuse were the cause or a contributing factor of one's homosexual desires, one would not be morally culpable for possessing the desires, though one most likely has some moral culpability for acting upon these desires, unless they could be considered truly uncontrollable obsessions.[58] And certainly some may be morally responsible for having homosexual desires; they may recklessly "experiment" with homosexual actions, and they may expose themselves to homosexual erotica and arouse desires in themselves that otherwise may not have been activated. But however the homosexual condition comes to be, whether one is morally culpable for acquiring the condition or not, Aquinas would still consider the condition a disordered condition—even if one's homosexuality were genetically determined. Aquinas would argue that those who are made lame by others, those who make themselves lame because of bad choices, and those who are born lame are all suffering some defect, some disorder in their being.

Boswell observes that some conditions that come about through defects are not in themselves defects. Boswell observes that although Aquinas thought that females came to be because of some defect in the semen or because of the presence of a moist south wind, Aquinas did not think females, for that reason, were without a natural purpose. Boswell reasons: "Since both homosexuality and femaleness occur 'naturally' in some individuals, neither can be said to be inherently bad, and both must be said to have an end." He observes that "the *Summa* does not speculate

[55] Ibid., p. 328.

[56] For an excellent discussion of these texts, see Daly, "Aquinas on Disordered Pleasures and Conditions".

[57] See Marie E. Tomeo et al., "Comparative Data of Childhood and Adolescence Molestation in Heterosexual and Homosexual Persons", *Archives of Sexual Behavior* 30, no. 5 (October 2001): 535–41.

[58] See Aquinas' *Commentary on Aristotle's Nicomachean Ethics* 7.5.

on what the 'end' of homosexuality might be, but this is hardly surprising in light of the prejudices of the day."[59] Boswell does some fancy distorting of texts to come to this conclusion. Women may be "naturally" inferior to males because, for instance, they are the passive as opposed to the active principle in procreation, but both maleness and femaleness are ordered to some good. There are many kinds of imperfection, one being something that is not a perfect instance of something (as a child is an imperfect adult), or something that is a privation of a good such as blindness. In Aquinas' view, homosexuality would be like blindness.

Moderns are unlikely to understand and accept Aquinas' analysis of homosexuality because we generally do not share his view of man's ontological dependence on God; we do not share his view that God wills each soul into existence and wants to share an eternity with every human being; we do not share his view that sexuality has a purpose designed by God and that we must live in accord with that purpose. Nor do we share his view that all of us must carry some portion of the cross. Original sin alone makes every human being disordered; many of us have acquired more specific disorders through our genetic heritage, our upbringing, our choices. Many of these make it difficult for us to avoid disordered and sinful actions. For Aquinas, homosexuality is simply one of those disordered conditions; he would assure us that God's grace is available to assist us in being healed of such a condition or of learning to live morally with such a condition by avoiding sinful behavior.

Refusal to acknowledge the centrality of the procreative meaning of sexual intercourse has led our culture to massive confusion about sexuality, to sexual practices that are destructive and perverse in many respects. Many in our culture seek intimacy and pleasure through sexual intercourse, intercourse often deprived of any procreative possibility by the choice of the agents. There is significant evidence that such sex does not contribute to the well-being of the individuals involved or of the societies in which such practices reign. When we attempt to remake the world in our flawed image rather than attempting to act as those created in God's perfect image, we cannot possibly attain the holiness to which we are called.

---

[59] Boswell, *Christianity, Social Tolerance, and Homosexuality*, pp. 326–27, and footnote 87.

A Lamentation of Eros

Challenging the Sexual Revolution
Fifty Years Later

Michele M. Schumacher, S.T.D., habil.

It's a most unlikely coincidence of anniversaries: the fiftieth anniversary of the sexual revolution and the fiftieth anniversary of *Humanae vitae*. The one told us to take off our clothes and put on condoms, the other to keep on our clothes and take off our condoms. The one claimed to make love not war, the other to make war—on our passions, that is—in the name of love. The one told us to release our sexual energies from the yoke of children; the other told us to keep those energies thriving through their fecundity.

Any such contradictory teachings could hardly survive together for long, and there is no doubt that the sexual revolution won far more converts than did Catholic sexual teaching—even among Catholics, judging from their contraceptive use, as has been well documented.[1] Among the general population, "great (infertile) sex is now a priority", concludes the renowned sociologist Mark Regnerus in his recent book mapping changes in sexual expression and intimacy among Americans. It is "a

---

[1] See, for example, Mary Rice Hasson and Michele M. Hill, *What Catholic Women Think about Faith, Conscience, and Contraception: Preliminary Report* (Fairfax, VA: Women, Faith, and Culture, 2012), http://s3.amazonaws.com/eppc/wp-content/uploads/2013/07/What _Catholic_Women_Think_Contraception-Aug_2012.pdf; Mark M. Gray and Mary L. Gautier, *Catholic Women in the United States: Beliefs, Practices, Experiences, and Attitudes* (Washington, DC: CARA / Georgetown University, 2018), pp. 30–31, https://cara.georgetown .edu/CatholicWomenStudy.pdf; Richard Fehring and Andrea Schlidt, "Trends in Contraceptive Use among Catholics in the United States: 1988–1995", *Linacre Quarterly* 68 (May 2001): 170–85.

hallmark of the good life, signaling that our genital and psychosexual life—sexual expression and how we experience it—is close to the heart of being human".[2] This victory is not without its casualties, however. Not only is "the Genital life ... leaving us lonelier";[3] it has also—and this is what is most ironic, given the promises of the sexual revolution— left us erotically impoverished.

Indeed, from this perspective, it is not Christianity with all its "commandments and prohibitions"—including, in the case at hand, the prohibition of contraception by *Humanae vitae*—that has "poisoned *eros*" and "turn[ed] to bitterness the most precious thing in life", as Friedrich Nietzsche argues in a passage cited by Pope Benedict in his first encyclical.[4] It is, rather, the sexual revolution that has done so, as Allan Bloom pointed out in his 1987 best seller, *The Closing of the American Mind*. The first promise of the sexual revolution was, Bloom points out, "happiness understood as the release of energies that had been stored up over millennia.... However, the lion roaring behind the door of the closet turned out ... to be a little, domesticated cat."[5] How could it be, the American philosopher and classicist asks, that parents—who only a generation earlier would have objected to "wayward" daughters darkening the family reputation—were only rarely protesting in the 1980s when boyfriends slept over in their homes? In response, his students explained matter-of-factly, "Because it's no big deal."[6]

That statement, Bloom comments, "says it all". It is the absence of passion that he considers "the most striking effect, or revelation, of the sexual revolution, and it makes the younger generation more or less incomprehensible to older folks".[7] In keeping, moreover, with the codes of a liberal society and out of fear of being considered "sexist" or of risking love in a culture of divorce, these students were unwilling or unable to seek stable marital relationships; whence Bloom's feeling of being "in the presence of

---

[2] Mark Regnerus, *Cheap Sex: The Transformation of Men, Marriage, and Monogamy* (Oxford/New York: Oxford University Press, 2017), p. 196.

[3] Ibid., p. 199.

[4] *Jenseits von Gut und Böse*, IV, 168, cited in Benedict XVI, encyclical letter *Deus caritas est* (December 25, 2005), no. 3 (hereafter cited as *DCE*), http://w2.vatican.va/content/benedict-xvi/en/encyclicals/documents/hf_ben-xvi_enc_20051225_deus-caritas-est.html.

[5] Allan Bloom, *The Closing of the American Mind: How Higher Education Has Failed Democracy and Impoverished the Souls of Today's Students* (New York: Simon and Schuster, 1987), p. 99.

[6] Ibid.

[7] Ibid.

robots". Their "lack of passion, of hope, of despair, of a twinship of love and death" was simply "incomprehensible" to him. "When I see a young couple who have lived together throughout their college years leave each other with a handshake and move out into life, I am struck dumb."[8]

In the interlude, large numbers of young men have become "convinced that their sexual responses have been sabotaged" by frequent exposure to pornography, as *Time* magazine reports,[9] and entire generations of men and women are now "lonely together"—no longer knowing, as Naomi Wolf puts it, "how to find each other again erotically, face-to-face."[10] It is not so much the paralysis of our passions, however, that will concern us in these pages as the loss of eros to which they are ordered. It is, I will argue more specifically, "that love between man and woman which is neither planned nor willed", as Pope Benedict described it, "but somehow imposes itself upon human beings"[11]—that is, among the most unsung casualties of the violation of the "the inseparable connection, established by God", and proclaimed by Paul VI, "between the unitive significance and the procreative significance" of the conjugal act.[12] By "making sex easy", the sexual revolution has, as Bloom puts it, "trivialize[d], de-eroticize[d], and demystify[ied] sexual relations".[13] This is hardly a minor matter, moreover; for in the absence of that which "tears man away from his finite existence and enables him, in the very process of being overwhelmed by divine power, to experience supreme happiness", the human person is arguably less human.[14]

An Intimacy Crisis

Given the ironic state of affairs among the first generation of sexual revolutionaries, Bloom could find no better word to describe the eroticism

[8] Ibid., p. 123.

[9] Belinda Luscombe, "Porn and the Threat to Virility", *Time*, March 31, 2016, http://time.com/4277510/porn-and-the-threat-to-virility/.

[10] Naomi Wolf, "The Porn Myth", *New York Magazine*, October 20, 2003, http://nymag.com/nymetro/news/trends/n_9437/index1.html.

[11] *DCE* 3.

[12] Paul VI, encyclical letter *Humanae vitae* (July 25, 1968), no. 12 (hereafter cited as *HV*), http://w2.vatican.va/content/paul-vi/en/encyclicals/documents/hf_p-vi_enc_25071968_humanae-vitae.html; cf. *Catechism of the Catholic Church*, no. 2366 (hereafter cited as *CCC*).

[13] Bloom, *Closing of the American Mind*, p. 100.

[14] *DCE* 4.

of his time than "lame".[15] In, moreover, the passing of nearly two generations of time since Bloom wrote of his own students, the lame have
arguably gotten only more crippled. Whereas the former University of
Chicago professor recognized his students as no longer having love affairs,
but only "relationships",[16] today's college students know—as numerous
psychiatrists, psychologists, sociologists, and journalists attest—that "relationships restrict freedom—they require more care, upkeep, and time
than anyone can afford to give.... They add pressure to the already heavily pressured, overscheduled lives of today's students." Therefore, many
have recourse instead to "hookups", allowing them "to get sex onto
the college CV without adding any additional burdens". Hookup sex, as
Boston University professor Donna Freitas puts it bluntly, "is fast, uncar-
ing, unthinking, and perfunctory". It is "bad sex, boring sex, drunken
sex you don't remember, sex you could care less about, sex where desire
is absent, sex that you have 'just because everyone else is, too,' or that
'just happens.'"[17] Students who engage in it—as Freitas knows from her
interviews of over twenty-five hundred students from seven U.S. colleges
and universities—are "'free' to forget about love, meaning, and commitment, 'liberated' to have sex with whoever comes along without any
strings".[18] In fact, as one journalist suggests, they might have sex before
they know each other's first names.[19]

Clearly ours is not so much a hookup culture as "an unhooked
culture",[20] with "cheap sex" becoming the "operative assumption"
over all.[21] Indeed, recent research shows that iGen-ers (those born in
the 1990s) are "on track to be the generation with the largest number
of single people in US history and the lowest birthrate on record",[22]

---

[15] Bloom, *Closing of the American Mind*, p. 132.

[16] "Love suggests something wonderful, exciting, positive and firmly seated in the passions.
A relationship is gray, amorphous, suggestive of a project, without a given content, and tenta-
tive. You work at a relationship, whereas love takes care of itself" (ibid., p. 124).

[17] Donna Freitas, *The End of Sex: How Hookup Culture Is Leaving a Generation Unhappy,
Sexually Unfulfilled, and Confused about Intimacy* (New York: Basic Books, 2013), pp. 1–2.

[18] Ibid., p. 62.

[19] See Tom Wolfe's comment in the introduction of Kathleen A. Bogle, *Hooking Up: Sex,
Dating and Relationships on Campus* (New York: New York University Press, 2008), p. 1.

[20] Laura Sessions Stepp, *Unhooked: How Young Women Pursue Sex, Delay Love and Lose at
Both* (New York: Riverhead Books, 2007), p. 6.

[21] Regnerus, *Cheap Sex*, p. 201.

[22] Jean M. Twenge, *iGen: Why Today's Super-Connected Kids Are Growing Up Less Rebel-
lious, More Tolerant, Less Happy—and Completely Unprepared for Adulthood* (New York: Atria
Books, 2017), p. 226.

and Europeans are not far behind. French sexologist Thérèse Hargot observes, for example, that the dissociation of sex and fecundity marking the thought of the first generation of sexual revolutionaries has led—in the present age of "sex friends"—to the further dissociation of sex and emotions.[23] As a case in point, one author—an American this time—points to website tips for those wishing to avoid "catching feelings" for their sex partners, thereby associating relational attachment with disease. Far worse than being considered a "slut" or a "prude" on a college campus today, as psychology professor Jean Twenge explains, is being labeled "desperate": a title provoked by acting "clingy", "as if you need someone".[24] In this environment, it is hardly shocking that one blogger—a Syracuse University student who goes by the name of "Blackout Blonde"—warns potential hookup partners, "Don't be surprised if you are to us, what we have always been to you, a toy, an object even."[25]

Sadly, these patterns are not unique to the campus scene, as Mark Regnerus has shown. From interviews with more than fifteen thousand Americans, most between the ages of twenty-four to thirty-five, he concludes that the "modal romantic relationship in America" is "sexual" before it is "official"—before, that is to say, a relationship has been established.[26] It's not so much that men are afraid to " 'man up' and commit", Regnerus argues in their defense. "They simply don't need to."[27] Women control the mating market, with sex as their collateral, he argues, and the current supply of willing sex partners, facilitated by Internet dating services and combined with virtual gratification, is— as research has aptly demonstrated—much higher than the (admittedly) high demand.

Ironically, however, at the very moment in which consent is being upheld as a panacea for putting a brake to the widespread sexual assault and harassment that the #MeToo movement has exposed, consent has fallen into the default position: like innocence in the case of an accused crime, consent is assumed unless it can be proven lacking. As might

---

[23] See Thérèse Hargot, *Une jeunesse sexuellement libérée (ou presque)* (Paris: Albin Michel, 2016), p. 103.

[24] Twenge, *iGen*, p. 217.

[25] In short, "lust doesn't mean love" (Blackout Blonde, "Boytoy", WordPress (blog), February 14, 2013, https://blackoutblonde.wordpress.com/2013/02/14/boytoy/).

[26] Regnerus, *Cheap Sex*, p. 106.

[27] Ibid., p. 16.

be expected in an environment wherein sex precedes relationship and pleasure trumps over emotional attachment, determining consent is bordering on impossible. As one young man put it in Vanessa Grigoriadis' appropriately entitled book *Blurred Lines*, "Not everyone is comfortable having that conversation [about consent] with someone we don't know that well but want to f——k."[28]

As for young women, many are sexually engaged "just because they want someone to talk to them", Grigoriadis reports. "Guys are resistant to giving girls a chance, or even getting to know you, unless you have sex with them. But once you have sex with them, most of them are done with you!" Not surprisingly, women tend to respond with a certain ambiguity to sexual propositions. "The problem has always been," as one female student told Grigoriadis, "that I didn't know how to say no.... It wasn't even that I wanted to say no. It's just that I didn't want to say yes."[29] At any rate, not all women would agree with Blackout Blonde when she writes, "In today's society females are on the prowl for hookups just as much as guys are."[30]

The Loss of Modesty and a Parallel Loss of Love

As this example serves to illustrate, women have come a long way since Lisa Sowle Cahill wrote in 1996 that the cultural norms of permissiveness and hedonism are still "gender unequal".[31] Many, furthermore, will applaud feminist Jessica Valenti's plea for a woman's equal opportunity to promiscuity. Such, after all, is what Bloom fittingly identifies as "central to the feminist project".[32] He reasons in his typically provocative style, "A woman who can easily satisfy her desires and does not invest her emotions in exclusive relationships is liberated from the psychological tyranny of men, to do more important things."[33]

[28] Vanessa Grigoriadis, *Blurred Lines: Rethinking Sex, Power, and Consent on Campus* (Boston/New York: Houghton Mufflin Harcourt, 2017), p. xxii.
[29] Ibid., pp. 35–36.
[30] Blackout Blonde, "You're Eskimo Sisters, Now What?", WordPress (blog), April 30, 2013, https://blackoutblonde.wordpress.com/2013/04/30/youre-eskimo-sisters-now-what/.
[31] Lisa Sowle Cahill, *Sex, Gender and Christian Ethics* (Cambridge/New York: Cambridge University Press, 1996), p. 206.
[32] Bloom, *Closing of the American Mind*, p. 101.
[33] Ibid., p. 100.

This is not to suggest that Valenti is wrong to insist that Western society break the double standard of "He's a stud; she's a slut." In turning girls making virginity pledges into "purity porn stars", however, whose primary purpose is to be "desirable to men",[34] Valenti does far more than dissuade them from offering themselves as commodities—to the male ego, if not to the male sex drive. Beyond this obviously applaudable goal, the young feminist also and more properly incites them, regrettably from my perspective, to break out of the "purity myth".

To be sure, it is not Valenti's attempt to put a clamp on puritanism in view of liberating eros that is objectionable, but rather her failure to grant female leverage in view of fostering authentic relationships—her insistence, in other words, upon the right to have a sex life according to the male model of "love 'em and leave 'em". Far from a reflection of woman's power, such an attitude is, in fact, Mark Regnerus astutely argues, "woman's subjugation to men's interests".

> If women were more in charge of how their relationships transpired—more in charge of the "pricing" negotiations around sex—we would be seeing, on average, more impressive wooing efforts by men, fewer hookups, fewer premarital sexual partners, shorter cohabitations, and more marrying going on (and perhaps even at a slightly earlier age, too). In other words, the "price" of sex would be higher: it would cost men more to access it.[35]

As for Bloom, his diagnosis of the problem of feminism, as he saw it already in his day, is that it precludes the one thing most likely to give rise to the mutual attraction of the sexes and thus to true and lasting eros—what he daringly identifies, even at the risk of being labeled masochist, phallocratic, and patriarchal, as "female modesty".[36] This—at least in Bloom's rendition—is *not* to be understood as a simple matter of keeping our cleavage up and our skirts down. Rather, female modesty, as Bloom proposes it, is that which "extends sexual differentiation from the sexual act to the whole of life", that, in other words, which encourages and fosters sexual complementarity.

[34] Jessica Valenti, *Purity Myth: How America's Obsession with Virginity Is Hurting Young Women* (Berkeley: Seal Press, 2009), p. 91. See also Jessica Valenti, *He's a Stud, She's a Slut, and 49 Other Double Standards Every Woman Should Know* (Berkeley, CA: Seal Press, 2008).

[35] Regnerus, *Cheap Sex*, p. 214.

[36] Bloom, *Closing of the American Mind*, p. 102.

It [female modesty] makes men and women always men and women. The consciousness of directedness toward one another, and its attractions and inhibitions, inform every common deed. As long as modesty operates, man and women together are never just lawyers or pilots together. They have something else, always potentially very important, in common— ultimate ends, or as they say, "life goals." Is winning this case or landing this plane what is important, or is it love and family? As lawyers or pilots, men and women are the same, subservient to one goal. As lovers or parents they are very different, but inwardly related by sharing the naturally given end of continuing the species.[37]

As the contrary of seduction, this increasingly uncommon aspect of the virtue of chastity repositions sexual intercourse as "central to a serious life". By impeding "free" love, it fosters the "the delicate interplay between the sexes", as Bloom acknowledges, and clears up the problem of ambiguous consent by making "acquiescence of the will as important as possession of the body".[38] Or, as Regnerus sees it, unlike the "Genital Life" built around cheap sex, which he characterizes as "misanthropic, ultimately anti-woman, and not sustainable", the classic view of sex within relationships built upon complementarity—sex that is not only procreative, but also unitive—"is deeply human. It fosters love when navigated judiciously. And it remains the historic heartbeat, and the very grammar, of human community and social reproduction."[39]

Rediscovering the Transcendental Dimension of Eros and the Goodness of Ends

Despite this obvious increase in sexual promiscuity since Bloom's teaching days, his diagnosis remains as timely as ever: "The problem," as he saw it nearly two generations ago, is that people "have no common object, no common good, no natural complementarity," because "selves ... have no relation to anything but themselves." They are like animals "grazing together" and "rubbing against one another", but there is no real intimacy.[40] This phenomenon of disappearing intimacy he

[37] Ibid.
[38] Ibid., pp. 101–2.
[39] Regnerus, *Cheap Sex*, p. 215.
[40] Bloom, *Closing of the American Mind*, p. 125.

attributed, in turn, to the dismantling "of the structure of involvement and attachment", which reduced sex "to the thing-in-itself".[41]

In the absence of truly erotic passion—the passion that Pope Benedict describes as "an ongoing exodus out of the closed inward-looking self towards its liberation through self-giving"—young men and women, and even not-so young ones, are being motivated by nothing more than "a moment of intoxication".[42] Sexual passion has, in other words, been flattened to the "here and now"—to what is more appropriately visualized as a simple point in time than a horizontal or even a vertical line. Lost, in any case it seems, is the transcendent dimension of what the ancients call eros, "the upward impulse of the human spirit toward what is true, good, and beautiful".[43] Or, as Bloom put it, "sexual passion no longer includes the illusion of eternity."[44] In short, sex has become, as it were, simply hopeless—without an objective, beckoning, upward focus, nor even a rooted profundity.

Of course, to insist on the timeliness of Bloom's diagnosis is not to admit that sex has simply lost all of its "magic". The intoxicating moment remains—at least as long as the orgasm does—but it has lost its bearings. The anchor that couples once cast out wildly into an unknown future each time they engaged in the sexual act—the "weight" that tied them down to serious consequences or secured their footing as they were lifted up in enthusiastic folly—has been hopelessly lightened by the rhetoric of "free" love, "safe" sex, and its accompanying "precautions". In the absence of uncertain, but nonetheless very imaginable (that is to say, foreseeable) consequences, including children and lasting promises, sex is not only dulled. It is also, and quite literally, unengaging—it neither expresses nor leads to commitment—and it is lifeless; it is no longer fruitful. "Free" love, like "safe" sex, is passionless, because there is nothing more at stake, that is, nothing to lose—or so they tell us!—and nothing to gain.

What I am suggesting by this commentary on passionless sex is not simply that it might be "redeemed"—even resurrected—within the

[41] Ibid., p. 102.
[42] DCE 6.
[43] John Paul II, General Audience (November 12, 1980), in *Man and Woman He Created Them: A Theology of the Body*, trans. Michael Waldstein (Boston: Pauline Books and Media, 2006), p. 319.
[44] Bloom, *Closing of the American Mind*, p. 106.

context of a monogamous relationship between husband and wife in view of founding a family. More fundamentally and more importantly, I am arguing for the very thing that renders such a fruitful relationship possible in the first place: that crazed élan of unrelenting love that is willing to sacrifice everything—even one's own self—to obtain the pearl of great price. Such, more specifically, is a force of attraction that cannot be imagined in the absence of the goodness or beauty that literally draws the lover toward itself. As any realist philosopher knows, it is impossible to speak of love in the absence of knowledge—whether sensitive or intellective—precisely because it is knowledge that incites love.[45] In fact, despite the common adage that "love is blind", poets, artists, and philosophers have always recognized erotic love as enkindled by beauty and goodness, and it is this causal relation that clears up any illusions that we might have about the power of human love.

For all its merits—and the history of art, music, and literature stands as proof that there is no shortage of praise for erotic love—we must not be deceived into thinking that it is capable of creating goodness and beauty. For, unlike God's love, which "infuses and creates goodness",[46] human love is a *response* to, and thus an *affirmation* of, goodness and beauty. As Saint Thomas Aquinas puts it straightforwardly, "Something is not beautiful because we love it; rather, it is loved by us because it is beautiful and good."[47] It follows that just as one cannot imagine the force of a magnet in the absence of a metal object, so also is it impossible to envision eros, or any passion for that matter, in the absence of the good that beckons and draws it forth in anticipation of unity, communion, or (in the case of the lesser passions) consummation. That is why Saint Thomas goes so far as to say that the "essence of goodness consists in this, that it is in some way desirable".[48]

Desirability, however, bespeaks at least as much of the one who desires as it does of the one, or the thing, desired. In both cases, we touch upon

---

[45] See St. Thomas Aquinas, *Summa theologiae* I–II, q. 27, a. 2 (hereafter cited as *ST*). See also Michael S. Sherwin, *By Knowledge & By Love: Charity and Knowledge in the Moral Theology of St. Thomas Aquinas* (Washington, DC: Catholic University of America Press, 2005).

[46] *ST* I, q. 20, a. 2.

[47] St. Thomas Aquinas, *In librum Beati Dionysii De divinis nominibus expositio*, c. 4, lect. 10, 439 (Taurini/Romae: Marietti, 1950): "non enim ideo aliquid est pulchrum quia nos illud amamus, sed quia est pulchrum et bonum ideo amatur a nobis."

[48] *ST* I, q. 5, a. 1: "Bonum est quod omnia appetunt" ("Good is what all desire").

the mystery of the Creator's intentions, whence the notion of suitability, fittingness, or connaturality. Not unlike the unity of man and woman, whom C. S. Lewis appropriately refers to as "a single organism" somewhat like "a lock and its key are one mechanism" or "a violin and a bow are one musical instrument", so also the natural human passions and their objects "were made to be combined together in pairs".[49]

The point to be made is that sexual passion, like marriage, is not simply arbitrary, nor is it an end in itself. Rather, it serves nature's own purpose, a purpose that in no way contradicts human freedom. Like a tree that grows upward in search of sunlight and downward in search of water, the sexual passions set man and woman "in motion toward each other"[50] in view of the unity that love, in the form of a free consent, will cement. Without denying that "excess, lack of control or obsession with a single form of pleasure" can soil and likewise lessen pleasure, Pope Francis thus recognizes sexual passion as "a gift from God that enriches the relationship of the spouses".

> A healthy sexual desire, albeit closely joined to a pursuit of pleasure always involves a sense of wonder, and for that very reason can humanize the impulses.... As a passion sublimated by a love respectful of the dignity of the other, it becomes a "pure, unadulterated affirmation" revealing the marvels of which the human heart is capable. In this way, even momentarily, we can feel that "life has turned out good and happy."[51]

Eros at the Service of the Unity of the Person and of the Family

Eros, to summarize, is that force of attraction that irresistibly draws us to the good signified by the beloved person, and this explains why Josef

---

[49] C. S. Lewis, *Mere Christianity* (New York: Fount Paperbacks/Collins, 1977), p. 93.

[50] See Pierre-Marie Emonet, *The Greatest Marvel of Nature: An Introduction to the Philosophy of the Human Person*, trans. Robert Barr (New York: Herder and Herder/Crossroads, 2000), p. 53.

[51] Francis, post-synodal apostolic exhortation *Amoris laetitia* (March 19, 2016), nos. 151–52, http://w2.vatican.va/content/dam/francesco/pdf/apost_exhortations/documents/papa-francesco_esortazione-ap_20160319_amoris-laetitia_en.pdf. The internal quotation is from Josef Pieper, *Über die Liebe* (Munich, 2014), 174. English: Josef Pieper, *On Love*, in *Faith, Hope, Love* (San Francisco: Ignatius Press, 1997), p. 256.

Pieper, who is cited in the above passage by Pope Francis, recognizes it as humanizing naked desire. Contrary to the modern tendency, following Descartes, of relegating the passions to the strictly subhuman domain, we are thus challenged to recognize them instead as "form[ing] the passageway and ensur[ing] the connection between the life of the senses and the life of the mind", as the *Catechism* puts it.[52] Indeed, from a holistic perspective of man as both body and soul, "moral perfection consists in man's being moved to the good not by his will alone, but also by his sensitive appetite".[53] That is why Pieper does not hesitate to speak of eros—that "first movement" and source of "all other affections" of the human heart toward the good[54]—as a "clamp that alone can hold together sex and agape".[55] In other words, eros might be understood as joining that which is most animal-like in the human person with that which is most divine. As such, it is also tightly bound to the virtue of chastity, which the *Catechism* presents as "the successful integration of sexuality within the person and thus the inner unity of man in his bodily and spiritual being".[56]

Of course, there is "an implication to calling eros a mediative power that unites the lowest with the highest in man", Pieper acknowledges, a power, that is to say, that

> links the natural, sensual, ethical and spiritual elements; that prevents one element from being isolated from the rest; and that preserves the quality of true humanness in all the forms of love from sexuality to *agape*. The implication is that none of these elements can be excluded as inappropriate to man, that all of them "belong". The great tradition of Christendom even holds that those aspects of man which derive from his nature as a created being are the foundation for everything "higher" and for all other divine gifts that may be conferred upon him.[57]

As "the elemental dynamics of our being itself, set in motion by the act that created us", eros—as it is presented by Pieper, who draws upon the

---

[52] *CCC* 1764; cf. *ST* I–II, q. 2, a. 2.

[53] *CCC* 1770.

[54] Ibid., 1766.

[55] Pieper, *On Love*, p. 255. "As long as eros reigns, it embodies in purest form the complete essence of love" (ibid., p. 254).

[56] *CCC* 2337.

[57] Pieper, *On Love*, p. 260.

Platonic tradition—is thus the "quintessence of all desire for fullness of being, for quenching of the thirst for happiness", that "primal impulse, which affects all our conscious decisions".[58]

Eros thus sets us before an ordering principle—that is to say, a norm—that is not of our making and that situates every romantic passion and every Platonic love, every concupiscent desire and every chaste affection, within the context of God's creative purposes for our lives. Such, more specifically, is the purpose revealed on the day of creation when God fashioned us as "male and female" and blessed us saying, "Be fruitful and multiply, and fill the earth" (Gen 1:27–28). *For this reason*, "a man ... clings to his wife, and they become one flesh" (Gen 2:24; cf. Mt 19:5; Mk 10:7; Eph 5:31).

In this way we are also invited to recognize both marital relationships and sexual intercourse—like all authentically human acts—within the very clear and unambiguous context of *purposefulness*. This, without a doubt, is what Pope Paul VI had in mind when he addressed what previous popes had presented as *ends* of the conjugal act—namely, marital unity and procreation—as *meanings*, or *significations*.[59] He invited us, more specifically, "to acknowledge" that we "are not the master[s] of the sources of life but rather the minister[s] of the design established by the Creator" and to do so precisely by using "this divine gift" in accord with "its meaning and purpose",[60] a meaning and a purpose that is "most serious", because it is the means chosen by the Creator for "the transmission of human life".[61]

Such, Pope Francis has recently remarked with reference to the teaching of his predecessor John Paul II, is " 'the nuptial meaning of the body and the authentic dignity of the gift'," which marks the "specifically human" dimension of sexuality.[62] The challenge, as John Paul II sees it, consists in this: "that what is 'erotic' " might be a reflection of the "true, good, and beautiful". If, on the other hand, one fails to acknowledge the Creator's intentions in the human body and its impulses, then "the

---

[58] Ibid., p. 222.

[59] See *HV* 12.

[60] Ibid., no. 13.

[61] Ibid., no. 1.

[62] *Amoris laetitia*, no. 151, quoting Catechesis (November 12, 1980), 1: Insegnamenti III/2 (1980), 1132; cf. John Paul II, General Audience (November 12, 1980), in Waldstein, *Theology of the Body*, p. 319.

very attraction of the senses and the passion of the body can stop at mere concupiscence, deprived of all ethical value, and man, male and female, does not experience that fullness of 'eros' ".[63]

It is to this end—that of respecting the Creator's purpose, so as to cooperate in a manner befitting our humanity—that the *Catechism* invites us to practice chastity, including *conjugal* chastity,[64] in view of "training ... human freedom"[65] toward "self-mastery"[66] and of integrating "the powers of life and love"[67] within us. Let there be no illusion, however. Mastering our passions is one thing; mastering love is another. The one who would win at the game of love is not a master. He is clearly *mastered*.

True Love Is Ecstatic

This claim—that the lover is necessarily surrendered in the game of love—is obviously not to admit that he might be compared to a rug that is trampled upon. The authentic lover is, however, quite likely to have the rug swept out from under his feet. True love is, in other words, *ecstatic*: it causes us to be expelled (*ex-*) from the very ground upon which we stand (*stasis*). Our lives are forever changed thereby, because they are quite simply disappropriated. They no longer belong to us alone. Whoever has not experienced this ecstatic "departure"[68] from himself and his world has not really loved, Saint Thomas Aquinas tells us. His is not a love of *ecstasy*, a love that draws one out of one's very self in view of an authentic communion with the beloved. Instead, this is a simple love of *concupiscence*, a love that seeks the pleasure accorded by the beloved more than the very person of the beloved. The final object of concupiscent love is, therefore, one's own self. "We use a most unfortunate idiom when we say, of a lustful man prowling the streets, that he 'wants a woman'", C. S. Lewis insightfully argues. "Strictly speaking, a woman

---

[63] John Paul II, General Audience (November 12, 1980), in Waldstein, *Theology of the Body*, p. 319.

[64] Cf. *CCC* 2349.

[65] Ibid., 2339.

[66] Ibid., 2346, 2395.

[67] Ibid., 2338.

[68] "To suffer ecstasy means to be placed outside oneself", St. Thomas teaches (*ST* I–II, q. 28, a. 3).

is just what he does not want. He wants a piece of apparatus [to satisfy his sexual desire]."[69]

To be sure, there is a certain spontaneity of the one who allows himself to be moved by his passions in such a perverted manner, but spontaneity is also proper to the one who is moved by authentic eros. Following the "impulses of one's own heart"[70] means, Pope John Paul II argues, settling for nothing less than the true good, the authentic truth and transcendent beauty. It means being freed of all that weighs down on eros, of all that hinders its upward movement, and this, in turn, means "mastering the instincts"[71] by way of discernment: the evaluating of the various attractive goods, in view of allowing oneself to be governed by transcendent goodness, truth, and beauty, in service of love. It means distinguishing "sensual arousal" from "the deep emotion" that involves both the "inner sensibility" and "sexuality" in response to the value of the beloved as a whole embodied person.[72] It also means acting as a whole embodied person, as one whose passions and emotions are intimately penetrated by reason.[73]

Mastering instincts does not, however, imply the destruction of authentic spontaneity. On the contrary, it liberates eros from all that infringes its upward movement—namely, vicious habits and the love of concupiscence. To be sure, "People often maintain that ethos takes away spontaneity from what is erotic in human life and behavior," as John Paul II acknowledges; "and for this reason they often demand detachment from ethos 'for the benefit' of eros.... Yet this opinion is mistaken," he insists.[74] It is mistaken, because it fails to acknowledge that far from suppressing eros, the virtue of chastity actually liberates the passions in view of obtaining the good that nature prescribes as befitting the human person.

---

[69] C. S. Lewis, *The Four Loves* (1960; repr., San Diego, CA: Harcourt Brace Jovanovich, 1991), p. 94.

[70] John Paul II, General Audience (November 12, 1980), in Waldstein, *Theology of the Body*, p. 319.

[71] Ibid., p. 321.

[72] Ibid., p. 320.

[73] See Marie-Dominique Chenu, "Les passions vertueuses", *Revue philosophique de Louvain* 72, no. 13 (1974): 11–18.

[74] John Paul II, General Audience (November 12, 1980), in Waldstein, *Theology of the Body*, p. 319.

Helpful in appreciating the spontaneous character of one who is governed by chastity is the distinction between continence and chastity. The continent man or woman is one who "contains", as it were, his or her sexual desires in view of protecting or fostering the greater good of marital unity and the fecundity of marital love—goods that might be threatened by those desires, when misdirected. The chaste man or woman, in contrast, is so entirely given over to the transcendent good that his or her desires are completely and *spontaneously* controlled by the true good. Lesser pleasures cannot entice one who has been won over by the greater good—not only because he or she has developed the habit of acting virtuously, but also because he or she has tasted the fruit of true goodness. Every other pleasure pales before it. The practice of chastity means freely submitting to the good in such a way that it might become, as the Belgium theologian Servais Pinckaers puts it, "the deepest source of spontaneity which shapes our willing".[75]

Erotic Love and Charity:
From Love of Spouse to Love of God

In the first instance, such an ethical evaluation in view of virtuous spontaneity entails identifying all that might hinder our authentic self-growth and Christian perfection, for *not every good* that might attract our passions—in accord with Saint Thomas' definition of love as the adaptation of our appetitive powers to some good[76]—is effectively good *for us*. "Nothing is hurt by being adapted to that which is suitable to it," the Angelic Doctor reasons; "rather, if possible, it is perfected and bettered. But if a thing be adapted to that which is not suitable to it, it is hurt and made worse thereby."[77] Far from leading us to authentic human perfection, eros might thus well be our downfall. "An intoxicated and undisciplined *eros*, then, is not an ascent in 'ecstasy' towards the Divine," Pope Benedict insists, "but a fall, a degradation of man."[78]

---

[75] Servais Pinckaers, *The Sources of Christian Ethics*, trans. Sr. Mary Thomas Noble (Washington, DC: Catholic University of America Press, 1995), p. 402.

[76] See *ST* I–II, q. 27, a. 1; cf. *CCC* 1765–66.

[77] *ST* I–II, q. 28, a. 5.

[78] *DCE* 4.

When, for example, eros is "reduced to pure 'sex' ", the human person risks becoming a mere "commodity"—that is, something to be "bought or sold".[79] By acting, moreover, under the influence of the sexual drive or the will to seduction *in the absence of an affirmation of the spiritual value of the person*—an affirmation that John Paul II recognizes in a pre-papal work as the "essence"[80] of love—we not only reduce *other* persons to their corporal dimension; we also diminish the value of our *own* persons by compromising our spiritual mode of operation: the exercise of our reason and will, which most properly characterizes us as persons. When, therefore, "we do not love the person in another human being, we thereby also degrade the person in ourselves."[81]

The saintly pope thus suggests that underlying the inseparable connection between the two meanings of sexual intercourse (the unitive and the procreative) is an inseparable connection between the sexual appetite and the rational appetite of the will, which are, after all, both rooted within the same human subject. There is nothing despotic about reason's reign in the emotional and affective field of the human being, he insists, precisely because of the inner unity of the person, who is both body and spirit.[82] Hence, as Pope Benedict reasons, "it is neither the spirit alone nor the body alone that loves: it is man, the person, a unified creature composed of body and soul, who loves."[83]

Again, this is not to deny that an authentically loving relationship is both humanly fulfilling and pleasurable. Nor—to return to Nietzsche's challenge—is this to admit that every romantic moment must be "chaperoned" by reason's cool-headed or calculatingly intervention and that passion's "folly" must be strictly banned from our lives. The act of reason might, after all, be interrupted in full accord with reason. If this were not the case, Saint Thomas reasons, it would be unreasonable to sleep.[84] Nor, for that matter, are we to be misled into thinking that the

---

[79] Ibid., no. 5.

[80] Karol Wojtyła, *Love and Responsibility*, trans. Grzegorz Ignatik (Boston: Pauline Books and Media, 2013), p. 26.

[81] Karol Wojtyła, "The Problem of Catholic Sexual Ethics: Reflections and Postulates", in *Person and Community: Selected Essays*, trans. Theresa Sandok (New York: Peter Lang, 1993), p. 287.

[82] See Chenu, "Les passions vertueuses".

[83] *DCE* 5. Similarly, "It is characteristic of mature love that it calls into play all man's potentialities; it engages the whole man" (ibid., no. 17).

[84] See *ST* II–II, q. 153, a. 2, ad. 2.

"exceeding" pleasure of the sexual act is opposed to virtue. On the contrary, this act is pleasurable *precisely because*, the Angelic Doctor further argues, the Creator has ordained it to the great good of preserving the human species.[85] Not surprisingly, then, the *Catechism* cites Pope Pius XII's teaching that "spouses should experience pleasure and enjoyment of body and spirit" in the sexual act *in accord with the Creator's intention*.[86] In the crazed love of eros that is "neither planned nor willed, but somehow imposes itself upon human beings", as Pope Benedict describes it,[87] we might thus recognize a sort of divine conspiracy in view of populating both earth and heaven.

This, however, is just one of the contriving tactics of divine providence. Because there appears to be, as Pope Benedict remarks, "a certain relationship between love and the Divine",[88] love's passions might also, he proposes, draw us to God. In virtue, more specifically, of its power to destabilize us, eros might also initiate us into the act of self-surrender, which is so essential to human fulfilment and Christian faith. In the words of the Second Vatican Council, which Pope John Paul II recognizes "can be said to sum up the whole of Christian anthropology",[89] "man, who is the only creature on earth which God willed for itself, cannot fully find himself except through a sincere gift of himself."[90] Under the influence of charity, chastity is, in fact, "a school of the gift of the person", as the *Catechism* acknowledges, for the self-mastery that is thereby entailed is actually "ordered to the gift of self".[91] As for the "noble and honorable" acts of conjugal union, wherein this gift of self is realized, "the truly human performance of these acts"—with respect, namely, to the "inseparable" character of their procreative and unitive meanings—"fosters the self-giving they signify", as the Second Vatican Council put it.[92]

---

[85] Ibid., corpus (I–II, q.153, a. 2). See also ibid., q. 151, a. 3, ad. 3.

[86] *CCC* 2362, quoting Pius XII, Discourse, October 29, 1951.

[87] *DCE* 3.

[88] Ibid., no. 5.

[89] John Paul II, *Dominum et vivificantem* (May 18, 1986), no. 59, http://w2.vatican.va/content/john-paul-ii/en/encyclicals/documents/hf_jp-ii_enc_18051986_dominum-et-vivificantem.html.

[90] Vatican Council II, Pastoral Constitution on the Church *Gaudium et spes* (December 7, 1965), no. 24, http://www.vatican.va/archive/hist_councils/ii_vatican_council/documents/vat-ii_cons_19651207_gaudium-et-spes_en.html.

[91] *CCC* 2346.

[92] *Gaudium et spes*, no. 49, quoted in *CCC* 2362.

Not surprisingly, the one who has been lured by love's promises of infinity, and eternity, is far more likely to utter his own promises: those of fidelity, love, and honor "in good times and in bad, in sickness and in health", for the duration of an entire lifetime. For what is love, Saint Augustine asks, if not "a kind of life which binds or seeks to bind some two together, namely, the lover and the beloved?"[93] Having experienced love's tenacious powers of attraction, such a person can hardly do otherwise than to "yield to love", as the famous Roman poet Virgil puts it.[94]

Such, I am suggesting, is also the way of faith, which entices us to give nothing less than our very selves. So passionate was the love of Saint Paul, for example, that he recognized himself as living only in Christ: "It is no longer I who live, but Christ who lives in me" (Gal 2:20). Similarly, as the great mystics have affirmed, and as Pope Francis does not hesitate to point out in his apostolic exhortation on the family, "a love lacking either pleasure or passion is insufficient to symbolize the union of the human heart with God."[95]

As this example serves to illustrate, passions that are ordered in accord with the demands of true love are like waters that are channeled into a roaring river. Focusing intently on the beloved, they draw the mind away from everything that does not serve their love.[96] For this reason that might also be likened to "flames of fire" (cf. Song 8:6) that burn away all that is unworthy of love, all that is not ordered "to the one thing necessary" (cf. Lk 10:42). That "one thing" is, of course, the love of him, who is "love" (1 Jn 4:8). "Tell me who you love," writes the nineteenth-century French novelist Arsène Houssay, "and I will tell you who you are."[97] As for the Christian, his first and final love, the one love that orders all the others is for him whose name he proudly bears (cf. Act 11:26; Rev 22:4).

---

[93] De Trinitate 8.10; St. Augustine, The Trinity, trans. Stephen McKenna, in The Fathers of the Church, vol. 45 (Washington, DC: Catholic University of America Press, 1963), p. 266. See also ST I–II, q. 28, a. 1.

[94] Virgil, Bucolics, X, 69, cited in DCE 4.

[95] Amoris laetitia, no. 142.

[96] Love, as St. Thomas points out, causes the lover to dwell upon the beloved (cf. ST I–II, q. 28, a. 2), "and to dwell intently on one thing draws the mind from other things" (a. 3).

[97] "Dis-moi qui tu aimes, je te dirai qui tu es" (Arsène Houssay, Le Roi Voltaire [Paris: Dentu, 1878], p. 103).

Conclusion

Despite appearances to the contrary, there is no contradiction between the radical attempt to master our passions, on the one hand, and the attempt to let go of all mastery, on the other. In both cases, what is sought is the alignment of our minds, bodies, and wills with the creative and redemptive intentions of the One who has mastered us by his love. This requires, of course, that we acknowledge the goodness of the created order, but also that we recognize our own weakness, especially our tendency to worship and serve "the creature rather than the Creator" (Rom 1:25). That is why "purification and growth in maturity are called for", as Pope Benedict acknowledges; "and these also pass through the path of renunciation. Far from rejecting or 'poisoning' *eros*, they heal it and restore its true grandeur."[98] The end, however, is not renunciation, but the joy of authentic, life-giving communion, which is an end, because it is a good. Such is the origin of the challenge of *Humanae vitae*: that of allowing our desires to be shaped by the transcendent good of communion—both human and divine—that truly suits the human person, the good that befits our humanity.

In the end, the best argument for chastity—including marital chastity—is not that it makes for *better sex*, but that it makes for *better love*. After all, chastity places the good that determines the passions far above the pleasures that result therefrom, and this is why to have surrendered in love is not the same as to have surrendered to concupiscence. It is the object of our love that makes all the difference. As Saint Augustine put it so well, "Whether for good or evil, each man lives by his love. It is his love and it alone that must be 'in order' for the person as a whole to be 'right' and good."[99]

---

[98] *DCE* 5.

[99] St. Augustine, *Contra Faustum* 5.10, Migne, *PL* 42:228: "quia ex amore suo quisque vivit, vel bene vel male". Cited by Pieper, *On Love*, p. 167.

Contraception and Abortion:
Fruits of the Same Rotten Tree?*

William Newton, Ph.D.

Consider the following proposition: Amnesty International is a major cause of the growing number of political prisoners in the world. The reason for this claim is as follows: Amnesty International promotes freedom of speech and opposes the locking up of political prisoners. But, its promotion of free speech leads to more people coming into conflict with tyrants and, hence, more political prisoners. Hence, Amnesty International is responsible for the increase in political prisoners.

I think that most people in their right mind would find it hard to assent to this kind of "logic", for Amnesty International is trying to free political prisoners, in part, so they can exercise free speech; it is others who are responsible for their imprisonment, which in itself is a limitation of freedom of speech.

Unfortunately, the same kind of illogic governs the thinking of those who blame the Catholic Church for the continued scourge of abortion. In an interview with the London newspaper *Telegraph*, Lord David Steel (the architect of the British abortion law) claimed that the Catholic Church's opposition to birth-control methods like condoms was "contributing to the use of abortion as a contraception".[1] The "logic" for this claim is: it is because the Catholic Church opposes contraception that many are forced to kill their unintentionally conceived unborn

---

* This essay originally appeared in *Linacre Quarterly* 82, no. 2 (2015): 135–48.

[1] Sophie Borland and Nicole Martin, "Abortions Used as Contraception, Claims Lord Steel", *Telegraph*, April 12, 2008, http://www.telegraph.co.uk/news/1567132/Abortions-used-as-contraception-claims-Lord-Steel.html.

children. Those reasoning this way fail to recognize that contraception leads to irresponsible sex, and it is irresponsible sex that leads to abortion. In opposing contraception and irresponsible sex, the Church is identifying a pattern of behavior that leads to much unhappiness—of which abortion is a part. Thus, it is irresponsible sex that leads to the "need" for abortion, not the Church's teaching on sexual morality.

Still, perhaps, on closer analysis, Lord Steel does have a point. Could we not mount a plausible argument that goes something like this? A major reason for abortion is that a woman conceives a baby that neither she nor her partner wants. The number of such unintended pregnancies might be reduced if contraception were more widely used. Hence, all those interested in the reduction of abortion should likewise support the greater use of contraception.

In this essay, I want to think through this question. We might rephrase it as this: What should the attitude of pro-life persons and the pro-life movement be toward contraception? Should one promote it, oppose it, or merely be indifferent?

The Facts

Let us first start with some facts and then later on move to some ideas; and in fairness to our esteemed interlocutor (Lord Steel), let us start with some studies that seem to support those who advocate contraception as a way to reduce abortion.

In Eastern Bloc countries during the Communist era, abortion rates rose to mind-boggling proportions. After the fall of Communism, the greater availability and use of modern forms of contraception seem to have lead to a dramatic reduction in these rates. In Russia, for example, the abortion rate between 1960 and 1990 ranged from between 102 to 165 per 1,000 women of childbearing age. Between 1990 and 2010 the rate fell from 114 to 42, as rates of modern contraceptive use increased.[2] While these figures are likely low since they don't include abortifacient contraceptives, it seems fair to say that contraception has had something to do with reducing rates of abortion in Russia. This, then, I would not

---

[2] Robert Johnston, "Historical Abortion Statistics, Russia", JohnstonsArchives.net, last updated March 25, 2018, http://www.johnstonsarchive.net/policy/abortion/ab-russia.html.

deny—namely, that in extreme cases contraception can trim off certain excesses.[3] But this really is in extreme cases because the rate of abortion in Russia (and other Soviet Bloc countries) was far higher than in other parts of Europe; for instance, the rate in England and Wales was 21 per 1,000 women of childbearing age for 2010.[4] The rate in Russia was, at its peak, eight times higher than this, and is still double the rate of most Western countries.

Russia, in the latter part of the Soviet era, was a culture in which the accepted standard form of family planning was abortion, and a country in which there was little or no cultural opposition to this. It is an extreme case rather than a typical case. Studies in other countries seem to show a different relationship between contraception and abortion. In Spain, a marked increase in the use of contraception between 1997 and 2007 (30 percent) was matched by a significant increase in abortion (48 percent). This represents an increase from 5.5 to 11.5 abortions per 1,000 women of childbearing age.[5]

Something similar can be seen in England and Wales, in which the use of contraception increased significantly among sexually active unmarried women between 1970 and 1990 from 26 percent to 97 percent (the use among married woman was already at saturation point), and this paralleled a similar increase in abortion from 8.8 to 19.9 per 1,000 women.[6]

Then again, in another study—this time in Turkey—we observe yet another pattern.[7] When abortion and contraception are liberalized we see a sharp increase in *both* contraceptive use and abortions. This seems

---

[3] See Cicely Marston and John Cleland, "Relationships between Contraception and Abortion: A Review of the Evidence", *International Family Planning Perspectives* 29, no. 1 (2003), http://www.guttmacher.org/pubs/journals/2900603.html.

[4] Robert Johnston, "Historical Abortion Statistics, England and Wales (UK)", Johnstons Archives.net, last updated October 22, 2017, http://www.johnstonsarchive.net/policy/abortion/uk/ab-ukenglandwales.html.

[5] José Luis Dueñas et al., "Trends in the Use of Contraceptive Methods and Voluntary Interruption of Pregnancy in the Spanish Population 1997–2007", *Contraception* 83 (2011): 82–87.

[6] For contraceptive use, see John McEwan et al., "Changes in the Use of Contraceptive Methods in England and Wales over Two Decades: Margaret Bone's Surveys and the National Survey of Sexual Attitudes and Lifestyles", *British Journal of Family Planning* 23, no. 1 (1997): 5–8.

[7] Pinar Senlet et al., "The Role of Changes in Contraceptive Use in the Decline of Induced Abortion in Turkey", *Studies in Family Planning* 32, no. 1 (2001): 41–52.

to follow the Spanish and British models. After a time, contraceptive use becomes saturated, though not ubiquitous (there will always be men and women in any society who do not use it). Once this level of use is attained, the abortion rate begins to drop, returning to somewhat above its initial preliberalization level.[8]

In these three cases (Spain, U.K., and Turkey), we observe a hand-in-hand increase in the use of contraception and the rate of abortion. The most plausible explanation for this is that both phenomena reflect a change in attitude toward sex and babies. Supported by increased use of contraception, extramarital sex becomes more prevalent, *and* women become psychologically orientated more and more to smaller family sizes: there is a more-sex-happening-less-babies-wanted dynamic developing.[9] This in turn is likely to lead to more pregnancies being unwanted and in turn to more abortions.[10]

---

[8] When the laws were first liberalized in 1983, 12 percent of all pregnancies ended in abortion. This increased to nearly 24 percent in 1988. However, by 1998 the rate decreased to 16 percent. The authors of the study claim that this is due to the greater availability of contraception. There has been fluctuation in this rate since, but by 2007 it had leveled at 17 percent. The 2007 rate of abortions is nearly 40 percent higher than before liberalization of contraceptive laws (see Senlet et al., "Role of Changes in Contraceptive Use"; Marston and Cleland, "Relationships between Contraception and Abortion").

[9] The argument here is not that the widespread availability of contraception is the *only* factor behind the sexual revolution and, in particular, the dramatic increase in premarital sexual intercourse. However, it cannot be denied that it is an indispensable element of this cultural change (see David M. Heer and Amyra Grossbard-Shechtman, "The Impact of the Female Marriage Squeeze and the Contraceptive Revolution on Sex Roles and the Women's Liberation Movement in the United States, 1960 to 1975", *Journal of Marriage and Family* 43, no. 1 [1981]: 49ff.; Jeremy Greenwood and Nezih Guner, "Social Change: The Sexual Revolution", PSC Working Paper 09-02, Population Studies Center, University of Pennsylvania, and Universidad Carlos III de Madrid, CEPR, and IZA, April 21, 2009, http://repository .upenn.edu/cgi/viewcontent.cgi?article=1011&context=psc_working_papers). In a similar way, the advent of cheap air travel is not the only reason for the explosion of foreign travel in the last forty years; but its absence in the past was a major restricting factor, which meant that formerly very few people traveled abroad for holidays.

[10] An important factor to consider here is the failure rate of contraception. For example, the failure rate for condoms is 2 percent with perfect use and 18 percent with typical use. This means that in typical use 18 women per 100 who use condoms as the sole means to prevent conception become pregnant each year (see James Trussell, "Contraceptive Failure in the United States", *Contraception* 83, no. 5 [May 2011], Table 1, http://www.ncbi.nlm.nih.gov /pmc/articles/PMC3638209/). The failure rate jumps to 72 percent in the case of poor cohabiting women under 20 years of age (see Haishan Fu et al., "Contraceptive Failure Rates: New Estimates from the 1995 National Survey of Family Growth", *Family Planning Perspectives* 31, no. 2 [March/April 1999]: 60–61, https://www.guttmacher.org/sites/default/files /pdfs/pubs/journals/3105699.pdf).

Certainly, in the case of Turkey the abortion rate dropped once contraception use saturated, but it never returned to where it began; rather, it leveled off at a rate that represents an overall 40 percent increase in abortions.

From the above data, it seems fair to conclude that there is no convincing way of arguing that contraception is a panacea for abortion. Even if the extremes of Soviet Russia can be somewhat mitigated, there appears to be in other situations a positive correlation between contraceptive use and abortions built upon the fact that contraception is an important element in changes in cultural attitudes, especially the attitude toward sex. To put this another way: we might say that contraception is the linchpin in a cultural revolution that has abortion as one of its principle effects. The overall result of this is that, far from liberating a culture from the scourge of abortion, contraception engrains and entrenches this practice into a culture that accepts it.

Let us be clear: even if contraception were a solution for abortion, we would be forced to oppose it as an immoral solution. But the fact is, it is not even an immoral solution—it is no solution at all, even on a practical level. I cannot, therefore, concur with the thinking of the aforementioned British statement. Rather, it seems right that I turn to the wisdom of a Polish pope who noted that "despite their differences of nature and moral gravity, contraception and abortion are often closely connected, as fruits of the same tree".[11] My goal, then, is to understand what the late pontiff meant when he made this statement. In order to do this we need now to move from facts to ideas.

Contraception as the Backbone of a Cultural Revolution

My principle argument here is that modern contraception is what is commonly called today "a game changer". The *Oxford Living English Dictionaries* defines "game changer" as "an event, idea, or procedure that

[11] John Paul II, encyclical letter *Evangelium vitae* (March 25, 1995), no. 13, http://w2.vatican.va/content/john-paul-ii/en/encyclicals/documents/hf_jp-ii_enc_25031995_evangelium-vitae.html .

effects a significant shift in the current way of doing or thinking about something."[12]

To a limited extent, the secular world recognizes the game-changing character of contraception, and it is on account of this that hormonal contraception is a frequent member in lists of "ten things that changed the world", alongside earlier inventions like the wheel, the compass, the printing press, the electric lightbulb, and newcomers such as penicillin and the Internet.[13]

When the secular world thinks of contraception as a game changer, it perhaps has in mind categories like giving women power over their bodies. However, the game-changing nature of contraception goes far beyond this. The dictionary says that a game changer effects a significant shift in ways of thinking. Contraception changes the way we think about very fundamental realities, because contraception changes attitudes to sex, to life, to science, to the human person, and to morality. Any one of these might have a significant impact on a society in terms of promoting a culture of death—together, as we shall see, they are devastating.

Contraception Changes the Meaning of Sex

The most fundamental reason why contraception tends to foster abortion is that contraception changes the meaning of sex, and not just in this or that act of sexual intercourse, but in the consciousness of whole cultures.

The key point is that contraception uncouples (in the mind of the individual who accepts it as normal behavior) the relationship of sexual intercourse to babies and to lifelong commitment; in a word, it trivializes sex because sex no longer has—or seems no longer to have—weighty consequences. Trivialized sex, in turn, leads inevitably to unwanted pregnancies, which inexorably leads to abortion.

To put this another way, when sex becomes recreational, individuals engage in sexual intercourse with persons whom they certainly would

---

[12] *Oxford Living English Dictionaries*, s.v. "game changer", OxfordDictionaries.com, accessed April 20, 2018, http://www.oxforddictionaries.com/definition/english/game-changer?search DictCode=all.

[13] Natalie Wolchover, "Top 10 Inventions That Changed the World", LiveScience.com, March 3, 2016, http://www.livescience.com/33749-top-10-inventions-changed-world.html.

not want to collaborate with in the long-term, demanding task of child-rearing. In this sense, contraception falls under what is known as the Peltzman effect. Samuel Peltzman was an economist who claimed that some road-safety regulations had no long-term benefits in terms of preventing serious accidents because, since they made people feel safer, they led to more reckless driving. Some claim that the Peltzman effect can be discerned in the area of ski safety. Apparently, the advent of ski helmets has led to more risky behavior on the slopes, and the "risk index" is higher for helmeted skiers rather than for nonhelmeted skiers.[14]

The point, of course, is that contraception seems to make sex less risky vis-à-vis pregnancy, and so people engage in sex with persons with whom they have no intention of raising children, and so when pregnancy does happen—as it undoubtedly does—*unwanted* pregnancies rise. This phenomenon can be seen particularly with teenage pregnancy and abortion.[15]

A report from Yale University and Duke University on the success (or otherwise) of programs to reduce teenage pregnancy noted: "Our

[14] Lana Ružić and Anton Tudor, "Risk-Taking Behavior in Skiing among Helmet Wearers and Nonwearers", *Wilderness and Environmental Medicine* 22, no. 4 (2011): 291–96.

[15] See Peter Arcidiacono, Ahmed Khwaja, and Lijing Ouyang, "Habit Persistence and Teen Sex: Could Increased Access to Contraception Have Unintended Consequences for Teen Pregnancies?", *Duke and Yale Universities Study*, January 22, 2011, http://public.econ. duke.edu/~psarcidi/teensex.pdf (later published in *Journal of Business and Economic Statistics* 30, no. 2 [April 2012]: 312–25; subsequent references are to the online edition); Sourafel Girma and David Paton, "Matching Estimates of the Impact of Over-the-Counter Emergency Birth Control on Teenage Pregnancy", *Health Economics* 15, no. 9 (2006): 1021–32; Sourafel Girma and David Paton, "The Impact of Emergency Birth Control on Teen Pregnancy and STIs", *Journal of Health Economics* 30, no. 2 (2011): 373–80; David Paton, "The Economics of Family Planning and Underage Conceptions", *Journal of Health Economics* 21, no. 2 (2002): 207–25 (abstract at http://www.sciencedirect.com/science/article/B6V8K-4537PJR-3/2/7b0ac0ed4 b84065fae3119e1663e50bc); Meg Wiggins et al., "Health Outcomes of Youth Development Programme in England: Prospective Matched Comparison Study", *British Medical Journal* 339, no. 72 (2009): 1–8, http://www.bmj.com/cgi/reprint/339/jul07_2/b2534; Karin Edgardh, "Adolescent Sexual Health in Sweden", *Sexually Transmitted Infections* 78, no. 5 (2002): 352–56, http://sti.bmjjournals.com/cgi/content/full/78/5/352. None of this is to deny that it is possible to find studies where aggressively targeted contraception campaigns on particular groups of women—offering them free long-term contraception and monitoring their use of it—can reduce the abortion rate of these women in comparison to their peers (cf. Kim Painter, "Free Birth Control Project Cuts Teen Births, Abortions", *USA Today*, October 4, 2012, updated October 5, 2012, http://www.usatoday.com/story/news/nation/2012/10/04 /free-birth-control-teen-birth-abortion/1613691/). However, promoting a culture of contraception (as opposed to individual projects) is bound to draw more women into sexual activity with resultant unwanted pregnancy.

results suggest that increasing access to contraception may actually in-crease long run pregnancy rates even when short run pregnancy rates fall. On the other hand, policies that decrease access to contraception, and hence sexual activity, may lower pregnancy rates in the long run."[16] The authors give reasons for this. They note that "should contraception become more available, those who switch from unprotected sex to protected sex will lower the teen pregnancy rate, while those who move from abstaining to protected sex will increase the teen pregnancy rate due to contraception failure."[17] In essence, this study (like others) shows that what contraception gives with one hand (in reducing abortions) it takes back with the other by bringing more women into the casual-sex–no-babies market.

Contraception Changes Our View of Life

In an attempt to lampoon Catholic attitudes toward child-rearing, the British comical ensemble Monty Python have a scene in one of their films (*The Meaning of Life*) in which the father of a very large group of ghetto-dwelling children tells us in song precisely why he is the father of so many. The song has the memorable refrain in which the father assures us that "every sperm is sacred, every sperm is great, if one sperm is wasted, God gets quite irate."[18]

This leans in the direction of suggesting that Catholics oppose contraception because it is a crime analogous to murder—the idea that every sperm (as well as every child) is sacred points in this direction.[19] It is clear from the quotation above from *Evangelium vitae* that John Paul II, at least, does not equate contraception with murder, because he says abortion and contraception are different in *nature* and not just different in *degree of seriousness*.

Nonetheless, there can be no doubt that contraception is an essential part of a culture that is ambivalent, at best, about the generation of new

[16] Arcidiacono, Khwaja, and Ouyang, "Habit Persistence and Teen Sex", p. 30.

[17] Ibid., p. 2.

[18] *Monty Python's The Meaning of Life*, directed by Terry Jones (Universal City, CA: Universal Pictures, March 31, 1983 [United States]; June 23, 1983 [United Kingdom]).

[19] Seemingly in this vein, St. Jerome wrote that "some go so far as to take potions, that they may insure barrenness, and thus murder human beings almost before their conception" (*Letter* 22.13).

life—it is antilife in a different way than abortion is antilife but, at the very least, it leads to the general idea of pregnancy as something to be guarded against as a potential disaster.[20]

Now, once this seed of doubt about the goodness of new life is planted and nurtured in the mind of a people, then the doors to abortion have been unbarred (if not opened); and as sure as day follows night, abortion will become law. Contraception turns pregnancy into a disease, opening up the way to drastic "curative" measures.

The antilife atmosphere nurtured by contraception goes a long way toward explaining why when countries permit contraception they very quickly follow up with laws permitting large-scale abortion. Just eight years separate the legalization of contraception and abortion in the United States (1965 and 1973); seven years in Britain (1961 and 1968); eight in France (1967 and 1975). Ireland held out longer, thirty-five years (1978 to 2013). I suspect this is a record but perhaps has something to do with the fact that Irish women could abort their babies in Great Britain. The point is that once contraception is legalized, its antilife inner character begins to do its work—the writing is on the wall. Of course, for many countries liberalized contraception and abortion come as a package under the euphemism of "reproductive health rights".

The antilife character of contraception is perhaps even more starkly evident in the acceptance of the morning-after pill, which sometimes works not by preventing pregnancy but by destroying a newly conceived human being. So-called emergency contraception is a testimony to how contraception "naturally" extends its inner logic toward abortion. Here is where the antilife essence of contraception spills over most directly into the antilife practice of abortion, since no longer is any effort made to separate these two realities.

Another way that contraception changes attitudes toward human life is that it engenders an exaggerated and ultimately despotic desire for power over the origins of human life. As John Paul II points out, to decide for contraception is to take the stance of an arbiter rather

---

[20] Some authors try to explain the Catholic Church's opposition to contraception primarily on the basis that it is antilife behavior, rather than appealing to the natural law perverted faculty argument (cf. William May, *Catholic Bioethics and the Gift of Human Life* [Huntington, IN: Our Sunday Visitor Publishing Division, 2008], pp. 141–44).

than a minister with regard to one's power to transmit human life.[21] In accepting contraception, mankind becomes forgetful that his role in the transmission of human life is one of partnership with God. After all, the mother and father can only contribute the material part of every new human being; the spiritual element must come directly from God.[22] In *Humanae vitae*, Paul VI reminds couples about this very point several times by using the word "munus" (meaning "mission" or "office") to describe the task assigned to spouses. If the task of transmitting human life is understood as an office bestowed upon the parents, the notion of collaboration with God is better preserved.[23]

But contraception fools us into thinking that we are in charge of the whole process of generating human life. This, in turn, leads to the perception that since we alone create a child, we alone can decide when we shall and shall not exercise this power. It gives the impression that we are the gatekeepers of human life. This totalitarian and autocratic notion of our power over the origins of human life easily leads to despotic attitudes with regard to unwanted and unplanned human life, as regards either pregnancies or the destruction of spare embryos resulting from in vitro fertilization.

Contraception Changes Our Notion of the Human Person

A few years ago, a colleague of mine told me a story about an experience of his own son at school. My colleague's wife was expecting their sixth child, and their eldest son had announced this happy news to one of his friends at school. This friend, on returning home to his own family,

---

[21] John Paul II, apostolic exhortation *Familiaris consortio* (November 22, 1981), no. 32, http://w2.vatican.va/content/john-paul-ii/en/apost_exhortations/documents/hf_jp-ii_exh_19811122_familiaris-consortio.html.

[22] It is impossible for the spiritual soul to emerge out of the material contribution of the parents. Nor (given the immaterial nature of the soul) is it reasonable to argue that the souls of the parents "split" in order to create the soul of the child. The soul must, therefore, be created directly by God (cf. Robert Brennan, *Thomistic Psychology* [New York: MacMillan, 1941], pp. 313–14). See also *Catechism of the Catholic Church*, no. 366.

[23] Janet Smith, "The Importance of the Concept of 'Munus' to Understanding *Humanae Vitae*", in *Why Humanae Vitae Was Right: A Reader*, ed. Janet E. Smith (San Francisco: Ignatius Press, 1993), p. 305.

asked his mother why they might not also have a new baby brother. The mother told her son that they would not be having any babies because she, the mother, had had one of those operations "like you give to rabbits" to stop that unfortunate type of thing happening.

To my mind it is significant that this mother explained things in terms of the fact that she had had an operation that had also been given to the pet rabbit in order to stop it from breeding. It strikes me that this explanation has embedded in it yet another powerful effect of the contraceptive culture—namely, the blurring of distinction between humans and animals. It is not too much to say that one of the very distinctive aspects of human beings is that they can control themselves in matters of sexuality—they can harness their sexual desires and integrate them into higher forms of love. This is, by my reading, the central thesis of Karol Wojtyła in *Love and Responsibility*, where the pope-to-be explains that human beings are able to bring reason to bear upon their sexual drive and thereby use it as raw material for self-sacrificing love.[24] Contraception is a discouraging phenomenon because it suggests that this is not really possible—in this way it conflates the difference between humans and animals in matters of sex. Something similar goes on in some forms of modern sex education. The view is taken that young women (and young men) are no more capable of developing virtue than are rabbits; so it is better just to give them some pills in order to chemically neuter them.

But this conflation of what is human and what is animal has implications for life issues. When techniques proper to the farm (such as neutering) are deemed suitable for human beings, then destructive forms of artificial fertilization are likewise seen to be acceptable. Here we can also see a logical link to euthanasia, because animals are routinely "put down" either when they are no longer useful or when they are sick and suffering.

In his 1994 Letter to Families, John Paul II touches upon a more subtle, but no less significant, shift in the attitude toward the human person that is brought about by contraception. This is closely tied to what the pope calls the reoccurrence of Manicheanism.[25] By this he

[24] Karol Wojtyła, *Love and Responsibility*, trans. Grzegorz Ignatik (Boston: Pauline Books and Media, 2013), pp. 125–57.
[25] John Paul II, Letter to Families (February 2, 1994), no. 19, https://w2.vatican.va/content/john-paul-ii/en/letters/1994/documents/hf_jp-ii_let_02021994_families.html.

means an exaggerated dualism in which the body is estranged from the person, being seen more like a mere tool or vehicle.

John Paul II believed that this exaggerated dualistic anthropology is implicit within a contraceptive mentality. His argument is as follows: when a couple engage in sexual intercourse and at the same time intentionally render themselves sterile (as they do by contraception), they are at one moment seeking to give themselves to each other for the sake of communion, and at the same time seeking not to give (or receive) something important—namely, their fertility. This only makes sense if the couple believe that the body (of which fertility is an important characteristic) need not be included in the personal communication because it is not really part of the person. The body is seen as a kind of tool used by the person to achieve union, but not part of the person and part of the personal gift of self that is inherent in sexual intercourse. In short, John Paul II is pointing out that contraceptive sex implicitly operates on the basis of an exaggerated dualistic anthropology.

Hence, the anthropology underlying contraception subtly but profoundly distorts our view of the human person and, thereby, removes a formidable psychological obstacle to abortion. It can translate into a belief that while a human body might well be present in the womb of the mother—by which is meant that matter of a human type is present—a human person is not present because, on account of the underlying contraceptive anthropology, the human body and the human person are radically distinct.

Contraception Contributes to a Change in Our Views of the Purpose of Science

It is instructive to consider two of the candidates for the ten inventions that changed the world, mentioned earlier. Penicillin and hormonal contraception stand side by side historically, because they were created within ten years of each other, in the first half of the twentieth century. However, what separates these two is, for our purposes, more interesting than what unites them. While both give to mankind a power over himself (over his body), one, namely, penicillin, fights against disease and promotes health and hence is clearly ordered to the true good of man, whereas the other, contraception, seeks to frustrate the operation of a healthy faculty, rendering it inoperative. As noted above, contraception treats fertility as though it were a disease.

This difference is very significant. Lauding hormonal contraception as one of the greatest achievements of mankind represents a quintessentially modern view of science. It sees progress as a task unconstrained by the question of what is really good for mankind. It is a manifestation of what Benedict XVI liked to call technocracy—meaning the ideology that what is *possible* is by that fact *good*.[26]

The key point is this: contraception embraces a notion of science and progress as the search for power unconstrained by the question of the good.[27] This philosophy of science has obvious and disastrous effects when it is applied to other life issues. It inevitably leads to a totalitarian claim over the origins of life itself, which manifests itself not just in abortion but in illicit forms of artificial procreation, cloning, and embryo experimentation—according to the logic of technocracy, as these technologies become possible, they become good.

Contraception Changes Our Moral Outlook

The final "game-changing" aspect of contraception is the way that it helps shape a culture's basic moral outlook.

In order to understand how contraception shapes the moral culture, it is necessary to focus on what is called the connection of the cardinal virtues. According to Saint Thomas, prudence, justice, fortitude, and temperance are so related that there cannot be growth in one without growth in the others, and, likewise, weakness in one is a weakening of all.[28] It is on account of this that, elsewhere, Aquinas can argue

[26] Benedict XVI, encyclical letter *Caritas in veritate* (June 29, 2009), nos. 69–71, http://w2.vatican.va/content/benedict-xvi/en/encyclicals/documents/hf_ben-xvi_enc_20090629 _caritas-in-veritate.html.

[27] This point is also evident in John Paul II's Theology of the Body, where he says that "the problem lies in maintaining the adequate relationship between that which is defined as 'domination ... of the forces of nature' (HV 2), and 'self-mastery' (HV 21), which is indispensable for the human person. Contemporary man shows the tendency of transporting the methods proper to the first sphere to those of the second" (John Paul II, *Man and Woman He Created Them: A Theology of the Body*, trans. Michael Waldstein [Boston: Pauline Books and Media, 2006], pp. 630–31).

[28] Cf. St. Thomas Aquinas, *Summa theologiae* I–II, q. 65.

that the thing that more than anything else undermines prudence is intemperance (and especially sexual intemperance, namely, lust).[29] As Josef Pieper notes, the "will-to-pleasure prevents [the unchaste man or woman] from confronting reality with that selfless detachment which alone makes genuine knowledge possible".[30]

We need now to factor in an insight of John Paul II concerning contraception—namely, that contraception contributes significantly to the problem of intemperance. This is, in fact, perhaps the major complaint leveled at contraception by John Paul II in the Theology of the Body. For him, contraception is not so much antilife as antilove, in the sense that it promotes concupiscence understood as sexual intemperance.[31] It does this because it totally removes from sexual relationships the need for self-control, and in a postlapsarian world this is a recipe for lust.

Hence, contraception fuels intemperance in cultures that accept it, and intemperance distorts and obscures our moral vision. The upshot of this is that intemperate persons and cultures see the world differently from temperate persons and cultures. This accounts for the disconcerting fact that unchaste cultures cannot see what is entirely obvious to the chaste—they even fail to see the humanity of the unborn child. It is not even a matter of bad will—intemperate cultures simply cannot see it, because they are blinded by their intemperance.

Or even worse, the unchaste are not able to see beauty. They cannot see it because the appreciation of beauty demands the appreciation of something "for its own sake". This is not possible for a person or a culture that is fixated on consumption—which is at the heart of intemperance. Only the pure can see beauty, so only the pure can see the beauty in and value of every life.

And finally, only the pure can see God. Jesus tells us in the Sermon on the Mount that "blessed are the pure in heart, for they shall see God" (Mt 5:8). To have a pro-life view of the world, one cannot do without this purity of heart. The ultimate reason to respect every human life, no matter how small or compromised it might be, is that every human life

---

[29] Cf. ibid., II–II, q. 53, a. 6.

[30] Josef Pieper, *The Four Cardinal Virtues* (Notre Dame, IN: University of Notre Dame Press, 1966), p. 161. Here I shall develop the relationship between intemperance, prudence, and abortion. Given the connection of the cardinal virtues, something similar could be said of intemperance, *injustice*, and abortion.

[31] *Familiaris consortio*, no. 32.

CONTRACEPTION AND ABORTION

is stamped through with the image of God; however, only the pure in heart can see this, because only they can see God.

Let us note here that all this points to a wider issue. I am taking contraception as a major contributor to intemperance in our culture, but it is not the only one—there is pornography, lurid music, various forms of immodesty, and consumerism. To the extent that these fuel intemperance, just like contraception they cloud our vision of the truth, and they are, therefore, elements of the culture of death.

A second way that contraception disturbs our moral compass is by way of undermining the notion of moral absolutes. John Finnis makes this point explicitly in his definitive work on moral absolutes. He notes that "the formal attack on the moral absolutes emerges, among Catholics, in response to the problem of contraception"[32] and that in its wake has come the denial of the moral absolutes of killing innocents (abortion), of telling lies (deceiving the public in matters of state security), of marital intercourse as the only legitimate form (masturbation, homosexual unions), of procreation as the result of marital intercourse (artificial forms of procreation and embryo freezing). His point is that contraception is the soft underbelly of moral absolutes. It seems a less serious issue than abortion and homosexual acts, for example. People are much more prepared to admit that there might be special cases in which married couples might do a little evil (use contraception) for the sake of the good, such as the good of marital intimacy. But once this is accepted, the horse has bolted.[33]

What I am arguing here is that the widespread acceptance of contraception, especially among Catholics, fatally undermines the opposition that can be mounted against abortion by the only organization that can mount a global challenge to the culture of death. This is because along with the acceptance of contraception comes the implicit acceptance of consequentialism and the denial of moral absolutes. This fatally undermines effective opposition to abortion, to euthanasia, to embryo experimentation, and so on. After all, the moral analysis that would justify contraception—namely, consequentialism—can certainly also justify these other elements of the culture of death in many cases.

[32] John Finnis, *Moral Absolutes* (Washington, DC: Catholic University of America Press, 1991), p. 85.
[33] Christopher Kaczor, "Proportionalism and the Pill: How Developments in Theory Lead to Contradictions to Practice", *Thomist* 63 (1999): 269–81.

There are, no doubt, other important connections between contraception and abortion (and other antilife activities) that I have not touched upon here. There is, for example, the legal connection, most evident in the case of the United States where the law permitting abortion is built upon a case law permitting contraception.[34] There is also undoubtedly a demographic connection—namely, that contraception contributes to a top-heavy population that stokes the flames of euthanasia.

Here, however, I have chosen to focus more on the psychological effects of contraception and how they have helped to bring about a cultural revolution that has itself ushered in the culture of death. One might say that as a mind-warping phenomenon the contraceptive pill is more powerful than a tablet of LSD. The latter only changes one's perception for an evening—the former has changed the minds of a whole culture and a whole generation.

I have been following closely here the teaching of John Paul II. However, on one thing I would humbly beg to differ. The late pontiff says that contraception and abortion are "fruits of the same tree".[35] I would suggest that another way of articulating this relationship would be to think of contraception not so much as the fruit of this tree but its rotten root—abortion, euthanasia, and embryo experimentation are the rotten fruits. Historically, contraception has predated these other evils, but this is only because these other crimes preexist in the logic of contraception, which inevitably takes time to unfurl.[36]

---

[34] It is quite well known that the decision of the U.S. Supreme Court that permitted abortion for the first time, the so-called *Roe v. Wade* (1973), hung on a previous case concerning contraception, *Griswold v. Connecticut* (1965) (cf. Janet E. Smith, *Right to Privacy?* [San Francisco: Ignatius Press, 2008]).

[35] *Evangelium vitae*, no. 13.

[36] This is not to deny that there might be some reality that underlies both contraception and abortion such that they are both fruits of that common reality. As Ratzinger notes: "Contraception and abortion both have their roots in that depersonalized and utilitarian view of sexuality and procreation which we have just described and which in turn is based on a truncated notion of man and his freedom" (Joseph Ratzinger, "Summary of the Consistory of Cardinals on Threats to Life", April 7, 1991, in "The Problem of Threats to Human Life" [Vatican City, April 4–7, 1991], from Teachings of the Catholic Church on Abortion, Priests for Life, http://www.priestsforlife.org/magisterium/threatstohumanlife.htm). Nonetheless, I have sought to argue here that at the level of cultural change, contraception and abortion align more as cause to effect than just as two unrelated effects of some third reality.

In conclusion then, I do not believe that the pro-life movement can be indifferent about the issue of contraception. In some way, it has to address the root of the culture of death. Every gardener knows from bitter experience that if the root of the weed is not entirely destroyed, then it grows back and often with a vengeance. We need to set the axe to the root of the culture of death, and this root is contraception.

The *Sensus Fidelium* and *Humanae vitae**†

Janet E. Smith, Ph.D.

For some theologians the fact that the vast majority of Catholics both approve of contraception and also practice contraception is powerful evidence that by the criteria of the *sensus fidelium* (sense of the faithful) the Church's teaching against contraception may or must be wrong.[1]

---

* In this essay I am going to prescind from the question whether the Church's teaching on contraception has been taught infallibly by virtue of the Ordinary Magisterium, which would render any consultation with the *sensus fidelium* moot. The literature on the subject is extensive; here let me note that the argument that the teaching of *Humanae vitae* is infallible can be found in John C. Ford, S.J., and Germain Grisez, "Contraception and the Infallibility of the Ordinary Magisterium", *Theological Studies* 39, no. 2 (1978): 258–312. For a response to this article, see Garth L. Hallett, S.J., "Contraception and Prescriptive Infallibility", *Theological Studies* 43, no. 4 (1982): 629–50. See also Ermenegildo Lio, O.F.M., *Humanae Vitae e Infallibilità: il Concilio Paolo VI e Giovanni Paolo II* (Vatican City: Libreria Editrice Vaticana, 1986). Monsignor Cormac Burke argues that the fact that the *sensus fidelium* "for centuries right up to the post-conciliar period" along with the teachings of the ordinary and universal Magisterium understood contraception to be wrong, is a sign of the infallibility of the teaching (Cormac Burke, *Authority and Freedom in the Church* [San Francisco: Ignatius Press, 1988], p. 172).

† "The *Sensus Fidelium and Humanae Vitae*", *Angelicum* 83 (2006): 271–97. Also published in *Called to Holiness and Communion: Vatican II on the Church*, ed. Rev. Stephen Boguslawski and Robert Fastiggi (Scranton, PA: University of Scranton Press, 2009).

[1] An earlier exploration of this possibility can be found in J. Komonchak, "*Humanae vitae* and Its Reception: Ecclesiological Reflections", *Theological Studies* 39, no. 2 (1978): 221–57. A recent statement of this position can be found in John E. Thiel, "Tradition and Authoritative Reasoning: A Nonfoundationalist Perspective", *Theological Studies* 56, no. 4 (1995): 627–51, http://cdn.theologicalstudies.net/56/56.4/56.4.1.pdf; see also Philip S. Kaufman, *Why You Can Disagree and Remain a Faithful Catholic* (New York: Crossroad, 1992); Luke Timothy Johnson, "Sex, Women and the Church: The Need for Prophetic Change",

John E. Thiel has argued that the principle of the *sensus fidelium* can be used to help discern which teachings of the Magisterium are in what he calls a state of "dramatic development". A "'dramatically' developing doctrine" is one "that is developing in such a way that its current authority as the authentic teaching of the magisterium will be lost at some later moment in the life of the Church, and that exhibits signs in the present moment that this final loss has begun to take place."[2] "Development" here does not mean discovering deeper and better understandings of a teaching or better justifications for a teaching, but means rejection of a teaching and replacement by another. Thiel states that "magisterial teaching that has not been received in belief and practice by a wide segment of the faithful, then, offers a more reliable, but still incomplete, criterion for judging when doctrine is currently in a state of dramatic development."[3]

To this criterion, what I call "reception of the faithful", Thiel adds two further criteria for judging doctrines to be in a state of dramatic development: (1) when the Magisterium is still in the process of providing theological argument for a teaching, it signals that the teaching is not stable, and (2) when the theological argument does not prove convincing to a wide segment of Catholic theologians, the teaching is still developing. Thiel crystallizes these three criteria into one; a doctrine in the state of dramatic development (i.e., one that is likely to be proved as inauthentic in the future) is "magisterial teaching that one judges not to have been widely received by the faithful and that presents its teaching through theological argument that does not prove convincing to a wide segment of theologians."[4]

Commonweal, June 25, 2004, https://www.commonwealmagazine.org/sex-women-church; and Luke Timothy Johnson, "Abortion, Sexuality and Catholicism's Public Presence", in *American Catholics, American Culture: Tradition and Resistance*, vol. 2 of *American Catholics in the Public Square*, ed. Margaret O'Brien Steinfels (Lanham, MD: Rowman and Littlefield, 2004), pp. 27–38. For a review of various positions concerning the *sensus fidelium* and *Humanae vitae*, see D. Finucane, *Sensus Fidelium: The Use of a Concept in the Post-Vatican II Era* (San Francisco: International Scholars Publications, 1996), pp. 379–401. I have defended the teaching numerous times; see particularly, *Humanae Vitae: A Generation Later* (Washington, DC: Catholic University of America Press, 1991).

[2] Thiel, "Tradition and Authoritative Reasoning", p. 627.
[3] Ibid., pp. 629–30.
[4] Ibid., p. 632.

Thiel uses the "reception"[5] of *Humanae vitae* as an example of a doctrine that is in a state of dramatic development. Although he is careful to state that he does not take polls as being the arbiter of who the faithful are who do or do not receive Church teaching, in fact his source for the claim that *Humanae vitae* has not been received by the faithful are polls that show that "a large percentage of Catholics do not practice the encyclical's proscription of artificial, preventive means of regulating births"[6] and his judgment that "few who practice such forms of birth control would regard their actions as tragic".[7] He thus concludes that "*Humanae vitae*'s prohibition of artificial, preventive means of birth control ... has not found reception among a wide constituency of the faithful."[8] He also finds abundant evidence that his other two criteria are met in respect to *Humanae vitae*.

Since my interest here is the *sensus fidelium*, I will respond in only the most cursory fashion to Thiel's claim concerning what we can conclude about the truth of *Humanae vitae* from the phenomena of magisterial theological argumentation in its favor and from the fact that many theologians do not find that argumentation persuasive. Let me briefly state that I believe the theological argument that is being provided for the teaching—and that argumentation is primarily Pope John Paul II's Theology of the Body—is, surprisingly, not defensive; that is, it seeks not so much to defend the teaching as to deepen our understanding why the teaching is true so it does not appear to be the work of someone desperate to defend the indefensible. That theologians are not being convinced by

---

[5] Ibid., pp. 629–30. The use of the term "reception" is variable in the theological literature. Thiel uses it here to refer to how the faithful have received a Church teaching. It also seems that "reception" can refer to the embracing in later magisterial documents of a teaching promulgated previously. See Francis A. Sullivan, S.J., *Creative Fidelity: Weighing and Interpreting Documents of the Magisterium* (Eugene, OR: Wipf and Stock Publishers, 2003), pp. 85–89. A classic treatment of the theory of reception is that by Yves Congar, "Reception as an Ecclesiological Reality", in *Election and Consensus in the Church*, ed. Giuseppe Alberigo and Antonius Weiler (New York: Herder and Herder, 1972), pp. 43–68; he makes no mention of the faithful rejecting a moral teaching as an instance of "reception".

[6] Thiel, "Tradition and Authoritative Reasoning", p. 633. Thiel then cites a 1994 *New York Times*/CBS poll that found "that 98% of American Catholics 18–29 years of age practice artificial birth control, 91% of those 30–44, 85% of those 45–64 and 72% of those 65 and older (*New York Times* [1 June 1994] B8)" (ibid., n. 14).

[7] Ibid., p. 633. His use of the word "tragic" here is puzzling; one would expect to read "wrong" or "sinful".

[8] Ibid.

the teaching is somewhat of a moot point since few of them have given due attention to John Paul II's Theology of the Body.[9] Indeed, it is very difficult to locate scholarly critical responses to it.[10] Furthermore, proportionalism, or revisionism, the moral theological system that has undergirded rejection of the Church's teaching on contraception, has arguably been rejected by the encyclical *Veritatis splendor*,[11] and thus the fact that proportionalists reject the teaching may have little force or relevance.

But I am not here to respond to the whole of Thiel's article;[12] rather, I wish to examine at some length the view that the nearly universal practice of contraception by Catholics and their de facto widespread rejection of the teaching is a manifestation of the *sensus fidelium* and thus a criterion for judging the truth of the doctrine. The question I am addressing here is whether in our times the laity as a whole is the portion of the Church that is discerning correctly the movements of the Spirit in sexual matters or whether there is some subgroup of laity that more

[9] Typical is the essay by Christine E. Gudorf entitled "Contraception and Abortion in Roman Catholicism", chap. 2 in *Sacred Rights: The Case for Contraception and Abortion in World Religions*, ed. Daniel C. Maguire (New York: Oxford University Press, 2003). The collection in which this article appears, edited by a Catholic theologian, purports to survey the views of major religions on the question of contraception. Gudorf's article reports on Roman Catholic teaching; she makes nary a mention of, let alone a response to, Pope John Paul II's views. Lisa Sowle Cahill in her *Sex, Gender and Christian Ethics* (Cambridge: Cambridge University Press, 1996) devotes a few pages to Pope John Paul II's defense of *Humanae vitae*. Her response is minimal; primarily she evaluates his view that each act of marital intercourse should be an act of "total self-giving" as being "a very romanticized depiction of sex" (p. 203). It is telling that she lists no scholarly responses to the thought of John Paul II in her footnotes. The most extended response I have found is that by biblical scholar Luke Timothy Johnson in his "A Disembodied 'Theology of the Body': John Paul II on Love, Sex and Pleasure", *Commonweal*, January 16, 2001 (online at https://www.commonwealmagazine.org/disembodied -theology-body). Surprisingly his critique is not directed toward John Paul II's use of Scripture but toward his understanding of marital sexuality. For a response to Johnson, see Christopher West, "A Response to 'A Disembodied "Theology of the Body": John Paul II on Love, Sex and Pleasure'", online at https://www.catholicfidelity.com/apologetics-topics /theology-of-the-body/a-response-to-the-critique-of-the-theology-of-the-body/.

[10] See my article "The Stale and Stalled Debate on Contraception", *Catholic World Report* (1993): 54–59, available online at http://www.lifeissues.net/writers/smith/smith_19humanae vitae.html.

[11] Aline H. Kalbian observes that since *Veritatis splendor* scholarly publication by proportionalists has been scarce. See her "Where Have all the Proportionalists Gone", *Journal of Religious Ethics* 30, no. 1 (2002): 3–22.

[12] I believe the second half of his paper, arguing for "nonfoundationalism", is as problematic as his utilization of proportionalism; just as proportionalism has been repudiated in *Veritatis splendor*, so has "nonfoundationalism" been repudiated by *Fides et ratio*.

fully embraces and lives that faith who more rightly should be consulted. Certainly it would seem that the Church's teaching on marital sexuality is one of those areas where the *sensus fidelium* should count for a lot, and perhaps especially its teaching on contraception since it is a matter about which Scripture does not speak explicitly.

This project requires us to establish what the *sensus fidelium* is, why it has any force in establishing Church teaching, what the limits of its authority are, what the *sensus fidei* (sense of the faith) is, and who the *fideles* (faithful) are. We shall be looking at the work of John Henry Newman, whose thought has provided a touchstone for understanding the concept *sensus fidelium*. We shall supplement his understanding with citations from more recent magisterial documents, documents, as we shall see, in harmony with Newman's thought. We shall attempt to establish what role the *sensus fidelium* plays in the proper assessment of the status of the Church's condemnation of contraception. In the end, I am going to try to make the case that the *sensus fidei*, a term that will receive explication below, is to be found in that small group of Catholics who practice natural family planning (NFP) when they need to limit their family size. I will not be arguing in a circular fashion—that is, that only those who accept the Church's teaching are proper judges of that teaching. Rather, I shall be arguing that it is their faithfulness *in other respects* and their *experience* of "natural sex" (to be explained below) that are key elements in qualifying them as judges of the Church's teaching. That is, I shall be arguing that those who exhibit themselves to be faithful Catholics in respect to fundamental Church teachings (apart from the teachings on sexuality) and who have had some extended experience of what I identify as "natural sex" have the connatural sense both of the faith and of sex that enable them to be proper interpreters both of the faith and of sexual morality.

What Is the *Sensus Fidelium*?

In an issue of the lay Catholic publication the *Rambler*,[13] John Henry Newman defended the right of lay Catholics to criticize English bishops

---

[13] I am following here the account of John Coulson in his introduction to John Henry Newman, *On Consulting the Faithful in Matters of Doctrine* (Kansas City: Sheed and Ward, 1961). See also Michael Sharkey, "Newman on the Laity", *Gregorianum* 68, nos. 1–2 (1987): 339–46.

about the way they handled a practical matter. In doing so, he undertook to explain when and why it was appropriate for the laity to speak about Church matters:

> Acknowledging, then, most fully the prerogatives of the episcopate, we do unfeignedly believe, both from the reasonableness of the matter, and especially from the prudence, gentleness, and considerateness which belong to them personally, that their Lordships really desire to know the opinion of the laity on subjects in which the laity are especially concerned. If even in the preparation of a dogmatic definition the faithful are consulted, as lately in the instance of the Immaculate Conception, it is at least as natural to anticipate such an act of kind feeling and sympathy in great practical questions, out of the condescension which belongs to those who are *forma facti gregis ex animo* [model for the flock].[14]

Newman was referring here to the fact that Pius IX just five years earlier had taken into account the views of the laity in his decision to pronounce the dogma of the Immaculate Conception. He notes that if the Holy Father thought the opinion of the laity was worthy of consultation in reference to a point of dogma, it would be even more appropriate to consider their views in a matter of practical consideration.[15]

Due to a negative episcopal response to his essay, in a subsequent issue of the *Rambler*, Newman provided an explanation of what he meant by consulting the faithful, in what has become known as his treatise "On Consulting the Faithful in Matters of Doctrine".[16] Since the faithful had just been consulted in the establishment of the dogma of the Immaculate Conception, it might have been expected that Newman would have used that event as his illustrative example. But in his essay Newman chooses to use the role of the laity in the settling of the Arian heresy; he reports extensively on how in the fourth century the laity were responsible for the defeat of Arianism when nearly all High Churchmen had gone over to Arianism. He states that while he was "not denying that the great body of the Bishops were in their internal belief orthodox; nor that there

[14] John Henry Newman, "Contemporary Events", *Rambler*, May 1859, in *Newman Reader—Works of John Henry Newman* (National Institute for Newman Studies, 2007), http://www.newmanreader.org/works/rambler/contemporary5-59.html.

[15] Newman was referring to a controversy over how far the Church should cooperate with the state in matters of education.

[16] John Henry Newman, "On Consulting the Faithful in Matters of Doctrine", *Rambler*, July 1859, in *Newman Reader*, http://www.newmanreader.org/works/rambler/consulting.html.

were numbers of clergy who stood by the laity, and acted as their centres and guides", he also boldly states that "there was a temporary suspense of the functions of the '*Ecclesia docens*' [teaching Church or magisterium]. The body of Bishops failed in the confession of the faith."[17]

Newman seems to have three scenarios in mind where the *sensus fidelium*[18] would be useful:

1. in formulating an unformulated dogma—that is, the Immaculate Conception;
2. in fighting heresy—that is, in defense of the Nicene Creed against the Arians;
3. in determining the best policy for the Church to follow in church and state affairs in respect to some concrete particular instance.

In these scenarios he does not include the case where the Church has constantly taught a doctrine and the faithful live in opposition to that doctrine.[19] At least from what he says about the *sensus fidelium*, it does not seem that he has in mind that the faithful might exercise a kind of "veto" over Church teaching manifested by nonadherence to the teaching. Benedict Ashley observes that historically Catholics have resisted many teachings of the Church: "There has often been a great deal of support for dueling and similar homicidal activities which the Church has condemned or at least sought to discourage. This is a good example of the fact that popular opinion, which approved such duels as noble and honorable, is not itself the *sensus fidelium* or the *vox Dei*, but requires to be instructed by the pastors of the Church witnessing authoritatively to the Gospel."[20]

---

[17] Ibid.

[18] In Newman and elsewhere we also find the term *consensus fidelium*, which seems generally to be used interchangeably with *sensus fidelium*. Edmund J. Dobbin, however, notes this difference: "More strictly speaking, *sensus* [*fidelium*] refers to the active discerning, or capability of discerning, the content of faith, whereas *consensus* [*fidelium*] is the 'consensual' result of that discerning" (Edmund J. Dobbin, "*Sensus Fidelium* Reconsidered", *New Theology Review* 2, no. 3 [1989]: 50). I am not so much concerned to distinguish these terms as to determine who are the faithful whose sense of the faith counts in judging the legitimacy of a doctrine or practice of the faith.

[19] For a view of the *sensus fidelium* as a kind of veto over Church teaching, see Daniel C. Maguire, "The Voice of the Faithful in a Clergy-Dominated Church", in *Just Good Company* vol. 1, no. 2 (April 2003), http://justgoodcompany.org/1.2/maguire.htm.

[20] Benedict M. Ashley, O.P., *Living the Truth in Love: A Biblical Introduction to Moral Theology* (New York: Alba House, 1996), p. 305.

Nor does Newman believe that the laity can always be trusted to discern what is compatible with the truth of faith. Indeed he acknowledges that at various times, different elements of the Church will carry the burden of defending the faith:

> Then follows the question, Why? [should the faithful be consulted] and the answer is plain, viz. because the body of the faithful is *one* [emphasis added] of the witnesses to the fact of the tradition of revealed doctrine, and because their *consensus* through Christendom is the voice of the Infallible Church.
>
> I think I am right in saying that the tradition of the Apostles, committed to the whole Church in its various constituents and functions *per modum unius* [as one], manifests itself *variously at various times* [emphasis added]: sometimes by the mouth of the episcopacy, sometimes by the doctors, sometimes by the people, sometimes by liturgies, rites, ceremonies, and customs, by events, disputes, movements, and all those other phenomena which are comprised under the name of history. It follows that none of these channels of tradition may be treated with disrespect; granting at the same time fully, that the gift of discerning, discriminating, defining, promulgating, and enforcing any portion of that tradition resides solely in the *Ecclesia docens*.[21]

Note that Newman recognizes that various parts of the Church are guardians of the faith at different times and also asserts that only the Magisterium is ultimately charged with determining what is authentic Church teaching.

Although the *sensus fidelium* is just one source of truth, it can be a mark of the infallibility of a teaching, as Newman notes. This position is affirmed in Vatican II.[22] *Lumen gentium* speaks explicitly of the infallibility of the universal agreement of the faithful about some matter of faith or morals:

> The holy people of God shares also in Christ's prophetic office; it spreads abroad a living witness to Him, especially by means of a life of faith and

---

[21] Newman, "Consulting the Faithful".

[22] It is not a claim new to Vatican II; Sullivan cites passages from several revered theologians dating back to the second century who express this view. See Francis A. Sullivan, "The Sense of Faith: The Sense/Consensus of the Faithful", in *Authority in the Roman Catholic Church: Theory and Practice*, ed. Bernard Hoose (Burlington, VT: Ashgate, 2002), pp. 85–93, especially p. 91.

charity and by offering to God a sacrifice of praise, the tribute of lips which give praise to His name. *The entire body of the faithful, anointed as they are by the Holy One, cannot err in matters of belief.* They manifest this special property by means of the *whole peoples'* supernatural discernment [*sensus fidei*] in matters of faith when *"from the Bishops down to the last of the lay faithful" they show universal agreement [universalem suum consensum] in matters of faith and morals.* That discernment in matters of faith [*sensu fidei*] is aroused and sustained by the Spirit of truth. It is exercised under the guidance of the sacred teaching authority, in faithful and respectful obedience to which the people of God accepts that which is not just the word of men but truly the word of God. Through it, the people of God adheres unwaveringly to the faith given once and for all to the saints, penetrates it more deeply with right thinking, and applies it more fully in its life.[23]

Note that the document does not speak of the *sensus fidelium* but of the *sensus fidei.* No definition of the term is given here, but it is a phrase akin to John Henry Newman's *phronema* (to be discussed below); it is a kind of connatural instinct for discerning what is compatible with the revelation of the Gospel and what is not.[24]

---

[23] Vatican Council II, Dogmatic Constitution on the Church, no. 12, in *The Sixteen Documents of Vatican II*, ed. Marianne Lorraine Trouvé, introduction by Douglas G. Bushman, S.T.L. (Boston: Pauline Books and Media, 1999), *Lumen gentium* (November 21, 1964), emphasis added. (The translation is that provided by the National Catholic Welfare Conference.) Some find reference to the *sensus fidei* in *Dei verbum*: "Tradition which comes from the apostles develops in the Church with the help of the Holy Spirit. For there is a growth in the understanding of the realities and the words which have been handed down. This happens through the contemplation and study made by believers, who treasure these things in their hearts (cf. Lk 2:10, 51), through a penetrating understanding [*intima intelligentia*] of the spiritual realities which they experience" (no. 8, in Trouvé, *Sixteen Documents of Vatican II*).

[24] Here we are interested in the *sensus fidei* as empowered to judge doctrine, but it should be noted that it has other powers as well. For instance, Pope Saint John Paul II speaks of it as guiding the laity in "concrete choices" (*Regina Coeli* [April 16, 1989], no. 2, http://www.vatican.va/liturgy_seasons/pentecost/documents/hf_jp-ii_reg_19890416_en.html), and as being key in the process of inculturation, in determining what portions of a culture are compatible with the faith and which are not ("Address of His Holiness John Paul II to the Plenary Assembly of the Pontifical Council for Culture", [Consistory Hall, March 18, 1994], https://w2.vatican.va/content/john-paul-ii/en/speeches/1994/march/documents/hf_jp-ii_spe_18031994_address-to-pc-culture.html); the *Catechism of the Catholic Church* refers to the *sensus fidelium* as knowing "how to discern and welcome in [private] revelations whatever constitutes an authentic call of Christ or his saints to the Church" (no. 67); in the *Directory for the Application of the Principles and Norms on Ecumenism*, the Pontifical Council for Promoting Christian Unity speaks of the need to consult the *sensus fidei* ([March 25, 1993], no. 179, http://www.vatican.va/roman_curia/pontifical_councils/chrstuni/general-docs/rc_pc_chrstuni_doc_19930325_directory_en.html).

The clearest statement of what the *sensus fidei* is, is found in the *Gift of Authority*, a joint statement of the Anglican–Roman Catholic International Commission:

> In every Christian who is seeking to be faithful to Christ and is fully incorporated into the life of the Church, there is a *sensus fidei*. This *sensus fidei* may be described as *an active capacity for spiritual discernment, an intuition that is formed by worshipping and living in communion as a faithful member of the Church*. When this capacity is exercised in concert by the body of the faithful we may speak of the exercise of the *sensus fidelium* (cf. *Authority in the Church: Elucidation*, 3–4). The exercise of the *sensus fidei* by each member of the Church contributes to the formation of the *sensus fidelium* through which the Church as a whole remains faithful to Christ. By the *sensus fidelium*, the whole body contributes to, receives from and treasures the ministry of those within the community who exercise *episcope*, watching over the living memory of the Church (cf. *Authority in the Church* I, 5–6). In diverse ways the "Amen" of the individual believer is thus incorporated within the "Amen" of the whole Church.[25]

The *sensus fidei* can be possessed by any member of the Church, laity, religious, and members of the hierarchy. When it guides the views of the faithful as a body, what emerges is the *sensus fidelium*.[26]

Who Are the *Fideles*?

Is being a *baptized* Catholic sufficient to qualify as one of the faithful who is to be consulted? Does one need to be a *practicing* Catholic? Does one need to *believe* the central *dogmas* of the faith? Are there any other qualifying criteria?

Newman makes some remarks that shed some light on whom he would consider worthy to be counted among the faithful. In support

---

[25] Anglican–Roman Catholic International Commission, *The Gift of Authority: Authority in the Church III* (September 3, 1998), no. 29, emphasis added, http://www.vatican.va/roman_curia/pontifical_councils/chrstuni/documents/rc_pc_chrstuni_doc_12051999_gift-of-autority_en.html.

[26] Sullivan discusses these terms and makes very much the same distinctions in his paper "Sense of Faith". See also Z. Alszeghy, S.J., "The *Sensus Fidei* and the Development of Dogma", in *Vatican II: Assessment and Perspectives: Twenty-Five Years After (1962–1987)*, vol. 1, ed. René Latourelle (New York: Paulist Press, 1988), pp. 139–56.

of the practice of consulting the faithful, Newman cites a passage from a treatise by the bishop of Birmingham written in support of the dogma of the Immaculate Conception:

> The more devout the faithful grew, the more devoted they showed themselves towards this mystery. And it is the devout who have the surest instinct in discerning the mysteries of which the Holy Spirit breathes the grace through the Church, and who, with as sure a tact, reject what is alien from her teaching. The common accord of the faithful has weight much as an argument even with the most learned divines. St. Augustine says, that amongst many things which most justly held him in the bosom of the Catholic Church, was the "accord of populations and of nations." In another work he says, "It seems that I have believed nothing but the confirmed opinion and the exceedingly wide-spread report of populations and of nations." Elsewhere he says: "*In matters whereupon the Scripture has not spoken clearly, the custom of the people of God, or the institutions of our predecessors, are to be held as law.*"[27]

Newman speaks here of "devout" Catholics and, as was noted earlier, he uses the conviction of the laity about the humanity of Christ during the Arian controversy to demonstrate the role that the fidelity of the laity can play in determining Church teaching. While Newman was adamant that the vast body of the laity opposed Arianism, he noted that the opposition was not unanimous; rather, he acknowledged that "some portions of the laity were ignorant, and other portions were at length corrupted, by the Arian teachers", and that "there were exceptions to the Christian heroism of the laity, especially in some of the great towns."[28] Nonetheless "all or even the majority of the laity opposed Arianism."

In speaking of what sort of laity Newman believes can be relied upon to preserve Church teaching in face of Protestantism, he states,

> What I desiderate in Catholics is the gift of bringing out what their religion is.... I want a laity, not arrogant, not rash in speech, not disputatious, but men who know their religion, who enter into it, who know just where they stand, who know what they hold, and what they do not, who know their creed so well, that they can give an account

---

[27] Newman, "Consulting the Faithful", emphasis added.
[28] Ibid.

of it, who know so much of history that they can defend it. I want an intelligent, well-instructed laity; I am not denying you are such already: but I mean to be severe, and, as some would say, exorbitant in my demands, I wish you to enlarge your knowledge, to cultivate your reason, to get an insight into the relation of truth to truth, to learn to view things as they are, to understand how faith and reason stand to each other, what are the bases and principles of Catholicism, and where lie the main inconsistencies and absurdities of the Protestant theory. I have no apprehension you will be the worse Catholics for familiarity with these subjects, provided you cherish a vivid sense of God above, and keep in mind that you have souls to be judged and to be saved. In all times the laity have been the measure of the Catholic spirit; they saved the Irish Church three centuries ago, and they betrayed the Church in England. Our rulers were true, our people were cowards. You ought to be able to bring out what you feel and what you mean, as well as to feel and mean it; to expose to the comprehension of others the fictions and fallacies of your opponents; and to explain the charges brought against the Church, to the satisfaction, not, indeed, of bigots, but of men of sense, of whatever cast of opinion.[29]

Here, Newman clearly states that the laity are not always reliable witnesses to the faith; he speaks of the time when they betrayed the Church in England and were cowards. In this passage, Newman identifies the faithful as those who know their faith; they are able to explain it and defend it and clearly also to believe it sincerely and live it.

What Justifies Consulting the Faithful?
What Is the *Sensus Fidei*?

Newman says very little in the "On Consulting the Faithful" about why the laity have this gift of the *sensus fidei*, but what he does say is extremely helpful. He speaks of the *consensus fidelium* "as a sort of instinct, or *phronema*, deep in the bosom of the mystical body of Christ".[30] By

[29] John Henry Newman, *Lectures on the Present Position of Catholics in England* (London: Longmans, Green, 1908), in *Newman Reader*, http://www.newmanreader.org/works/england /lecture9.html.
[30] Newman, "Consulting the Faithful".

way of explanation of *phronema*, he cites a passage from Father Perrone, the Jesuit theologian who promoted the role of the faithful in defining the Immaculate Conception:

> The Spirit of God who directs and animates the Church, in becoming united to a human being, engenders a distinctively Christian sensitivity which shows the way to all true doctrine. This common sensibility, this consciousness of the Church, is tradition in the subjective sense of that word. What, from that point of view, is tradition? It is the Christian mentality, existing in the Church and transmitted by the Church; a mentality, however, inseparable from the truths it contains, because it is formed out of and by those very truths.[31]

This is all that Newman says about the *phronema* in "On Consulting the Faithful", but as other scholars have observed, this *phronema* has "close affinity with his own teaching on the 'illative sense' involved in the assent of faith".[32] The word itself recalls what Aristotle and Aquinas spoke of as the virtue of prudence.[33] At this point I am going to let my deliberations be guided by the Aristotelian/Thomistic understanding.

Prudence is that virtue or *habitus* possessed by the person who has authentic and reliable knowledge of the reality to which some moral precept applies, as well as, of course, an understanding and acceptance of the precept as well. The understanding of the precept is not the understanding of the philosopher or the expert; it is the understanding that can be described as the acceptance of the truth of the precept as corresponding to the truth of reality. Aquinas' concept of connaturality is applicable here;[34] as an analogy we might speak of the horse trainer who knows horses so well that he can judge quickly when a horse is ill or out of sorts and knows how to remedy its condition; or the connoisseur of wine who can identify to what region and year a wine belongs. These

---

[31] John Henry Newman, "'On Consulting the Faithful in Matters of Doctrine', *The Rambler, July 1859*", in *John Henry Newman, Conscience, Concensus and the Development of Doctrine: Revolutionary Texts by John Henry Cardinal Newman*, ed. James Gaffney (repr., New York: Image/Doubleday, 1992), pp. 392–428, from the Internet Modern History Sourcebook, Fordham University, ed. Paul Halsall, October 1998, http://www.fordham.edu/halsall/mod/newman-faithful.html.

[32] Dobbin, "*Sensus Fidelium* Reconsidered", p. 56.

[33] Ibid., p. 57.

[34] Sullivan also understands the *sensus fidei* to be equivalent to Aquinas' connaturality (see "Sense of Faith", p. 86).

individuals know a great deal about horses and wines generally and also of horses and wines in particular. The person who possesses prudence is one who has lived a virtuous life and has extensive knowledge of the realm of life in which he must make his moral judgment. The faithful spouse needs not only to know that adultery is wrong, but must know what presents a temptation to infidelity for him or herself, and also have the virtues to avoid or extricate one's self from such situations.

Connaturality is also reliable in matters of faith, but requires knowledge both of general principles and experience of relevant lived realities. That the bishops consulted the faithful about Mary's Immaculate Conception makes sense only if they believed that the faithful had an intimate knowledge of Mary—acquired, one supposes, through having acquired a knowledge of Mary's role in salvation, most likely through instruction and through prayerful practice of Marian devotions.

The *sensus fidei* depends upon *phronema*, upon knowledge both of general principles and lived realities. So the question is, how do we know who possesses *phronema*? Who are the Catholic faithful who possess the *sensus fidei* in respect to sexuality?[35] Again, is being a baptized Catholic sufficient to qualify as one of the faithful who is to be consulted? Does one need to be a practicing Catholic? Does one need to believe the central dogmas of the faith? As noted above, when the Church refers to "universal" agreement she does not mean unanimity of all believers. So, if we are to consult some subgroup, which of the many subgroups who call themselves Catholic should we consult? What experience or knowledge of sex must be had by those who are to be consulted about matters of sexuality?

Donum veritatis addresses directly the question of the status of the opinion of the laity as manifestation of the *sensus fidelium*. It is worthy of being cited at some length:

> Dissent sometimes also appeals to a kind of sociological argumentation which holds that the opinion of a large number of Christians would be a direct and adequate expression of the "supernatural sense of the faith".

[35] Newman seemed to vacillate in sometimes equating the "faithful" with the laity and sometimes including priests among the faithful. In one passage he distinguished the "faithful" from priests and the episcopacy: "I mean ... the 'faithful' do not include the 'pastors'" (Coulson, *On Consulting the Faithful*, p. 65); in another, he includes priests among the laity: "And again, in speaking of the laity, I speak inclusively of their parish-priests (so to call them), at least in many places" (ibid., p. 110).

278 WHY *HUMANAE VITAE* IS STILL RIGHT

Actually, the opinions of the faithful cannot be purely and simply identified with the "sensus fidei". The sense of the faith is a property of theological faith; and, as God's gift which enables one to adhere personally to
the Truth, it cannot err. This personal faith is also the faith of the Church
since God has given guardianship of the Word to the Church. Consequently, what the believer believes is what the Church believes. The
"sensus fidei" implies then by its nature a profound agreement of spirit
and heart with the Church, "sentire cum Ecclesia".

Although theological faith as such then cannot err, the believer can still
have erroneous opinions since all his thoughts do not spring from faith.
Not all the ideas which circulate among the People of God are compatible with the faith. This is all the more so given that people can be swayed
by a public opinion influenced by modern communications media. Not
without reason did the Second Vatican Council emphasize the indissoluble
bond between the "sensus fidei" and the guidance of God's People by the
magisterium of the Pastors. These two realities cannot be separated. Magisterial interventions serve to guarantee the Church's unity in the truth of the
Lord. They aid her to "abide in the truth" in face of the arbitrary character
of changeable opinions and are an expression of obedience to the Word of
God. Even when it might seem that they limit the freedom of theologians,
these actions, by their fidelity to the faith which has been handed on, establish a deeper freedom which can only come from unity in truth.[36]

Several important points are made here: (1) the opinions of the Catholic
community are not equivalent to the *sensus fidelium*; (2) it is only those
who *sentire cum Ecclesia* (see below for an explanation of this term) that
have the *sensus fidei*;[37] (3) the faithful can easily be swayed by trends of
the time, which implicitly means that only those laity who understand
what the Church teaches are reliable interpreters of the faith.

---

[36] Congregation for the Doctrine of the Faith, Instruction on the Ecclesial Vocation
of the Theologian *Donum veritatis* (May 24, 1990), no. 35, http://www.vatican.va/roman
_curia/congregations/cfaith/documents/rc_con_cfaith_doc_19900524_theologian
-vocation_en.html. ·

[37] Ormond Rush in his "*Sensus Fidei*: Faith 'Making Sense' of Revelation", *Theological
Studies* 62 (2001): 231–61, extensively considers the *sensus fidei* as the possession of an individual believer; he states, "There is perhaps no more succinct definition of sensus fidei than this:
sensus fidei is faith seeking understanding, interpretation, and application" (p. 234). I believe
his definition does not exactly correspond to the sense it manifests in Church documents, for
he focuses largely on how the *sensus fidei* helps the individual believer understand the faith and
apply it to his life rather than to the *sensus fidei* as a means of discerning what is compatible
with the faith on a doctrinal level.

The phrase *sentire cum Ecclesia* illuminates what we are looking for. It would be wrong, I think, to understand *sentire cum Ecclesia* to mean "agree with the Church"; that would make an appeal to a *sensus fidei* circular—those who are to be consulted about Church teaching are those who accept Church teaching. Rather, I believe *sentire cum Ecclesia* means something like "to think as the Church does", or, that is, that the thoughts of such a thinker flow from the same source as the teachings—they flow from an acceptance of Christ and his teachings and from the guidance of the Holy Spirit. Such individuals need not be highly educated, to be sure, but would need to be in love with Christ and his Church, devoted to receiving the sacraments and other pious practices and to being instructed in the teachings of the Church.

The need for a laity that knows the faith is stated in many documents of Pope John Paul II. Early in his pontificate, Pope John Paul II made this statement to the bishops of India upon their *ad limina* visit:

> In the community of the faithful—which must always maintain Catholic unity with the Bishops and the Apostolic See—there are great insights of faith. The Holy Spirit is active in enlightening the minds of the faithful with his truth, and in inflaming their hearts with his love. But these insights of faith and this sensus fidelium are not independent of the magisterium of the Church, which is an instrument of the same Holy Spirit and is assisted by him. *It is only when the faithful have been nourished by the word of God, faithfully transmitted in its purity and integrity, that their own charisms are fully operative and fruitful.* Once the word of God is faithfully proclaimed to the community and is accepted it brings forth fruits of justice and holiness of life in abundance. But the dynamism of the community in understanding and living the word of God depends on its receiving intact the depositum fidei; and for this precise purpose a special apostolic and pastoral charism has been given to the Church. It is one and the same Spirit of truth who directs the hearts of the faithful and who guarantees the magisterium of the pastors of the flock.[38]

---

[38] Address of John Paul II to the Bishops from India on Their *Ad Limina* Visit (May 31, 1979), emphasis added, http://www.vatican.va/holy_father/john_paul_ii/speeches/1979/may/documents/hf_jp-ii_spe_19790531_ad-limina-india_en.html. The Holy Father reiterated this claim a year later in his address to the bishops of Liverpool (see Messages of John Paul II for the Opening of the National Pastoral Congress in Liverpool [May 2, 1980], http://www.vatican.va/holy_father/john_paul_ii/speeches/1980/may/documents/hf_jp-ii_spe_19800502_pastorale-liverpool_en.html).

Clearly the faithful are those whose faith has been nurtured, who have been taught the faith in its purity and integrity, and who possess the *sensus fidei.*

The above passage asserts that the opinions of the Catholic community are not equivalent to the *sensus fidei.* We find similar statements elsewhere. One of the clearest statements about the nature and limits of the *sensus fidelium* appears in *Familiaris consortio,* certainly directed toward the question of contraception. First it acknowledges that the laity has a special power of discernment concerning "temporal reality" and then further speaks of those who are married as having a special charism concerning marriage:

> Discernment is accomplished through the sense of faith, which is a gift that the Spirit gives to all the faithful, and is therefore the work of the whole Church according to the diversity of the various gifts and charisms that, together with and according to the responsibility proper to each one, work together for a more profound understanding and activation of the word of God. The Church, therefore, does not accomplish this discernment only through the Pastors, who teach in the name and with the power of Christ but also through the laity: Christ "made them His witnesses and gave them understanding of the faith and the grace of speech (cf. Acts 2:17–18; Rv. 19:10) so that the power of the Gospel might shine forth in their daily social and family life" (Second Vatican Council, *Lumen gentium,* 35). The laity, moreover, by reason of their particular vocation have the specific role of interpreting the history of the world in the light of Christ, in as much as they are called to illuminate and organize temporal realities according to the plan of God, Creator and Redeemer.[39]

And further:

> Christian spouses and parents can and should offer their unique and irreplaceable contribution to the elaboration of an authentic evangelical discernment in the various situations and cultures in which men and women live their marriage and their family life. They are qualified for this role by their charism or specific gift, the gift of the sacrament of matrimony.[40]

[39] John Paul II, apostolic exhortation *Familiaris consortio* (November 22, 1981), no. 5, http://www.vatican.va/holy_father/john_paul_ii/apost_exhortations/documents/hf_jp-ii_exh_19811122_familiaris-consortio_en.html.

[40] Ibid.

Yet, being married in itself is not sufficient to make spouses reliable interpreters of the faith. *Familiaris consortio* responds to those who argue that majority opinion constitutes the *sensus fidei*:

> The "supernatural sense of faith" however does not consist solely or necessarily in the consensus of the faithful. Following Christ, the Church seeks the truth, which is not always the same as the majority opinion. She listens to conscience and not to power, and in this way she defends the poor and the downtrodden. The Church values sociological and statistical research, when it proves helpful in understanding the historical context in which pastoral action has to be developed and when it leads to a better understanding of the truth. Such research alone, however, is not to be considered in itself an expression of the sense of faith.
>
> Because it is the task of the apostolic ministry to ensure that the Church remains in the truth of Christ and to lead her ever more deeply into that truth, the Pastors must promote the sense of the faith in all the faithful, examine and authoritatively judge the genuineness of its expressions, and educate the faithful in an ever more mature evangelical discernment.[41]

Clearly, *Familiaris consortio* holds that only an educated laity are reliable interpreters of the faith.

In articles that deal with the *sensus fidelium*, the claim is routinely made that a simple poll of Catholics would not serve to determine what the *sensus fidelium* is about a given issue.[42] After all, many claim to be Catholics who have not attended Church in years, who attend sporadically, or who believe very few of the key dogmas of the faith—witness such organizations as Catholics for Choice, a pro-abortion organization. One reliable study gives this picture of the beliefs of Catholics; those polled

[41] Ibid.

[42] Thiel, for instance, states: "Sociological findings may be helpful in locating teaching not received by the faithful, but polling results alone cannot establish the extent of doctrinal reception. In addition, there remains the theological issue of how one understands *Lumen gentium*'s reference to 'the whole body of the faithful' in which infallibility resides. Does this phrase refer to the baptized, to practitioners of the faith, or more self-referentially to those who do indeed possess the unerring sense of the faith, however difficult it may be to determine its character or their number?" (Thiel, "Tradition and Authoritative Reasoning", p. 630). But see Kaufman, *Why You Can Disagree and Remain a Faithful Catholic*, who asks, "In our day, cannot carefully taken and carefully evaluated sociological surveys be a tool for determining that 'mind of the faithful'?" (p. 79).

were parishioners in Indiana as well as nationwide Catholics (numbers are percentages):[43]

	Pre-Vatican II (born 1940 or earlier)	Vatican II (born 1941–1960)	Post-Vatican II (1961–76)
The Catholic Church is the one true church. Strongly agree.	58	34	30
It is important to obey Church teachings even when one doesn't understand them. Strongly agree.	38	24	11
One can be a good Catholic without going to Mass. Strongly agree.	26	32	45
Artificial birth control is "always wrong".	20	6	4
Premarital sex is "always wrong".	55	26	20

If the beliefs of parishioners constituted the *sensus fidelium* and thus are infallible, clearly much Church teaching would need to change. The fact that those who are in the younger age groups are less likely to accept Church teaching across the board may be due to weak catechesis and failure to practice the faith and also to the influence of the surrounding culture rather than inner sense of the faith.

If all those who identify themselves as Catholics or even all those who belong to parishes do not qualify as *fideles* possessing the *sensus fidei*, who does? I have found no proposed set of standards that might be used to discern who qualifies as the *fideles* who are to be consulted,

---

[43] I have reproduced with some slight modifications for clarity the chart found in Dean R. Hoge et al., *Young Adult Catholics: Religion in the Culture of Choice* (Notre Dame, IN: University of Notre Dame Press, 2001), p. 35; he is reporting on a study done by James D. Davidson, *The Search for Common Ground: What Unites and Divides Catholic Americans* (Huntington, IN: Our Sunday Visitor, 1997), and A. Williamson and J. D. Davidson, "Catholic Conceptions of Faith: A Generational Analysis", *Sociology of Religion* 57, no. 3 (Fall 1996): 273–90.

as those who *sentire cum Ecclesia*.[44] Let me tentatively offer a few criteria that perhaps should be on any list by which we might discern who are those who *sentire cum Ecclesia*:

1. those who think that missing Mass on Sundays and Holy Days would be a serious sin;[45]
2. those who believe in the Real Presence of Christ in the Eucharist and who believe all the claims of the Creed;
3. those who know the basic duties of their faith (such as yearly reception of the Sacrament of Reconciliation if in a state of mortal sin);
4. those who support the work of the Church in some way such as through financial contributions or apostolic work,
5. those who practice some form of regular devotion, such as daily Scripture reading, daily Rosary, or daily Mass.

Let me for the moment call the individuals described above, those who *sentire cum Ecclesia*, the "SCEs"; since they *orare et vivere cum Ecclesia*—that is, they pray and live with the Church—it seems right to infer that they therefore *sentire cum Ecclesia*.

To be a SCE would be essential to being counted among the faithful to be consulted concerning the *sensus fidelium*. But as noted above, not only must one be a prayerful, practicing Catholic; one must also

---

[44] Thomas Dubay, S.M., "The State of Moral Theology: A Critical Appraisal", in *Readings in Moral Theology*, no. 3, ed. C.E. Curran and R.A. McCormick, S.J. (New York: Paulist Press, 1982), pp. 332–63, gives a fairly vague set of criteria: "I would presume that both theology and common sense would reply [to the question who the faithful are] that 'the faithful' are precisely that, namely, faithful. They are, it seems to me, those who accept the whole Gospel, who are willing to carry the cross every day, who lead a serious prayer life, who accept the teaching magisterium commissioned by Christ. We could hardly call faithful those who reject knowingly anything Jesus has taught or established" (p. 353).

[45] For a survey of the views of "self-described" Catholics, see Hoge et al., *Young Adult Catholics*, p. 208; 77 percent answer yes to "can you be a good Catholic without going to Church every Sunday?"; 72 percent to "without accepting the teaching on birth control"; 68 percent to "without obeying the hierarchy's teaching regarding divorce and remarriage"; 53 percent to "without obeying its teaching on abortion". Only 8 percent of those who are twenty to thirty-nine years old go to Mass weekly and are active in the parish and another 42 percent attend two or three times a month but are not involved in a parish (ibid., p. 71). See also Kenneth C. Jones, *Index of Leading Catholic Indicators: The Church since Vatican II* (St. Louis: Oriens Publishing, 2003).

have some knowledge or experience of the reality that one is judging; that is, those who are to judge the truth of claims about Mary must be a practitioner of Marian devotions—one must possess *phronema* or connaturality about Mary. Possessing *phronema* about sex may be difficult in a culture where having multiple sexual partners before marriage is the norm, and where divorce is widely practiced—for instance, practices at odds with what the Church teaches about sexuality regarding natural law. The *fideles* need to have had some knowledge or experience of authentic sexuality, a sexuality in keeping with natural law.

Knowledge of Natural Sex

Many propose that the Church's teachings on sexuality are suspect because they have been articulated largely by those who are celibates and who have not lived active sexual lives. It certainly is possible to challenge that claim since the majority of the most active advocates of the Church's teaching and the promoters of methods of natural family planning are married laypeople. Those who make this objection seem oblivious to the fact that many of those who defend the Church's teaching and who run the organizations that promote natural family planning are married.[46] Is it true that only those who are married can pronounce upon the compatibility of contraception with the vocation of marriage? What kind of experience qualifies one to speak to any issue? Does one have to have been raped to understand that rape is wrong? To have been robbed to know that theft is wrong? The experience or knowledge required for *phronema* can be of different kinds. Indeed, simply having direct experience of a reality is not sufficient to give one *phronema*, and lack of *direct* experience does not prohibit a kind of *phronema*. That is, those who have not been to war may know a great deal about war because of what they have heard or read about war; because of their power of imagination; because of what they know about human nature. Some spouses who have been abused within marriage may know little about the realities of an authentic marriage. Those who have lived in

---

[46] Consider for instance the work of Dr. John and Lynn Billings, John and Sheila Kippley, Mercedes Wilson, William May, Germain Grisez, John Finnis, Joseph Boyle, and Christopher West.

a culture where severe injustice is practiced may not have an accurate understanding of justice. What is necessary for any kind or degree of *phronema* is that, however acquired, one's "experience" or "knowledge" of a reality must be of the truth of the relevant reality.

So who in the Catholic community are qualified to judge whether some teaching of the Church on sexual morality is in accord with the values of the Gospel? I have suggested above that it is not necessarily the case that individuals need to have direct lived experience of a reality in order to judge it accurately; that is, one need not have fornicated or committed adultery to know that these actions are immoral—thus one need not have had an experience of contracepted sex to be able to judge its morality or consistency with the values of the Gospel.

Yet the fact is that most Catholics have experienced or at least been exposed to a wide variety of sex. In fact, presently it is somewhat difficult to find Catholics in their fertile years who have not had sex outside of marriage or who have had an extended experience of noncontracepted sex. Even many (likely most) of those who use natural family planning had premarital sex and contracepted.[47] It is important to keep in mind that most of those who use natural family planning have at one time contracepted, but most of those who contracept have little experience of noncontracepted sex[48]—both their sex before marriage and their sex after marriage is dominated by the use of contraception or ultimately by sterilization.

Here I want to suggest that most sexually active Catholics presently do not have the kind of experience that would give them the *phronema* necessary to make them good judges of the Church's teaching on contraception. Certainly it is true that few have read, been taught, studied, or prayed about the Church's teaching on contraception.[49] It is well known that theologians largely rejected *Humanae vitae* and quite

---

[47] Mercedes A. Wilson, "The Practice of Natural Family Planning versus the Use of Artificial Birth Control: Family, Sexual and Moral Issues", *Catholic Social Science Review* 7 (2002): 185–211; see the chart on p. 196. Another report of the study analyzed by the previous article is A. C. Pollard and M. A. Wilson, "Correlates of Marital Satisfaction in a Sample of NFP Women", *Integrating Faith and Science through Natural Family Planning*, ed. Richard J. Fehring and Theresa Notare (Milwaukee, WI: Marquette University Press, 2004), pp. 139–65.

[48] Ibid.

[49] Avery Dulles, S.J., observes, "It is not surprising that the teaching on contraception and women's ordination is not universally welcomed. On the grassroots level it is not so much a question of dissent as of ignorance. To accept church teaching one has to be exposed to

immediately upon its promulgation instructed the laity that they were free to reject its teaching.[50] Since few priests at the time[51] and perhaps even now accept the teaching, it can reasonably be assumed that it has rarely been taught in any fashion in the parishes or schools. Indeed, the bishops of the Philippines have acknowledged that they failed in their duty to teach the Church's teaching about contraception:

> It is said that when seeking ways of regulating births, only 5% of you consult God. In the face of this unfortunate fact, we your pastors have been remiss: how few are there among you whom we have reached. There have been some couples eager to share their expertise and values on birth regulation with others. They did not receive adequate support from their priests. We did not give them due attention, believing then this ministry consisted merely of imparting a technique best left to married couples.
>
> Only recently have we discovered how deep your yearning is for God to be present in your married lives. But we did not know then how to help you discover God's presence and activity in your mission of Christian parenting. Afflicted with doubts about alternatives to contraceptive technology, we abandoned you to your confused and lonely consciences with a lame excuse: "follow what your conscience tells you." How little we realized that it was our consciences that needed to be formed first. A greater concern would have led us to discover that religious hunger in you.[52]

---

credible presentations of it. Catholics who hardly know the doctrines of their church except through the fragmentary and often biased reporting of the secular media can scarcely be expected to assent in difficult cases" (Avery Dulles, S.J., "*Humanae Vitae* and *Ordinatio Sacerdotalis*: Problems of Reception", in *Church Authority in American Culture: The Second Cardinal Bernardin Conference*, introduction by P.J. Murnion [New York: Crossroad, 1999], p. 26).

[50] Karl Rahner, S.J., lent his considerable theological stature to this effort quite immediately upon the promulgation of *Humanae vitae* in "On the Encyclical 'Humanae Vitae'", in *Theological Investigations XI*, trans. D. Bourke (New York: Seabury Press, 1974), pp. 263–87, originally in *Stimmen der Zeit* 182 (1968): 193–210. J.G. Milhaven announced it to be a dead letter in "The Grounds of the Opposition to 'Humanae Vitae'", *Thought* 44 (1969): 343–57. For a collection of essays by prominent theologians justifying dissent, see *Contraception: Authority and Dissent*, ed. C.E. Curran (New York: Herder and Herder, 1969). For a concise history of the dissent against *Humanae vitae*, see Megan Hartman, "*Humanae Vitae*: Thirty Years of Discord and Dissent", *Conscience* 19, no. 3 (Autumn 1998): 8–16.

[51] Komonchak, "*Humanae vitae* and Its Reception", p. 221, cites a study by Andrew M. Greeley that stated that only 29 percent of the "lower clergy" accepted the teaching (Andrew M. Greeley, William C. McCready, and Kathleen McCourt, *Catholic Schools in a Declining Church* [Kansas City: Sheed and Ward, 1976], p. 153).

[52] From *Love Is Life* by the Catholic Bishops' Conference of the Philippines issued October 7, 1990, from section A, in *Birth Control: What's Behind the Population Program*, vol. 3, no. 12 (Manila, Philippines: Documentation Service, 1990), p. 7.

In spite of the lack of instruction, perhaps most Catholics would know that the Church *has* taught that contraception is wrong, but many would be confused about whether or not the Church still teaches that and how free they are to abide by the teaching or not. Few would be able to identify the reasons why she teaches that contraception is intrinsically evil.

But I not only want to say that most Catholics do not have sufficient understanding of the teaching to be able to have opinions about it that must be given much weight. Rather I want to make a bolder assertion. It is perhaps ironic that in an age where most people start acquiring sexual experience when they are young and when most experience a wide exposure to a variety of sexual activities through the entertainment world, not to mention through use of pornography, the pool of those who have an experience of what might be called natural sex may be dangerously small. It is plausible that very few Catholics have an experience of the true realities of sex. Yes, they have had lots of sex, but few have had much if any experience of what the Church would call natural or real sex. Natural sex is sex that is meant to be an expression of committed love; it is sex within marriage and sex that is open to children—not just sporadically in a quasi-utilitarian way, but in a way in which children are seen to be the natural and good outcome of sexual intercourse and in which they would be understood as completing the marital commitment. I think it is arguable that perhaps even most people today do not first and foremost think of sexual intercourse as properly an expression of love. They began their sexual involvement quite young and were frequently motivated more by curiosity and a desire for pleasure than motivated by the dynamics of love and affection. Likely most of the sexual relationships they had before marriage were initiated long before they could claim to have feelings of love for their sexual partner. Sex is largely seen as an act performed for the purposes of pleasure between individuals who experience an attraction for each other, or sometimes between individuals who simply are available for sexual intercourse.[53] Such individuals often are nearly incapable of understanding what is meant by sex as an expression of love; they no more can appreciate such a reality than those who have only read comic books can understand

---

[53] It is, perhaps, unnecessary to support this claim, but a good place to start might be the article by Benoit Denizet-Lewis entitled "Friends, Friends with Benefits, and the Benefits of the Local Mall", *New York Times Magazine*, May 30, 2004.

what people are talking about when they speak of great literature, or than those who have only drunk cheap wine can understand what those who have tasted the finest wines can be raving about.

Most Catholics have multiple sexual partners before marriage; they also contracept both before and after marriage. They stop contracepting, however, in order to conceive a child or two, and then many of them get sterilized.[54] The sexual beliefs and lives of most modern Catholics have been shaped much more by the culture in which they live rather than by the Church. They have never had a prolonged experience of a sexual relationship based on the understanding that sexual intercourse is only moral and good between those who have a lifetime commitment to each other based on love and who would welcome children as a natural result of the sexual act—something for which they should be prepared and which they should welcome.

Of course the question must be asked why Catholics rushed to use contraception in the first place; certainly at one time, if only because contraception was not available, most Catholics did not contracept. Why did they embrace contraception? Part of the explanation would be that contraception was promoted as a kind of miracle solution to marital tensions; couples could now have spontaneous sexual relationships without the possibility of a pregnancy. Predictions were that marriages would be much happier once the fear of an unwanted pregnancy was removed from sexual intercourse. It was supposed that women would be happier in that they could pursue careers since they would not be so burdened by childcare. Families would also be happier because of the extra income.[55] The prospect of being able to have sex prior to marriage was seen (and still is largely seen) as a means of ensuring longer lasting marriages since the partners could discern their compatibility before marriage. With such expectations, it is perhaps not surprising that so many turned to contraception. The fact that the doubling of the divorce rate coincided with the widespread use of contraception suggests that

---

[54] For a report on how many Catholics use contraception and NFP, and for data on the rate of sterilization, see Guttmacher Institute, "Who Needs Contraceptives?", Contraceptive Use in the United States Fact Sheet, September 2016, https://www.guttmacher.org/fact-sheet/contraceptive-use-united-states.

[55] For illuminating testimonies of couples who mostly abided by the Church's teaching on contraception before *Humanae vitae*, but who supported a change in Church teaching, see Michael Novak, *The Experience of Marriage* (New York: Macmillan, 1964).

those promises may have been false.[56] Here is not the place to do a full consideration of the possible causes of the great increase in divorce, but certainly the widespread use of contraception should not be ruled out (more about this below).

The willingness of Catholic couples to embrace contraception can be likened to the eagerness with which women were prepared to forgo breastfeeding and embrace bottle feeding. Bottle feeding was promoted as healthy and efficient and sophisticated. And for a period of time, bottle feeding was more popular than breastfeeding, but there has been a gradual return to breastfeeding as the health and psychological benefits have become more apparent.[57]

Although Catholics may have embraced contraception because it promised happier marriages, wouldn't we expect that those who had experienced natural sex prior to the use of contraception to have eventually noticed a diminution in the quality of their sexual experience once they began using contraception? Possibly they did, but failed to attribute it to contraception. I know of no studies that examine comparative satisfaction of sexual intercourse for those who have not contracepted for a period of time and then chose to practice contraception. On the other hand, we do have at least some information about the satisfaction of those who at one time contracepted and then adopted natural family planning,[58] and it overwhelmingly suggests that sexual satisfaction increased with the cessation of contraception and the subsequent use of natural family planning.

[56] For documentation on the connection between the use of contraception and divorce, see the following by Robert Michael: "The Rise in Divorce in Divorce Rates, 1960–1974: Age Specific Components", *Demography* 15, no. 2 (1978): 177–82; "Determinants of Divorce", in *Sociological Economics*, ed. L. Levy-Garboua (London: SAGE Publications, 1979), pp. 223–54; "Why Did the U.S. Divorce Rate Double within a Decade?", in *Research in Population* (Greenwich: JAI Press, 1988), pp. 361–99.

[57] Among the benefits to breastfeeding are included increased intelligence of the baby, increased protection from various diseases, decreased propensity to obesity, easier weight loss for mothers, and decreased incidence of breast cancer; see "What Are the Benefits of Breastfeeding?", Eunice Kennedy Shriver National Institute of Child Health and Human Development, accessed May 11, 2018, https://www.nichd.nih.gov/health/topics/breastfeeding/conditioninfo/benefits.

[58] Those who find personal testimonies to be a source of evidence and insight will find of interest the following: John Long, ed., *Sterilization Reversals: A Generous Act of Love* (Dayton, OH: One More Soul, 2001), and S. Joseph Tham, M.D., *The Missing Cornerstone* (Hamden, CT: Circle Press, 2003).

We should also be open to the possibility that not all noncontra-cepted sex, even between the married, fully incorporates all the values of "natural sex". The Church understands sexual intercourse rightly experienced to be the expression of a committed lifetime union based on love and open to children as a great good, but that is not enough. "Natural sex", sex fully in accord with the goods of human nature, must also be sexual intercourse that flows not just from sexual desire but which is under the influence of the virtue of chastity. A significant level of chastity or self-mastery is required to ensure that acts of sexual intercourse are pursued as acts of expression of love and commitment and not just opportunities to experience sexual pleasure or release sexual tension. Perhaps few individuals have experience of sexual appetites governed by the virtue of chastity and thus free from lust.

Nonetheless there is some evidence that what I am calling natural sex is in fact more enjoyable sex and sex that leads to happier and longer lasting marriages. Many of those who use NFP have at one time contracepted, and most of these testify that their marriages and sexual lives improved once they embraced NFP as their means of spacing or limiting children.[59] Very significantly, in contrast to the rest of the population whose divorce rate is rapidly approaching 50 percent, they almost never divorce.[60]

In determining the *sensus fidelium* concerning contraception, I think sociological data can be very helpful. Indeed, I challenge theologians to take a very close look at the data that sociologists provide—not just the data of how many are willing to assume the title of Catholic who contracept and reject the Church's teaching on contraception, but the data of how happy and strong are the marriages of those who do accept and live by the Church's teaching, the data of the success of the marital relationships of those who contracept, and the data indicating the damaging effects of contraception on our culture.[61]

Almost everyone currently has contraceptive sex before marriage; the number of those who remain virgins before marriage is small, but they are a group whose marriages are remarkably more stable than those who

[59] Wilson, "Practice of Natural Family Planning".

[60] Ibid.

[61] See, for instance, Lionel Tiger, *The Decline of Males* (New York: Golden Books, 1991).

are not.[62] Studies have shown for some time that those women who enjoy sex the most are Evangelical Protestants—women who more likely have been chaste before marriage and faithful within marriage. Consider this finding: "Women without religious affiliation were the least likely to report always having an orgasm with their primary partner—only one in five. On the other hand, the proportion of [Evangelical] Protestant women who reported always having an orgasm was the highest, at nearly one-third."[63] Although no data was given about the contraceptive practices of these Evangelical women, it is likely that they contracept at the same rate as the rest of the population. So would it be right to conclude that their lower divorce rate in spite of contraception indicates that use of contraception within marriage is not a threat to the marriage? It may be premature to draw that conclusion. Certainly their experience of sex may be better and their marriages stronger because they did not have sex prior to marriage; one might suppose they may be more able to be trusting of their husbands; they may benefit from not comparing their spouses to previous sexual partners or being compared to previous sexual partners; they experience at least one of the characteristics of natural sex, sex with someone with whom one has a lifetime commitment (those who cohabit and then marry seem to have a weaker commitment to their spouses). I have not seen studies that show the comparative happiness of those who were virgins upon marrying and who contracepted after marriage with those who were virgins upon marrying and did not contracept after marriage, but it is not implausible that the second group would have even happier and more stable marriages. I propose these possible reasons: (1) the wives are not experiencing the bad physical and psychological effects of contraception; (2) the spouses do not need to interrupt the sexual act to put on a condom or insert a diaphragm; (3) the spouses appreciate the gift of fertility; (4) the spouses attain the virtue of chastity or self-mastery; (5) the spouses communicate better and understand each other better; (6) they are open to more children and experience family life more fully. (Those who use NFP generally have more children than those who do not—not, evidently, because NFP is less reliable, but because the spouses gain a greater respect for their

---

[62] Edward O. Laumann et al., *The Social Organization of Sexuality: Sexual Practices in the United States* (Chicago: University of Chicago Press, 1994), pp. 503–5.

[63] Ibid., p. 115.

fertility and want more children. In spite of the fact that having children puts a strain on marriage, those who have children have longer lasting marriages than those who don't.[64])

In the last few years a new concern has shown up in popular publications—a concern with the phenomenon of sexless marriages.[65] These are marriages where the spouses have simply stopped having sex. No one has precisely identified the cause, but the most commonly offered explanation is that the demands of double careers, household management, and raising children simply leave spouses too fatigued. Yet I know few people who have more demands made on them than mothers and fathers of large families, especially those who homeschool, and reports are that love making among that group is very alive and well. Chemical contraceptives have as a side effect a reduced libido for the female, and may reduce the attractiveness of females to males,[66] so they may be a contributing factor to this diminished interest in sex among the married.

So, if I am correct about who belongs to the "faithful" who possess the *phronema* about sex that is necessary for the *sensus fidei* to do its proper work of discernment, it is a very small group of Catholics indeed.

Grex Parvus

Indeed, Newman certainly believes that it is sometimes the few who have the power to maintain fidelity to God in the midst of an attack on the faith. He states:

> Your strength lies in your God and your conscience; therefore it lies not in your number. It lies not in your number any more than in intrigue, or combination, or worldly wisdom. God saves whether by many or by few;

---

[64] Carolyn Pape Cowan and Philip A. Cowan, *When Partners Become Parents: The Big Life Change for Couples* (New York: Basic Books, 1992); Jay Belsky and John Kelly, *The Transition to Parenthood* (New York: Dell, 1994); Tim B. Heaton, "Marital Stability throughout the Child-Rearing Years", *Demography* 27 (1990): 55–63; Linda Waite and Lee A. Lillard, "Children and Marital Disruption", *American Journal of Sociology* 96 (1991): 930–53.

[65] See for instance the cover story of *Newsweek Magazine*, "No Sex, Please, We're Married", June 30, 2003.

[66] Tiger, *Decline of Males*, pp. 36–39.

you are to aim at showing forth His light, at diffusing "the sweet odour of His knowledge in every place:" numbers would not secure this. On the contrary, the more you grew, the more you might be thrown back into yourselves, by the increased animosity and jealousy of your enemies.

It is not giants who do most. How small was the Holy Land! yet it subdued the world. How poor a spot was Attica! yet it has formed the intellect. Moses was one, Elias was one, David was one, Paul was one, Athanasius was one, Leo was one. *Grace ever works by few; it is the keen vision, the intense conviction, the indomitable resolve of the few*, it is the blood of the martyr, it is the prayer of the saint, it is the heroic deed, it is the momentary crisis, it is the concentrated energy of a word or a look, which is the instrument of heaven. Fear not, *little flock*, for He is mighty who is in the midst of you, and will do for you great things.[67]

Now the phenomenon of which he speaks in the above passage, the phenomenon of the effective witness of the few or even of the one, may not be what he means by the *sensus fidelium* or the *consensus fidelium*. It may in fact be another means by which the faith is preserved. Perhaps this should be called the sensus *fidei gregis parvi*, "the sense of the faith of the small flock".

What this *sensus fidei gregis parvi* has in common with the *sensus fidelium* is that its worthiness as a test of legitimacy of doctrine or practice is not the authority of office or the extent of education or the worthiness of argument. What makes their witness powerful is that they believe and live the faith and also have an experience of the reality under question; they thus are in a position to have a nearly instinctual sense of what is or is not compatible with the faith.

As was noted earlier, in virtually every essay concerning the *sensus fidelium* the claim is made that a simple poll of those calling themselves Catholic does not suffice to determine the *sensus fidei*. Here I have attempted to identify some criteria that may be useful in determining who the *fideles* are. I have also argued that careful attention must be paid not only to what level of faith is possessed by those who would be numbered among the faithful but also to the level of experience of the reality that is being judged. Currently most Catholics are sadly without the knowledge of the basics of their faith and also are not fully faithful

[67]John Henry Newman, "Duties of Catholics towards the Protestant View", in *Newman Reader*, emphasis added, http://www.newmanreader.org/works/england/lecture9.html.

to the practice of the faith, which would disqualify them from being numbered among the *fideles*. It is also of no little importance that they are also without knowledge of the reality of sex that enables them to be able to be counted among those with *phronema* or connatural knowledge. There is within the Church a small flock, a *grex parvus*, who know and live their faith, who have a knowledge both of the sexual reality that involves fornication and contraception and of the sexual reality that would confine sexual activity to marriage and finds the procreative power of the sexual act to be a defining feature of that act. It is of more than a little interest that this *grex parvus* affirms the wisdom of the Church concerning sexual morality.

Conscience, Contraception, and Catholic Health-Care Professionals*

Janet E. Smith, Ph.D.

Introduction and Historical Perspective

The Church's teachings are often very challenging. It can require a great deal of resoluteness and courage to be faithful to those teachings. Those in the health-care professions who conduct their practices in accord with Church teaching or who give witness to the truth of Church teaching to their colleagues can certainly expect misunderstanding and even rejection from their colleagues—Catholic as well as non-Catholic. One of the most difficult teachings of the Church is its claim that contraception is not in accord with God's plan for sexuality. Surely it is a challenge for Catholic physicians both to be faithful to that teaching in their practice and to give witness to others of the truth of that teaching.

On July 25, 1968, *Humanae vitae* hit the world like a bomb.[1] It really surprised and distressed the world and many in the Church when Pope Paul VI pronounced that the Church's teaching on contraception is God's law, not man's law. The resistance to *Humanae vitae* and rejection of its teaching was swift. Father Charles Curran, who was a young professor of moral theology at Catholic University of America, held a press conference within twenty-four hours of the promulgation

* This essay previously appeared in *The Linacre Quarterly* 77, no. 2 (May 2010): 204–28.

[1] Refer to Paul VI, encyclical letter *Humanae vitae* (July 25, 1968), trans. Janet E. Smith, in Humanae Vitae: *A Challenge to Love* (New Hope, KY: New Hope Publications, 2006) (hereafter cited as *HV*).

of *Humanae vitae*.[2] He announced that Catholics were not obliged to follow the teaching of *Humanae vitae*; he judged that it was based on an inadequate understanding of natural law and thus Catholics were free to follow their conscience in regards to this teaching.

Although many bishops around the world issued statements in support of *Humanae vitae*, some of those statements were lamentably weak. For instance, the Canadian bishops stated:

> In accord with the accepted principles of moral theology, if these persons [people who do not accept *Humanae vitae*] have tried sincerely but without success to pursue a line of conduct in keeping with the given directives, they may be safely assured that whoever honestly chooses that course which seems right to him does so in good conscience.[3]

The line "chooses that course which seems right to him" is problematic, as is the conclusion that this can be done "in good conscience". Here we have an elevation of individual judgment over Church teaching.

Should a Catholic prefer his own judgment over Church teaching? Certainly Catholics should act in "good conscience", but what does that mean, especially when one's judgment goes against Church teaching?

Many have a false view of what the conscience is. One thing the conscience is not is our opinion about what is right and what is wrong. We hear this phrase all the time—"You have your opinion, I have mine. Who is to say what is right and what is wrong?" Many in our time seem to think an appeal to conscience is an appeal to base our actions on whatever we think is acceptable; what we think will not cause us too much guilt. Conscience, however, is not an opinion or even our own well-considered judgments. It is not about what I think; it is about what God thinks. It is not about what I want; it is about what God wants.

John Henry Cardinal Newman, one of the great writers about conscience, talked about people who took refuge in "conscience" to do

[2] Father Curran has published a large number of works about contraception and dissent, e.g., Charles E. Curran, *Contraception, Authority, and Dissent* (New York: Herder and Herder, 1969).

[3] "The Winnipeg Statement: Canadian Bishops' Statement on the Encyclical *Humanae vitae* (On Human Life)", no. 26, in *The Birth Control Debate*, ed. Robert G. Hoyt (Kansas City: National Catholic Reporter, 1968), pp. 169–70; also see http://www.u.arizona.edu/~aversa /modernism/winnipeg.html.

whatever they wanted. He said: "When men advocate the rights of conscience, they in no sense mean the rights of the Creator, nor the duty to Him, in thought and deed, of the creature; but the right of thinking, speaking, writing, and acting, according to their judgment or their humour, without any thought of God at all."[4]

Regrettably, we are all susceptible to such behavior; in "good conscience" a person may take a couple of reams of paper from the office, because he reasons that he worked three hours overtime on Saturday and the paper is just compensation that his boss would permit. The problem is not so much that he took the paper, for he may even be right that he is justified in taking the paper. The problem is that he did not consult his conscience; he just made a quick judgment about taking some paper when he wanted it and came up with some rationalization for taking it. People often never really ask the question "What does God think?" or "What would God think about this action?" They just ask whether they feel justified. The conscience, however, seeks to know how *God* would evaluate an action; it does not seek to determine how the agent evaluates an action or how guilty or not guilty an agent will feel about an action.

In the last fifty years, priests rarely if ever speak about contraception from the pulpit. Regrettably, those who were taught in seminaries from about 1970 until the mid-1990s were told *not* to teach this doctrine. In fact, in recent decades priests rarely preach about *any* moral issue from the pulpit. Priests do not preach against racism or greed, for instance; rather, they generally give gentle exhortations to be kind and forgiving. Most hearing those homilies do work on being more kind and forgiving, but they likely would work on other sinful behavior if it were called to their attention. Certainly, few priests speak against fornication or contraception as well as such contemporary issues as in vitro fertilization and embryonic stem-cell research or how to make moral decisions about end-of-life issues. Parishioners are left without guidance on such difficult matters. For several decades priests were taught simply to "break open" the Gospel and not to make any application of Christ's teaching to difficult or controversial moral issues, as they might cause division and upset people. Sadly, many priests were told that the Church might be

[4]John Cardinal Newman, "Letter to the Duke of Norfolk", sect. 5, in the *Newman Reader—Works of John Henry Newman* (Pittsburgh: National Institute for Newman Studies, 2007), http://www.newmanreader.org/works/anglicans/volume2/gladstone/section5.html.

wrong in some of her moral teachings, so they should just remain silent about moral issues until the Church reformed.

It was not always that way. In her book *Catholics and Contraception*, Leslie Woodcock Tentler tells us that from the early decades of the twentieth century until about 1960, Catholics were very well instructed on the Church's teaching on contraception.[5] Parishes regularly hosted missions during Advent and Lent led by Passionists, Redemptorists, and Jesuits. During those missions, usually on a Wednesday night, they would give a talk about sexual morality. Often basing their instruction on personalist principles, they would teach the Church's teaching and speak against fornication, adultery, masturbation, and contraception. They did not threaten hellfire and damnation for those who did not abide by sexual morality, but urged individuals to realize that sexual immorality was against their human dignity and other human goods, that they were more likely to find happiness following the Church's teaching than violating it. Studies show that Catholics found these presentations persuasive and for the most part lived by the Church's teaching on sexual morality.

In 1960, most Catholics had never contracepted,[6] and these Catholics were by that time living in a very contraceptive culture. The Pill did not come out until around 1960, but the rest of the culture, including non-Catholic Christians, had embraced regular use of condoms and the diaphragm, and easily accepted the Pill. American culture by 1960 was a largely contracepting culture, but Catholics were not a part of it. Part of the reason is that, as we just noted, Catholics were well informed of the Church's teaching. While Professor Tentler herself rejects the Church's teaching on contraception, her book indicates that Catholics were very proud of being Catholic and were proud of having large families. They felt that they were living a radically Christian life and were avoiding the materialism to which the rest of the culture had succumbed.

Sadly, since *Humanae vitae*, Catholics have neither been instructed to be obedient to the Church nor been instructed on the justification for the Church's teaching on contraception. In 1990, the Philippine bishops acknowledged their failure to do their job with respect to this teaching in a remarkable statement. They said:

[5] Leslie Woodcock Tentler, *Catholics and Contraception: An American History* (Ithaca, NY: Cornell University Press, 2007).

[6] Ibid., pp. 133–34.

It is said that when seeking ways of regulating births, only 5 percent of you consult God. In the face of this unfortunate fact, we your pastors have been remiss: how few are there among you whom we have reached. There have been some couples eager to share their expertise and values on birth regulation with others. They did not receive adequate support from their priests. We did not give them due attention, believing this ministry consisted merely of imparting a technique best left to married couples. Only recently have we discovered how deep your yearning is for God to be present in your married lives, but we did not then know how to help you discover God's presence and activity in your mission of Christian parenting. Afflicted with doubts about alternatives to contraceptive technology, we abandoned you to your confused and lonely consciences with a lame excuse: "follow what your conscience tells you." How little we realized that it was our consciences that needed to be formed first. A greater concern would have led us to discover that religious hunger in you.[7]

Again, it is likely that the bishops were told in seminary that they should not teach the Church's teaching—as they state, their consciences "needed to be formed".

Conscience

Simply speaking, the conscience is the voice of God within helping us to choose good and avoid evil. Simple enough, perhaps, but one major problem is that we have many interior voices speaking to us. Indeed, we engage in lively internal dialogues all day long, and sometimes it seems that there is a dialogue between a good angel debating with a bad angel—even getting out of bed can be a moment of wrestling with the devil. We have such conversations all day long with many voices, the voice of our culture and our peers, for instance. The voice we need to train ourselves to listen to most closely is the voice of God because that is the conscience. Learning to distinguish God's voice from all the other voices competing for our attention requires that we should be people of

[7] Catholic Bishops' Conference of the Philippines, *Love Is Life*, October 7, 1990, in *Birth Control: What's Behind the Population Program*, vol. 3, no. 12 (Manila, Philippines: Documentation Service Theological Centrum, 1990), p. 7.

prayer. When we consult our conscience we are seeking the guidance of the Holy Spirit. We are trying to hear the voice of God and allow him to help guide our choices. After all, it is a certain truth that God's will is better than ours.

Veritatis splendor, one of John Paul II's outstanding encyclicals, discusses the conscience at some length. He talks about the very erroneous view of conscience that moderns have. We live in a society that tends to think there is no such thing as truth. Here is what *Veritatis splendor* says:

> Once the idea of a universal truth about the good, knowable by human reason, is lost, inevitably the notion of conscience also changes. Conscience is no longer considered in its primordial reality as an act of a person's intelligence, the function of which is to apply the universal knowledge of the good in a specific situation and thus to express a judgment about the right conduct to be chosen here and now.[8]

Our conscience is meant to help us figure out what we are meant to do here and now. The most laudable feature of the human person is the desire to find the truth and live by it. That, again, is the conscience.

Too many, however, have an erroneous view of the conscience—they do not seek *the* truth; they simply act in accord with their "own" truth. *Veritatis splendor* says:

> Instead, there is a tendency to grant to the individual conscience the prerogative of independently determining the criteria of good and evil and then acting accordingly. Such an outlook is quite congenial to an individualist ethic, wherein each individual is faced with his own truth, different from the truth of others. Taken to its extreme consequences, this individualism leads to a denial of the very idea of human nature.[9]

Any priest who has done marriage preparation regularly encounters this erroneous view of conscience. The vast majority of engaged couples are cohabiting; they generally evidence no discomfort or shame in disclosing that. When reminded that the Church teaches that sex outside

---

[8] John Paul II, encyclical letter *Veritatis splendor* (August 6, 1993), no. 32, http://w2 .vatican.va/content/john-paul-ii/en/encyclicals/documents/hf_jp-ii_enc_06081993 _veritatis-splendor.html.
[9] Ibid.

of marriage is seriously immoral, they allow that the Church has a right to its "own opinion" and they have a right to theirs.

Veritatis splendor also says:

> Although each individual has a right to be respected in his own journey in search of the truth, there exists a prior moral obligation, and a grave one at that, to seek the truth and to adhere to it once it is known. As Cardinal John Henry Newman, that outstanding defender of the rights of conscience, forcefully put it: "Conscience has rights because it has duties."[10]

Everyone has the right to follow his conscience only because the conscience has the ability to discover the truth. We have the *duty* to seek the truth. *Rights* of conscience follow upon the *duty* of the conscience to seek the truth. If someone says that he has the right to his opinion, he is correct, but if his opinions are unintelligent, uninformed, and unthoughtful, they are of no use no use to himself or others. Opinion and, certainly, conscience have to be shaped.

The *Catechism*, quoting *Gaudium et spes*, provides an excellent description of the conscience:

> Deep within his conscience man discovers a law which he has not laid upon himself but which he must obey. Its voice, ever calling him to love and to do what is good and to avoid evil, sounds in his heart at the right moment.... For man has in his heart a law inscribed by God.... His conscience is man's most secret core and his sanctuary. There he is alone with God, whose voice echoes in his depths.[11]

Notice here the claim that there are laws within us that we did not lay upon ourselves but we know we must obey. From a very early age, we understand that lying, stealing, and harming others is wrong. We learn these truths easily; we know we did not make them up and even that our parents did not, but that they are somehow laws of the universe that must be obeyed.

---

[10] Ibid., no. 34. The quotation is from John Henry Newman, *A Letter Addressed to His Grace the Duke of Norfolk: Certain Difficulties Felt by Anglicans in Catholic Teaching*, Uniform ed., vol. 2 (London: Longman, Green and Company, 1868–1881), p. 250.

[11] Vatican Council II, Pastoral Constitution on the Church in the Modern World *Gaudium et spes* (December 7, 1965), no. 16, quoted in the *Catechism of the Catholic Church*, no. 1776 (hereafter the *Catechism* is cited as *CCC*).

One time at a conference, a woman told me that her conscience was perfectly clear in regards to the accepted use of contraception. I expressed surprise and noted that, although Pope John Paul II prayed many hours every day for the guidance of the Holy Spirit, he never heard the Holy Spirit tell him that contraception was moral. Somehow the Holy Spirit has decided to let her know that contraception is moral but was not able to get through to John Paul II. I did not mean to mock her and embarrass her, but it was a question that needed to be asked. She had not really consulted her conscience—she was not seeking God's views on the matter; she asked only whether she was comfortable with contraception. With some chagrin, she acknowledged that my questions gave her pause.

Years ago, a nurse told me that she worked in a hospital where, after a woman had a baby, it was her job to hand a stack of pamphlets on contraception to the new mother. The nurse would tell the new mothers, especially those who were Catholic, that they did not need to follow these pamphlets. When the women would protest that their doctors advised them to use contraception, she would recommend that they pray about it: "Ask what Jesus wants you to do. Let God guide you on that decision, not a pamphlet." Often she would find the pamphlets tossed in the garbage can.

The *Catechism* says:

> Moral conscience, present at the heart of the person, enjoins him at the appropriate moment to do good and to avoid evil. It also judges particular choices, approving those that are good and denouncing those that are evil. It bears witness to the authority of truth in reference to the supreme Good to which the human person is drawn, and it welcomes the commandments. *When he listens to his conscience, the prudent man can hear God speaking.*[12]

Too many people think that the commandments of God are designed to rob us of pleasure: no fornicating, no adultery, no contraceptives. It can seem like God does not want us to have any fun! God, however, is telling us what is poisonous to our lives. The commandments are like the little skulls on cleaning fluids; they tell us these chemicals will

---

[12] *CCC* 1777, emphasis added.

kills us. God is not just putting up arbitrary fences to keep us out of the gardens of delight and telling us that if we manage to stay between these arbitrary fences we will get a big present at the end of time. That is not what he is doing. The commandments are keeping poison out of our system. These commandments are not something from a wicked God who will not let us have fun. Yes, it can be hard not to have sex before marriage. It can be hard to be faithful during marriage. It can be hard not to look at pornography. It also can be very hard not to be proud, not to be lazy. It can be hard to eat well and exercise regularly. Generally what is good for us requires some self-denial, some self-discipline, but the results of failing to exercise that discipline are often disastrous and the results of gaining self-discipline are beautiful. Through the commandments God is doing for us what Christ has done for the Church, the giving of "himself up for her, that he might sanctify her, having cleansed her by the washing of water with the word, that he might present the Church to himself in splendor, without spot or wrinkle or any such thing, that she might be holy and without blemish" (Eph 5:26–27).

An Erroneous Conscience

Despite our best efforts, trying to form our consciences does not always result in the right answer. On issues on which the Church has an explicit definite teaching, we need to read those teachings and shape our consciences accordingly. On some particular matters, there is no explicit Church teaching, so we need to pray and consult those who are wise. Unfortunately sometimes our advisors give us wrong or bad advice—even when it comes to matters in which there is explicit Church teaching. I have heard from too many people that they have heard from priests that in their case, contraception, sterilization, or in vitro fertilization would be permitted. These acts are never right, but some people are misinformed about them. We need to seek reliable, faithful advisors.

Yet the conscience is so important that we must follow it even when it is wrong. The *Catechism* says:

A human being must always obey the certain judgment of his conscience. If he were deliberately to act against it, he would condemn himself. Yet it can happen that moral conscience remains in ignorance and makes erroneous judgments about acts to be performed or already committed.[13]

Even if our conscience is wrong, we need to follow it. Aquinas tells us that even an "erroneous" conscience binds.[14] This does not mean, of course, that we must follow a conscience we know to be wrong! The reason we should follow even an erroneous conscience is that the conscience is our highest internal moral guide: if we are not following our consciences, we are following something else—most likely our disordered passions.

It is ignorance that makes a conscience erroneous. If the guidance of our conscience is erroneous because of what is called "vincible" ignorance, we do not escape culpability. Sometimes we are responsible for not knowing what we should know that would lead us to a moral decision. We may neglect, for instance, to get all the information we need to make a good decision, and sometimes we do not seek the information because we do not want to discipline our passions. This is the case when an individual " 'takes little trouble to find out what is true and good, or when conscience is by degrees almost blinded through the habit of committing sin.' In such cases, the person is culpable for the evil he commits."[15]

For instance, consider a doctor who, because he is in a hurry, does not read a patient's chart carefully and does something like prescribe penicillin for a patient who was allergic to penicillin. Ignorance in this case does not absolve him of culpability.

It is the same with a Catholic in respect to Church teaching. As Catholics we have an obligation to learn what the Church teaches about matters and why. The *Catechism* lists these as common sources of error in moral judgment: "ignorance of Christ and his Gospel, bad example given by others, enslavement to one's passions, assertion of a mistaken notion of autonomy of conscience, rejection of the Church's authority and her teaching, lack of conversion and charity".[16]

We should be trying to know Christ better all the time. We should follow the example of good and not of bad people. We should be trying to be free of the domination of our passions. We should strive to

[13] Ibid., 1790.
[14] *Summa theologiae* I–II, q. 19, aa 5–6.
[15] CCC 1791, quoting *Gaudium et spes*, no. 16.
[16] CCC 1792.

understand the nature of conscience and Church authority. We should undergo conversion and practice charity because if we did so we would be less likely to commit errors of judgment.

Yet not all ignorance is culpable; sometimes we are what is called invincibly ignorant. Invincible ignorance means that we could not have known what we needed to know—for some reason the information just wasn't available to us. In emergency situations, a physician who was not able to get a patient's medical history may treat a patient in a way that is safe for the vast majority of people, but that would be harmful to another. He is not culpable for his wrong choice.

The example that I often use to explain invincible ignorance to my students is that of a thirteen-year-old girl taken to Planned Parenthood for an abortion by her mother. Her mother and all her advisors tell her that abortion is not the killing of a human being; it is the removal of tissue. Objectively what she has done is very wrong—it is killing an innocent human being. Although she is not culpable, this does not mean the abortion will not have profound impact upon her, whether or not she ever comes to realize how wrong abortion is, but especially if she does. We cannot engage in seriously wrong behavior, even innocently, and not be harmed by it.

What are we to think of all the cohabiting couples? Are they acting in accord in vincible or invincible ignorance? If their culture and their parents approve of cohabitation and present it as good preparation for marriage, what culpability do they have? If they are churchgoing and never hear cohabitation condemned, what culpability do they have? I tend to think that those who truly consult their consciences, who sincerely try to hear God's voice on the morality of cohabitation, might quickly come to realize that it is immoral. If a couple spent about fifteen minutes in front of the tabernacle asking God whether he approved of cohabitation, I suspect most would hear his voice.

But, then again, how many people have been taught what the conscience is and what it means to consult it? I suspect that an enormous number of Catholics in our culture, including many health-care professionals, may be invincibly ignorant when it comes to contraception. They may know that the Church teaches that it is wrong, but may think that for some reason that the teaching is not binding on t hem. They may have been told that if their consciences are comfortable with contraception, they should follow their consciences.

Recall that in 1968 the Canadian bishops basically told Catholics they were free to follow their consciences about contraception. In 1973, however, they somewhat backtracked on their original statement. They said:

> A believer has the absolute obligation of conforming his conduct first and foremost to what the Church teaches, because first and foremost for the believer is that Christ, through his Spirit, is ever present in his Church, in the whole Church to be sure, but particularly with those who exercise services within the Church and for the Church, the first of which services is that of the apostles.[17]

The Canadian bishops are essentially saying that while they had advised couples to follow their consciences, they did not do a good job telling them how to do so, so they issued a second statement. They clarified that Catholics have a responsibility to form their conscience in respect to what the Church teaches. Blessedly, in this day and age there are really an abundance of resources available to Catholics who desire to know Church teaching. Church documents are readily available on the Internet; there are many good commentaries and YouTube lectures, good radio stations, and conferences. Catholics who seek to know what and why the Church teaches anything will not find it difficult to satisfy that desire. A challenge, of course, is igniting that desire in them. That is a subject for another essay, but if Catholics were convinced that Christ established the Church and guides the Church through the Holy Spirit, then Catholics would realize that a teaching of the Church is not just another "opinion" and would consider any teaching of the Church a great blessing.

Conscience Formation for Physicians

Humanae vitae was issued in 1968. It is a short, readable document, and only about thirty-five pages long. It would probably take about an hour or so to read. I once had the pleasure of hearing a Protestant minister

---

[17] Canadian Catholic Conference, "Statement on the Formation of Conscience", December 1, 1973, no. 39, www.consciencelaws.org/religion/religion040.aspx.

address a crowd of priests; he, along with a large number of family members, had converted to Catholicism the preceding Easter. During his address he held a copy of *Humanae vitae* up in the air and said, "You priests think that if you start preaching this people are going to leave the Church. I want to tell you that people are going to come in. I sat down and I read this document; I read it once, I read it twice, I read it three times. I wanted to belong to a Church that teaches something like that." He said if priests started preaching the truth of *Humanae vitae*, it would draw people into the Church and not drive them away. I suspect that Rex Moses was particularly susceptible to accepting the truth about contraception because he was already very active in the pro-life movement.

We need to read and study Church documents and ask God, "If this is true, open my mind, open my heart to it. Let me be shaped by your word and your teaching."

Humanae vitae states:

> The Church can only conduct herself as did the Divine Redeemer: she knows mankind's weakness; she has compassion on the multitude, and she forgives their sins. She cannot, however, do otherwise than to teach the law which is proper to human life restored to its original truth and guided by the Spirit of God.[18]

The Church is essentially saying, "We cannot change this teaching, any more than we could say adultery is right or abortion is right." This is God's law, not man's law. The document continues:

> The teaching of the Church about the proper spacing of children is a promulgation of the divine law itself. No doubt many will think this teaching difficult to keep, if not impossible. And truly, just as with all good things outstanding for their nobility and utility, [keeping] this law requires strong motivation and much effort from individual Men, from families, and from society. Indeed, this law is not able to be kept without the abundant grace of God, upon which the good moral choices of Men depend and from which they get their strength. Moreover, those who consider this matter thoroughly will see that [their] efforts [to keep God's law] increase human dignity and confer benefits on human society.[19]

[18] *HV* 19.
[19] Ibid., no. 20.

The Church knows it is going to be hard for people to accept and live by the truth about contraception. Thus we have to ask God for the graces to help us do what is difficult to do.

This is what *Humanae vitae* says to health-care professionals:

> Likewise we hold in the highest esteem those doctors and members of the nursing profession who, in the exercise of their calling, endeavor to fulfill the demands of their Christian vocation before any merely human interest. Let them therefore continue constant in their resolution always to support those lines of action which accord with faith and with right reason. And let them strive to win agreement and support for these policies among their professional colleagues. Moreover, they should regard it as an essential part of their skill to make themselves fully proficient in this difficult field of medical knowledge. For then, when married couples ask for their advice, they may be in a position to give them right counsel and to point them in the proper direction. Married couples have a right to expect this much from them.[20]

A book entitled *Physicians Healed* features the testimonies of fifteen courageous physicians who do not prescribe contraception.[21] They testify to how hard it was for them to stop doing something that their practice and training taught was good to do, but how satisfying it is to practice medicine in accord with God's will and with a clear conscience.

Another item that physicians should familiarize themselves with is the *Ethical and Religious Directives for Catholic Health Care Services* issued by the United States Conference of Catholic Bishops.[22] In directive 70 we find: "Catholic health care organizations are not permitted to engage in immediate material cooperation in actions that are intrinsically immoral, such as abortion, euthanasia, assisted suicide, and direct sterilization." The footnote to directive 70 reads:

> Any cooperation institutionally approved or tolerated in actions which are in themselves, that is, by their nature and condition, directed to a

---

[20] Ibid., no. 27.

[21] Cleta Hartman, ed., *Physicians Healed* (Dayton, OH: One More Soul, 1998).

[22] United States Conference of Catholic Bishops, *Ethical and Religious Directives for Catholic Health Care Services*, 5th ed. (November 17, 2009), http://www.usccb.org/issues-and-action/human-life-and-dignity/health-care/upload/Ethical-Religious-Directives-Catholic-Health-Care-Services-fifth-edition-2009.pdf .

contraceptive end ... is absolutely forbidden. For the official approbation of direct sterilization and, *a fortiori*, its management and execution in accord with hospital regulations, is a matter which, in the objective order, is by its very nature (or intrinsically) evil.[23]

Not only are institutions that perform or permit such actions as abortion, euthanasia, sterilization, and contraception engaging in intrinsically evil actions; they are also causing scandal. Directive 71 states: "The possibility of scandal must be considered when applying the principles governing cooperation." Any Catholic institution or any Catholic physician who engages in a forbidden action causes scandal— that is, they lead others into sin. Some priests are rightly hesitant to allow couples who are cohabiting to have a large wedding ceremony, because they fear they are giving the impression that the Church approves. In the same way, many look at Catholic doctors prescribing contraceptives and conclude that contraception cannot be bad, because otherwise good Catholic physicians would not prescribe it. Consider how powerful is the witness if Catholic physicians stop prescribing contraceptives. Certainly, and sadly, they would likely initially suffer significant financial loss, the loss of patients from their practice, and the loss of the respect of some of their colleagues. On the other hand, others, observing their brave witness, might be moved to imitate their courageous action and put aside sin in their lives.

There are a number of reasons why Catholic doctors continue to prescribe contraception. Many want to help women avoid unwanted pregnancies and abortions, especially unmarried women. It seems to make sense to urge a young woman who already has several children born out of wedlock to learn how to use contraception reliably. But that rarely helps—contraceptives just enable her to maintain the lifestyle that is already making a mess of her life. How much better if she encounters a doctor who tells her of the bad physical side effects of contraception and also helps her see how her life choices may not be good ones. I know of several physicians who enabled their patients to have the courage to stop fornicating by helping them understand the harms of contraception.

---

[23] Ibid., quoting "Reply of the Sacred Congregation for the Doctrine of the Faith on Sterilization in Catholic Hospitals" (*Quaecumqu Sterilizatio*) (March 13, 1975), in *Origins* 6 (1976): 33–35.

We often hear the claim that young people are going to have sex anyway, so we should at least urge them to be responsible and use a contraception. But oddly, we do not give young people who want to smoke low-nicotine cigarettes; rather, we tell them that smoking is bad for them. We do not tell those who drive while drunk that they should wear their seatbelts and drive slowly in uncongested areas. Sex outside of marriage and contraceptive sex in general can have similarly negative consequences as smoking or driving drunk. Why should we be facilitating such bad choices?

Morality of Prescribing Contraceptives for Therapeutic Reasons

Physicians prescribe the hormones found in contraceptives for various conditions. The Church teaches that it is morally permissible to prescribe the hormones in contraceptives for conditions for which they are helpful as long as the primary intention is not to cause infertility. *Humanae vitae* states:

> The Church, moreover, does allow the use of medical treatment necessary for curing diseases of the body although this treatment may thwart one's ability to procreate. Such treatment is permissible even if the reduction of fertility is foreseen, as long as the infertility is not directly intended for any reason whatsoever.[24]

Certainly physicians should try to determine whether vitamins or natural sources for hormones might help; but if the hormones that are present in the Pill are truly necessary to treat a condition, it is morally permissible to prescribe them since women taking the hormones in contraceptives are not doing so with a contraceptive intent. In fact, they are not contracepting, and the physicians are not prescribing a contraceptive. They are prescribing the hormones that are in the contraceptive. Contraception as a moral category is deliberately doing something that interferes with the sexual act in such a way as to prevent conception specifically. Those taking the hormones that are in the Pill for various medical conditions

[24] *HV* 15.

are not doing so to prevent conception; their infertility is a side effect of their choice.

We have seen in recent years that there are many in positions of power who want to force all physicians to prescribe contraceptives and do abortions, all health-care facilities to provide for them, all employers, even orders of nuns, to pay for contraception. I had a debate recently with a lady lawyer who told me that a pharmacist should not let his personal "preferences" stand in the way of "health care for patients". I challenged her statement and said, "The pharmacist was not acting on his preferences but on deeply held moral convictions."

Our culture does not even know what a deeply held moral conviction is. What our culture thinks are moral judgments are simply preferences, not much different from one person preferring chocolate ice cream while another prefers vanilla ice cream. Some people approve of abortion; some do not—those, according to our culture, are just preferences.

I also challenged the lady lawyer's claim that a pharmacist who refused to fill a prescription for contraceptives would be refusing health care to a client. After all, contraception is not health care; it cures no diseases and in fact suppresses natural healthy fertility. Contraceptives are prescribed not to cure a disease but to facilitate lifestyles. The lady lawyer could no more understand this point than she did the clarification of the distinction between preferences and deeply held convictions. Her reasoning was very simplistic in that she believed that since physicians are responsible for health care, and since they prescribe contraceptives, contraceptives therefore must be health care.

Margaret Sanger did a brilliant thing when she was able to persuade the world that physicians should prescribe contraceptives. Perhaps we should make contraceptives over-the-counter and put them where they belong: over in the porn section of the drugstore or with the cigarettes or even with the junk food—items that are not good for people but we allow them to have nonetheless. Contraceptives, cigarettes, and junk food are not things health-care professionals should be prescribing or recommending. Indeed, is it not the case that we require that contraceptives be available only through a physician's prescription because we know they are bad for women? The physician is giving a woman something that is risky and could endanger her health, and thus he needs to monitor her use of contraceptives. A patient discontinues antibiotics, high blood pressure medicine, and chemotherapy when they are no longer needed to advance his health. If contraceptives were a medication for an unhealthy condition, once the woman achieved health, she would discontinue the use of the contraceptive.

No doctor, Catholic or non-Catholic, should be prescribing contraceptives. Catholic physicians have a special responsibility not to prescribe contraceptives because they belong to a Church that has preserved wisdom on sexuality that many in the Church have forgotten. They have an obligation to form their consciences in accord with this teaching—no physician should be prescribing drugs that do not heal a condition and that pose significant danger to physical health and facilitate serious social dysfunction.

In our culture, most people have committed serious sins in respect to sexuality. Most Catholic health-care professionals have violated Church teaching in serious ways. Many of them have done so out of a desire to attempt to relieve people's suffering. Much experience shows that violation of Church teaching more often than not leads to heartbreak and tattered, if not shattered, lives.

Conclusion

Christ came not to make us feel miserable about our bad choices but to relieve us of the guilt and misery that we may experience because of our bad choices. He not only forgives us but gives us the graces to help us change our ways and make better choices. We have an all-powerful Father who sent us his Son to show us his love; he sent the Holy Spirit to guide us, often through the Church. We Catholics should take full advantage of the gifts that God has given us.

How *Humanae vitae* Has Advanced Reproductive Health[*]

Derek Doroski, Ph.D.

In 1968 Pope Paul VI issued the encyclical entitled *Humanae vitae*.[1] He has been hailed as a prophet[2] for accurately predicting some of the negative consequences of widespread use of contraception.[3] In his encyclical

---

[*] This essay was originally published in *Linacre Quarterly* 81, no. 3 (August 2014): 286–94. It was previously presented orally in an abbreviated form as follows: Derek M. Doroski, *Response to "Scientific, Spiritual, and Marital Dynamics of Natural Family Planning"* (presented at the conference "*Humanae vitae* at 45: Life, Liberty, and the Pursuit of Holiness", Franciscan University of Steubenville, Steubenville, OH, September 27, 2013).

[1] Paul VI, encyclical letter *Humanae vitae* (July 25, 1968) (hereafter cited as *HV*), http://w2.vatican.va/content/paul-vi/en/encyclicals/documents/hf_p-vi_enc_25071968_humanae -vitae.html.

[2] Mary Eberstadt, "The Prophetic Power of *Humanae Vitae*: Documenting the Realities of the Sexual Revolution", *First Things*, April 2018, https://www.firstthings.com/article /2018/04/the-prophetic-power-of-humanae-vitae (pp. 15–31 in this volume). See also Archbishop Angel Lagdameo, "*Humanae Vitae:* Controversial but Prophetic" (homily during the Mass celebrating the fortieth anniversary of *Humanae vitae* at the Manila Cathedral, July 9, 2008), *Catholic News Agency*, accessed April 9, 2018, http://www.catholicnewsagency.com /resources/life-and-family/humanae-vitae/humanae-vitae-controversial-but-prophetic/; and Janet E. Smith, Humanae Vitae: *A Prophetic Document* (Washington, DC: United States Conference of Catholic Bishops, Secretariat for Pro-Life Activities, 1988), http://www.usccb .org/prolife/programs/rlp/HVProphetic88.pdf.

[3] See *HV* 17. "Fertility control" or "fertility suppressor" may be a more accurate term than "contraception". A contraceptive acts by preventing the union of sperm and egg (or more properly the oocyte). Some methods such as condoms are indeed wholly contraceptive in their method of action. However, other interventions that are commonly called "contraceptives" also have other mechanisms of actions such as preventing implantation (i.e., an interceptive) or disrupting implantation after it has already occurred (i.e., a contragestive). Hormonal methods such as the Pill and the IUD may have interceptive and contragestive mechanisms of action, and thus it would not be fully accurate to refer to them as "contraceptives". On the other

Pope Paul VI also noted the morality of limiting intercourse to only the infertile times of a woman's fertility cycle.[4] In this way a couple could space births without interfering with the fertility of any particular conjugal act. Natural family planning (NFP) and, more recently, fertility awareness–based methods (FABMs) are the names often given to methods that space births in this manner.[5]

In this essay, I suggest that crediting *Humanae vitae* for predicting negative consequences of contraception is not going far enough. *Humanae vitae* should also be praised for promoting what future generations will see as dramatic improvements in reproductive health care. These improvements are occurring because (1) *Humanae vitae* encouraged the development of NFP and (2) the application of NFP-based approaches has promoted significant developments in reproductive health care. In addition, it will also be shown that health care based on a contraceptive mentality has stunted the development of reproductive science. Therefore, *Humanae vitae* should also be credited for discouraging methodologies rooted in the contraceptive mentality.

So how has *Humanae vitae* encouraged the development of NFP? At the end of *Humanae vitae* there are a number of pastoral directives. The one addressed "to men of science" states, "It is supremely desirable ... that medical science should by the study of natural rhythms succeed in determining a sufficiently secure basis for the chaste limitation of offspring".[6] The pastoral directive addressed to "doctors and members of the nursing profession" states, "Let them therefore continue constant in their resolution always to support those lines of action which accord with faith and with right reason."[7] These directives encouraged doctors and scientists to develop alternatives to contraception that would be based on understanding natural fertility rhythms. Dr. Thomas Hilgers is an example of a doctor who followed this directive. He specifically cites

---

hand, all of these so-called contraceptive measures have the goal of controlling and suppressing the healthy fertility of a couple. While the author believes that "fertility control" or "fertility suppressor" is a more accurate term, the term "contraceptive" will be used for greater ease of understanding.

[4] Ibid., no. 16.

[5] "Fertility awareness–based method" (FABM) is sometimes used synonymously with NFP, although the terms can have different connotations.

[6] *HV* 24.

[7] Ibid., no. 27.

Humanae vitae as his inspiration for developing the Creighton model of NFP,[8] and other developers of NFP have also been inspired by *Humanae vitae*.[9] From the development of the science of NFP even greater goods have followed.

According to Catholic teaching, the healthy function of our bodies is a good and noble thing. The *Catechism* states that "the human body shares in the dignity of 'the image of God' ".[10] Therefore, doctors who are informed by Catholic teaching, and especially by *Humanae vitae*, generally see the healthy function of the reproductive system as something good. They will naturally seek to understand the reproductive system better, cooperate with it, and heal its defects. In contrast, a contraceptive approach to the reproductive system sees our fertility as a problem, and thus treats it as a defect or disease, a thing to be suppressed, subverted, overcome, or destroyed.

The practical effects of this distinction may be illustrated with a comparison between a contraceptive approach to infertility and an approach in union with *Humanae vitae*. A review of some of the details of fertility and the marital act should help bring this distinction in focus. In the womb, a five-month-old female conceptus may have up to seven million of the germ cells that will create her future supply of "eggs".[11] By the time she is born, the number of germ cells will have dropped to a mere two million. At puberty only tens of thousands to hundreds of thousands of germ cells remain in the form of oocytes, which are nearly mature "eggs". Of these thousands of oocytes, up to fifty may start to mature during each fertility cycle.[12] Each oocyte suppresses the development of the other oocytes in an effort to become the lone dominant oocyte. After a dominant oocyte has been established, it will be released from the ovary during ovulation. The final result over a woman's lifetime is that only a few hundred oocytes will ever be ovulated (at most) out of a possible seven million germ cells. In other words, only about

---

[8] "Vision Statement", Pope Paul VI Institute for the Study of Human Reproduction, accessed April 9, 2018, http://www.popepaulvi.com/about.php.

[9] The developers of the Marquette model of NFP have mentioned their inspiration from *Humanae vitae* in conversations with the author.

[10] *Catechism of the Catholic Church*, no. 364 (hereafter cited as *CCC*).

[11] Bruce Carlson, *Human Embryology and Developmental Biology*, 4th ed. (Philadelphia: Mosby/Elsevier, 2009), pp. 4–5.

[12] Ibid., p. 13.

1 percent of 1 percent of the original germ cells ever reach ovulation and have an opportunity to be fertilized. Why are so many germ cells created in the first place if such a small number have the opportunity to be used for a new organism? This tremendous level of germ cell reduction may be a selection process that ensures that only the healthiest of oocytes will eventually be ovulated. In turn, a healthy oocyte increases the probability that a healthy organism will result from fertilization.

A similar process occurs with the sperm from a man. When a husband and wife come together in marital intercourse it is normal for hundreds of millions of sperm to enter the vagina.[13] Seminal fluid will protect the sperm from the acidic environment of the vagina for approximately ten minutes. This gives sperm the time that is needed to make it to the narrow part of the womb called the cervix. Ninety percent of sperm will die in this first step in their journey through the female reproductive system.[14] More sperm will be lost as they travel through the womb and the uterine tubes and seek out an oocyte to fertilize. Only hundreds to thousands of sperm will ever make it anywhere near the oocyte.[15] This translates into less than 1 percent of 1 percent of the initial sperm deposited ever making it anywhere near the oocyte. As with the oocyte, this reduction of sperm numbers may be a selection process that ensures that only the healthiest sperm have the opportunity to fertilize the oocyte. In turn, a healthy sperm increases the probability that a healthy organism will result from this fertilization. With these details established, we are now ready to look at potential treatments of infertility.

For many couples struggling with infertility, in vitro fertilization (IVF) will seem like the obvious solution to their problem. The first step in this technique is hyperstimulating the woman's ovaries to promote the production of multiple oocytes. Next, sperm will be collected from the man, usually through masturbation.[16] At this point one sperm may be selected and injected directly into the oocyte in a process called

---

[13] Ibid., p. 29.

[14] Ibid., p. 39.

[15] Ibid., p. 30; and Keith L. Moore, T. V. N. Persaud, and Mark G. Torchia, *Before We Are Born: Essentials of Embryology and Birth Defects*, 8th ed. (Philadelphia: Elsevier, 2013), p. 19.

[16] Sperm could licitly be obtained through the use of a perforated condom employed during intercourse. However, this method is rarely used in IVF. Even if sperm are licitly obtained, other steps used in the process of IVF would remain illicit.

intracytoplasmic sperm injection (ICSI). Alternatively, a number of sperm may be selected and deposited into an area around the oocyte. After the oocytes are fertilized, the resulting embryos that are to be used for pregnancy will be transferred into the mother's womb. Embryos not used to achieve a pregnancy are typically frozen for potential future use.[17]

While most IVF procedures are undertaken using sperm and eggs from the intended parents, some IVF procedures involve sperm and eggs donated from other people. This means that the sperm and eggs may be genetically distinct from those of the intended parents. Donor eggs are used in 3.2 percent of procedures, and both donor eggs and donor sperm are used in 6.0 percent of procedures to create donor embryos.[18] *Donum vitae* refers to these procedures as *"heterologous artificial fertilization"* and notes that they are *"contrary to the unity of marriage, to the dignity of the spouses, to the vocation proper to parents, and to the child's right to be conceived and brought into the world in marriage and from marriage."*[19] In other words, it is illicit for a man to fertilize the egg of a woman other than his wife and for a woman to allow herself to become pregnant by a man other than her husband. The moral problems of procreating with someone other than one's spouse are present whether the means are technological or through more old-fashioned methods.[20]

---

[17] Carlson, *Human Embryology*, pp. 36–37.

[18] Centers for Disease Control and Prevention, American Society for Reproductive Medicine, and Society for Assisted Reproductive Technology, *2015 Assisted Reproductive Technology Success Rates: National Summary and Fertility Clinic Reports* (U.S. Department of Health and Human Services, 2017), p. 8 (hereafter cited as CDC).

[19] Congregation for the Doctrine of the Faith, Instruction on Respect for Human Life in Its Origin and on the Dignity of Procreation *Donum vitae*—Replies to Certain Questions of the Day (February 22, 1987), II, A, 2, emphasis in original (hereafter cited as *DV*), http://www.vatican.va/roman_curia/congregations/cfaith/documents/rc_con_cfaith_doc _19870222_respect-for-human-life_en.html.

[20] One way in which heterologous artificial fertilization may be a violation of the one-flesh union involves the phenomenon of fetal microchimerism. Fetal microchimerism refers to the presence of cells in a mother's body that come from children she carried in her womb. These cells can be grafted in a variety of organs such as her lungs, spleen, liver, kidneys, and heart. As a result a mother will have cells inside her body that are genetically related to her husband, a kind of cellular one-flesh union. If a woman undergoes heterologous artificial fertilization, she will have cells in her body with DNA related to a man other than her husband or even from another woman. This microchimerism may be a kind of one-flesh union with a man other than her husband and possibly even another woman. For examples of fetal microchimerism, see Emilie C. Rijnink et al., "Tissue Microchimerism Is Increased During Pregnancy: A Human Autopsy Study", *Molecular Human Reproduction* 21, no. 11 (2015): 857–64.

It should be noted that even when the sperm and the eggs are both obtained from the intended parents, the IVF process promotes reproduction without the use of marital intercourse. Using the language found in *Humanae vitae*, one could say that IVF separates the unitive meaning of marital intercourse from the procreative meaning. Interestingly, *Humanae vitae* uses the term "procreation" rather than "reproduction".[21] It does so because human life is radically different from all other animal life: human beings have an immortal soul and only God can create an immortal soul. Thus, God is directly involved in the creation of every new human life. Spouses help God in "the transmission of human life"[22] and thus participate in his creative act. Animals "reproduce": they bring about another member of the species; human beings "procreate" something much more than just another member of the species. *Humanae vitae* teaches that the unitive and procreative meanings are both essential aspects of the marital act[23] and that "depriving it, even if only partially, of its meaning and purpose, is equally repugnant to the nature of man and of woman, and is consequently in opposition to the plan of God and His holy will."[24] By promoting reproduction outside of conjugal union, IVF brings the procreative meaning outside of the conjugal act and thus would be an approach that is not in union with the teachings of *Humanae vitae*.[25]

Furthermore, the contraceptive mentality present in IVF can also be seen by the contrast between procreation achieved through conjugal union and the methods used to achieve reproduction in IVF. While healthy function of a woman's reproductive system normally produces one oocyte at a time, IVF hyperstimulates the ovaries to produce multiple oocytes. While conjugal union delivers sperm to the female reproductive tract, IVF delivers sperm to oocytes in a dish. In addition, the sperm used for IVF are normally gathered through masturbation instead of conjugal

---

[21] *HV* 7, 9, 11, 14–15.

[22] Ibid., no. 1.

[23] Ibid., no. 12.

[24] Ibid., no. 13.

[25] Other magisterial documents also attest to the problem of substituting a procedure for the conjugal act. For examples see Congregation for the Doctrine of the Faith, Instruction on Certain Bioethical Questions *Dignitas personae* (June 20, 2008), no. 12, http://www.vatican .va/roman_curia/congregations/cfaith/documents/rc_con_cfaith_doc_20081208_dignitas -personae_en.html; see also *DV*, II, B, 4, a; and *CCC* 2377.

union. While conjugal union results in selection of sperm by the female reproductive tract, IVF achieves sperm selection through the choices of the IVF practitioner. Each of the IVF practices highlighted here subverts the normal process inherent in the marital act or even goes completely outside of the natural means of the body, thus treating the reproductive system as something to be overcome. Therefore, it is apparent that IVF has a foundation in the contraceptive mentality. One could suggest that IVF is a positive outcome of the contraceptive mentality if one believes that IVF is an advance in reproductive science. However, its success rate suggests otherwise.

IVF costs approximately $13,000 to $16,000 per attempt.[26] On average, this results in a 37 percent birth rate per attempt.[27] The surprising fact is that this success rate does not seem be much greater than that of treatments available decades ago. A maternity nursing textbook from 1971 suggests that 30 percent of infertile marriages can be rendered fertile.[28] The first birth resulting from IVF was in 1978. This means that after thirty years of development, IVF may not be much more successful than treatments available seven years before IVF existed. Studies from 1979 and 1981 of treatments for infertility due to tubal factors, endometriosis, or polycystic ovarian syndrome reported similar or higher treatment rates compared to IVF used today for the same problems.[29]

---

[26] Wendy S. Vitek et al., "Management of the First In Vitro Fertilization Cycle for Unexplained Infertility: A Cost-Effectiveness Analysis of Split In Vitro Fertilization-Intracytoplasmic Sperm Injection", *Fertility and Sterility* 100, no. 5 (2013): 1381–88.

[27] The live-birth rate is 37 percent each time that embryos are transferred to the womb. The success rate is 24 percent for those who start IVF and 27 percent when oocytes (eggs) are successfully gathered. (CDC, p. 13.)

[28] Elise Fitzpatrik et al., *Maternity Nursing*, 12th ed. (Philadelphia: J.B. Lippincott, 1971), p. 62.

[29] Live birth rate after tubal factor infertility was 28 percent in 1979 ("An Analysis of Macrosurgical and Microsurgical Technique in the Management of Tuboperitoneal Factor in Infertility", *Fertility and Sterility* 32 [1979]: 377) vs. 24 percent for IVF in 2015 (CDC, p. 26). Live birth rate after endometriosis was 54 percent in 1981 (J.F. Daniell and C. Christianson, "Combined Laparoscopic Surgery and Danazol Therapy for Pelvic Endometriosis", *Fertility and Sterility* 35, no. 5 [1981]: 521) vs. 27.6 percent for IVF in 2015 (CDC, p. 35). Rates of conception after treatment for polycystic ovarian syndrome was 73 percent in 1981 (E.Y. Adashi et al., "Fertility Following Bilateral Ovarian Wedge Resection: A Critical Analysis of 90 Consecutive Cases of Polycystic Ovary Syndrome", *Fertility and Sterility* 36, no. 3 [1981]: 320) vs. 26 percent through 34 percent for IVF in 2010 (Y.J. Kim et al., "A Comparative Study on the Outcomes of In Vitro Fertilization between Women with Polycystic Ovary Syndrome and Those with Sonographic Polycystic Ovary-Only in GnRH Antagonist Cycles", *Archives*

This evidence suggests that the contraceptive mentality, by promoting a focus on IVF, has stunted medical progress and may have even caused it to go backwards.[30]

So how does an approach in union with *Humanae vitae* fare in comparison? The American College of Obstetricians and Gynecologists (ACOG) has recommended monitoring of menstrual cycles (as is done in NFP) for health reasons.[31] I agree with ACOG that monitoring menstrual cycles through NFP should be an integral part of reproductive health care. One of the fundamental health benefits of using NFP-based approaches to overcome infertility is that they promote procreation by improving upon decreased reproductive function. They seek to heal defects of the reproductive system in order to enhance the effectiveness of the marital act. Since NFP-based approaches strengthen the connection between the unitive and procreative meanings of conjugal union, they are in union with the teachings of *Humanae vitae*. Overall, NFP-based approaches have higher published success rates (61 percent–66 percent) than IVF (37 percent) for treating infertility.[32] The increased ability to treat infertility remains even when a couple has already tried IVF once and failed (see Fig. 1) or when compared to repeated cycles of IVF

---

of Gynecology and Obstetrics 282, no. 2 [2010]: 199). See also A. M. Siegler and V. Kontopoulos, "An Analysis of Macrosurgical and Microsurgical Technique in the Management of Tubo-peritoneal Factor in Infertility", *Fertility and Sterility* 32, no. 4 (1979): 377–83; Daniell and Christianson, "Combined Laparoscopic Surgery and Danazol Therapy", pp. 521–25; CDC, p. 26; Adashi et al., "Fertility Following Bilateral Ovarian Wedge Resection", pp. 320–25; Kim et al., "Comparative Study on the Outcomes of In Vitro Fertilization", pp. 199–205.

[30] It should be noted that these comparisons do not meet the highest level of evidence (i.e., randomized controlled trials). However, it would be difficult, if not impossible, to make comparisons of this type across time with a randomized controlled trial. Comparison of similar studies is the best available evidence that we have at this point. Therefore, given the available evidence, it would seem reasonable to conclude that IVF has not resulted in much historical success.

[31] American Academy of Pediatrics and American College of Obstetricians and Gynecologists, "Menstruation in Girls and Adolescents: Using the Menstrual Cycle as a Vital Sign", *Pediatrics* 118, no. 5 (2006): 2245–50.

[32] E. Tham, K. Schliep, and J. Stanford, "Natural Procreative Technology for Infertility and Recurrent Miscarriage: Outcomes in a Canadian Family Practice", *Canadian Family Physician* 58, no. 5 (2012): e267–74; J. B. Stanford, T. A. Parnell, and P. C. Boyle, "Outcomes from Treatment of Infertility with Natural Procreative Technology in an Irish General Practice", *Journal of the American Board of Family Medicine* 21, no. 5 (2008): 375–84; CDC, p. 13.

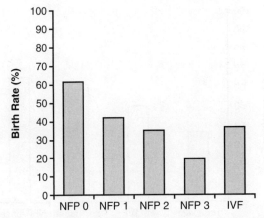

Figure 1. Success rates in treating infertility when an NFP-based approach is used after IVF has previously failed. NFP 0: birth rate using an NFP-based approach if IVF has not been previously attempted. NFP 1: birth rate using an NFP-based approach if IVF has previously been attempted and failed once. NFP 2: birth rate using an NFP-based approach if IVF has previously been attempted and failed twice. NFP 3: birth rate using an NFP-based approach if IVF has previously been attempted and failed three times. IVF: birth rate per cycle of IVF. This figure is adapted from published data.[33]

(see Fig. 2).[34] The contrast in success can be even more dramatic when treating specific causes of infertility such as endometriosis.[35]

In a certain sense, the success rates of IVF are even worse than these results suggest because IVF does not actually treat the causes of infertility. When IVF-based approaches succeed, a couple has a baby, but is still infertile. This is due to the fact that IVF goes outside of the reproductive

---

[33] Stanford, Parnell, and Boyle, "Outcomes from Treatment of Infertility"; CDC, p. 13.

[34] It should be noted that some of these comparisons do not meet the highest level of evidence (i.e., randomized controlled trials). In some cases, comparisons of similar studies are the best available evidence that we have at this point. This evidence points to the superiority of NFP-based approaches for treating infertility compared to IVF. Another important factor to consider is that it would be illicit to do a randomized control trial that included IVF. This limits the ability of promoters of NFP-based approaches to show that these approaches definitively are superior to IVF.

[35] J. S. Campbell et al., "Preliminary Meta-Analysis Comparing In Vitro Fertilization with Surgical Treatment for Moderate and Severe Endometriosis", *Journal of the American Association of Gynecologic Laparoscopists* 2, no. 4 (1995): S6–S7.

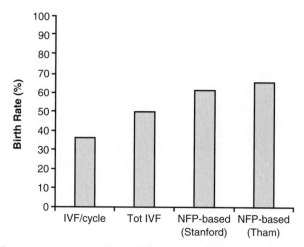

Figure 2. Success rates in treating infertility with IVF or NFP-based approaches. IVF/cycle: birth rate per cycle of IVF. Tot IVF: cumulative birth rate when all IVF cycles that a couple has participated in are included. NFP-based: birth rate of NFP-based based approaches from the respective citations. This figure is adapted from published data.[36]

system to achieve its effect and does not heal the reproductive system as part of its methodology. In contrast, NFP-based approaches will heal the underlying pathology of the reproductive system that is causing infertility. Therefore, when NFP-based approaches succeed, a couple has a baby and is no longer infertile.

Not only does IVF have a lower success rate in treating infertility compared to NFP-based approaches, but IVF is also accompanied by added complications that are minimal or absent in marital intercourse. Many of the complications of IVF are strongly linked to the ways in which IVF subverts the natural reproductive process. For example, the condition known as ovarian hyperstimulation syndrome (OHSS) does not arise in the context of natural marital intercourse. OHSS is a risk factor of IVF that arises due to the fact that the ovaries are stimulated to

[36] CDC, p. 13; V.A. Moragianni and A.S. Penzias, "Cumulative Live-Birth Rates After Assisted Reproductive Technology", *Current Opinion in Obstetrics and Gynecology* 22, no. 3 (2010): 189–92; Stanford, Parnell, and Boyle, "Outcomes from Treatment of Infertility"; Tham, Schliep, and Stanford, "Natural Procreative Technology".

produce multiple oocytes,[37] unlike the situation normally promoted by the reproductive system (i.e., only one oocyte). This can lead to severe pain, blood clots, and even possible kidney failure.[38] While ovulation may be promoted in NFP-based approaches, this stimulation is always targeted toward restoring normal ovulatory function (i.e., promoting ovulation of one oocyte only) and seeks to avoid stimulating the ovaries to function beyond their natural design.[39] As a result, OHSS is not a risk of NFP-based approaches.[40]

In addition to OHSS, IVF also appears to be associated with an increased risk of birth defects compared to marital intercourse.[41] While the precise cause of these birth defects is uncertain,[42] there is reason to believe that IVF may promote birth defects independent of maternal factors.[43] One potential explanation relates to how the oocytes and sperm are harvested in IVF. As previously noted, the reproductive system has an inherent selection process that results in making only 1 percent of 1 percent of potential sperm/oocytes available for fertilization. Since IVF goes outside the reproductive system to achieve its ends, this natural selection process is absent. Oocytes that would not naturally be ovulated will now be harvested from the hyperstimulated ovary. Even assuming that an IVF practitioner can select the best 1 percent of sperm for fertilization, this still pales in comparison to the natural sperm selection process. The end result is that there is a greater likelihood that sperm and oocytes will be used in IVF that would never have been used in the natural process of reproduction. It would be reasonable to suppose that some of these sperm and oocytes will therefore be less healthy and

[37] Arianna D'Angelo, "Ovarian Hyperstimulation Syndrome Prevention Strategies: Cryopreservation of All Embryos", *Seminars in Reproductive Medicine* 28, no. 6 (2010): 513–18.

[38] P. R. Brinsden et al., "Diagnosis, Prevention and Management of Ovarian Hyperstimulation Syndrome", *British Journal of Obstetrics and Gynaecology* 102, no. 10 (1995): 767–72.

[39] Thomas W. Hilgers, *The NaProTECHNOLOGY Revolution: Unleashing the Power in a Woman's Cycle* (New York: Beaufort Books, 2010), pp. 120–21, 217.

[40] Stanford, Parnell, and Boyle, "Outcomes from Treatment of Infertility".

[41] M. Hansen et al., "Assisted Reproductive Technology and Birth Defects: A Systematic Review and Meta-Analysis", *Human Reproduction Update* 19, no. 4 (2013): 330–53.

[42] J. Reefhuis et al., "Assisted Reproductive Technology and Major Structural Birth Defects in the United States", *Human Reproduction* 24, no. 2 (2009): 360–66.

[43] Lorraine Kelley-Quon et al., "Congenital Malformations Associated with Assisted Reproductive Technology: A California Statewide Analysis", *Journal of Pediatric Surgery* 48, no. 6 (2013): 1218–24.

may promote increased rates of birth defects. Interestingly, reproductive techniques that employ the natural selection mechanisms of the reproductive system, such as intrauterine insemination and ovulation induction (without hyperstimulation), may have a lower risk of birth defects than IVF and may not even have an increased risk compared to marital intercourse of fertile couples.[44] In contrast, while there is no published data on the prevalence of birth defects when NFP-based approaches are used, it is reasonable to suppose that these approaches would not promote increased levels of birth defects compared to those resulting from natural marital intercourse since promoting natural marital intercourse is how these methods achieve fertility.

A final complication of IVF is the increased risk of a multiple pregnancy.[45] Since IVF has a relatively low success rate, more than one embryo is usually transferred to the womb[46] in order to improve chances of a viable pregnancy. When more than one embryo is transferred to the womb there is a dramatic increase in the likelihood that multiple embryos will implant.[47] A multiple pregnancy is considered a disadvantage since it increases the risk of premature birth and low birth weight.[48] In contrast, the rate of multiples with NFP-based approaches is very low.[49] The low multiple rate with NFP-based approaches should not be a surprise since natural reproduction rarely results in the transport of multiple embryos to the womb.[50] The common theme in each of these risks is that the subversion of natural reproduction, which causes IVF to conflict with the teachings of *Humanae vitae*, seems to be promoting negative reproductive health consequences. In other words, the very things that cause IVF to conflict with *Humanae vitae* are also resulting in practical

[44] Ibid.; and Christine K. Olson et al., "In Vitro Fertilization Is Associated with an Increase in Major Birth Defects", *Fertility and Sterility* 84, no. 5 (2005): 1308–15.

[45] CDC, p. 18.

[46] Ibid., p. 32.

[47] There is a 2.1 percent chance of multiples when one embryo is transferred. The rate is 34.2 percent when two embryos are transferred, 25 percent for three, and 21.8 percent for four or more. See ibid., p. 35.

[48] Michael O. Gardner et al., "The Origin and Outcome of Preterm Twin Pregnancies", *Obstetrics and Gynecology* 85, no. 4 (1995): 553–57.

[49] Stanford, Parnell, and Boyle in "Outcomes from Treatment of Infertility" reported a multiple rate of 4.5 percent, and Tham, Schliep, and Stanford in "Natural Procreative Technology" reported no cases of multiples (0 percent).

[50] Carlson, *Human Embryology*, p. 54.

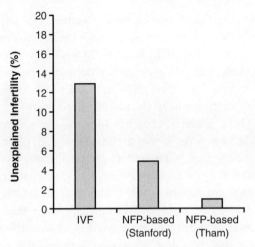

Figure 3. Cases of unexplained infertility after IVF or an NFP-based approach is used to treat infertility. This figure is adapted from published data.[51]

detriments. In contrast, the NFP-based approaches do not have these negative consequences, since reproduction is achieved in the context of natural marital intercourse.

Another dramatic effect of NFP-based approaches is that they are very effective in diagnosing the cause of reproductive pathologies. In multiple studies, NFP-based approaches have identified root causes of infertility that had not been previously identified (Fig. 3). Many of the couples in these studies had already tried IVF without a successful diagnosis of the cause of their infertility. Miscarriage treatments are another dramatic example of the power of NFP-based approaches. The treatments for miscarriage listed on the Mayo Clinic website include expectant management, medications to cause expulsion of the placenta, and dilation and curettage (D&C).[52] The medications and D&C remove the remains of the conceptus after the miscarriage has already occurred. Expectant management allows the remains of the conceptus

[51] CDC, p. 5; Stanford, Parnell, and Boyle, "Outcomes from Treatment of Infertility"; Tham, Schliep, and Stanford, "Natural Procreative Technology".

[52] Mayo Clinic, "Miscarriage: Treatment", July 20, 2016, https://www.mayoclinic.org /diseases-conditions/pregnancy-loss-miscarriage/diagnosis-treatment/drc-20354304.

to be expelled naturally. None of these treatments is targeted toward healing the underlying causes of miscarriage or improving the chances that gestation can continue.[53] In fact, the Mayo Clinic website suggests that there is nothing that can generally be done to prevent a miscarriage before it occurs[54] and does not suggest testing for underlying causes until after multiple miscarriages have already occurred.[55]

In contrast, NFP-based approaches can actually predict the risk of miscarriage before a woman is ever pregnant and then provide treatment to prevent the miscarriage.[56] There has been similar success in diagnosing and treating ovarian cysts, endometriosis, PMS, postpartum depression, and many other conditions.[57] NFP-based approaches are creating dramatic advances in reproductive health care even though there are many people, including doctors, who still don't know about them. This is an amazing gift that the Church is giving to the world, and it has been built on the foundation of *Humanae vitae*. Catholics should be proud of the amazing contributions to reproductive health care that the Church has promoted through Pope Paul VI's encyclical.

[53] The Mayo Clinic provides advice on avoiding known risk factors such as smoking and drinking. However, this advice appears to be focused on patients who have already experienced a miscarriage. For example, the overview section says, "Take a step toward emotional healing by understanding what can cause a miscarriage", which suggests that the person reading has already experienced miscarriage. While "hormonal problems" are identified as a potential cause of miscarriage, no methods for evaluating healthy pre-pregnancy hormone levels are noted in the diagnosis or prevention sections. In addition, there are no treatments listed that are targeted toward preventing a miscarriage in women at pre-pregnancy or early pregnancy state. See Mayo Clinic, "Miscarriage: Symptoms & Causes", July 20, 2016, https://www.mayoclinic.org/diseases-conditions/pregnancy-loss-miscarriage/symptoms-causes/syc-20354298.

[54] Mayo Clinic, "Miscarriage: Prevention", July 20, 2016, https://www.mayoclinic.org/diseases-conditions/pregnancy-loss-miscarriage/symptoms-causes/syc-20354298.

The term "threatened miscarriage" is used to refer to a point where the conceptus is alive, but in danger of miscarriage. Therefore it could be reasonable to assume that a search for the term "threatened miscarriage" might provide information on preventing miscarriage. However, a search for "threatened miscarriage" does not bring up any further results.

[55] The exact wording is as follows: "If you experience multiple miscarriages, generally two or three in a row, consider testing to identify any underlying causes." See Mayo Clinic, "Miscarriage: Treatment; Future Pregnancies", July 20, 2016, https://www.mayoclinic.org/diseases-conditions/pregnancy-loss-miscarriage/diagnosis-treatment/drc-20354304.

[56] Hilgers, *NaProTECHNOLOGY Revolution*, pp. 259–69.

[57] Thomas W. Hilgers, *The Medical & Surgical Practice of NaProTECHNOLOGY* (Omaha: Pope Paul VI Institute Press, 2004).

The United States Bishops vs.
the HHS Contraception Mandate

A Question of Religious Freedom, Moral Truth, or Both?*

Peter J. Colosi, Ph.D.

The U.S. bishops' deployment of the Fortnight for Freedom in 2012 was an astonishing unified confrontation with modern U.S. culture that did enormous good in calling attention to and resisting attacks against religious liberty. In the face of such an impressive effort, it may seem churlish to criticize aspects of it and especially to criticize those Church

---

* This chapter builds upon previous pieces I have authored on the U.S. Department of Health and Human Services (HHS) mandate: "The HHS Mandate: A Question of Religious Freedom or the Life Issues?", *Life and Learning* XXV, *Conference Proceedings of the Twenty-Fifth University Faculty for Life* (The Bronx: University Faculty for Life, 2017), pp. 159–88; "The HHS Mandate: A Question of Religious Freedom or the Life Issues?", *The Catholic Social Science Review* 20 (2015): 53–73; "The HHS Mandate: What Now, in Light of the Supreme Court Ruling?", *Crisis Magazine*, July 2, 2012, http://www.crisismagazine.com/2012/the-hhs-mandate-what-now-in-light-of-the-supreme-court-ruling; "The HHS Mandate: This Is about Contraception", *Crisis Magazine*, June 28, 2012, https://www.crisismagazine.com/2012/the-hhs-mandate-this-is-about-contraception; "The HHS Mandate: A Question of Religious Freedom or the Life Issues?", *Crisis Magazine*, June 27, 2012, http://www.crisismagazine.com/2012/the-hhs-mandate-a-question-of-religious-freedom-or-the-life-issues; "False Premises", *Crisis Magazine*, February 23, 2012, http://www.crisismagazine.com/2012/false-premises; "Is the Catholic View of Contraception Immoral?", *Catholic Exchange*, February 20, 2012, https://catholicexchange.com/is-the-catholic-view-of-contraception-immoral; "Contraception and the Fight against the HHS Mandate Ruling", *Catholic Exchange*, February 7, 2012, https://catholicexchange.com/142703.

leaders who boldly led the efforts against the HHS mandate. I in no way mean to diminish the greatness of what they did and a certain prudence with which they acted. But because there will undoubtedly be attacks against religious liberty in the future, we need to learn from our various engagements with the government and culture. This essay will suggest that along with making a defense of religious freedom, the Church also needs to undertake a concerted effort to implement the Church's teaching on contraception (or on whatever teaching is part of an attack) to Catholics and non-Catholics alike. Not only will this advance the human happiness the teaching is designed to promote, but it would help in the defense of religious liberty, for the case could and should be made that religious liberty is not in service of some idiosyncratic, unobserved Catholic teaching but of a teaching that truly is crucial to human well-being. Indeed, the U.S. bishops have for some time been building their website on marriage and family, and individually and collectively are doing more to teach the Church teaching on contraception. This essay seeks to help us learn from recent missed opportunities and to encourage ongoing efforts to catechize the laity about Catholic teachings at odds with the culture.

Historical Context

On March 23, 2010, President Obama signed into law the Affordable Care Act (ACA), also known as Obamacare. The act contained a provision requiring that many preventative health services be fully covered by health insurance plans and with no co-pay. There were many services listed; two such, for example, were mammograms and smoking-cessation aids. On August 1, 2011, Secretary of Health and Human Services Kathleen Sebelius added a whole range of female contraceptives, including temporary, permanent, and abortifacient ones, to the list of such services, and set the date by which this revision to the rule would be legally enforceable for one year later, August 1, 2012. This meant that Catholic institutions and businesses would be required to participate in the contraceptive industry and thus to support, via health insurance policies, intrinsically immoral actions of their employees. This was a clear violation of religious freedom.

A Teaching Moment Unparalleled since 1968

The events just described created a situation strikingly similar and yet in one key respect much different from that of 1968 when *Humanae vitae* was promulgated. The similarity was that in both 1968 and 2012 the whole world had its ears perked up concerning Catholicism and contraception—and, basically, heard nothing from the pulpit. I would like to suggest that the deafening silence in 1968 was understandable for two reasons: (1) not only did many priests and theologians dissent from *Humanae vitae*; bishops and priests were not prepared to explain the reasons behind the teaching,[1] and (2) people were not prepared to hear it. Things are very different now: (1) many priests and lay Catholics can ably explain the reasons supporting the goodness and beauty of the Church's teaching on contraception from every possible perspective, including physical health, medical, psychological, environmental, spousal, family-relational, spiritual, and more;[2] and (2) the sexual and relational mess of our times indicates that people may be more receptive to this teaching.[3]

Pope Francis has noted that one of the principal settings for the New Evangelization is "that of '*the baptized whose lives do not reflect the demands of Baptism.*' ... The Church, in her maternal concern, tries to help them experience a conversion which will restore the joy of faith

---

[1] For an analysis of the dissent from *Humanae vitae*, see Peter M. Mitchell, *The Coup at Catholic University: The 1968 Revolution in American Catholic Education* (San Francisco: Ignatius Press, 2015). For a subtle treatment of the question on the international level, see John Joseph Williams, "Bishops' Conferences in the Wake of Humanae Vitae: Commentaries That Missed the Mark", *Catholic Social Science Review* 22 (2017): 171–87.

[2] For just three excellent examples, see Angela Franks, "The Gift of Female Fertility", in *Women, Sex, and the Church: A Case for Catholic Teaching*, ed. Erika Bachiochi (Boston: Pauline Books and Media, 2010), pp. 97–119; Adrian Walker, " 'What God Has Conjoined, Let No Man Put Asunder': A Meditation on Fruitfulness, Fidelity, and the Conjugal Embrace", *Communio*, Summer 2014, pp. 372–79; and Simcha Fisher, *The Sinner's Guide to Natural Family Planning* (Huntington, IN: Our Sunday Visitor, 2014).

[3] See Jennifer Fulwiler, "We're Finally Ready for *Humanae Vitae*", postscript in Pope Paul VI, *On Human Life: Humanae Vitae*, foreword by Mary Eberstadt, afterword by James Hitchcock (San Francisco: Ignatius Press, 2014), pp. 103–7; and Marie Anderson, "Contraception, Wrestling with Reality", in *Breaking Through: Catholic Women Speak for Themselves*, ed. Helen M. Alvaré (Huntington, IN: Our Sunday Visitor, 2012), pp. 33–48.

to their hearts and inspire a commitment to the Gospel."[4] We find a striking illustration of Pope Francis' concern in a study of millennials by the Public Religion Research Institute, showing that what millennials are deeply seeking is love, support, and companionship. The study also found that 71 percent of millennials consider contraception morally acceptable; 72 percent of white Catholics and 74 percent of Hispanic Catholics said that "safe sexual practices and contraception was more effective than abstinence."[5] Millennials do not seem to know that contraception and the uncommitted sex it enables work against their desire for love, support, and companionship. *Humanae vitae* notes, "None can achieve true happiness, the happiness that they desire with the strength of their whole soul, unless they observe the laws inscribed on their nature by the Most High God. To be happy human beings must prudently and lovingly cultivate these laws."[6] Keeping the laws is possible, but for the faithful to observe them wisely and lovingly, a deeper understanding of their truth, goodness, and beauty is essential.

The bishops took the lead opposing the mandate on the grounds that it undercuts religious freedom. They chose not to focus on the morality of contraception. While the lack of knowledge among the Catholic faithful could not have been completely remedied by the antimandate campaign, that moment was a clear wake-up call to the problem of the nonacceptance of the Church's teaching on contraception and should have been embraced as a proverbial teaching moment, not only for Catholics but for the many others who were wondering what the Catholic Church thinks about contraception. Moreover, had the Catholic laity been better informed about the immorality of contraception, as

---

[4] Francis, apostolic exhortation *Evangelii gaudium*, no. 15, emphasis in original, quoting Benedict XVI, Homily at Mass for the Conclusion of the Synod of Bishops (October 28, 2012), in *AAS* 104 (2102): 890, http://w2.vatican.va/content/francesco/en/apost_exhortations/documents/papa-francesco_esortazione-ap_20131124_evangelii-gaudium.html.

[5] Carol Zimmermann, "New Survey Shows Millennials' Attitudes about Contraception, Abortion", Catholic News Service, March 30, 2015, http://catholicphilly.com/2015/03/news/national-news/new-survey-shows-millennials-attitudes-about-contraception-abortion/. Strictly speaking, the quotation given is logically inconsistent since abstinence is 100 percent effective.

[6] See Paul VI, encyclical letter *Humanae Vitae*, no. 31, trans. Janet E. Smith, in Humanae Vitae: *A Challenge to Love* (New Hope, KY: New Hope Publications, 2006 (hereafter cited as *HV*).

well as its health risks to women,[7] they may have been more aggressive in supporting the bishops' effort.

This essay suggests a two-pronged effort to strengthen the Church's opposition to attacks on religious liberty that push for Catholic funding of contraception (or supporting other immoral actions): the political effort must (in this instance) include (1) showing that contraception is not health care (and, rather, poses serious health risks) and (2) catechizing the faithful regarding the moral objections to contraception in light of a holistic vision of human life and love.

More importantly, people of today yearn for an abiding happiness and for true love, and thus they need a Church with courage and an overall plan to teach them about the necessary foundations to achieve those desires.

Legal Battles and Pastoral Responsibilities

Some of this work has already begun. One excellent resource developed by the bishops is their webpage covering multiple dimensions of marriage and family from a Catholic perspective.[8] This is a superb, clear, and easy-to-navigate resource. Sadly, it is likely that most Catholic laity are unaware of this website, thus steps must be taken to ensure that parish priests and qualified laity work together to create opportunities to introduce this rich material to their fellow parishioners.

One inspiring recent example comes from Archbishop Samuel Aquila of Denver, who has written an excellent, short, and easily accessible pastoral letter honoring the fiftieth anniversary of *Humanae vitae* titled *The Splendor of Love*.[9] The archbishop encourages the priests and

---

[7] See Kathleen M. Raviele, "Reproductive Health and the Practice of Gynecology", in *Catholic Witness in Health Care: Practicing Medicine in Truth and Love*, ed. John M. Travaline and Louise A. Mitchell (Washington, DC: Catholic University of America Press, 2017), pp. 105–69.

[8] See "Marriage", United States Conference of Catholic Bishops, accessed May 7, 2018, http://www.usccb.org/issues-and-action/marriage-and-family/marriage/. (Additional information is available for Spanish-speaking couples by clicking on the Por tu Matrimonio website icon.)

[9] Archbishop Samuel Aquila, *The Splendor of Love*, Archdiocese of Denver, February 2, 2018, http://archden.org/wp-content/uploads/2018/02/splendor-of-love_web.pdf.

deacons of his diocese to proclaim the truth of God's plan for human love with charity and gentleness, and to accompany their people in their difficulties living this out.[10] The archbishop also says that in Denver—as he did when he was bishop of Fargo, North Dakota—he requires all couples in marriage preparation to attend a full course of NFP (natural family planning) training for three to four months. He recounts beautiful and moving stories of the positive effects of this policy, even though there was sometimes initial resistance to it.[11] Another excellent example is the pastoral letter of Bishop David D. Kagan of Bismarck, North Dakota, titled "And the Two Shall Become One".[12] Letters like these, accompanied by well-planned implementation across the entire country, would do very much good.[13] As Archbishop Aquila notes in his letter, the fifty-year anniversary of *Humanae vitae* presents the perfect opportunity to do just that.[14] We expect to see a great deal of activity from the bishops supporting the teaching of *Humanae vitae* during this year. Catholic University of America, which can justly be called the "bishops' university", held a significant conference on *Humanae vitae* in April 2018, and the bishops of Michigan are responding to the resolution of the U.S. bishops to promote *Humanae vitae*, by preaching about it at several central parishes.[15]

It needs to be noted that the criticism below of some remarks of the bishops who took the lead in opposing the HHS mandate is not at all meant to suggest that these particular bishops have been opposed to

---

[10] See ibid., no. 42 (reference is to the paragraph number).

[11] See ibid., no. 3.

[12] For an explanation of the pastoral letter, see "Bishop: Marriage Sacrament Allows Man and Woman to Carry Out God's Will", Catholic News Service, March 30, 2015, http://catholicphilly.com/2015/03/ news/national-news/bishop-marriage-sacrament-allows -man-and-woman-to-carry-out-gods-will/.

[13] In a recent article, Joan Frawley Desmond noted that "only 12 U.S. Catholic dioceses presently require natural family planning (NFP) instruction in their pre-Cana programs" (Joan Frawley Desmond, "'Humanae Vitae' Generates Greater Public Support 50 Years On", *National Catholic Register*, April 13, 2018, http://www.ncregister.com/daily-news /humanae-vitae-continues-to-generate-dissent-greater-public-support-50-years). According to the USCCB's website, there are 196 archdioceses/dioceses and one Personal Ordinariate in the United States (see "Bishops and Dioceses", United States Conference of Catholic Bishops, updated January 2018, http://www.usccb.org/about/bishops-and-dioceses/index.cfm).

[14] See Aquila, *Splendor of Love*, 50.

[15] See Daniel Meloy, "Bishops to Preach about '*Humanae Vitae*' in Today's Church", *Michigan Catholic*, April 20, 2018, http://www.themichigancatholic.org/2018/04/bishops -to-preach-about-humanae-vitae-in-todays-church/.

Humanae vitae; indeed, they have been among those who have defended Church teaching on contraception and deserve gratitude for that. The suggestions here are made to advance that work of defense and to encourage bringing it to the next level.

Statements of the U.S. Bishops in 2012

"Not about Contraception"

The unity, work, and leadership of the bishops in the fight for religious freedom was indeed something unique and wonderful to behold. They began by clearly identifying the wrongheaded notions built into the HHS mandate: (1) "an unwarranted government definition of religion",[16] (2) "a mandate to act against [the] teachings"[17] of our religion, and (3) "a violation of personal civil rights".[18] Regardless of the specific provisions of that mandate in regard to contraception, legalizing these notions violates the nature of freedom and conscience, and the laws and customs of this country.[19] The same would be true had the government forced the Amish to participate in car sales in ways that violated their beliefs. To isolate and name such erroneous notions is necessary, and the bishops did that clearly.

After identifying these problems within the mandate, the bishops made the following statement:

> This is *not* about access to contraception, which is ubiquitous and inexpensive, even when it is not provided by the Church's hand and with the Church's funds. This is *not* about the religious freedom of Catholics

---

[16] By this the bishops mean both that it is beyond the role of a government to define a religion and also that the definition of a "religious employer" given by the government in the HHS mandate is false. That definition is that a religious employer is one who hires and serves primarily members of its own faith. For their development of this two-part meaning of "unwarranted government definition of religion", see Administrative Committee of the United States Conference of Catholic Bishops, "March 14 Statement on Religious Freedom and HHS Mandate", March 14, 2012, http://www.usccb.org/issues-and-action/religious -liberty/march-14-statement-on-religious-freedom-and-hhs-mandate.cfm.

[17] Ibid.

[18] Ibid.

[19] Ibid.

only, but also of those who recognize that their cherished beliefs may be next on the block. This is *not* about the Bishops' somehow "banning contraception," when the U.S. Supreme Court took that issue off the table two generations ago. Indeed, this is *not* about the Church wanting to force anybody to do anything; it is instead about the federal government forcing the Church—consisting of its faithful and all but a few of its institutions—to act against Church teachings. This is *not* a matter of opposition to universal health care, which has been a concern of the Bishops' Conference since 1919, virtually at its founding.[20]

The bishops repeatedly stated that the fight was not about contraception.

For instance, in a high-profile interview, Timothy Cardinal Dolan, a great champion in the fight against the HHS mandate, stated: "We have to be very vigorous in insisting that this is not about contraception. It's about religious freedom."[21] And in a *Wall Street Journal* interview, he emphasized the point by stating: "We've grown hoarse saying this is not about contraception, this is about religious freedom."[22] And although Dolan aptly noted the Church's concern about religious freedom, it should perhaps be acknowledged that for the Obama administration, the issue *was*—even primarily so—about providing contraception free of charge and only secondarily about religious freedom.

While the focus on the assault on religious liberty was certainly justified, focusing the discussion exclusively on religious freedom unfortunately may have left the impression with many people that Catholics were allowing an idiosyncratic, largely ignored teaching to stand in the way of needed "health care". So although religious liberty was a key issue, it is also true that it is a serious matter for Catholics to be forced to pay for insurance plans that pay for contraception—contraception is not a trivial matter, nor is it a moral issue only for Catholics, and thus in order for the Church to make its case against forcing it to provide contraception, the case against contraception should be made.

---

[20] Ibid., emphasis in original.

[21] Catholic News Agency, "Cardinal Dolan: We Bishops Will 'Vigorously' Continue Fight against HHS Mandate", *National Catholic Register*, March 30, 2012, http://www.ncregister.com/daily-news/cardinal-dolan-we-bishops-will-vigorously-continue-fight-against-hhs-mandat.

[22] James Taranto, "When the Archbishop Met the President", *Wall Street Journal*, March 31, 2012, https://online.wsj.com/article/SB10001424052702303816504577311800821270184.html.

The Parable of the Kosher Deli

Archbishop William Lori of Baltimore, chairman of the U.S. bishops' Ad Hoc Committee for Religious Liberty during the fight against the HHS mandate, has long been a noble defender of *Humanae vitae*: on its fortieth anniversary, he wrote a wide-ranging explanation of the document and the resistance to it.[23] Yet, I believe an analogy he used to speak against the mandate while strong in some ways could leave a false impression. In his testimony before Congress on February 16, 2012, he used what he called "the parable of the kosher deli" to make his point. If the government were to require orthodox Jews to serve pork in their delis, any person of good will would easily grasp both the reason why religious freedom should be respected in that case and the absurdity of not respecting it, for people can easily buy pork (or contraceptives, so the analogy goes) inexpensively at the grocery store next door.[24] This analogy is helpful in that it serves to highlight a very serious general trajectory of the mandate—namely, the complete dismantling of the First Amendment, which would open the door to legal intrusions on religious freedom in many other areas. The parable is also potentially helpful in that it could aid in gaining a broad coalition of concerned citizens, many of whom have no qualms about using contraception but share the concern about establishing a very worrisome precedent. Archbishop Lori's parable was an important part of this fight, and made the contribution just outlined.

The weakness of the analogy—and all analogies break down at some point—is the equating of teachings by particular religions based on features distinctive of them with teachings based on universal human nature. For instance, the Torah contains various dietary proscriptions that God gave to the Jewish people and which were not required for non-Jews. The Amish do not drive cars because of beliefs distinctive

---

[23] See "Humanae Vitae Part I", Archdiocese of Baltimore, August 21, 2008, https://www.archbalt.org/humanae-vitae-part-i/; "Humanae Vitae Part II", Archdiocese of Baltimore, August 28, 2008, https://www.archbalt.org/humanae-vitae-part-ii/; "Humanae Vitae Part III", Archdiocese of Baltimore, September 4, 2008, https://www.archbalt.org/humanae-vitae-part-iii/.

[24] Keith Fournier, "The Parable of the Kosher Deli: Bishop Lori before Congress Defending Religious Liberty", *Catholic Online*, February 21, 2012, https://www.catholic.org/news/national/story.php?id=44808.

336 WHY *HUMANAE VITAE* IS STILL RIGHT

of them. Although Christians are not bound by Jewish dietary law, we have full respect for the Jewish commitment to obeying those laws. And although Catholicism is not opposed to cars, Catholics have respect for the decision of the Amish not to drive cars.

There is, however, a very important *difference in kind* between the argumentation that is supportive of the Catholic teaching that using contraception is immoral and the argumentation used in the Amish and Jewish prohibitions on driving and on eating pork that these examples may unfortunately obscure. This difference derives from the fact that one can show the immorality of contraception on the basis of the natural moral law and its roots in human nature. Perhaps in a brief congressional testimony, it was practical for Archbishop Lori to develop the analogy only as far as he did. Strictly speaking, however, Archbishop Lori's parable does not provide a telling argument against the position of those who are not swayed by religious claims and who hold that there is a moral imperative to "reproductive rights". If you asked the authors of the HHS mandate whether they think Orthodox Jews are being *immoral* in not allowing their people to eat pork, or whether they think the Amish are *immoral* in not teaching their children to drive cars, they would likely say, "No, those prohibitions are not immoral." They do, however, think that the Catholic Church is committing an *immoral, irrational*, and *inhuman* act—indeed, an *abuse* against women—in prohibiting contraception on moral grounds. To let that charge stand unaddressed is tacitly, if unintentionally, to give the impression that it is accurate. And if accurate, why should anyone be granted freedom, religious or otherwise, to refuse to include contraception coverage in health insurance? Thus, a follow-up, perhaps in a different venue, by the bishops on the difference between contraception and the Jewish dietary restriction could have shown why this fight for religious liberty was also a fight for the natural law and the common good.

Another way to see this point is to consider Kathleen Sebelius' press release of January 20, 2012, in which she said: "I believe this proposal strikes the appropriate balance between respecting religious freedom and increasing access to important preventive services."[25] Her remark

---

[25] U.S. Department of Health and Human Services, "A Statement by U.S. Department of Health and Human Services Secretary Kathleen Sebelius", news release, January 20, 2012, https://wayback.archive-it.org/3926/20150121155601/http://www.hhs.gov/news/press/2012pres/01/20120120a.html.

corresponds with the view of many who see the Church's teaching that contraception is immoral as equivalent to proscriptions of other religions that in reality are not parallel. One such example is the Jehovah's Witnesses' belief that blood transfusions are immoral. The conventional wisdom on dealing with that issue is to require the children of Jehovah's Witnesses who need blood transfusions to receive them, even against their parents' wishes by means of a court order, but to allow adult Jehovah's Witnesses to refuse blood transfusions because they are of the age of consent.[26] Now, to people who are not Jehovah's Witnesses, this practice seems tragic and wrong, but it is allowed. Possibly, Sebelius sees the Catholic prohibition of contraception as like the Jehovah's Witnesses' prohibition of blood transfusions. Just as society limits to the bare minimum those who can refuse blood transfusions, she wants to limit to the bare minimum those who do not receive free access to FDA-approved contraceptives and abortifacients. But, again, it must be made clear that, unlike blood transfusions, contraceptives are not health care; they, in fact, suppress the healthy condition of fertility—the choice to use contraception is a lifestyle choice, not a health choice.[27]

Sebelius and company think of contraception and Catholicism in the exact same way as the readers of this book may think of blood transfusions and Jehovah's Witnesses. On this view, contraception and blood transfusions are simply sources of good health that make the world a better place. Anyone who has a principled opposition to either of those things is odd, if not outright mistaken. To fail to address that premise tacitly affirms it. As noted above, contraception is not health care, and this needs to be explained.

---

[26] For a helpful discussion of this situation, see Rev. Albert S. Moraczewski, O.P., "Religious Freedom and Pastoral Care", in *Catholic Health Care Ethics: A Manual for Practitioners*, ed. Edward J. Furton (Philadelphia, PA: National Catholic Bioethics Center, 2009), pp. 249–50.

[27] The therapeutic use of the Pill has been argued to be morally licit under the principle of double effect, as that is permitting the use of the hormones present in the Pill to control such conditions as the growth of ovarian cysts and endometriosis, and in those cases the prescription is not intended for contraceptive purposes, though fertility will be suppressed. The hormones in the Pill do not cure any underlying condition but only treat symptoms, have other negative side effects on health, and are potentially abortifacient. More and more physicians are finding ways to treat the underlying conditions and find the therapeutic use of the Pill to be unnecessary and in this way also protect the fertility of the patient. For recommendations for natural treatments, see "Treating Disorders", Natural Womanhood, accessed May 7, 2018, https://naturalwomanhood.org/learn/treating-disorders/.

Warning about Future Ramifications

Another approach was that taken by the late Francis Cardinal George of Chicago, a courageous supporter of orthodoxy, who wrote: "If you haven't already purchased the Archdiocesan Directory for 2012, I would suggest you get one as a souvenir.... On page L-3, there is a complete list of Catholic hospitals and health care institutions in Cook and Lake counties.... Two Lents from now, unless something changes, that page will be blank."[28] Cardinal George's letter also made a contribution to the fight. Besides accurately foretelling what very well could have happened in the near future, it was also supposed to rally the laity to do something to prevent hospital closures. Yet, I suspect many hearing George's statement would think it to be hyperbolic. Or, if not as hyperbole, they might just wonder why he doesn't acquiesce to the law since the hospitals do so much good work in other areas. It would seem to many, if not most, to be a strange imbalance to close Catholic hospitals in order to deny a non-Catholic employee access to contraception.

Cardinal George also wrote: "I expect to die in bed, my successor will die in prison, and his successor will die a martyr in the public square." In the rest of the passage, often left out in citations of his remarks, he continued, "His successor will pick up the shards of a ruined society and slowly help rebuild civilization, as the Church has done so often in human history."[29] But we need to do something similar now, at this moment, to rebuild the public's perception and knowledge of Church teaching on human sexuality gradually. The most promising place to begin is with our own people in the pews.

Contraception Is the Wrong Question

Archbishop Charles Chaput has been one of the most outspoken leaders of the Catholic Church in our times, about *Humanae vitae* as well

[28] Thomas Cloud, "Cardinal George: Catholic Hospitals Will Be Gone in 'Two Lents' Under Obamacare Regulation", *CNSNews.com*, February 28, 2012, http://cnsnews.com/news/article/cardinal-george-catholic-hospitals-will-be-gone-two-lents-under-obamacare-regulation.

[29] Francis Cardinal George, O.M.I., "The Wrong Side of History", *Chicago Catholic*, October 21, 2012, http://legacy.chicagocatholic.com/cnwonline/2012/1021/cardinal.aspx.

as a myriad of other issues.[30] His opposition to the HHS mandate was powerful. Yet the Church remains vulnerable to attacks on her religious liberty especially when it involves contraception because so many Catholics do not follow the teaching. Thus, when the Church fights against legislation providing free access to contraception, it seems hypocritical. The charge of hypocrisy is implicit in the question when Chaput was asked about the fact that many Catholics use contraception and also support abortion rights. He answered:

> That's the wrong question. Plenty of self-described Catholics also commit adultery and cheat on their taxes. That doesn't make them right, and it doesn't make their behaviors "Catholic." The central issue in the HHS-mandate debate isn't contraception. Casting the struggle as a birth-control fight is just a shrewd form of dishonesty. The central issue in the HHS debate is religious liberty. The government doesn't have the right to force religious believers and institutions to violate their religious convictions. But that's exactly what the White House is doing.[31]

Clearly Chaput saw that the supporters of the HHS mandate thought Catholics are vulnerable on the matter of contraception and that if they could make the HHS mandate succeed, future attacks on religious liberty would be easier to win. He was correct to point out that the Obama administration was trying to focus the fight on contraception and neatly showed the logical irrelevance of the charge that Catholics do not live by the Church's teaching. On that account it was prudent not to allow the administration's focus on contraception to dictate the terms of the debate, especially since the culture is not yet ready to engage in a serious reexamination of the morality and consequence of abortion.

Nonetheless the hypocrisy of the situation does serve to undermine efforts to protect religious liberty. Surely we need to reduce the Church's vulnerability in all areas, especially in those where its teaching is at great odds with the culture. We hope we can get to a point where

[30] See "Archbishop Chaput's Address at Catholic University: Humanae Vitae and Its Legacy, April 4, 2018", Archdiocese of Philadelphia, April 11, 2018, http://archphila.org/archbishop-chaputs-address-at-catholic-university-humanae-vitae-and-its-legacy-april-4-2018/.

[31] Archbishop Charles Chaput, "Ringing a Bell for Liberty", interview by Kathryn Jean Lopez, *National Review Online*, April 2, 2012, http://www.nationalreview.com/articles/294990/ringing-bell-liberty-interview.

the charge cannot be made that many Catholics use contraception and support abortion rights and that Catholics will be mobilized to convert the rest of the culture.

But also, the administration in fact did see the controversy as primarily about access to contraception, sterilization, and abortifacient drugs and devices (e.g., IUDs). Their willingness to attack religious freedom, which they did by building large fines into the law for institutions that chose not to abide by it,[32] served as a powerful means to achieve their goal, since many religions oppose the mandate's coverage of one or more of these practices. Thus, asking about the fact that many Catholics use contraception is a legitimate question, and not the wrong question.

Explaining the Reasons for Clerical Silence

The widespread and well-known discrepancy between Catholic practice and Catholic teaching[33] was one key foundation for the success of the Obama administration's approach, and it constituted a genuine obstacle to our side in the battle for religious freedom. It was one reason among two others noted by Cardinal Dolan for clerical silence.

In the *Wall Street Journal* interview mentioned above, Cardinal Dolan admitted candidly to three reasons why many bishops and priests are silent on questions of contraception and Church teachings on human sexuality: (1) the enormity of the catechetical challenge, (2) the priestly sexual abuse scandal, and (3) the aftermath of *Humanae vitae*.[34] Here is the first quotation of Cardinal Dolan: "I'm not afraid to admit that we have an internal catechetical challenge—a towering one—in convincing

---

[32] The Little Sisters of the Poor calculated that they would have been fined $70 million per year. See "Nuns Could Face 'Frightening' $70m-a-Year Fine in Birth Control Case", by staff reporter, *Catholic Herald*, March 24, 2016, http://catholicherald.co.uk/news/2016/03/24/nuns-could-face-frightening-70m-a-year-fine-in-birth-control-case/; for full details, see the Becket Fund for Religious Liberty webpage that is dedicated to the Little Sisters of the Poor case at https://www.becketlaw.org/case/littlesisters/.

[33] See Jennifer Ohlendorf and Richard J. Fehring, "The Influence of Religiosity on Contraceptive Use among Roman Catholic Women in the United States", *Linacre Quarterly* 74, no. 2 (May 2007): 135–44, and Richard J. Fehring, "Under the Microscope, The Facts about Faithful Catholics and Contraception", *Current Medical Research* 23, nos. 1 and 2 (Winter/Spring 2012): 13–19.

[34] Taranto, "When the Archbishop Met the President".

our own people of the moral beauty and coherence of what we teach. That's a biggie.... We have gotten gun-shy ... in speaking with any amount of cogency on chastity and sexual morality."[35] The towering challenge today would perhaps not be quite so towering, were it not for the lack of previous catechesis on these matters among so many of the faithful. Yet, people nowadays do have a sense that something is amiss. Many do not have an intellectual understanding concerning why this is so, but their own experience of contraception and related issues has left them aware that it is not the be-all and end-all that they had thought it would be. Maybe they are clinging to it because they do not think that there is an alternative. Perhaps they are afraid of change, or perhaps the wounds and possible guilt that emerge seem too difficult. The pastoral problem is undoubtedly immense, but God is infinite. He desires nothing more than to forgive us, and he can make all things new.

In his interview, Cardinal Dolan implied that this lack of catechesis explains why Church spokesmen, when asked about that teaching, kept saying that the battle was not about contraception. It is time to act upon the plea that Pope Paul VI made in *Humanae vitae* when speaking to his fellow bishops:

> We make this urgent request of you: We ask all of you to take the lead with the priests who assist your sacred ministry, and all your faithful. With complete zeal and with no delay, devote yourselves to keeping marriage safe and holy, so that the life of married couples may draw more closely to its proper human and Christian perfection. Truly consider this as the greatest responsibility [opus] of your mission [*munus*] and the greatest work [onus] committed to you at the present time. As you well know, [your] mission [*munus*] requires a certain coordination of pastoral ministry in all areas of human activity, including economic, social and cultural matters.[36]

The urgency of that summons was due to the ripeness of the teaching moment; we have a similar moment now. As mentioned, initiatives by the bishops collectively and individually in this fiftieth-year anniversary of *Humanae vitae* are encouraging, but we cannot let it be a "flash-in-the-pan" moment—the educational efforts must be thorough and ongoing.

[35] Ibid.
[36] HV 30.

There are glimmers of hope that priests are ready to preach on *Humanae vitae* and parishioners are ready to listen. For an example of one priest, and there were others, who rose to the occasion in 2012, consider Jennifer Fulwiler's heartening account of a homily by her parish priest, Fr. Jonathan Raia, on contraception. After a few moments of pregnant silence, the congregation erupted in applause.[37] A concerted effort is needed, with clear direction from the bishops, to foster such informative and rousing homilies.

The second reason that Cardinal Dolan gave for the clerical silence is the priestly sexual abuse scandal: "[It] intensified our laryngitis over speaking about issues of chastity and sexual morality, because we almost thought, 'I'll blush if I do.... After what some priests and some bishops, albeit a tiny minority, have done, how will I have any credibility in speaking on that?' "[38] But this view underestimates the ability of people to realize that the majority of bishops and priests are not guilty of sexual misconduct and that priests altogether deplore the horrific behavior of fellow priests. The scandal does not constitute a reason to remain silent on these matters; quite to the contrary, it constitutes a reason to speak more, and with direct clarity and firm conviction and even to show the connection between the mistaken view of sexuality promoted by contraception and misuses of sexuality, among them sexual abuse by priests.[39]

Undoubtedly, some humiliations will come if the bishops and priests begin to teach on these matters, but they can be assured of widespread support and encouragement from the laity who also teach on these matters, and I suspect from many more, if the anecdote recounted by Jennifer Fulwiler is any indication. In any case, we must all speak the truth "in season and out of season" (2 Tim 4:2). And, in fact, in the very same interview, Taranto reported that Cardinal Dolan "sees a hunger, especially among young adults, for a more authoritative Church voice on sexuality".[40] The cardinal is right about this, and it is a reason for the authorities to speak.

---

[37] See Fulwiler, "Ready for *Humanae Vitae*", pp. 103–7.

[38] Taranto, "When the Archbishop Met the President".

[39] See Peggy Noonan, "The Sexual-Harassment Racket Is Over", *Wall Street Journal*, November 23, 2017, https://www.wsj.com/articles/the-sexual-harassment-racket-is-over-1511470096.

[40] Taranto, "When the Archbishop Met the President".

With great candor, Cardinal Dolan offered a third reason for the silence of the bishops when he says that *Humanae vitae*

> brought such a tsunami of dissent, departure, disapproval of the Church, that I think most of us—and I'm using the first-person plural intentionally, including myself—kind of subconsciously said, "Whoa. We'd better never talk about that, because it's just too hot to handle." We forfeited the chance to be a coherent moral voice when it comes to one of the more burning issues of the day.[41]

We must not forfeit another chance to be a "coherent moral voice". As mentioned above, there may have been some understandable reasons fifty years ago for a reticence to speak, but now there are many reasons to speak with confidence, and the aftermath of *Humanae vitae* is one of those reasons. Pope Saint John Paul II thematized his papacy with the words "Do not be afraid",[42] and now is the time to apply those words to this topic—bishops, priests, and laity together.

A Stark Contrast concerning Contraception and the Common Good

The Obama administration believed that the Catholic position prohibiting contraception is both irrational and immoral, and they saw widespread access to contraception as the solution to some of the world's problems. This became very clear when, after objections to the mandate mounted from Catholic and other religious nonprofits and businesses, the Obama administration issued, at different times, modifications purportedly to assuage these concerns. The modifications were called "accommodations", and none of them removed the difficulties Catholics have in complying with the unjust law. Consider this argument of the administration when presenting one of their accommodations: "If a woman's employer is a charity or a hospital that has a religious objection to providing contraceptive services as part of

---

[41] Ibid.

[42] Homily of His Holiness John Paul II for the Inauguration of His Pontificate (October 22, 1978), no. 5, http://w2.vatican.va/content/john-paul-ii/en/homilies/1978/documents/hf_jp-ii_hom_19781022_inizio-pontificato.html.

their health plan, the insurance company—not the hospital, not the charity—will be required to reach out and offer the woman contraceptive care free of charge, without co-pays and without hassles."[43] This carefully crafted statement implied that the religious objection represents the opposite of "reaching out" and "offering care" and is therefore immoral. It also clearly suggests a lack of charity in the religious objection by mentioning "hassles", which are deemed irrational, as is the rejection of free contraceptive "care". In other words, this was nothing other than doubling down on the same ploy to make the Church look out of touch with reality.

Statements like that should also not be left standing and unchallenged. The reason is that according to the Church's own social teaching, the State *does* have a responsibility to regulate society.[44] To take an extreme example, if there were a religion carrying out human sacrifices, the State would be playing its rightful role in stopping that practice and legislating against it. And so, rather than standing by and silently allowing the false premises in the above statement to sink into the minds of those who hear it, those premises must be exposed, debunked, and replaced with the truth. Otherwise, it appears that the State is simply playing its proper role of regulation with the HHS mandate by stopping the Catholic Church from imposing its odd prohibition on employees at its numerous institutions.

But the core reason why the approach encapsulated in the mandate is a complete and utter error is expressed in this simple statement by Pope Benedict XVI: "When a society moves towards the denial or suppression of life, it ends up no longer finding the necessary motivation and energy to strive for man's true good."[45] The contrast of worldviews could not be starker. We need the leaders of the Church to explain why this statement of Pope Benedict is true and rooted in the two ideas of

[43] "Remarks by the President on Preventive Care", White House, Office of the Press Secretary, February 10, 2012, http://www.whitehouse.gov/the-press-office/2012/02/10/remarks-president-preventive-care.

[44] See Pontifical Council for Justice and Peace, *Compendium of the Social Doctrine of the Church* (June 29, 2004), nos. 351–55, 393–98, http://www.vatican.va/roman_curia/pontifical_councils/justpeace/documents/rc_pc_justpeace_doc_20060526_compendio-dott-soc_en.html.

[45] Benedict XVI, encyclical letter *Caritas in veritate* (June 29, 2009), no. 28, http://www.vatican.va/holy_father/benedict_xvi/encyclicals/documents/hf_ben-xvi_enc_20090629_caritas-in-veritate_en.html.

the blessings of children and the relation between the family and the common good.[46]

That explanation will perhaps not be given widespread coverage on television news interviews, although even in those settings, one should be prepared with some appropriate, brief, and clear defense that might make a thoughtful viewer consider the possibility of its truth. In other settings, such as parishes and dioceses, an all-out effort is needed, and particularly if there is a teaching moment like in 2012 when everyone was following the story. There are well-trained lay Catholics in all fields ready and willing to help, who would enthusiastically respond to an invitation from their bishop or priest.

If such an invitation were issued and a practical plan developed, then gradually the many Catholics who have accepted the false premises that contraception is a kind of health care and that it promotes the common good could be shown the positive alternatives. Failing such an effort, the striking rhetorical question of Paul VI makes perfect sense: "Would anyone blame those in the highest offices of the state for employing a solution [contraception] considered morally permissible for spouses seeking to solve a family difficulty, when they strive to solve certain difficulties affecting the whole nation?"[47] In other words, if Catholics and other citizens think that contraception is helpful in their own personal lives, then we have lost any basis on which to blame a government for deeming to use it on a wider scale to solve larger problems that it perceives.

And furthermore, it is not just against individual government mandates that we must fight. There are, in fact, forces at the highest level of global politics and industry working toward the goal of spreading "reproductive rights". Consider, for example, that at the very same time that the HHS mandate was being promoted in the United States, the government of the United Kingdom and the Bill and Melinda Gates

[46] For an autobiographical account of going from a fear of children to the awareness of the blessings of children, see Helen M. Alvaré, "Fear of Children", in Alvaré, *Catholic Women Speak for Themselves*, pp. 19–32. For a helpful explanation of the relation between the family and the common good as seen through the lens of Catholic social teaching, see Carl Anderson and José Granados, *Called to Love: Approaching John Paul II's Theology of the Body* (New York: Doubleday, 2009), pp. 226–44. And for a description of what he terms the "demographic suicide" of Europe and evidence of its reality from numerous statistical studies, see George Weigel, *The Cube and the Cathedral* (New York: Basic Books, 2005), pp. 21–23, and the notes given there.

[47] *HV* 17.

Foundation hosted a family-planning summit in London; its goal was "to generate unprecedented political commitment and resources from developing countries, donors, the private sector, civil society and other partners to meet the family planning needs of women in the world's poorest countries by 2020".[48] In 1995 in *Evangelium vitae* (The Gospel of Life), Pope John Paul II described this situation in the following way:

> The Pharaoh of old, haunted by the presence and increase of the children of Israel, submitted them to every kind of oppression and ordered that every male child born of the Hebrew women was to be killed (cf. Ex. 1:7–22). Today not a few of the powerful of the earth act in the same way. They too are haunted by the current demographic growth, and fear that the most prolific and poorest peoples represent a threat for the well-being and peace of their own countries. Consequently, rather than wishing to face and solve these serious problems with respect for the dignity of individuals and families and for every person's inviolable right to life, they prefer to promote and impose by whatever means a massive programme of birth control.... Aside from intentions, which can be varied and perhaps can seem convincing at times, especially if presented in the name of solidarity, we are in fact faced by an objective "conspiracy against life", involving even international Institutions, engaged in encouraging and carrying out actual campaigns to make contraception, sterilization and abortion widely available.... [The] culture ... presents recourse to contraception, sterilization, abortion and even euthanasia as a mark of progress and a victory of freedom, while depicting as enemies of freedom and progress those positions which are unreservedly pro-life.[49]

John Paul is making two main points. First, that there are power structures in place implementing well-developed plans to bring it about gradually that the practices of the culture of death become widespread and commonplace as solutions to life's challenges. And second, that these forces have as part of their plan to generate the impression that the

---

[48] United Kingdom Department for International Development, "Family Planning: UK to Host Summit with Gates Foundation", March 6, 2012, http://www.dfid.gov.uk/News /Latest-news/2012/Family-planning-UK-to-host-summit-with-Gates-Foundation/.

[49] John Paul II, encyclical letter *Evangelium vitae* (March 25, 1995), nos. 16–17, http:// w2.vatican.va/content/john-paul-ii/en/encyclicals/documents/hf_jp-ii_enc_25031995 _evangelium-vitae.html.

pro-life forces are out of touch with contemporary life and reality, and thus irrationally restrictive and backwards.

For all of these reasons, a well-thought-out educational effort by the Church needs to be implemented.

Some Practical Suggestions

The three false premises that need to be directly addressed are (1) that contraception is health care, (2) that contraception is good for society, and (3) that to oppose contraception is immoral. The Church should proclaim with zeal, confidence, and joy the many dimensions of the good news of Church teaching on love and procreation:[50] the blessings of children,[51] responsible parenthood, fertility awareness,[52] the benefits of waiting until marriage,[53] and the Catholic view of the goodness of the body.[54] We should point out the many risks that contraception

[50] Pope St. John Paul II's Theology of the Body has many profound dimensions, and one of those is certainly a rich commentary on *Humanae vitae*. See John Paul II, *Man and Woman He Created Them: A Theology of the Body*, trans. Michael Waldstein (Boston: Pauline Books and Media, 2006), 118–25 (references are to the audience numbers). Together with friends in Europe, I have co-organized a series of international symposia on John Paul II's Theology of the Body in four different countries. The videos of those presentations, by experts from every scientific field, as well as pastoral and popular presentations can be viewed online; see the website of the TOB [Theology of the Body] International Symposia at www.tobinterna tionalsymposia.com.

[51] The USCCB has a ready-made, three-part teaching tool, including a video, study guide, and parish night outline, available at http://www.marriageuniqueforareason.org/children -video/. See also Jason T. Adams, *Called to Give Life: A Sourcebook on the Blessings of Children and the Harm of Contraception*, foreword by Archbishop Charles J. Chaput (Dayton, OH: One More Soul, 2003), available at http://onemoresoul.com/catalog/called-to-give-life -pdf-p1119.html.

[52] See Richard J. Fehring, "Fertility Care Services", in *Catholic Witness in Health Care*, ed. John M. Travaline and Louise A. Mitchell (Washington, DC: Catholic University of America Press, 2017), pp. 170–208; the website of FACTS: Fertility Appreciation Collaborative to Teach the Science at https://www.factsaboutfertility.org/; and the website of the Friends of FertilityCare Philadelphia at http://www.fertilitycarefriends.org/.

[53] See Bridget Maher, "Why Wait: The Benefits of Abstinence until Marriage", Family Research Council, accessed May 23, 2018, https://downloads.frc.org/EF/EF11B20.pdf.

[54] See Peter J. Colosi, "The Christian Personalism of John Paul II as the Foundation of Theology of the Body" (lecture given at the National Theology of the Body Congress in Philadelphia, held July 28–30, 2010). For the audio version of my lecture, see Peter J. Colosi, "Christian Personalism and Theology of the Body", PeterJColosi.com, April 18, 2012, http:// peterjcolosi.com/christian-personalism-and-theology-of-the-body/.

poses to relationships,[55] health,[56] the common good, and respect for women.[57]

It is very heartening that priests and laypeople have started speaking on all of these topics, and many rose to the occasion precisely because of the 2012 debate. There is the marvelous talk given by Gloria Purvis at the Catholic Information Center on February 27, 2012.[58] Several good homilies have been posted online, for example, one by Philadelphia priest Father Philip Forlano (given on March 4, 2012, at St. Stanislaus Roman Catholic Church in Lansdale, Pennsylvania),[59] and another by Father Ben Cameron of the Confraternity of Our Lady of Mercy (in Auburn, Kentucky).[60] Both of these homilies combined boldness, clarity, and compassion. Tom Hoopes, a layman, gave a moving personal testimony.[61] There is also an excellent website (Natural Womanhood) that explains many of the facts in an accessible and beautiful way, with depth.[62] Bishops could invite speakers from the Culture Project[63] and other chastity education ministries to their dioceses. There is also the important, thorough, widely used, and easily accessible work of Dr. Janet E. Smith.[64] Dr. Christopher Tollefsen presents a clear, quick-read

[55] See the talk given by Janet E. Smith entitled "Contraception: Cracking the Myths", Our Lady of Good Counsel Catholic Church, Plymouth, Michigan, October 4, 2011 (the third version of "Contraception: Why Not"); the CD is available at Lighthouse Catholic Media at https://www.lighthousecatholicmedia.org/store/title/contraception-cracking-the-myths.

[56] See Maricela P. Moffitt et al., "CMA Women Physicians Respond to Women Senators' Column", Catholic Medical Association, February 22, 2012, http://www.cathmed.org/cma-women-physicians-respond-to-women-senators-column/.

[57] See Valerie Pokorny, "Opinion: Contraception Denigrates Me as a Woman", *In America* (blog), CNN, February 15, 2012, http://inamerica.blogs.cnn.com/2012/02/15/contraception-denigrates-me-as-a-woman/.

[58] Gloria Purvis, "HHS Mandate Is Anti-Woman: Catholics Need to Speak Up", YouTube video, 7:02, March 7, 2012, http://www.youtube.com/watch?v=UvoBPVsjdog.

[59] See Katie van Schaijik, "A Priest Lays Out the Wrong of the HHS Mandate", March 6, 2012, http://www.thepersonalistproject.org/comments/a_priest_explains_the_objection_to_the_hhs_mandate.

[60] Father Ben Cameron, "Artificial Birth Control", Fathers of Mercy, YouTube video, 8:50, January 16, 2008, http://www.youtube.com/watch?v=IBjxtXJQXFg&list=UUdLDRDAlpQloMuyRnokfNOA&index=17&feature=plcp.

[61] Tom Hoopes, "Contraception Opposed Me First", CatholicVote.org, April 2, 2012, http://www.catholiclane.com/contraception-opposed-me-first/.

[62] Natural Womanhood's website can be found at https://naturalwomanhood.org/.

[63] Culture Project's website can be found at http://www.restoreculture.com/.

[64] Janet E. Smith, *Self-Gift:* Humanae Vitae *and the Thought of John Paul II* (Steubenville, OH: Emmaus Academic, 2018); *Why* Humanae Vitae *Was Right: A Reader*, ed. Janet E. Smith

argument based on the new natural law theory.[65] "The Vindication of *Humanae vitae*", written for the fortieth anniversary of *Humanae vitae*, and its companion piece for the fiftieth anniversary, "The Prophetic Power of *Humanae vitae*", by Mary Eberstadt, are gripping articles constituting a sort of definitive proof that Pope Paul VI was right on every count.[66] And from the medical point of view, there is the work of the Pope Paul VI Institute,[67] as well as all of the other fertility awareness methods.[68] From a Christian personalist perspective, see the book *Love, Marriage and the Catholic Conscience* by Dietrich von Hildebrand.[69] There are a large number of videos that explain the Church's teaching from many perspectives, and many institutes that do the same. Indeed, the Couple to Couple League and the Theology of the Body Institute provide special training sessions for priests.[70]

Conclusion

The purpose of this essay has been to assess the approaches of various bishops to the HHS mandate in the year 2012, and to express gratitude

---

(San Francisco: Ignatius Press, 1993); Janet E. Smith, Humanae Vitae: *A Generation Later* (Washington, DC: Catholic University of America Press, 1991); and Smith, "Contraception: Cracking the Myths".

[65] Christopher Tollefsen, "Contraception and Catholicism", *National Review Online*, February 16, 2012, http://www.nationalreview.com/articles/291220/contraception-and-catholicism-christopher-tollefsen.

[66] Mary Eberstadt, "The Vindication of *Humanae vitae*", *First Things*, August 2008, https://www.firstthings.com/article/2008/08/002-the-vindication-of-ihumanae-vitaei, and Mary Eberstadt, "The Prophetic Power of *Humanae vitae*: Documenting the Realities of the Sexual Revolution", *First Things*, April 2018, https://www.firstthings.com/article/2018/04/the-prophetic-power-of-humanae-vitae.

[67] The website of the Pope Paul VI Institute for the Study of Human Reproduction can be found at http://www.popepaulvi.com/.

[68] For helpful overviews and explanations see Fehring, "Fertility Care Services", and the website of FACTS: Fertility Appreciation Collaborative to Teach the Science.

[69] Dietrich von Hildebrand, *Love, Marriage and the Catholic Conscience: Understanding the Church's Teachings on Birth Control* (Bedford, NH: Sophia Institute Press, 1998). For a philosophical analysis of Hildebrand's approach, see Maria Fedoryka, "*Finis* Superabundant *Operis*": Refining an Ancient Cause for Explaining the Conjugal Act", *American Catholic Philosophical Quarterly* 90, no. 3 (Summer 2016): 477–98.

[70] The main page for Couple to Couple League, which has a search engine to locate classes around the country, is https://ccli.org/. On their website at http://tobinstitute.org/programs/in-the-person-of-christ/, the Theology of the Body Institute offers information about the In the Person of Christ: Clergy Enrichment Program.

and admiration for all of those approaches achieved; but the purpose has also been to point out one important dimension of this issue that needs more direct attention: courage to explain the truth, rooted in both a conviction of the goodness of that truth and also in a love for the faithful whose lives are suffering for not having heard it. Studying the resources cited above, and very many others that are available, will provide the means to build a case for speaking truth not only to the faithful, but also to the wider public, about the Catholic teaching on human sexuality, which can be proclaimed with courage, confidence, and joy. And surely when future attacks on religious liberty arise, Catholics will not only be better able to defend the Church's right to teach the truth, but also able to defend the truth that she teaches.

Now is the time to begin in earnest. For Pope Paul VI was right when he said: "People of our time, we think, are especially able to understand that this teaching is in accord with human reason."[71] What we have found, however, is that people need help in seeing this harmony, help that is not hard to find but is not widely disseminated. A source of hope in this regard is that many people of today, particularly Catholics who have not yet heard it, want to hear this teaching. As Cardinal Dolan suggests, we need to respond to the "hunger, especially among young adults, for a more authoritative Church voice on sexuality".[72] The cardinal is right, and people today want explanations, and they listen intently. Talks by laypeople on these matters are very helpful, yet preaching from the pulpit has great impact too. The best would be if we had both, working together.

With respect to the culture at large, it may be the longest of long shots to try to shut down the contraceptive industry by means of convincing people to stop purchasing contraceptives out of a deep understanding of the goodness of the truth about conjugal relations, but that is what the Church is called to do. That effort is surely aided by the growing acknowledgment of the disintegration of our culture, especially in respect to sexual issues: social scientists and others are beginning to realize the long-term consequences of single parenthood, abandoned women, fatherless children, and attacks on fatherhood—phenomena rooted in a

---

[71] *HV* 12.
[72] Taranto, "When the Archbishop Met the President".

contraceptive culture.[73] Furthermore, unless a critical mass of lay Catholics become inspired to live according to Church teaching because they themselves understand its goodness, it will not be possible to garner their support in fights for religious freedom. For, in order for a specific truth to have a positive impact on the culture, there has to be a critical mass of people who grasp that truth deeply and live what they grasp.[74] That critical mass does not exist on this teaching, and it needs to be fostered.

As mentioned above, the bishops' webpage on marriage and family is an impressive achievement and numbers among the excellent online resources that can be of great help in restoring some sanity to our culture. In addition, there are very many well-trained lay Catholics in all fields who have a deep desire to share these life-affirming and enriching truths, in charity and joy, with others. Now is the time for the bishops and priests to reach out to the lay resources in their dioceses, who are yearning to be asked and will respond with grateful enthusiasm. Together we can develop a courageous plan to introduce all of this new knowledge to the wider Catholic community.

Many have rightly pointed out that all of the dire predictions made by Pope Paul VI have, sadly, come to pass. However, in addition to the prescient and severe warnings in *Humanae vitae*, the pope included a positive and beautiful prediction following directly on his call to bishops cited above. Let us be inspired by its hope and heed its call:

> If progress is gained on all of these fronts at the same time, then not only will family life of parents and children be more tolerable, it will be easier and happier. Once the plan God conceived for the world is faithfully kept, fellowship in society will be richer in fraternal charity and more safely grounded in a true peace.[75]

---

[73] See Mark Regnerus, *Cheap Sex: The Transformation of Men, Marriage and Monogamy* (Oxford: Oxford University Press, 2017); Mary Eberstadt, *Adam and Eve after the Pill: Paradoxes of the Sexual Revolution* (San Francisco: Ignatius Press, 2013); and Mark Regnerus and Jeremy Uecker, *Premarital Sex: How Young Americans, Meet, Mate, and Think about Marrying* (Oxford: Oxford University Press, 2011).

[74] In a series of dialogues with Jürgen Habermas and Marcello Pera, Joseph Ratzinger developed his idea on the role of Christian minorities influencing the broader culture. In the following article I tried to summarize and capture the main points of those dialogues: Peter J. Colosi, "Ratzinger, Habermas and Pera on Public Reason and Religion", *Logos: A Journal of Catholic Thought and Culture* 19, no. 3 (Summer 2016): 148–69.

[75] *HV* 30.

Self-Gift: The Heart of *Humanae vitae*[*]

Janet E. Smith, Ph.D.;
John S. Grabowski, Ph.D.;
J. Budziszewski, Ph.D.; and
Maria Fedoryka, Ph.D.

1. Introduction

The Catholic Church's teaching on sexuality is based on the dignity of the human person as being made in the image and likeness of a loving God. The gift of life is a great gift, not only because it enables us to enjoy the marvelous goods of this world but, even more importantly, because it enables us to anticipate and strive for eternal life, where there will be an everlasting enjoyment of all goods, made possible by union with our loving Father.

Humanae vitae begins by referencing the "extremely important [*gravissimum*] mission [*munus*] of transmitting human life" that God has entrusted to spouses.[1] It speaks of parents as those who render God a great service. After all, God wants to share his limitless goodness with souls; that is why he created the universe. Having and raising children is an act of immense generosity and dignity, and it enables us to participate in an act of inestimable value: the act of assisting God in bringing a new immortal soul into existence.

---

[*] This essay was first published in *National Catholic Bioethics Quarterly* 16, no. 3 (Autumn 2016): 449–74. Additional contributors are Richard J. Fehring, Ph.D., R.N., F.A.A.N.; Gerard M. Nadal, Ph.D.; and Gregory K. Popcak, Ph.D.

[1] Paul VI, encyclical letter *Humanae vitae* (July 25, 1968), trans. Janet E. Smith, in Humanae Vitae: *A Challenge to Love* (New Hope, KY: New Hope Publications, 2006) (hereafter cited as *HV*).

In August 2016, the Wijngaards Institute in the United Kingdom released a statement challenging Church teaching on contraception.[2] Our statement provides the big picture of the Church's teaching rather than a point-by-point rebuttal of the Wijngaards statement, although responses to the Wijngaards claims are included here. Among many erroneous claims is the assertion that *Humanae vitae* is based primarily on biological laws. As the opening sentences of *Humanae vitae* indicate, that is very far from the truth. The biological reality that sexual intercourse can lead to the conception of new life is undeniably relevant to any consideration of contraception, but biology in no sense provides the primary basis for the Church's teaching. To start there is to start in the wrong place.

1.1. God Is Love and the Source of New Life

The Church's teaching on sexuality begins with an understanding of God as love and an understanding of love as a power that overflows into new love and new life. The human persons he creates have an immortal destiny. He has bestowed on spouses the tremendous gift of being participators with him in the creation of new persons, a gift that requires complete self-giving. The statement in this essay makes this clear and shows that many compelling reasons have been put forth to justify the claims of *Humanae vitae*. These reasons are based on Sacred Scripture, Sacred Tradition, several theories of natural law, and the real-life consequences of contraception on women's bodies, on non-marital and marital sexual relationships, and on society. None of these reasons have been addressed by the Wijngaards statement. The intent here is not to provide a full-scale defense of *Humanae vitae*. It is, rather, to give a sketch of some powerful defenses of the doctrine found in the encyclical and to show that love, rather than biology, animates all of them.[3]

[2] Wijngaards Institute, "Catholic Scholars' Statement on the Ethics of Using Contraceptives", August 2016, http://www.wijngaardsinstitute.com/statement-on-contraceptives/.

[3] The footnotes in this essay as well as an online list of resources offer additional in-depth support for these defenses; a comprehensive bibliography and list of resources is available on the website of the School of Theology and Religious Studies at the Catholic University of America at http://trs.cua.edu/res/docs/HV-Bibliography-Resources.pdf.

1.2. Multiple Defenses

It is possible to explain the wrongness of many moral issues by a variety of defenses. Adultery, for instance, can be argued to be wrong because (1) it is against God's will, (2) it violates the sixth commandment, (3) it contravenes the nature of marriage, (4) it is incompatible with the virtues of fidelity and self-mastery, (5) it violates a valid promise, (6) it violates the rights of a spouse, (7) it has been considered by virtually all civilizations at all times and all places to be wrong and has been prohibited by law, and (8) it can be harmful to one's self, spouse, children, other relationships, financial status, and society. Some of these arguments lead to the conclusion that adultery is always wrong, and some to the conclusion that is almost always wrong. Thus, they do not all have the same strength, but all weigh heavily against adultery.

It must be noted that there are also weak arguments against adultery— for example, that it is unpleasant to be known as an adulterer; but just because an argument is weak does not mean that the claim it is meant to support is false. Nor is it true that such an argument is necessarily philosophically valid or strong simply because it leads to a true conclusion.

1.3. Fundamental Truths

Not everyone who collaborated on this document accepts all its arguments or sees them as equally valid, but each author and contributor does accept the Church's teaching that contraception is never in accord with God's plan for sexuality, and each holds that one or more of the arguments presented, rightly understood, establishes that contraceptive intercourse is an action that is always incompatible with the goods of marriage.

The claims below state our shared understanding.

1.3.1. God Is Love. The God who made our beautiful and ordered world is loving and good. All of his creation is a loving gift to mankind. Even after the Fall, God continued to reach out to his people, gradually revealing himself and the depths of his love and mercy. God the Father's gift of his Son, Jesus, whose life was poured out on the Cross, was the ultimate and complete self-gift. This great and radical love is borne out in Scripture, where the authors of the Old Testament often speak of God as husband and his people as his wife, and the authors of the New Testament describe Christ as the Bridegroom and the Church as his Bride. Throughout the history of the Church, many have seen this spousal imagery as a key to understanding God's relationship to every human soul.

1.3.2. Made in God's Image. Because God is love, a communion of the Divine Persons, he made men and women in his image: able to reason and to choose freely, with the capacity to love and to be in loving relationships.

1.3.3. Complete Gift of Self. God invites all people to share in his love. Every person, therefore, is beloved by God and is made to be in loving relationships; every person is created to make a gift of self to God and to others. This gift need not include any sexual dimensions; it means living in a way that promotes the good of everyone, especially those with whom one is in a close relationship.

1.3.4. Marriage: A Unique Communion of Persons. Marriage was designed by God to enable a man and a woman to live out humanity's core identity as lovers and givers of life—to enable the two to become "one flesh" (Gen 2:24) and that one flesh to "be fruitful and multiply, and fill the earth" (Gen 1:28). Human sexual relations fulfill God's intent only when they respect the procreative meaning of the sexual act and involve a complete gift of self between married partners.

1.3.5. God's Law, Not Man's. In the words of *Humanae vitae*, "The doctrine that the Magisterium of the Church has often explained is this: there is an unbreakable connection [*nexu indissolubili*] between the unitive meaning and the procreative meaning [of the conjugal act], and both are inherent in the conjugal act. This connection was established by God, and Man is not permitted to break it through his own volition."[4] The teaching that contraception is always against God's plan for sexuality, marriage, and happiness is not based on human law: "The teaching of the Church about the proper spacing of children is a promulgation of the divine law itself."[5]

1.3.6. Faith and Reason. God has revealed the truths about sexuality to man through the biblical vision of the human person and has also made them accessible to our reason. Several well-argued versions of natural

[4] *HV* 12.
[5] Ibid., no. 20.

law defenses support the Church's teaching that contraception is not in accord with God's plan for sexuality and marriage. Each begins with different basic truths, and thus each constructs its arguments differently.

1.3.7. The Theology of the Body: Pope Saint John Paul II's Contribution. John Paul II's Theology of the Body[6] (virtually ignored by the Wijngaards statement) provides a powerful defense of the view that contraception is not in accord with the understanding of the human person as conveyed by Sacred Scripture and Sacred Tradition. He speaks of the language of the body and shows that to violate the procreative meaning of the marital act is also to violate its unitive ("commitment-expressing") meaning. He demonstrates that our very bodies have a language and a spousal meaning—that they express the truth that we are to be in loving and fruitful relationships with others.

1.3.8. Humanae vitae as Prophetic. Humanae vitae speaks against the distorted view of human sexuality and intimate relationships that many in the modern world promote. The encyclical was prophetic when it listed some of the harms that would result from the widespread use of contraception. Many studies show that contraception, such as hormonal contraceptives and intrauterine devices, can cause serious health problems for women. The widespread use of contraception appears to have contributed greatly to the increase of sex outside of marriage, nonmarital pregnancies, abortion, single parenthood, cohabitation, divorce, poverty, and the exploitation of women. It has contributed to declining marriage rates as well as declining population growth in many parts of the world. There is also growing evidence that chemical contraceptives harm the environment.

1.3.9. A Practical Help to Husbands and Wives—Fertility Awareness–Based Methods. In order to live God's design for married love, husbands and wives need moral family planning methods. Fertility awareness–based methods of family planning (FABMs)—that is, the many forms of natural family planning (NFP)—respect the God-given spousal union and the potential to procreate. FABMs are fully consistent with the Church's teaching on marital chastity, and couples using these methods do not thwart the power of acts that could result in the creation of new human persons. They respect God's design for sexuality, help individuals grow

---

[6]John Paul II's Theology of the Body consists of a series of addresses regarding the human body and sexuality, given during his Wednesday audiences between 1979 and 1984.

in self-mastery, have the potential to strengthen marriages, and respect the physical and psychological health of women. Moreover, scientific studies show that FABMs are highly effective in helping couples both limit their family size when necessary and conceive when appropriate.

1.3.10. Respect for Cultural Values and Freedom. International organizations and governments should respect the values and beliefs of families and cultures that see children as a gift and therefore should not impose practices that are antithetical to those values and beliefs about children and family planning. Governments and international organizations should make instruction in FABMs a priority, because these methods are based on a solid scientific understanding of a woman's fertility cycle, are easily learned by women in developing countries, are virtually without cost, and promote respect for women.

1.3.11. Christ Provides Grace. Because of original sin, men and women are subject to temptations that sometimes seem insuperable. Christ came not just to restore our original goodness but to enable us to achieve holiness. The Catholic Church invites married couples to participate in the life of Christ and in the sacraments, especially Reconciliation and the Holy Eucharist. The Church asks the faithful to deepen their relationship with God the Father, to be open to receiving the direction of the Holy Spirit, and to ask Christ to provide the graces needed to live in accord with God's will for their married lives, even when doing so requires living the difficult moral truths.

1.4. Theology of the Body

The big picture conveyed by these fundamental truths encompasses much more than the Wijngaards statement. It includes the view that the teaching on love and marriage in Holy Scripture shows that contraception is incompatible with God's plan for sexuality and the dignity of the human person. The Wijngaards statement never mentions John Paul II's *Love and Responsibility*[7] or his Theology of the Body; indeed, the statement shows no awareness of it or of the fact that conferences have been held and institutes have sprung up all over the world (largely founded by married laity) to instruct people about John Paul II's profound

[7] Karol Wojtyła, *Love and Responsibility* (1981; repr., San Francisco: Ignatius Press, 1993).

philosophical defense of the Church's teaching on sexuality in *Love and Responsibility* nor of his meditations on Scripture and his exposition of the spousal meaning of the body, found in his Theology of the Body.[8] Nor does the Wijngaards statement acknowledge that John Paul II's insights have led countless couples away from the use of contraception to an appreciation of the great joy found in embracing God's plan for sexuality. Never claiming that Scripture explicitly condemns contraception but claiming that Church teaching arises from the logic of the text, John Paul II shows the ways in which contraception is incompatible with Scripture's clear teaching about love and marriage. Focused as the Wijngaards statement is on promoting sterile sex, it is perhaps unsurprising that it barely mentions love or marriage.

Pope Saint John Paul II's teaching on sexuality forms the basis of the explanation of the Church's teaching on contraception presented here, but it also sketches other natural law arguments and draws upon the findings of science to demonstrate the validity and the strength of the Church's teaching.

2. John Paul II's Philosophical Defense of the Church's Teaching on Sexuality

This section briefly lays out a philosophical defense of the Church's teaching on contraception developed by John Paul II, writing as Karol Wojtyła before he became pope, and presented primarily in *Love and Responsibility*. The purpose of that book is to explain how to transform the self-seeking sexual urge into an impetus for self-giving love in marriage.

2.1. The Personalistic Norm

The first principle Wojtyła establishes is that, because they are free, human persons are never to be used, and they thus have an innate

---

[8] Consider, for instance, the facts that the John Paul II Pontifical Institute for Marriage and Family Sciences and its affiliated campuses exist on all of the continents, with the exception of Antarctica (see https://www.johnpaulii.edu/about/the-institute-worldwide/); that there are many lay-run apostolates promoting chastity that are based on the Theology of the Body; and that most seminaries and many universities now use the Theology of the Body as the preferred explanation of the Church's teaching on sexuality.

dignity that must be respected. Indeed, he enunciates what he calls the personalistic norm, which states that the only just response to a person is love; by love he means "seeking what is good for another". In spousal love, each spouse seeks the good of the other in a context of total mutual self-giving.

2.2. "Conscious Parenthood" and Mutual Affirmation

Central to Wojtyła's sexual ethics is the claim that the dignity of human persons resides in the ability to know the truth and to choose freely to live in accord with it. Wojtyła speaks of two goods toward which the marital act is directed: a deep union through total mutual self-giving and the common good of conceiving and raising a child.

Wojtyła holds that in the order of nature, the sexual act can lead to the coming-to-be of a new member of the human species, whereas in the order of the person, the sexual act leads to two persons becoming parents of a new human person. Thus, to reject one's own or another's fertility but to enjoy sexual pleasure from another is to reject the person and to allow one's self to use or be used by another. Wojtyła maintains that being aware of these truths and making decisions in accord with them is the foundation of moral choices about sexual matters. Wojtyła refers to the recognition that sex leads to parenthood and the lively embrace of that as a good that dictates moral behavior, as "conscious parenthood".[9] To be willing to be a parent with another is an act of great affirmation of the other, for one thereby unites one's entire life to another. Moreover, since love by its inner logic is life-giving, blocking the creative dimension of the act of love between the spouses poses a threat to the love itself.

2.3. Justice to the Creator

Love and Responsibility has a chapter titled "Justice to the Creator", in which Wojtyła speaks of each person as God's own and explains that using another person is an offense against God. Wojtyła shows how in

[9] For a discussion of this concept, see Janet E. Smith, "Conscious Parenthood", *Nova et Vetera* 6:4 (2008): 927–50.

conjugal relations the body serves as a means, not otherwise open to spouses, for a new and deeper union between them. That is, for human beings, God has made the order of nature not to be separate from but to participate in the order of persons, which explains why the bodily act of union—no longer a merely biological reality—can be incorporated into the act of love. Wojtyła shows that by a divinely established order, the body also serves the fruitfulness integral to spousal love by giving it a new, awe-inspiring scope: the possibility of the creation of new human life. On the basis of this integration of the bodily act into the order of person and love, Wojtyła makes it clear that by rejecting the possibility of parenthood in any individual act, the spouses reject the authority of the Creator, act against the inner logic of love, and take up an attitude of use.

Elsewhere, John Paul II speaks of sexuality and the ability to participate in the act of creating a new human person as a great gift from God: human persons engage in the physical act that provides God with the opportunity to create a new immortal soul. The male provides the sperm, the female provides the ovum, and God provides the soul. God acts out of love; so, too, should the spouses. Justice to the Creator requires that we do nothing to thwart the possibility of the creation of a new human soul. John Paul II explains that confining one's sexual acts to the infertile period for the purposes of responsible parenthood does not thwart the possible creation of a new human soul and permits the spouses to affirm each other as integral wholes through the marital act.

2.4. Thomism and Personalism

The above sketch, which provides the main lines of John Paul II's philosophical defense of the position that contraception conflicts with the dignity of the human person, is based on both Thomistic principles and personalist principles. From Thomism he takes the objective truth that what God creates is good, and that it is good to live in accord with the natures and essences of what God has created. From personalism he takes the view that the ability of each person to choose in accord with the truth and thereby to shape his character is the source of human dignity: such creatures deserve to be loved. These principles, along with the principles of the Theology of the Body, are being utilized more and more in both magisterial documents and statements produced by episcopal conferences and dioceses throughout the world. The Wijngaards statement evinces no knowledge of them.

3. Several Approaches to Natural Moral Law

3.1. Natural Moral Law

3.1.1. The Role of Natural Moral Law in the Church's Teaching on Contraception. Since the close of the Second Vatican Council and its call to renew moral theology, the Church has witnessed several approaches to natural moral law over the past five decades. Those scholars and schools of thought that have worked broadly in the Thomistic tradition and who maintain fidelity to the Magisterium have developed various theories to understand the law that Saint Paul taught is "written on their hearts" (Rom 2:15). The proponents of these theories do not all see eye-to-eye on how to understand natural moral law properly. But all agree that the natural moral law is rooted in the created order, that there is an objective moral order, and that certain acts, such as contraception that is freely engaged in, are not compatible with God's plan for his created order and for sexuality in particular. Thus, although these theories of moral law are not in every respect harmonious, all are united in affirming absolute moral norms, including that contraception is contrary to the natural moral law.

3.1.2. Biological Laws. It is essential to note that none of the theories of natural moral law hold that biological laws are sufficient to ground a condemnation of contraception. The Church does not object to violating biological laws in respect to sex among animals: animals neither achieve personal union nor procreate. Animals achieve bodily union; humans seek intimate personal union. Animals reproduce; persons procreate. Human biology is not directed merely to the continuation of the species but to the creation of new human persons who have an eternal destiny with God. Interfering with a process that simply blocks another member of a species from coming into being is very different from preventing the coming-to-be of a new immortal soul and refusing to respect God's plan for marriage and human sexuality.

This teaching of natural moral law, which *Humanae vitae* says is also "illuminated and made richer by divine revelation",[10] is grounded in both the nature of the human person as a body-soul unity and Church teaching about the nature of marriage as a one-flesh reality, which is open to both union and procreation.[11] This openness is not only a moral truth to guide conscience, but a truth about the human person and the meaning of human sexuality as well.[12] Therefore, the view in the Wijngaards statement, which would caricature the Church's teaching against contraception as being based on a physicalist or biologistic understanding of natural law, is greatly mistaken.

3.2. Thomistic Theory of Natural Moral Law

Thomistic metaphysics, which entails a teleological understanding of nature, has for centuries provided the foundation for the Church's moral teachings. It holds that natural things have purposes; that those purposes are good; and that for things to flourish, their natures must be respected. Mainstream Thomistic natural moral law is not based on biological laws but on the fact that things have essences or natures. The natures of many things are instrumental. Indeed, all of creation, except for human persons, was created for the good of human persons. Thus, we can use other things for our purposes. Wood, for instance, can be used for many human goods. Human persons, however, are a good in themselves and should never be used as things for the advantage of others.

What is good for all other things may not be good for human persons. Marriage, for instance, is not an institution needed by animals, since animals do not need intimate relationships, have immortal souls, or require the wise guidance of parents to help them develop virtue and holiness. Animal and human sexuality have radically different purposes. Animal sexuality has as its purpose the reproduction of species whose destiny is only temporal. Human sexuality has the purpose of providing a way for a male and female to join in a special kind of love and friendship that

---

[10] *HV* 4.

[11] See also Gen 2:24 and Mt 19:5.

[12] See John Paul II, apostolic exhortation *Familiaris consortio* (November 22, 1981), no. 32, http://w2.vatican.va/content/john-paul-ii/en/apost_exhortations/documents/hf_jp-ii_exh_19811122_familiaris-consortio.html.

enables them to bring forth new human beings who have an eternal destiny. Since human beings have intrinsic value, the very processes that bring about a new human being share in that intrinsic value. To violate the purposes of the sexual act is to violate the purposes that God has embedded in it. Therefore, contraception is always wrong.

Although traditional Thomistic natural law theory did not speak of contraception being a violation of the personal meaning of sexual intercourse, implicitly it held that contraception is always wrong for persons, because they are persons. This is the view of Wojtyła. Thus, as we shall see, the personalism of John Paul II draws out of Thomism something that is already there but that needed to be expanded and expressed in more modern terms.

3.3. Contraception Is Contralife

Another version of natural moral law theory is known as "new natural law theory"—it understands morality as a matter of living in accord with basic human goods and not acting in such a way as to violate those goods. *Humanae vitae* defines and excludes as morally wrong "all acts that attempt to impede procreation, both those chosen as means to an end and those chosen as ends."[13] For the new natural law theorists, the encyclical's definition of contraception thus makes it clear that what is relevant is not the behavior involved but the intention to impede procreation, no matter how that intention is carried out. What is wrong with contraception is that it precedes from a contralife will.

According to this view, although contraception presupposes an act of intercourse, it is not itself a sexual act, for it involves a distinct choice. A couple chooses contraception when they have already decided to have intercourse and fear it will result in the conception of a child. Their decision to use contraception is aimed precisely at preventing the child they fear will come into existence from actually doing so. Contraception, then, is a contralife act.

By rejecting contraception as contralife, the Church makes it clear that, like other choices, the choice to contracept has an intrinsic meaning. A couple cannot reasonably define the act purely in terms of the

[13] *HV* 14.

end they have in mind and discount the significance of their chosen means. A married couple may well intend the good end of enjoying intercourse without risking conception when their other responsibilities would make it irresponsible for them to conceive. If, however, contraception is their chosen means, then one of the reasons for its wrongness is that it is a contralife choice.[14]

This problem becomes especially clear when one considers the relation of the couple to the child when contraception fails—since they tried to prevent that child from existing, they almost invariably to some extent regret the fact that the child has come to exist. Given that conception is seen as a failure, it is not difficult to see how it can lead to abortion, for it is all too easy for the couple to follow the fatal logic of taking the life of the child they failed to prevent. While they will likely come to accept and love their child, the fact is that their choices have caused them to some extent to have a contralife will.

It is worth noting that couples who practice natural family planning never make such a choice. Since they make the sacrifice of abstaining whenever they think conception is possible, they never make the distinct contralife choice of trying to prevent a child from coming into existence. Nevertheless, if a child is conceived, they may initially be emotionally distraught, but they are morally secure. No change of heart is necessary.

In short, *Humanae vitae*'s definition of contraception perfectly captures the idea that contraception is contralife—wrong precisely *because* it is intended to prevent a new person from coming to be.

4. The Differences between Natural Family Planning and Contraception

4.1. Different Methods

Fertility awareness–based methods (FABMs), or natural family planning (NFP) methods, describe the scientific, natural, and moral methods of family planning that can help married couples either achieve or postpone pregnancy. Most women and too many physicians have little knowledge

---

[14] For a detailed treatment, see Germain Grisez, *The Way of the Lord Jesus*, vol. 2 of *Living a Christian Life* (Quincy, IL: Franciscan Press, 1993), pp. 506–19.

of a woman's patterns of fertility and the various signs that indicate when she is fertile and when she is not.

The majority of these methods provide a thorough education in the combined fertility of a man and a woman. Most NFP methods are based on the daily observation of the naturally occurring signs and symptoms of the fertile and infertile phases of a woman's menstrual cycle, such as a variation in the mucus she secretes, a rise in temperature after she ovulates, and a change in her cervix. These methods treat each woman and cycle as unique; therefore, all women, despite varying lengths of menstrual cycles, can use most NFP methods. In addition, because of the variety of NFP methods, women from different cultures and educational backgrounds can find a method of NFP that is effective for them.[15] Finally, women who learn to chart their own patterns of fertility can often discover various hormonal imbalances that may be causing infertility or other health issues.[16]

4.1.1. Effectiveness. Research demonstrates that NFP methods can be up to 99 percent successful in postponing or avoiding pregnancy when couples understand the methods, are motivated to use them according to their family planning intentions (spacing or limiting births), and follow the guidelines consistently.[17]

4.1.2. NFP and the Couple Relationship. Research also shows that couples who switch from a contraceptive to an NFP method improve their relationships, feel more respected by their partners, and are more in control of their fertility.[18] In fact, some evidence suggests a positive correlation between NFP and lower divorce rates. Anecdotal studies and nonpopulation comparison studies, for example, consistently show low levels of divorce among couples who use NFP.[19]

---

[15] Leona VandeVusse et al., "Couples' Views of the Effects of Natural Family Planning on Marital Dynamics", *Journal of Nursing Scholarship* 35, no. 2 (April 2003): 171–76.

[16] For answers to frequently asked questions about NFP, see "What Is Natural Family Planning?", United States Conference of Catholic Bishops, accessed March 29, 2018, http://www.usccb.org/issues-and-action/marriage-and-family/natural-family-planning/what-is-nfp/index.cfm.

[17] European Society for Human Reproduction and Embryology, "Natural Family Planning Method as Effective as Contraceptive Pill, New Research Finds", *Science Daily*, February 21, 2007, https://www.sciencedaily.com/releases/2007/02/070221065200.htm.

[18] VandeVusse et al., "Couples' Views", pp. 171–76.

[19] Richard J. Fehring, *Current Medical Research* 24:3–4 (Summer/Fall 2013): 12–16, http://www.usccb.org/issues-and-action/marriage-and-family/natural-family-planning/medical-research/upload/CMR-Summer-Fall-2013-Divorce-and-NFP-edited.pdf; and Mercedes Arzú Wilson, "The Practice of Natural Family Planning versus the Use of Artificial Birth Control: Family, Sexual, and Moral Issues", *Catholic Social Science Review* 7 (2002): 185–211.

4.2. Moral Differences

The Church teaches that couples are to discern prayerfully when it is right to limit their family size, and praises couples who generously and prudently decide to have large families as well as those who responsibly limit their family size when health, financial, psychological, or sociological reasons indicate that they should do so.[20] These families are protecting the good of fertility rather than violating it.

Many people fail to see any moral difference between contraception and NFP. They think that since both a couple using contraception and one using NFP do not want to have a child and intend to have sexual intercourse that does not issue in a child, their actions amount to the same thing.

A succinct justification for the use of NFP can be made this way: there is nothing wrong with deciding, for good reasons, that it is not a good time to have another child. There is nothing wrong with abstaining from sex at any time, including during the period of fertility. There is nothing wrong with having marital intercourse during the infertile time. Therefore, there is nothing wrong with using NFP, which simply involves not having marital intercourse during the fertile time and having it during the infertile time when the spouses, for good reasons, have made the decision not to have another child.

Still, there is more that can be said. The distinction between means and end is certainly operative here. Although both couples may have equally good reasons for wanting to limit their family size, one couple chooses the means of thwarting their fertility, engaging in potentially fertile acts while simultaneously working to destroy that fertility. They engage in an act that gives only partially of themselves; they give and refuse to give at the same time. The other couple respects their fertility, and when not prepared to accept a child, they refrain from fertile acts. They do not diminish the gift of self; rather, they give all they have at that moment. A standard example demonstrating the difference between contraception and NFP is the rough analogy with bulimia. Some individuals who wish to avoid weight gain eat and then force themselves to vomit. They want the pleasure of eating but not the consequences. Others who wish to avoid weight gain do not eat fattening foods. They abstain from rich foods and only eat them when

[20] HV 10.

prepared for the consequences. The parallels with contraceptive sex and NFP are clear.

The differences between the two means of birth control are much greater than this brief argument conveys. Contraception treats fertility as though it were a defect to be corrected rather than a gift to be cherished. Moreover, there is something radically antifemale about contraceptives—their use suggests that it is better to have a male body that can engage in sexual intercourse and not become pregnant. Many women resent contraceptives for their unpleasant side effects and also resent the men who want them to use contraceptives. Women who use NFP, on the other hand, are generally very positive about it, because it does not in any way threaten their health. NFP respects their fertility, whereas contraception, as noted above, treats it as a liability. They have confidence in the love of their husbands, who revere their fertility to the extent that they do not wish to interfere with it. They understand abstaining to be another form of love. After all, many save the gift of self until marriage, precisely out of love for their beloved.

There is no denying that the abstinence required for NFP can be difficult, more for some than for others; those who have abstained before marriage usually bring self-mastery into the marriage, whereas those who indulge in sex before marriage (which is nearly everyone in the current culture) have to learn new habits to use NFP. Nonetheless, spouses who use NFP nearly always find that, in spite of the difficulties (which, like those of dieting, can be considerable), there are great benefits realized over time both for their relationship with each other and for their relationship with God. NFP enables a couple to understand and cooperate with the plan of God their Creator, while contraceptives tempt them into thinking that they can control their destinies without any reference to the order of creation. Finally, NFP invites a married couple to build a greater intimacy, grounded in communication and mutual self-mastery, while contraceptives lull them into thinking that technology can replace patience and virtue.

5. Authority, Infallibility, and the *Sensus Fidelium*

5.1. Authority and the Criteria for Infallible Teachings

While an encyclical is a particularly solemn expression of papal authority, the significance of *Humanae vitae* is to be found primarily not in the status of the document but in the teaching it contains. The core of that teaching—contraception is always wrong—"is rooted in natural law, illuminated and made richer by divine revelation."[21] Indeed, as John Paul II showed at length in his Theology of the Body, when this teaching is set against the fuller context of biblical anthropology, one sees that it "belongs not only to the natural moral law, but also to the *moral order revealed by God*".[22]

It is clear that Catholics are bound to follow the teaching of the Church on contraception because of the Church's teaching authority. How binding is the teaching? Some argue that the Church's teaching on contraception is infallible by virtue of her universal Ordinary Magisterium.[23] Vatican II clearly sets out the conditions that must be met for bishops dispersed throughout the world to proclaim Christ's teaching infallibly. They must "maintain communion with one another and with Peter's successor, authoritatively teach on a matter of faith and morals, and agree in one judgment as something to be held definitively".[24] The required universality cannot be undone even by a later lack of consensus.[25] The historical evidence makes it abundantly clear that all of these conditions have been met.[26] A list of highlights must suffice here:

- Certain Fathers of the Church condemned contraception, and none ever approved it.
- Throughout the ages, many bishops have taught that acts intended to prevent conception are always wrong, as have non-bishops who are canonized saints and some who are also Doctors of the Church. No saint or Doctor of the Church ever approved

---

[21] *HV* 4.

[22] John Paul II, General Audience (July 18, 1984), no. 4, emphasis in original, in John Paul II, *Man and Woman He Created Them: A Theology of the Body*, trans. Michael Waldstein (Boston: Pauline Books and Media, 2006), p. 621.

[23] For a defense of this claim, see John C. Ford and Germain Grisez, "Contraception and the Infallibility of the Ordinary Magisterium", *Theological Studies* 39, no. 2 (May 1978): 258–312.

[24] Peter Ryan and Germain Grisez, "Indissoluble Marriage: A Reply to Kenneth Himes and James Coriden", *Theological Studies* 72, no. 2 (June 2011): 410. For a consideration of the meaning of these conditions, see pp. 410–11.

[25] Ibid., pp. 411–12.

[26] See Ford and Grisez, "Contraception and Infallibility of the Ordinary Magisterium", pp. 277–86.

contraception. And there is no evidence of a Catholic theologian teaching otherwise until at least 1962.

- From the thirteenth century until 1917, the Church's canon law included a canon severely condemning contraception. Needless to say, canon law has never suggested that contraception is licit.
- Until 1962, there was a constant consensus among modern theologians in support of the received teaching on contraception, and bishops authorized the use of these theologians' works in seminaries.
- When Pope Pius XI reaffirmed the teaching in his 1930 encyclical *Casti connubii*, bishops did not object but readily accepted it, and many supported it with their own statements and programs.
- No evidence has shown that bishops handed on this teaching as a private opinion, a probable judgment, or an ideal that need not be realized. It was always authoritatively proposed as a grave moral obligation.
- The teaching was often proposed as a divinely revealed moral norm, which by definition must be held definitively.

The teaching that contraception is always wrong has not been formally defined by the Church. Nevertheless, theologians have never refuted—indeed, they have largely ignored—the claim that the teaching is infallible, because Catholic bishops in communion with each other and the pope have authoritatively proposed it in one judgment to be held definitively.

5.2. Sensus Fidelium

Some, of course, claim that widespread dissent from the Church's teaching on contraception manifests a *sensus fidelium*, or sense of the faithful. But this raises the question of what counts as being faithful. That sense is not authentic if it contradicts revelation, tradition, and the Magisterium. Moreover, to affirm the claim, one must deny that those who accept the teaching on contraception, including almost all Catholics before the 1960s and the great majority of other Christians until several decades earlier, had a sense of the faithful. Reasonable people will reject such culturally myopic chauvinism.

6. The Use of Condoms to Prevent Transmission of HIV

There has been a debate in the Catholic Church on the morality of using condoms to prevent the transmission of HIV (human immunodeficiency virus). Some theologians maintain that the use of a condom is intrinsically contraceptive and that even if one's primary intention is to avoid the transmission of HIV, the use of a condom is morally wrong, since it is never morally permissible to do a moral wrong to achieve a good. The argument is also made that the use of a condom is immoral because it is immoral to engage in incomplete sexual acts, and having sex with a condom makes the sexual act incomplete: although penetration occurs, the union of bodies does not truly take place, because the man deposits his semen not in a woman's vagina but in a condom.

Those who argue that one may use a condom to prevent the transmission of HIV without violating Church teaching maintain that the moral evaluation of the act must be determined by the intentionality of the agent. Since the intention is to avoid transmission of HIV and the structure of the act remains the same, the use of a condom is good because the fact that conception cannot take place is not the defining feature. (The Magisterium has not made a determination on this matter.) It is very important to keep in mind that the distribution and use of condoms in developing countries has proved to be very ineffective in reducing the rate of transmission of HIV; abstinence-based programs are the only ones that have succeeded.[27]

7. Medical, Psychological, Environmental, Social, Legal, and Cultural Consequences of Contraception

7.1. Medical Consequences

Although much of the public believes that contraceptives provide substantial health benefits, it has long been established in professional medical and scientific literature that contraceptives carry substantial risks to life and health, as well as being relatively ineffective in preventing disease

---

[27] See Matthew Hanley and Jokin de Irala, *Affirming Love, Avoiding AIDS: What Africa Can Teach the West* (Philadelphia: National Catholic Bioethics Center, 2010).

transmission. At the outset of its fact sheet on condom effectiveness, the Centers for Disease Control and Prevention (CDC) states, "The most reliable ways to avoid transmission of sexually transmitted diseases (STDs), including human immunodeficiency virus (HIV), are to abstain from sexual activity or to be in a long-term mutually monogamous relationship with an uninfected partner."[28]

In other words, the CDC has recapitulated traditional Christian moral teaching: abstinence (virginity) followed by fidelity. This core component of God's design for human sexuality carries the very health benefits that the CDC and the medical establishment have failed to secure with condoms. Notice, too, that the CDC does not include the condom among the most reliable ways to avoid disease transmission. In fact, they go on in the document to say, "Genital ulcer diseases and HPV [human papillomavirus] infections can occur in both male and female genital areas that are covered or protected by a latex condom, as well as in areas that are not covered.... Condom use may reduce the risk for HPV infection and HPV-associated diseases (e.g., genital warts and cervical cancer)."[29]

Beyond the threats to life and health from their failure, condoms have not lived up to their promise in preventing unintended pregnancies. According to *Contraceptive Technology*, a widely respected textbook in the field, the male latex condom is only slightly more effective than the withdrawal method, 18 and 22 percent, respectively.[30] Considering the narrow window of fertility in the monthly cycle and the fact that *Contraceptive Technology* defines a failure as a resultant pregnancy, it must be deduced that the absolute mechanical failure rate of condoms is much higher than the 18 percent of the time their use results in pregnancy.

If the disease prevention and pregnancy data on condoms are less than reassuring, the inherent risks of hormonal contraceptive use are even more alarming. In addition to the well-known role of oral contraceptives

---

[28] "Condoms and STDs: Fact Sheet for Public Health Personnel", Centers for Disease Control and Prevention, last updated March 25, 2013, https://www.cdc.gov/condomeffec tiveness/docs/condoms_and_stds.pdf.

[29] Ibid.

[30] James Trussell, "Percentage of Women Experiencing an Unintended Pregnancy during the First Year of Typical Use and the First Year of Perfect Use of Contraception, and the Percentage Continuing Use at the End of the First Year", table 3–2, in *Contraceptive Technology*, 20th rev. ed., ed. Robert A. Hatcher et al. (New York: Ardent Media, 2011). Trussell's table is also available at http://www.contraceptivetechnology.org/wp-content/uploads/2013/09/CTFailureTable.pdf.

in causing the most common forms of breast cancer, their use raises the risk of the deadliest and most difficult-to-treat form of cancer: premenopausal triple-negative breast cancer. According to a 2009 study, the elevated risk ranges from 250 percent for women who start oral contraceptives at age twenty-two or older, to 540 percent for women who start using them before age eighteen.[31] This should not come as a surprise. The International Agency for Research on Cancer (IARC), a part of the World Health Organization, has classified estrogen-progestogen (progestin) oral contraceptives as group 1 carcinogens for breast, cervical, and liver cancers.[32] Oral contraceptives also increase a woman's risk of possibly lethal and always disabling pulmonary embolism, myocardial infarction, and cerebral vascular accidents as well as her susceptibility to the HIV and HPV viruses with their attendant morbidity. Both the estrogen-progestin combined pill and the progestin-only pill have also contributed greatly to the incidence of ectopic pregnancies, which are fatal for the baby and life-threatening for the mother.[33] Oral contraceptives have failure rates of close to 10 percent with typical use.[34]

These data show that the more people use these contraceptive technologies, the higher the incidence of unintended pregnancy and disease. None of these data existed fifty years ago in the run-up to *Humanae vitae*, and many people who were not aware of the rationale behind the Church's clear and consistent teaching believed in good faith that contraceptives might be a modern and humane way of addressing all manner of social ills. That was then. In the ensuing half century, the clear teaching that the Church explicated in the simplest language has been tragically underscored by the failures inherent in the contraceptive culture and the overwhelming number of its victims. God's wise design

---

[31] Jessica M. Dolle et al., "Risk Factors for Triple-Negative Breast Cancer in Women under the Age of 45 Years", *Cancer Epidemiology, Biomarkers and Prevention* 18, no. 4 (April 2009): 1159.

[32] Group 1 agents are those that have been shown to be carcinogenic to humans; they include known carcinogens such as tobacco, radium, plutonium, and all types of ionizing radiation. The classification of carcinogenic agents is published in the *IARC Monographs*, which can be located on IARC's website at http://monographs.iarc.fr/. See especially the IARC tables "Agents Classified by the *IARC Monographs*, Volumes 1–120" (http://monographs.iarc.fr/ENG/Classification/List_of_Classifications.pdf), and "List of Classifications by Cancer Sites with Sufficient or Limited Evidence in Humans, Volumes 1 to 120" (http://monographs.iarc.fr/ENG/Classification/Table4.pdf), last updated March 29, 2018.

[33] Walter L. Larrimore and Joseph B. Stanford, "Ectopic Pregnancy with Oral Contraceptive Use Has Been Overlooked", Letter, *BMJ* 321, no. 7258 (August 12, 2000): 450.

[34] Trussell, "Women Experiencing Unintended Pregnancy".

is not a no to happiness, but a protection of life and health. The numbers tell the story.

7.2. Psychological Consequences: Hormones and Relationships

Although research into the psychological and behavioral effects of hormonal contraceptives has been insufficient until recently, a review of scholarly research to date finds significant cause for concern. One author states, "Women who use HCs [hormonal contraceptives] report higher rates of depression, reduced sexual functioning, and higher interest in short-term sexual relationships compared to their naturally cycling counterparts. Also, hormonal contraceptives use may alter women's ability to attract a mate, as well as the mate retention behaviors in both users and their romantic partners. Some evidence even suggests that hormonal contraceptive use alters mate choice and may negatively affect sexual satisfaction in parous women, with potential effects on future offspring."[35] Regarding mate attraction and retention, a subsequent study supported those findings. It found that women are attracted to different types of men depending on whether or not they are taking hormonal contraceptives, and that marital stability can be negatively affected when a woman who was on hormonal contraceptives at the beginning of her relationship subsequently discontinues their use.[36]

7.3. Chemical Contraception and the Environment

It is an inconvenient truth that chemical contraceptive use is wreaking havoc on the environment. The chemical ethinyl estradiol (EE2) in hormonal contraceptives is transferred directly to the water supply through urination. There is no practical or economic way to remove these toxins from the water supply using standard treatment methods.[37]

[35] Lisa L. M. Welling, "Psychobehavioral Effects of Hormonal Contraceptive Use", *Evolutionary Psychology* 11, no. 3 (July 2013): 718, doi: 10.1177/147470491301100315.

[36] V. Michelle Russell et al., "The Association between Discontinuing Hormonal Contraceptives and Wives' Marital Satisfaction Depends on Husbands' Facial Attractiveness", *Proceedings of the National Academy of Sciences of the United States of America* 111, no. 48 (December 2, 2014): 17081–86, doi: 10.1073/pnas.1414784111.

[37] Wynne Parry, "Water Pollution Caused by Birth Control Poses Dilemma", *LiveScience*, May 23, 2012, https://www.livescience.com/20532-birth-control-water-pollution.html.

Because of this, artificial reproductive hormones are accumulating in both natural and drinking water supplies and are having significant negative environmental effects, especially on fish populations living in inland estuaries and, in particular, near water treatment plants.[38] Male fish are feminized and have less reproductive success, to the point where population collapse has occurred among some species in certain locations.[39] Vertebrates, including male amphibians and rats, appear to be similarly affected.[40]

The evidence of intersex and other fertility-related disorders in higher-order male vertebrates contributes to the growing concerns that environmental EE2 toxicity may be a significant contributor to the decades-long global increase in the rates of poor reproductive health among men, including increased rates of hypospadias, undescended testicles, testicular cancer, and low sperm count.[41]

7.4. Social and Personal Consequences

For decades, scholars have documented the harmful social effects of contraception.[42] One of the most harmful effects is the astronomical

---

[38] Lund University, "Estrogen in Birth Control Pills Has a Negative Impact on Fish", *ScienceDaily*, March 4, 2016, https://www.sciencedaily.com/releases/2016/03/160304092230.htm. See also Adam R. Schwindt et al., "An Environmental Oestrogen Disrupts Fish Population Dynamics through Direct and Transgenerational Effects on Survival and Fecundity", *Journal of Applied Ecology* 51, no. 3 (June 2014): 582–91, doi: 10.1111/1365-2664.12237.

[39] Matthew R. Mills et al., "Removal of Ecotoxicity of 17α-Ethinylestradiol Using TAML/Peroxide Water Treatment", *Scientific Reports* 5, e-pub (June 12, 2015): 1–10, doi: 10.1038/srep10511.

[40] Stephanie Tamschick et al., "Sex Reversal Assessments Reveal Different Vulnerability to Endocrine Disruption between Deeply Diverged Anuran Lineages", *Scientific Reports* 6, e-pub (March 31, 2016): 1–8, doi: 10.1038/srep23825. See also Lisa A. Vrooman et al., "Estrogenic Exposure Alters the Spermatogonial Stem Cells in the Developing Testis, Permanently Reducing Crossover Levels in the Adult", *PLOS Genetics* 11, no. 1, e-pub (January 23, 2015): 1–20, doi: 10.1371/journal.pgen.1004949.

[41] L. M. Zorrilla et al., "The Effects of Ethinyl Estradiol on Spermatogenesis in the Adult Male Rat", presented at Triangle Consortium of Reproductive Biology, Research Triangle Park, NC, February 6, 2010, available at https://cfpub.epa.gov/si/si_public_record_report.cfm?dirEntryId=218968. See also Vrooman et al., "Estrogenic Exposure".

[42] Lionel Tiger, *The Decline of Males: The First Look at an Unexpected New World for Men and Women* (New York: St. Martin's Press, 2000). See also Francis Fukuyama, *The Great Disruption: Human Nature and the Reconstitution of Social Order* (New York: Free Press, 2006); and Mary Eberstadt, *Adam and Eve after the Pill: Paradoxes of the Sexual Revolution* (San Francisco: Ignatius Press, 2013).

increase in sex outside of marriage and, when contraception fails, in single parenthood. This has led to the sadness of countless children being raised in fatherless households. Social science findings have repeatedly demonstrated that growing up in an intact home benefits children and, conversely, that growing up in a single-parent home increases the risks of sexual abuse, criminality, truancy, emotional disorders, and other childhood and adolescent harm.

Moreover, the widespread use of contraception has led to a rise in both illegitimacy and abortion. In *Evangelium vitae* John Paul II speaks of contraception and abortion as fruits of the same tree.[43] It is an easily observable fact that trend lines for both contraception and abortion rise in parallel. To say that the relation is only a correlation and not a sign of causation is to refuse to see what is obvious. It is hard to deny that contraceptive use leads to abortion, in part because it contributes to the perception that unintended pregnancy is a failure or an accident that can be remedied by killing the unborn child.

Those who advocate for increased use of contraception should realize that it not only increases the number of abortions but also leads to gendercide, the form of abortion that targets unborn children of a specific sex. Across the planet, millions more unborn girls are killed by abortion than boys. In some cultures, this happens because parents want boys to carry on the family legacy; in others, it is a result of the consumer mentality reinforced by widespread contraception—we want what we want when we want it—which extends to killing children whose sex does not match our preferences.

In many ways, the harmful effects of contraception are closely connected to a consumer mentality. Men can come to treat women as interchangeable partners for recreational sex, rather than as potential partners in a lifelong relationship that involves commitment to each other and the shared task of child-rearing. *Humanae vitae* predicted that the sexual revolution would lessen respect for women among men.[44] The accumulated data from studies of happiness suggest that female unhappiness has increased since the sexual revolution took hold. One study found that during the past thirty-five years, women's self-reported feelings

[43] See John Paul II, encyclical letter *Evangelium vitae* (March 25, 1995), no. 13, http://w2.vatican.va/content/john-paul-ii/en/encyclicals/documents/hf_jp-ii_enc_25031995_evangelium-vitae.html.

[44] *HV* 17.

of well-being have declined both absolutely and relatively compared to men's.[45]

The enthusiasm for contraception arose when people thought the world would soon be overpopulated to the point of annihilation. Today, in contrast, more and more scholars and leaders are realizing the damage done to economies and cultures when birth rates fall below replacement levels. Indeed, some countries fear that the wealthier nations try to impose their contraceptive lifestyles on developing nations because they fear competition.[46]

The multiple ways that contraception contributes to social decay have been catalogued elsewhere; suffice it to say here that the writers of the Wijngaards statement are naïve to speak of proven benefits without acknowledging the harms. Certainly there are great benefits to spouses in being able to control the size of their family, but that can be done using NFP methods, which are very effective, lack bad health consequences, are virtually free, and contribute to marital stability and happiness.

7.5. Legal Consequences

Pope Paul VI spoke prophetically in *Humanae vitae* when he warned that with widespread contraception, governments would begin violating human rights:

> [Let reasonable individuals] also carefully consider that a dangerous power will be put into the hands of rulers who care little about the moral law.... Who will prevent public authorities from favoring what they believe to be the most effective contraceptive methods and from mandating that everyone must use them, whenever they consider it necessary? And clearly it will come about that Men who desire to avoid the difficulties that are part of the divine law, difficulties that individuals, families, or society may experience, will hand over to the will of the public authorities the power of interfering in the most exclusive and intimate mission [*munus*] of spouses.[47]

---

[45] Betsey Stevenson and Justin Wolfers, "The Paradox of Declining Female Happiness", *American Economic Journal: Economic Policy* 1, no. 2 (August 2009): 190–225, doi: 10.1257/pol .1.2.190.

[46] Matthew Connelly, *Fatal Misconception* (Cambridge, MA: Belknap Press of Harvard University Press, 2010).

[47] *HV* 17.

Once a large segment of society accepts contraception as a social good, it takes but a few short steps for governments to begin to force this "good" on others. This process begins with the elimination or reduction of legal impediments to contraceptive access, followed by heavy state subsidization of contraceptive drugs and devices and active suppression of religious, familial, and cultural opposition to contraception. It takes the form of mandatory sexual education in public schools (which may also be extended to private and religious schools) that indoctrinates children and erodes parental authority. School administrators, counselors, and teachers thus assume the role of primary educators in sexual matters. In some schools, children receive condoms and instructions on their use at school, with no possibility of opting out, while school officials disingenuously claim that they are leaving the moral question of contraceptive use to families. But once the state decides to promote contraceptives, its position on the moral question is clear: having accepted contraception as a societal good, the state will treat it as such.

When concentrated government power supports an ideology of radical sexual autonomy, the religious freedom of all also comes under assault. In the United States, the government actualized this threat by mandating near-universal coverage of contraceptives and abortion-inducing drugs and devices by employers and insurance companies. Private business owners and religious nonprofits who objected, including a religious order that serves the poor, were threatened with millions of dollars in fines if they followed their faith and refused to collaborate in the provision of contraceptives. Although narrowly decided court decisions have so far protected such groups from government coercion, the durability of those rulings remains to be seen.

In any event, it is clear that government has come to see religious authority as an obstacle to government-endorsed goals for contraceptive use and thus an obstacle to progress. Religious institutions may thus be targeted by the state for exclusion from the public square and public programs if they do not adopt or endorse the government's views on human sexuality.

It is the vulnerable populations served by religious institutions—be they women, racial and ethnic minorities, the poor, or the undereducated—that will be induced and ultimately coerced by governments into accepting contraceptive practices. One need only look at forced sterilization programs in India, Africa, and South America or forced abortions in

China to see this this dynamic in practice. As Paul VI states in *Humanae vitae*, people under individual or societal pressure "will hand over to the will of the public authorities the power of interfering in the most exclusive and intimate mission [*munus*] of spouses." Once this authority is ceded, it will not easily be restored.

7.6. Cultural Consequences

Many African nations have been under enormous pressure for decades to distribute contraceptives. Since the Catholic Church provides nearly 50 percent of the health care in most African nations, there have also been attempts to coerce Catholic institutions to distribute contraceptives. This is a serious violation of religious liberty. *Humanae vitae* provides a solid line of defense for bishops, religious, and laity who are committed to both following the Church's teaching and refusing to be used by governments and international agencies for their agendas. Ecclesial and lay Catholic leaders have seen the harms, if not devastation, to which the widespread use of contraceptives has contributed in developed countries. They are convinced that the values honored by FABMs are more compatible with the family values of their cultures. It is scandalous that international agencies in some cases refuse to provide food and health care unless a government institutes population-control measures based on widespread distribution of contraceptives and access to abortion. Africans love their children: they do not so much want fewer of them as want food and health care for them. The money spent providing contraception and promoting abortion could easily fund universal instruction on FABMs, with large amounts remaining for food, clean water, and health care.

8. The Challenge of Infertility and Contraception

Just as the language of marital love requires spouses to accept each other in all of their dimensions, richness, and wholeness (here, fertility), so spouses must welcome each other in their weaknesses, limitations, and lack of wholeness (here, infertility). In the case of spouses suffering from infertility, the temptation can be strong to seek another partner to fulfill the natural (but sometimes obsessive) desire for children. The absence of children, much like the failure to find a good spouse, can be experienced as an insuperable barrier to happiness, a void that cannot be filled, leading sometimes to permanent heartbreak. Yet abandoning one's spouse for this reason is a grave breach of love, a betrayal, and amounts to using the new partner with whom one seeks to have children. Those who have experienced the heavy cross of infertility can testify to what a great gift fertility is.

The struggles with infertility yield an important perspective on the question of contraception, since those who are infertile can come to reject their spouses, a rejection that is implicit in the use of contraception, as well. For spouses to love the fertility they offer to and receive from each other is just as necessary as loving each other when infertility is a part of the relationship. Rejecting the gift of fertility by the use of contraception amounts to telling one's spouse that he or she is not loved in all respects. Spouses who use contraception reject a key element of their marital pledge and thereby wound their love at its very core.

9. The Reality of Grace

Although living by the Church's teaching that it is good for each and every act of marital sexual intercourse to retain its openness to life can present many challenges that seem insuperable, the Gospel, or Good News, *is* good news. We are not on our own. Our Savior, Jesus Christ, came to make available to us the graces that enable us to live up to the demands and greatness of our nature. He is eager to take our burdens onto himself and has provided many sources of grace, such as prayer, the Eucharist, and the Sacrament of Reconciliation. At times, we must all practice what can seem a frightening, radical reliance on the Lord, but we must have confidence that he is there to help us: "Cast all your anxieties on him, for he cares about you" (1 Pet 5:7). The time we spend worrying would be better spent in prayer, for there we can hear the voice of the Lord and learn his plan for us, a plan he will help us achieve.

10. Conclusion

Catholics deserve to be taught the Church's teaching on contraception in the most attractive and persuasive way. The fate of their marital and familial happiness depends a great deal upon living in accord with God's plan for sexuality, as does the fate of their individual souls. Bishops and their delegates should ensure that young people, especially those preparing for marriage, are well taught about contraception and NFP; priests and lay educators should be well trained in teaching and promoting the Church's teaching on sexuality. Health-care professionals should work to refine the methods of natural family planning.

The evidence from both sociological research and common sense seems to challenge the popular belief that access to contraception will provide a kind of freedom and help people attain, if not long-lasting love, at least some degree of happiness. People should ask whether they are healthier or happier from contraceptive use and the sexual behavior that accompanies it.

We do not presume to tell people what to believe, but we do urge all people of good will to question the status quo—especially the healthiness of contraceptive use with regard to both their personal lives and society in general.

We also invite all people to read *Humanae vitae*, test the claims made against it, and appreciate its wisdom.

CONTRIBUTORS

Joseph Atkinson, S.T.D, is associate professor of Sacred Scripture at the Pontifical John Paul II Institute in Washington, D.C. He has written numerous articles on the domestic church and the biblical view of the family, including the role of the family in salvation history. He produced a thirteen-part series for EWTN on the domestic church. He has written a book entitled *The Biblical and Theological Foundations of the Family: The Domestic Church* (Catholic University of America Press, 2014) and founded the Theology of the Family Project, which promotes topics of interest to the family and places them in a biblical context (http://www.theologyofthefamily.com).

Peter J. Colosi, Ph.D., is assistant professor of philosophy at Salve Regina University; he also taught at St. Charles Borromeo Seminary in Philadelphia, and at Franciscan University of Steubenville at its campus in Gaming, Austria. He organizes the International Symposia on Pope St. John Paul II's Theology of the Body. He has published numerous scholarly book chapters and articles, as well as popular and online pieces, in the areas of medical ethics, contemporary philosophical personalism, Franciscan studies, among others. His personal website is www.peterjcolosi.com, where his work in video and audio format can be found.

Derek Doroski, Ph.D., is associate professor of biology, an engineering instructor, and director of the Pre-Engineering Program at the Franciscan University of Steubenville. His experimental research is focused on stem cells and tissue engineering. His scientific work has been published in journals such as *Biomaterials* and *Tissue Engineering*. In addition to his experimental work, Dr. Doroski has published and presented on topics related to biology and the Church. He co-authored a paper on the metaphysics of twinning in *Theoretical Medicine and Bioethics* and has presented work demonstrating the dominance of adult stem cells in clinical trials to the Society for Catholic Social Scientists.

Mary Eberstadt is a senior research fellow at the Faith and Reason Institute. She is author of several books, among them *It's Dangerous to Believe: Religious Freedom and Its Enemies* (Harper, 2016); *How the West Really Lost*

God: A New Theory of Secularization (Templeton Press, 2014); and *Adam and Eve after the Pill: Paradoxes of the Sexual Revolution* (Ignatius Press, 2012). An adaptation of her 2010 novel *The Loser Letters: A Comic Tale of Life, Death, and Atheism* (Ignatius Press) premiered at Catholic University's Hartke Theater in 2016. She has written for many publications, including *TIME, First Things, National Review*, the *Weekly Standard*, and the *Wall Street Journal*.

Obianuju Ekeocha, from Nigeria, is trained in microbiology and biomedical science. She works as a specialist biomedical scientist in Canterbury, England. She writes and speaks internationally on abortion and contraception. She is the founder of Culture of Life Africa. She is the author of *Target Africa: Ideological Neocolonialism in the Twenty-First Century* (Ignatius Press, 2018).

Maria Fedoryka, Ph.D., is associate professor of philosophy at Ave Maria University. Coming from a background in phenomenological realism and personalism, and specializing in issues related to the philosophy of love, she has published and lectured on the thought of Aquinas, Edith Stein, Dietrich von Hildebrand, and John Paul II. Among her recent publications are the pamphlet *The Special Gift of Women for God, the Family and the World*, and an article on *Humanae vitae* in the *American Catholic Philosophical Quarterly* entitled "*Finis* superabundant *Operis*: Refining an Ancient Cause for Understanding the Spousal Act".

John Grabowski, Ph.D., is an associate professor of theology at the Catholic University of America. He and his wife were appointed members of the Pontifical Council for the Family in 2009. He serves as a theological advisor to the U.S.C.C.B. Committee on Laity, Marriage, Family, and Youth. In 2015 he was appointed by Pope Francis to serve as an expert (*adiutor*) at the Synod of Bishops on the Family. His books include *Sex and Virtue: An Introduction to Sexual Ethics* (Catholic University of America Press, 2003), *Transformed in Christ: Essays on the Renewal of Moral Theology* (Sapientia Press, 2017), and *One Body: A Program of Marriage Formation for the New Evangelization* with Claire Grabowski (Emmaus Road Press, 2018).

Angela Lanfranchi, M.D., is a clinical assistant professor of surgery at Rutgers Robert Wood Johnson Medical School. A retired breast cancer surgeon, she is co-founder and president of the Breast Cancer Institute, which reports on all risks of breast cancer, including induced abortion and hormonal contraception. Along with Ian Gentles and Elizabeth Ring-Cassidy, she co-authored *Complications: Abortion's Impact on Women* (DeVeber

Institute for Bioethics and Social Research, 2013). She has published in the *Linacre Quarterly, Ethics and Medics,* and *Issues in Law and Medicine.*

William Newton, Ph.D., is a professor of theology at Franciscan University of Steubenville; for ten years he taught at the International Theological Institute in Austria. He has written two books, *A Civilization of Love: The Catholic Vision for Human Society* (Gracewing Publishing, 2011), and *"What God Has Joined": The Biblical Foundations for Traditional Christian Sexual Morality* (CreateSpace Independent Publishing Platform, 2015). He has authored many articles and lectures widely on a wide range of Catholic topics. He co-founded the Aquinas Institute, which runs an annual summer program to promote the writings of Saint Thomas (aquinasinstitute.ie).

Deborah Savage, Ph.D., teaches at the St. Paul Seminary School of Divinity in St. Paul, Minnesota, where she directs the Masters in Pastoral Ministry Program. In such journals as *Nova et Vetera,* the *Lonergan Review,* and *Logos,* she has published on the nature of woman and man; the genius of both man and woman; on the central place of lived experience in Karol Wojtyla's account of the person; on woman as knower; among other topics. She speaks on and publishes in the areas of neo-Thomism, philosophical anthropology, and John Paul II's thought and Theology of the Body. She is co-founder of the Siena Symposium for Women, Family, and Culture at the University of St. Thomas, Minnesota.

Michele M. Schumacher, S.T.D., habil., is a private docent at the University of Fribourg, Switzerland, where she teaches sexual morality. She founded and directed the Office of Family Life and Social Justice for the Diocese of Yakima, Washington. She has written *A Trinitarian Anthropology: Adrienne von Speyr and Hans von Balthasar in Dialogue with St. Thomas Aquinas* (Catholic University of America Press, 2014), and she is the editor and contributor to *Women in Christ: Towards a New Feminism* (Eerdmans, 2004). She has also authored many articles on such topics as gender, feminism, marriage, the family, and the theology of the body.

Janet E. Smith, Ph.D., is the Father Michael J. McGivney Chair of Life Ethics at Sacred Heart Major Seminary. She is the author of *Humanae Vitae: A Generation Later* (Catholic University of America Press, 1991), and *The Right to Privacy* (National Catholic Bioethics Center; Ignatius Press, 2008). *Self-Gift* (Emmaus Academic, 2018) is a volume of her already published essays on *Humanae vitae* and the thought of John Paul II. She edited *Why Humanae Vitae Was Right: A Reader* (Ignatius Press, 1993), *Life Issues, Medical*

Choices: Questions and Answers for Catholics (with Christopher Kaczor; Servant Books, 2016), and *Living the Truth in Love: Pastoral Approaches to Same-Sex Attraction* (with Father Paul Check; Ignatius Press, 2015).

Michael Waldstein, Ph.D., Th.D., is a Distinguished Fellow of the St. Paul Center for Biblical Theology and a professor of New Testament at the Franciscan University of Steubenville. He has taught at Ave Maria University and the University of Notre Dame. He was the founding president of the International Theological Institute in Gaming, Austria, where he held the position of St. Francis of Assisi Professor of New Testament. He has published many books and articles on biblical and theological topics in such journals as *Nova et Vetera*, *Communio*, and *Anthropotes*. He translated John Paul II's *Man and Woman He Created Them: A Theology of the Body* (Pauline Books and Media, 2006). He served on the Pontifical Council for the Family, 2003–2009.

George Weigel is a Distinguished Senior Fellow of the Ethics and Public Policy Center where he holds the William E. Simon Chair in Catholic Studies. He is the *New York Times* bestselling author of two dozen books, including his internationally acclaimed biography of Saint John Paul II, *Witness to Hope* (HarperCollins, 1999), and its sequel, *The End and the Beginning* (Image, 2010). He wrote a memoir of his experiences with Saint John Paul II: *Lessons in Hope—My Unexpected Life with St. John Paul II* (Basic Books, 2017).

Christopher West is senior lecturer of theology and Christian anthropology at the Theology of the Body Institute and is founder and president of the Cor Project, a global outreach promoting Pope Saint John Paul II's Theology of the Body. Among his many books are *Theology of the Body Explained: A Commentary on John Paul II's* Man and Woman He Created Them (Pauline Books and Media, 2007); *Love Is Patient, but I'm Not: Confessions of a Recovering Perfectionist* (Beacon Publishing, 2017); *Fill These Hearts: God, Sex, and the Universal Longing* (Image, 2013); *At the Heart of the Gospel: Reclaiming the Body for the New Evangelization* (Image, 2012); *Heaven's Song: Sexual Love as It Was Meant to Be* (Ascension Press, 2008).